America and the Vie

The Vietnam War was one of the most heavily documented conflicts of the twentieth century. Although the events themselves recede further into history every year, the political and cultural changes the war brought about continue to resonate, even as a new generation of Americans grapples with its own divisive conflict.

America and the Vietnam War: Re-examining the Culture and History of a Generation reconsiders the social and cultural aspects of the conflict that helped to fundamentally change the nation. With chapters written by subject area specialists, *America and the Vietnam War* takes on subjects such as women's role in the war, the music and the films of the time, the Vietnamese perspective, race and the war, and veterans and post-traumatic stress disorder.

Features include:

- Chapter Summaries
- Timelines
- Discussion Questions
- Guides to Further Reading
- A Companion Website with primary source documents and tools (such as music and movie playlists) for both instructors and students

Heavily illustrated and welcoming to students and scholars of this infamous and pivotal time, *America and the Vietnam War* is a perfect companion to any course on the Vietnam War era.

Andrew Wiest is Professor of History and Co-director of the Center for the Study of War and Society at the University of Southern Mississippi. He is the author of *Vietnam's Forgotten Army: Heroism and Betrayal in the ARVN*.

Mary Kathryn Barbier is Associate Professor of History at Mississippi State University. She is the author of *D-Day Deception: Operation Fortitude and the Normandy Invasion*.

Glenn Robins is Associate Professor of History at Georgia Southwestern State University. He is the author of *The Bishop of the Old South: The Ministry and Civil War Legacy of Leonidas Polk*.

America and the Vietnam War

Re-examining the Culture and History of a Generation

Edited by
Andrew Wiest
Mary Kathryn Barbier
and
Glenn Robins

Routledge
Taylor & Francis Group
NEW YORK AND LONDON

First published 2010
by Routledge
270 Madison Avenue, New York, NY 10016

Simultaneously published in the UK
by Routledge
2 Park Square, Milton Park, Abingdon, Oxon OX14 4RN

Routledge is an imprint of the Taylor & Francis Group, an informa business

© 2010 Taylor & Francis

Typeset in Bell Gothic and Perpetua
by Keystroke, Tettenhall, Wolverhampton
Printed and bound in the United States of America on acid-free paper
by Edwards Brothers Inc.

All rights reserved. No part of this book may be reprinted or reproduced or utilized in any form or by any electronic, mechanical, or other means, now known or hereafter invented, including photocopying and recording, or in any information storage or retrieval system, without permission in writing from the publishers.

Trademark Notice: Product or corporate names may be trademarks or registered trademarks, and are used only for identification and explanation without intent to infringe.

Library of Congress Cataloging in Publication Data
America and the Vietnam War : re-examining the culture and history of a generation / edited by Andrew Wiest, Mary Kathryn Barbier, and Glenn Robins.
    p. cm.
"Simultaneously published in the UK"—T.p. verso.
Includes bibliographical references and index.
1. Vietnam War, 1961–1975—Social aspects. 2. Vietnam War, 1961–1975—Study and teaching. I. Wiest, Andrew A. II. Barbier, Mary. III. Robins, Glenn.
DS559.8.S6A46 2009
959.704′3—dc22
2009026811

ISBN10: 0–415–99529–9 (hbk)
ISBN10: 0–415–99530–2 (pbk)
ISBN10: 0–203–86288–0 (ebk)

ISBN13: 978–0–415–99529–0 (hbk)
ISBN13: 978–0–415–99530–6 (pbk)
ISBN13: 978–0–203–86288–9 (ebk)

Contents

List of illustrations — vii

Introduction: Vietnam in history and memory — 1
Mary Kathryn Barbier

1 Vietnam divided: regional history and the Vietnam wars, 1598–1975 — 15
Martin Loicano

2 Historians and the origins of the Vietnam War — 35
Matthew Masur

3 The "other" Vietnam War — 55
Andrew Wiest

4 The Women's Army Corps goes to Vietnam — 77
Heather Stur

5 The Black Panthers and the Vietnam War — 101
Curtis Austin

6 Patriots for peace: people-to-people diplomacy and the anti-war movement — 121
Amy Scott

7 Vietnam and the conscientious objector experience — 143
Philip Szmedra

CONTENTS

8	The American POW experience Glenn Robins	165
9	Post-traumatic stress disorder and healing from the war Raymond M. Scurfield	187
10	The Vietnam War and literature Maureen Ryan	209
11	Vietnam and film Thomas Doherty	231
12	The soundtrack of Vietnam Kim Herzinger	255
13	The legacy of the Vietnam War for the US Army James H. Willbanks	271
14	Iraq as "the good war" as opposed to Vietnam, the bad war Lloyd Gardner	291
Contributors		312
Index		315

Illustrations

FIGURES

0.1	Map of Vietnam	4
0.2	Vietnam Veterans Memorial, Washington, DC	7
1.1	Statue of Trần Hưng Đạo, downtown Saigon, 1968	19
1.2	President Nguyên Văn Thiệu	28
2.1	President Dwight D. Eisenhower and Secretary of State John Foster Dulles greet South Vietnam's President Ngo Dinh Diem at Washington National Airport, May 8, 1957	39
2.2	President Lyndon B. Johnson meeting with Joint Chiefs of Staff around a picnic table on the L.B.J. Ranch front lawn, December 22, 1964	45
2.3	President Kennedy confers with General Maxwell Taylor and Secretary of Defense Robert McNamara in the cabinet room, 25 January 1963	49
3.1	President Ngo Dinh Diem of South Vietnam	59
3.2	Hue City from the air during Tet	64
3.3	American advisers and Army of the Republic of Vietnam troops	66
3.4	Army of the Republic of Vietnam troops on operations near the Laotian border in 1969	68
4.1	a and b: "Opportunity Awaits You in the Women's Army Corps"	78–9
4.2	"Meet Today's WAC Officer"	82
4.3	Untitled Women's Army Corps recruitment pamphlet, 1959	85
4.4	"Long Binh Wacs Provide a Study in Women's Lib"	93
4.5	"Wac of the Week: One of 85 in 'Nam"	95
5.1	Yellow Peril, Oakland, CA 1969	107
6.1	US poster regarding the recruitment of black soldiers to fight in Vietnam, 1967	126
6.2	Actress Jane Fonda and North Vietnamese soldiers and peasants near Hanoi in July 1972	136

ILLUSTRATIONS

7.1	The author with his mother and younger brother prior to his graduation from Penn State University, University Park, Pennsylvania, in June 1969	147
7.2	a and b: The author's draft cards indicating changes in draft status	150
8.1	American POWs	168
8.2	"The Vietnamese Rope Trick"	172
8.3	American POWs who participated in the Hanoi March were surrounded by hostile crowds and were punched, kicked, and cursed	177
8.4	POWs meeting with Canadian journalists	180
9.1	Raymond M. Scurfield working with Vietnamese civilians during his tour on one of the US Army's two psychiatric teams in Vietnam	189
9.2	Raymond M. Scurfield at the 98th Medical Attachment, 8th Field Hospital, during the Vietnam War	196
9.3	Raymond M. Scurfield seated with Vietnam veterans Roy Ainsworth and Charles Brown during a trip back to Vietnam in 2000	203
10.1	Combat scenes	212
10.2	"A female demonstrator offers a flower to military police . . ."	216
10.3	Viet Cong soldiers moving forward under covering fire from a heavy machine gun during the Vietnam War, ca. 1968	224
10.4	Arrival of South Vietnamese refugees, Eglin Air Force Base, Florida, May 1975	225
11.1	Director-star John Wayne on the Hollywood set of *The Green Berets* (1968), his World War II-style combat film about Vietnam	235
11.2	Rambo (Sylvester Stallone) rescues American POWs still languishing in Vietnam in *Rambo: First Blood Part II* (1985)	242
11.3	Charlie Sheen and Keith David as grunts in Oliver Stone's *Platoon* (1986)	244
11.4	Marine drill Sergeant Hartman (Lee Ermey) expresses his displeasure about jelly doughnuts to Private Pyle (Vincent D'Onofrio) in Stanley Kubrick's *Full Metal Jacket* (1987)	245
12.1	Jimi Hendrix performing live at the Royal Albert Hall, London, February 24, 1969	257
12.2	British pop group the Beatles pose with the cover of their new album, *Sgt. Pepper's Lonely Hearts Club Band*	260
12.3	Creedence Clearwater Revival, ca. 1970	267
13.1	General William DePuy, chief architect of the new American military doctrine of "Active Defense"	276
13.2	US Marines from Alpha Company, 1st Tank Battalion, provide security in an M1A1 Abrams tank while Marines from Regimental Combat Team 2 search for weapons caches along a section of the west bank of the Euphrates River, March 9, 2007, north of Hit, Iraq	280
13.3	General Donn Starry, chief architect of the US doctrine of AirLand Battle	281

13.4	An Army AH-64 Apache helicopter, one of the chief weapons systems of AirLand Battle that made possible the stunning coalition victory in Operation Desert Storm	284
14.1	President George W. Bush speaks to an audience in the Pentagon auditorium on March 19, 2008	293
14.2	Army Spc. Anthony Dowden of the 3rd Infantry Division presents a plaque made from a piece of armor that saved him from a sniper's bullet to Donald H. Rumsfeld in Baghdad, Iraq, on April 12, 2005	301
14.3	American troops during the Iraq War, a conflict that, to many in the American public, brought back uncomfortable reminders of Vietnam	304
14.4	Commander of US Central Command Gen. David H. Petraeus talks with members of Combined Joint Task Force 101 at Combat Outpost Marghah, Afghanistan, on November 6, 2008	307

Introduction

Vietnam in history and memory

Mary Kathryn Barbier

In *Pickett's Charge in History and Memory*, Carol Reardon demonstrates how the "fog of war," soldiers' recollections, and newspaper accounts shaped a historical memory that glorified Pickett and his men at the expense of the other participants, both Southern and Northern, and suggested that the event was a major turning point in the Civil War. Reardon's book demonstrates how the memory of the events, which differs from the history of the events, was used by Northerners and Southerners to promote sectional reconciliation. Conversely, the memory of the Vietnam War has been tied to assigning blame because the war has traditionally been viewed as a mistake and a national tragedy. The memory of, and the historical writing on, the conflict in Vietnam have both occurred within the context of the tumultuous 1960s. Only recently has a type of post-Vietnam generation memory and history begun to emerge.

Many factors influence the development of historical memory and perhaps make the telling of history much more difficult. Writing the history of contentious events, such as the Vietnam War, can, as a result, be challenging, particularly for the historian. Although the United States' involvement in Vietnam dates back to World War II, most Americans remember it only in terms of the turbulent 1960s, because it was not until then that most Americans became aware of the small Asian country and the role that American troops were playing there. Thinking of the 1960s brings back memories of social unrest, of revolution: the Civil Rights Movement, "sex, drugs, and rock and roll," political demonstrations on college campuses, Woodstock, flower children and communal living, Ed Sullivan, the Beatles, and Elvis Presley, and, yes, the Vietnam War.

By 1975 most Americans had concluded that even though American troops had won every battle, they had lost the war. Someone had to be blamed, and there was enough blame to spread around. Surely both the military and the government were at fault, and Americans no longer completely trusted either. The social and political upheaval that occurred as a result of, and in conjunction with, the Vietnam War colored Americans' perceptions of the war and of the military and of society as a whole, and those perceptions influenced movies, literature, music, and, to some extent, the writing of the history of the war. Over time, memories of the Vietnam War have softened, but the current conflict in Iraq has brought those memories back to the surface and has evoked comparisons with the conflict in Vietnam.

Today's college students are a generation removed from the Vietnam War, and while some have been told about the war by relatives who served, most have learned about it from movies as widely varied as *Forrest Gump* and *Apocalypse Now*. The curious ones read books by George C. Herring or David Halberstam or take courses at their university. Unfortunately, because the Vietnam War, like most wars or defining moments in history, was complex and multifaceted, it is very difficult for students to get an accurate historical picture of the war from one or two books, or even from a college course. In addition, although there has been some effort recently to change this, most books tell only one side of the story—the American side, which generally suggests that the war was simply one to stop the spread of communism. The Vietnam War was, however, much more than that. It was a war for independence, for religious freedom, for democracy, for communism, for freedom from oppression, for a Vietnamese way of life, for a government free of corruption, for a better way of life. It was a war that spilled over into American society even though it was being fought a world away. It had an impact on all aspects of American life—the economy, politics, society—and the war, in conjunction with the anti-war movement, the sexual revolution, and the Civil Rights Movement, destroyed the "June Cleaver" perfect American world.

As is the case with the Civil War, many discussions about the Vietnam War revolve around history, defeat, and memory. It is one of the few wars in which the debate over its memory commenced even before direct American involvement in the war began. In 1956, Graham Greene published *The Quiet American*, which was made into a motion picture starring Audie Murphy two years later. Greene wrote about political intrigue and what Halberstam later called the "quagmire" that was becoming apparent in Vietnam. In 1967, Bernard B. Fall described the last major battle in the French war in Indochina in *Hell in a Very Small Place: The Siege of Dien Bien Phu*, in which he argued that the political and psychological aspects of Dien Bien Phu were much more significant than its military aspects. This was an argument that was generally ignored by the United States as it became increasingly embroiled in the "quagmire" and ignored the lessons of the French military and political experience in Vietnam.

As the conflict progressed, the debate over the war's meaning and eventual memory became more and more entrenched with journalists like Halberstam and Neil Sheehan, who succeeded in establishing what has become known as the orthodox view or interpretation of the war. Although not all journalists or historians agreed with Halberstam and like-minded journalists at the time, this view and the collective memory of the war have dominated the "history" of the Vietnam War for twenty-five years. With the post-Vietnam generation of historians, however, there is a shift in perspective. These historians have begun to question some of the old memories and to present new views, new interpretations, and new methodologies for writing about the war.

INTRODUCTION

EXPANDING THE VIEW OF THE VIETNAM WAR

The debates over the memory and legacy of the Vietnam War have resulted in at least four basic tenets, which have arisen from the orthodox view. These beliefs are that: (1) the war and its origins are American in nature; (2) the military won every battle, but fought in the service of a dysfunctional South Vietnam; (3) the war was lost because of dissension on the home front; and (4) the war had a considerable aftermath. Understanding these tenets is critical to understanding the war. To further that understanding, each of these themes will be explored briefly here, but in more depth throughout this volume. The following discussions will demonstrate the fact that these four themes are actually much more complex than the orthodox history suggests.

Most Americans arrogantly believe that the Vietnam War and its origins were American in nature. They tend to ignore the other major players in the conflict—the North and South Vietnamese—and the fact that the origins could actually predate US involvement. In fact, the Vietnamese call it the "American War." The conflict in Vietnam, however, was not simply an American war. Its origins are rooted in so much more. The war in Vietnam was part of the Cold War, a regional conflict, a civil war, a class war, a religious war, and a colonial war all at the same time. These different wars merged at times while at other times they collided with each other. Consequently, it is difficult to define the conflict, or conflicts, in Vietnam.

If one limits an examination of the different wars to the period 1965–73, then the "American-ness" of the war becomes more apparent because the American military, to a large extent, dominated the way in which the war was fought; but the war was much more than that. One could, however, easily expand those dates, which would then dictate the inclusion of other players, including the French and the North and South Vietnamese. Ho Chi Minh might have argued that the war began in 1941 when he returned to his native land to unite the Vietnamese people against the Japanese invaders, and he received some US support for the struggle. For the French, who tried to re-establish control over their Asian colony, hostilities commenced in late 1946. By 1950, when President Harry S. Truman sent the first US military advisers to Vietnam to help the French, the United States had become involved in the country again. President Dwight D. Eisenhower chose to let the advisers remain, and in fact increased their number, to help the fledgling government that was created in South Vietnam under Ngo Dinh Diem.

Not all Americans, however, concurred with the nature of US involvement in Vietnam during the 1950s. Rufus Phillips first went to Vietnam in 1954 as a young CIA officer. He returned to the United States a couple of years later, but found himself back in Vietnam running the Office of Rural Affairs in 1960. By the mid-1960s, Phillips argues, US military advisers, as well as the senior diplomatic staff in Vietnam, had no real conception of how to "fight the war." In addition, some Army of the Republic of Vietnam (ARVN) officers, according to Phillips, did have the right idea and were working hard to establish a good relationship with local populations, which he believed would foster support for Diem's government. While Phillips and

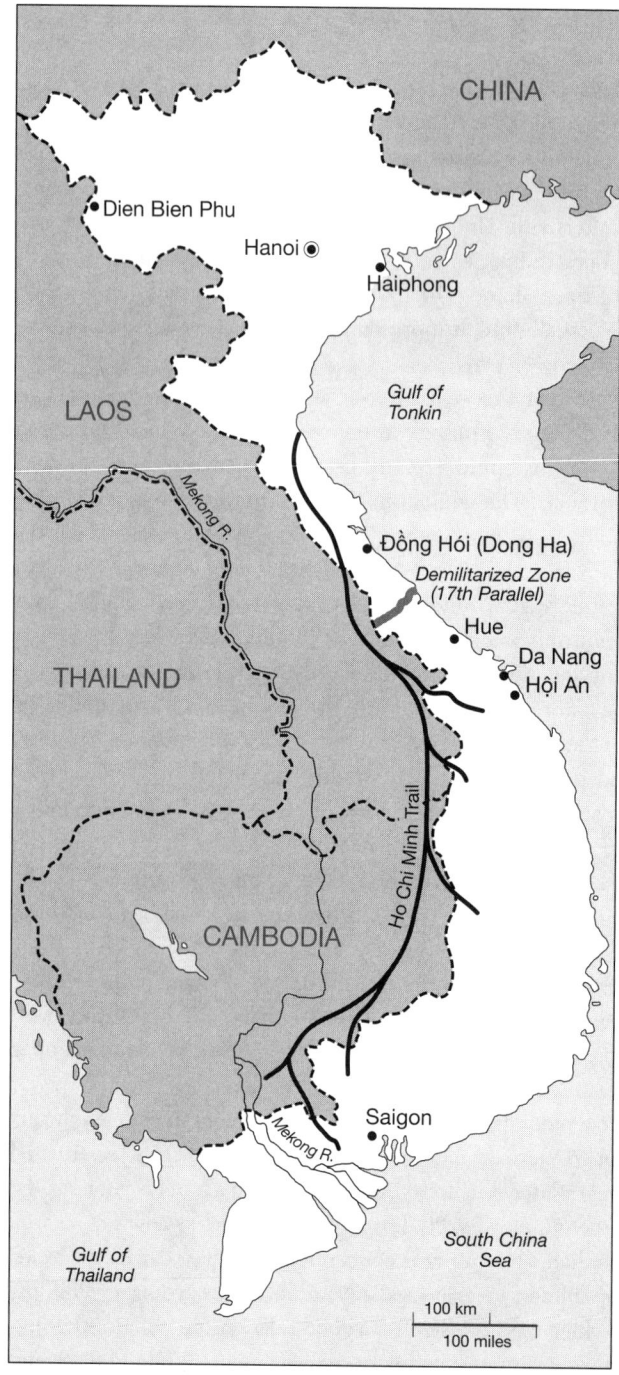

Figure 0.1 Map of Vietnam.

others pushed for a grassroots effort to win over the local populations, the military advisers and the diplomats argued that the United States had to increase its military effort. Consequently, bombings and military operations on the ground, dominated by US doctrine and desires, overshadowed South Vietnamese interests. The South Vietnamese had to win the war, according to Phillips, and could do so with US help. It was not up to the United States to win the war with minimal assistance from its South Vietnamese counterparts. Too few US officials bothered to discover what the South Vietnamese interests and goals were then, and many historians have generally ignored them when writing a history of the war. As Phillips demonstrated, the conflict in Vietnam was not just an "American" war.

The most sacred piece of Vietnam dogma is the idea that American forces won all of the battles they fought during the conflict. Even this, though, is under contention at present. Historians such as Andrew Krepinevich in *The Army and Vietnam* (1988), Harry G. Summers Jr. in *On Strategy: A Critical Analysis of the Vietnam War* (1982), and Mark Moyar in *Phoenix and the Birds of Prey: Counterinsurgency and Counterterrorism in Vietnam* (2007) debate even the fundamental question of how the US military chose to accomplish its strategic mission in Vietnam. At the same time, the debate over the military nature of the war has broadened. Initially, historians writing in the 1970s, 1980s, and 1990s did tend to argue that the US military won every battle, but fought in the service of a dysfunctional South Vietnam. Another traditional version suggests that the US military won every battle, but lost the war because the US government restricted what the military was allowed to do in waging the war. However, even these most standard modes of understanding the American war in Vietnam have come under close scrutiny from a newer generation of historians.

Few historians, however, have made the connection between the US military and the South Vietnamese state. Was the US military in the service of a dysfunctional state, as many historians have argued? Most present a typical view of Diem as a corrupt, tyrannical leader. In addition, few question whether or not South Vietnam actually fought hard in the conflict and seem to suggest that US forces did all of the heavy work and supported the corrupt, inept Army of the Republic of Vietnam (ARVN). There must, however, be more here than meets the eye despite the prevailing view that is articulated in much of the literature. Only in recent years, though, have some post-Vietnam War historians begun to question the standard interpretation.

Not all of the literature about the Vietnam War focuses on military aspects of the conflict. Some historians address the dissension on the American home front and make a connection between it and the military loss of the war. Somehow, draft dodging, race, the evolving and expanding women's rights movement, the anti-war movement, music, the media—THE SIXTIES—have been seen as the reason for the loss in Vietnam. The 1960s was a tumultuous time in American history. American society seemed to be turned upside down, and many, even at the time, made the connection between the social unrest at home and the war in Vietnam. There seems to be a feedback loop between Vietnam and the 1960s, for while the upheaval of the 1960s is cited as the cause for the US defeat in Vietnam, at the same time the Vietnam War is blamed for, at the very least, contributing to the disruption of American society during that decade. By suggesting that they would not win the war on the battlefield but would win it in the streets of America, North Vietnamese officials managed to use the social unrest—particularly the anti-war movement—in the United States to their advantage.

In a conversation that occurred during the four-party military talks in Hanoi in April 1975 the North Vietnamese interpretation becomes even more apparent. President Gerald Ford had just conceded defeat in the Vietnam War. Colonel Harry G. Summers Jr., then the chief of the US delegation's negotiating team, was chatting with his North Vietnamese counterpart, Colonel Tu. "'You know you never defeated us on the battlefield,' said the American colonel. The North Vietnamese colonel pondered this remark a moment. 'That may be so,' he replied, 'but it is also irrelevant.'"[1] Tu's obvious implication was that it did not matter how well the American military had done against the North Vietnamese on the battlefield. The determining factor was how the war played out on the American home front. Many evaluators of the war in Vietnam have concurred. Historians need to explore this more deeply to understand more fully the complex and dynamic relationship between the war in Vietnam and American society.

The fourth tenet, perhaps the most recognizable to Americans, is that Vietnam had a considerable aftermath which involved both physical and psychological manifestations. The most obvious physical one, besides thousands of physically disabled Vietnam veterans, is the Vietnam Veterans Memorial in Washington, DC—"the Wall." Newscasters, reporting over Memorial Day weekend, show crowds of veterans and civilians visiting the Wall. It is an image that most Americans have seen at least once. One of the most poignant scenes in the film *Dear America: Letters Home from Vietnam* is the closing one in which the camera pans the memorial while voices in the background read some of the letters that visitors have left at the Wall. Few viewers can avoid tears, particularly when the voices reading the letters crack and are charged with emotion. Those images are a constant reminder that the Vietnam War is ever-present in American memory. Consequently, the Wall, or rather the response to the creation of the Wall and the response of the visitors at the Wall, is a component of the conflicting memories of the Vietnam War.

The psychological legacy of the war is less tangible and harder to see. Many Americans came to distrust the government during this time, and in some respects that mistrust remains a part of current American society. In addition, thousands of Vietnam veterans suffer from post-traumatic stress disorder (PTSD), and their families live each day with its effects. It is only when a troubled veteran does something dramatic and newsworthy that Americans are forced to acknowledge this particular legacy. Even the federal government was reluctant for many years to recognize that PTSD was a real diagnosis and to allocate funds for treatment at Department of Veterans Affairs facilities. That reluctance fueled the veterans' disillusionment with the government and fostered the feeling that they had been forgotten. Today people are much more willing to assign the PTSD diagnosis, but it frequently has little to do with veterans, particularly Vietnam veterans. One of the most recent examples that comes to mind is September 11, 2001. As the media faithfully reported, many firemen and policemen who responded on 9/11 now suffer from PTSD. While their experiences were quite different from

Figure 0.2 Vietnam Veterans Memorial, Washington, DC. Digital Image Archives. Copyright Shutterstock/SACarroll.

those of Vietnam veterans, the assignment of the PTSD diagnosis provides a tenuous link between the two groups. Although more commonly used today, the term PTSD is also a reminder that the legacy of the Vietnam War remains in American memory.

Another manifestation of the aftermath of the Vietnam War concerns image—America's image—an image that was tarnished by the "Vietnam syndrome," the legacy of failure and defeat. In the wake of the war, Americans no longer trusted the federal government, and more importantly, in some ways, they totally distrusted the military, which had fought the longest war in which the United States had ever been involved—and lost. The image that the United States presented to the world was one of a victor, the champion of the underdog, of the oppressed, of the less fortunate. The outcome of the war, even though President Richard M. Nixon claimed that he was ending the war with honor, destroyed the "feel-good" image that most Americans had of their country. As a result, the US military fought an uphill battle to repair—and in some ways reinvent—its image at home in order to project a better one abroad. To do so, however, they had to overcome the legacy of the Vietnam War.

Ultimately, this book is a response to the challenge posed by the traditional histories and an answer to the question about whether or not there are in fact new perspectives of the Vietnam War to consider. It also posits a challenge to the reader: to re-examine the four basic tenets that are generally reinforced by standard texts on the war. Consequently, this book seeks to address these contexts, questions, and centralities of the war.

NEW PERSPECTIVES ON THE VIETNAM WAR

In his review of Andrew Wiest's award-winning book *Vietnam's Forgotten Army: Heroism and Betrayal in the ARVN*, Matt Steinglass of *The Nation* remarked, "No book about the Vietnam War can be simply a book about the Vietnam War."[2] Given the cultural and historic meaning of Vietnam, no book is just that—about Vietnam. Its meaning carries further, along with the ghosts of the war, and is compared, in some cases, to the ongoing war in Iraq. Unfortunately, too many monographs about the Vietnam War do not heed Steinglass's advice. They present facts about the political and military aspects of the war and draw the appropriate conclusions, but they fail to include the other aspects of the war that will allow them to complete the picture adequately. Unless one seeks out a book written by a Vietnamese historian or wartime participant, one learns little about the Vietnamese side of the story. The same can be said about African Americans and women. This book presents new ways in which to examine the Vietnam War and seeks to educate the reader even more about the impact of the war on *all* aspects of Vietnamese and American society and culture. Consequently, the topics covered in these chapters are vital to a complete understanding of the Vietnam War. Rather than view this book sequentially, however, the reader should look at the chapters as they relate to four dominant themes: origins, the military experience, the anti-war movement, and the legacy, which can be perceived as a cultural legacy and as a military/diplomatic legacy.

INTRODUCTION

Origins

In "Vietnam divided: regional history and the Vietnam Wars, 1598–1975," Martin Loicano's discussion goes beyond the traditional dates that most historians assign to the Vietnam War, because, in his view, the war was defined by more than just US involvement. He provides the voice of the people who were fighting for independence, for communism, for democracy, for land reform, and for political, religious, and economic freedom. Loicano concludes that the war in Vietnam was much more complex and deeply rooted than most people understand. He utilizes Vietnamese sources to suggest that perhaps the master Vietnamese narrative of the war, which argues that Ho Chi Minh was the only natural successor to Vietnam's long history of staving off foreign domination, can be proven to be flawed and that South Vietnam actually had historical precedent and even the ability to survive.

Matthew Masur, on the other hand, in "Historians and the origins of the Vietnam War" focuses on a historiographical look at why the United States got involved in the war and when the American government reached a point of no return regarding its commitment in Vietnam. He includes a discussion of Ngo Dinh Diem, as well as questions about why the United States supported him. In addition, he critiques the orthodox view that Diem was a problem or a failure and explores the revisionist takes on Diem and more nuanced orthodox views as well. Masur argues that questions about the Vietnam War remain pertinent today, and as a result "the scholarship on Vietnam will remain passionate, vibrant, and contentious."

The military experience

Many monographs about the Vietnam War fail to take into account one of the major players: the Army of the Republic of Vietnam (ARVN). Andrew Wiest attempts to rectify that situation in his chapter entitled "The 'other' Vietnam War." In doing so, he suggests that the prevailing view that the ARVN performed poorly on the battlefield was not entirely correct. He challenges the orthodox conclusions about the ARVN, conclusions that became entrenched in the American military's assessment of their South Vietnamese counterparts by the early 1960s. Although he does not redeem all ARVN officers, Wiest's conclusions mirror those of Rufus Phillips, who worked with ARVN officers, both good and bad, on a grassroots level.

Like Wiest, Heather Stur introduces another voice—that of women—in "The Women's Army Corps goes to Vietnam." Stur examines the experiences of WACs in Vietnam and "the ways in which ideas about appropriate gender roles shaped the WAC image." She also notes the differences between the image and the reality. In addition, Stur explores the motivations for service held by WACs, the difficulties women faced while serving in the US military, and ultimately what the experience meant to the women who served in Vietnam.

Women were not the only people to have another experience in Vietnam. That was also the case for the approximately 800 American servicemen who were incarcerated in prison camps in both North and South Vietnam. Few monographs focus on POWs, and although that has begun to change in recent years, their voices need to be incorporated into the Vietnam War narrative. In "The American POW experience," Glenn Robins gives voice to that change. He examines the prisoner of war experience both chronologically and geographically within the broader context of "no official or master POW narrative." As a result, Robins uncovers a variety of experiences when contrasting the POWs of the jungle camps of the South with the urban camps of the North.

Finally, as is the case in all conflicts, war has an impact on the soldiers who fight and survive it. During World War I, soldiers suffered from shell shock, while soldiers who fought in Vietnam received a different diagnosis, a new diagnosis—PTSD—a diagnosis that is no longer given exclusively to soldiers. Raymond M. Scurfield explores PTSD in "Post-traumatic stress disorder and healing from the war." He examines the effect that PTSD had and continues to have on the soldiers, whom he calls "living casualties of the war," and their families in an effort to educate the public about the real, wide-ranging impact the war had on those who fought it.

The anti-war movement

While most general texts about the Vietnam War briefly discuss the anti-war movement in the United States, they often fail to delve more deeply into the different types of resistance movements that emerged during the war. Amy Scott's chapter, "Patriots for peace," moves beyond the traditional focus on student activists and includes a sophisticated analysis of the role liberal internationalists, radical pacifists, and religious-minded dissenters played in the anti-war movement. Scott also examines how Black Power and Chicano activists in America used the anti-war movement to create the message of a "global liberation struggle." Scott devotes attention to the visits anti-war activists made to both South and North Vietnam. As a result, a dominant theme throughout the chapter is the impact US bombing had on Vietnamese civilians. Scott concludes that the anti-war movement fashioned a legacy that contributed to the "people to people diplomacy or citizenship diplomacy" of the late Cold War era."

Not all opponents of the Vietnam war participated in anti-war groups. Some chose to work within the established system. In "Vietnam and the conscientious objector experience," Philip Szmedra draws upon his own experiences as a conscientious objector from 1970 to 1973 to examine the entire conscientious objector (CO) experience. In addition to identifying increased political awareness and moral consciousness as the reasons why some men chose to become COs, he also explores the process he and other COs had to follow to officially declare themselves a CO, what life for a CO was like, why some men declared themselves a CO, and how they tried to move on after the war.

African Americans became involved in a number of resistance movements, including the Black Panthers, as Curtis Austin notes in "The Black Panthers and the Vietnam War." Unlike previous studies, such as Wallace Terry's *Bloods: An Oral History of the Vietnam War by Black*

Veterans, which examines the Vietnam War and its impact through the experience of African American soldiers, Austin discusses the impact the soldiers had on the Black Panther Party. He explains the origins of the Black Panther Party and its vitriolic attack on the "white man's" Vietnam War. The Black Panther Party recruited black Vietnam veterans who possessed military training and experience in guerrilla warfare and utilized them, according to Austin, in an armed defense of the black community against the white power structure of local, state, and the federal governments.

The legacy

The multifaceted legacy of Vietnam in the United States is evident in all aspects of American culture, including literature, films, and music, a full understanding of which calls for something beyond the standard historical methodological approach. Literary scholar Maureen Ryan, author of "The Vietnam War and literature," discusses depictions of the Vietnam War in three genres: fiction, drama, and poetry. She argues that "this vast assemblage of literary treatments of the war, its aftermath, and the home front testify to the lingering influence of the Vietnam War in American society." She also suggests that literary texts—novels, memoirs, drama, and poetry—reflect that influence and "personally and powerfully recreate a variety of experiences of the war and its era." Although she focuses primarily on the American perspective, Ryan does devote a section to the "voices of the Vietnamese." Ryan uses several literary examples, such as the traditional combat novel, novels about the home front and the aftermath of the war, and Vietnam memoirs, to demonstrate the ways in which the legacy of the Vietnam War continues to have an impact on American society.

One can also see the influence of the Vietnam War on American society through the movies that were produced beginning in the 1960s as Thomas Doherty discusses in "Vietnam and film." Noting the two waves of Vietnam movies, he analyzes films that were about the war without being explicitly about the war, those that were critical of the war, and others that attempted to persuade the viewer that Vietnam veterans were heroes. Doherty argues that the films have come full circle and accomplished what *The Green Berets* did not: "turned Vietnam into a World War II movie."

In his discussion, Doherty identifies the key components of a Vietnam War movie, including one of the most memorable—music—which is the topic of Kim Herzinger's chapter, "The soundtrack of Vietnam." Concluding that rock music provided the background to the Vietnam era and quoting lyrics to make his case, Herzinger traces some of the reasons why rock music achieved this extraordinary cultural resonance and why it came to be such a fitting expression of the Vietnam era's sensibility, and suggests some of the ways that rock music expressed that sensibility.

In addition to its cultural legacy, the Vietnam War also has a military legacy. James H. Willbanks presents a new take on a traditional topic—the US military—in "The legacy of the

Vietnam War for the US Army." He argues that the US Army of 1991 that achieved success in the First Gulf War "was shaped by the legacy of the Vietnam War and in turn today's Army continues to be shaped by the Army's response to that war." Willbanks examines how the American military reacted to the failure of Vietnam. Reeling from defeat, the military attempted to redefine the American "way of war." In a series of revolutionary developments, the American Army transformed itself into a professional, technologically adept force. However, its reliance on technology, though it made the Army the dominant conventional force in the world, left the military vulnerable to another insurgency.

In the current political and media-dominated climate, both politicians and journalists have analyzed the American military's performance in Iraq and, as a result of accusations that the military has implemented the wrong strategy, have made connections between Iraq and Vietnam. Lloyd Gardner addresses these correlations in "Iraq as 'the good war' as opposed to Vietnam, the bad war." As the title suggests, Gardner offers a comparison between Vietnam and Iraq, a debate that has been conducted in the media, in classrooms, and by academics since the start of the Iraq War. As Gardner claims, many of the terms used to describe the conflict in Iraq are reminiscent of "Vietnam rhetoric." He invites a comparison between the two wars, but he also discovers that the Vietnam syndrome, the legacy of failure and defeat, the so-called bad war, prompted the Bush administration to frame the Iraq War in terms reminiscent of World War II, America's so-called "good war."

The issues surrounding the Vietnam War and its legacy are too complex to be dealt with in a traditional "here is what happened" textbook. No single text or specialist can do it all. Still, one must try. Thus, this is the reason for this collection and why it is so different from other works. Taken together, the chapters in this volume offer new perspectives of Vietnam War history. They add to the discussion of the war in an important way because, in many cases, they give voice to viewpoints previously neglected in the debate about the war. They also persuade the reader to look at the conflict in new ways. These exciting, thought-provoking chapters fill the gaps in the prevailing histories of the Vietnam War and reflect the continued interest in the war that exists even today in American society.

Designed to supplement standard textbooks about the Vietnam War, this volume has several features, including a website, that will make history come alive. Each chapter includes a timeline that will enable readers to place events about which they are reading in the broader context of the war, as well as visual images of different aspects of the conflict. Each chapter also includes suggested readings and a list of questions that will help the readers better analyze the presented material. In addition, there is a website for the book that includes a number of different items: primary documents for each chapter, excerpts from Vietnam literature, and links to music that can be downloaded to an iPod, and to film clips. Readers who access these features will have a better understanding of the complexity of the Vietnam War. The website can be accessed at: **www.americaandthevietnamwar.com** or **www.americaandthevietnamwar.co.uk**.

SUGGESTED READING

Herring, George C. *America's Longest War: The United States and Vietnam, 1950–1975*. 4th ed. New York: McGraw-Hill, 2002.
Karnow, Stanley. *Vietnam: A History*. New York: Penguin Books, 1991.
McMaster, H. R. *Dereliction of Duty: Johnson, McNamara, the Joint Chiefs of Staff, and the Lies That Led to Vietnam*. New York: Harper Perennial, 1998.
Moyar, Mark. *Phoenix and the Birds of Prey: Counterinsurgency and Counterterrorism in Vietnam*. Winnipeg: Bison Books, 2007.
Phillips, Rufus. *Why Vietnam Matters: An Eyewitness Account of Lessons Not Learned*. Annapolis, MD: Naval Institute Press, 2008.
Schulzinger, Robert D. *A Time for War: The United States and Vietnam, 1941–1975*. New York: Oxford University Press, 1997.
Summers, Harry G. Jr. *On Strategy: A Critical Analysis of the Vietnam War*. Novato, CA: Presidio, 1982.
Military History Institute of Vietnam. *Victory in Vietnam: The Official History of the People's Army of Vietnam, 1954–1975*. Lawrence: University Press of Kansas, 2002.
Wiest, Andrew. *Vietnam's Forgotten Army: Heroism and Betrayal in the ARVN*. New York: New York University Press, 2008.

NOTES

1. Conversation in Hanoi, April 1975, in *On Strategy: A Critical Analysis of the Vietnam War* by Harry G. Summers Jr. (Novato, CA: Presidio, 1984), 1, 7n.
2. Max Steinglass, "Questions of Loyalty," *The Nation*, April 3, 2008, http://www.thenation.com/doc/200804.21/steinglass.

TIMELINE EVENTS

111 BC – First Chinese Occupation of Vietnam

1288 – Vietnamese victory over the Mongols

1600 – Nguyễn Hoàng' decides to create an independent southern principality

1698 – Founding of Saigon

1802 – Unity of Vietnam under the Nguyễn

1860 – End of Vietnamese unity under the Nguyễn

1862 – Beginning of French colonial era in Vietnam

1949 – Bảo Đại takes control of Associated State of Vietnam

1954 – End of French colonial era in Vietnam

1963 – Assassination of Ngô Đình Diệm

1967 – Nguyễn Văn Thiệu becomes President of South Vietnam

1975 – Fall of Saigon

Chapter 1

Vietnam divided
Regional history and the Vietnam wars, 1598–1975

Martin Loicano

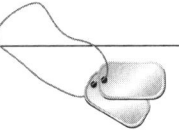

CHAPTER SUMMARY

When noticed at all in the West, Vietnamese history is usually viewed through the lens of an imagined past of a single, united Vietnam offering continuous resistance to foreign invaders culminating in Hồ Chí Minh's August Revolution in 1945. However, recent scholarship has indicated the presence of a much more complex Vietnamese past—one that involved disunity, struggle, and emerging cultural differences. Viewed from the vantage point of this more nuanced version of Vietnamese history, the American war in Vietnam carries a new meaning as part of a long history of South vs. North struggle in the region.

The Vietnam War can only be understood in the context of both Vietnamese regional history and the complex international relationships of the Cold War. General histories of the war usually include a brief and simplistic version of Vietnamese history, an imagined past of a single, united Vietnam offering continuous resistance to foreign invaders culminating in Hồ Chí Minh's August Revolution in 1945. The defeat of France and the United States in the twentieth century comprises simply another chapter in this version of Vietnam's complex history. This narrative is conceptually centered on resistance and geographically oriented toward Hanoi and the Red River Delta. However, the Vietnamese people have a varied and nuanced story that has included a number of civil wars and rival Vietnamese states. When the Republic of Vietnam (RVN) came into being in 1954, it was a state with important historical precedents, not merely an American creation. South Vietnam's problem was not historical legitimacy; it was the failure to use the past to suit its aims and the problem of facing a powerful, determined military threat from the North.

If we are to understand the complicated reasons why the Vietnam War began, we must reconsider the way in which we teach Vietnamese history as it pertains to the twenty-five-year Second Indochina War. Both South and North Vietnam of the 1950s evolved in ways based on their regional past, and Vietnamese on both sides found causes they could support to varying degrees. On the whole, the Republic of Vietnam's relationship to regional history and its genesis and development have been mischaracterized. The RVN is portrayed as an entirely illegitimate and hopelessly flawed entity, while the Democratic Republic of Vietnam (DRV) to the north has been inaccurately depicted as the sole heir to Vietnam's past traditions and author of an independent popular revolution.

When the seventeenth parallel divided competing Vietnamese states for the second time into North and South in 1954, both sides had already entered into complex international entanglements in different ways for their own reasons. When the world's powers backed rival claimants to political control of a divided Vietnam, this was in some ways the perpetuation of a centuries-old conflict that overlay the more recent concerns of the Cold War. Only by thinking of this war as a Vietnamese event, with historical precedents on both sides of the Demilitarized Zone (DMZ), can we begin to help our students understand the causes and course of this bitter conflict.

In this vein, it is worthwhile to consider some of the prevailing notions about the twentieth-century South Vietnamese state and its military. When considered in historical context, few frequent criticisms of the Republic of Vietnam retain their merit, and so we must look elsewhere for answers to important questions about the history of the long war fought from 1954 to 1975. Historians have argued that the Republic of Vietnam was an American creation, a place with no roots in the Vietnamese past, and so this state could never have the same legitimacy as that perceived to have accrued around Hồ Chí Minh and the communist government in Hanoi. As recently as early 2008, historian James Carter's *Inventing Vietnam* continued to perpetuate the intertwined myths that South Vietnam had no historical basis in the Vietnamese past, that it was an American creation, and that it was doomed to fail from the beginning.[1]

Critics also argue (despite the fact that nearly all of these authors lack the tools to explore materials in Vietnamese) that successive South Vietnamese governments failed the people of the South, never representing their interests or making efforts to improve their lot. Along the same lines, scholars have argued that the South's army was a disaster, that rampant and somehow peculiar self-interest and incompetence among southern military and civilian officials crippled efforts at state building and war making. The RVN was thus an illegitimate entity that never transcended its purportedly dubious origins. In this line of reasoning, shared by conventional scholarship and, coincidentally, the Communist Party of Vietnam, South Vietnam was merely an aberration in the natural and historic unity of the Vietnamese people. In each instance, Vietnamese communism is presented as the polar opposite: an independent, popular, effective, and solely legitimate arbiter of nationalist revolution. However, Hanoi's government and its leaders successfully constructed this image in spite of the historical record. The story of the

Vietnamese in both the southern and northern regions was more complex and more inclined to validate the existence of a separate state than is generally recognized.

Regional and local identities played a complicated role in the Second Indochina War. In South Vietnam a unique and potent regional identity formed over the centuries preceding the war —one reason that substantial numbers of Vietnamese people could not identify with either northern rule or communism. At the same time as regionalism served as a basis for an independent southern state, the rivalry between South Vietnam's two principal cities, Saigon and Hue, and the presence of large numbers of northern Vietnamese refugees, prevented the conflict from operating on a sectional basis. The Republic of Vietnam also faced the strongly dissimilar character of its three regions (north, south, and central) and the challenge of forming a national narrative and Vietnamese identity that appealed to these three groups. At the same time, maintaining a sufficiently strong distinction from the communist northerners was a critical challenge for the RVN. Much as scholars have legitimized North Vietnam's war in the context of Vietnamese history, we must look to the Vietnamese past to find antecedents for the foundations of the Republic of Vietnam.

Widely read general accounts by George Herring, Stanley Karnow, George Donelson Moss, and Spencer Tucker make mention of the division of Vietnam from the late sixteenth century in passing, but a more lengthy examination of the period from 1558 to 1895 reveals some relevant antecedents to conflicts in the Second Indochina War. These same prominent general accounts also cling to recent communist historiography, positing the joined themes of antipathy to China and all foreigners, and storied resistance to them as the principal themes of the Vietnamese past. George Moss typifies this approach in his *Vietnam: An American Ordeal*: "Eternal war was the primal theme of Vietnamese history, but there was also the corollary theme as well—the myth of indomitability."[2] Of general accounts of the war in English, only Mark Moyar's *Triumph Forsaken* has made a more accurate assessment of the Sino-Vietnamese relationship between the tenth and twentieth centuries:

> In general, amicability characterized relations between China and Vietnam during these thousand years. Having been a Chinese province and a popular destination for Chinese emigrants during the preceding thousand years, Vietnam had thoroughly absorbed the customs, ideas, and religions of China.[3]

Rather than viewing the Vietnamese past as a series of foreign disruptions of a natural unity of a single people, history tells us that the Vietnamese had been divided for centuries for reasons still valid to some degree today. These general accounts obscure the actual nature of the relationship between China and the Vietnamese, replacing a story of cultural borrowing and mutually beneficial cooperation with one of storied resistance that began with the first Chinese occupation of Vietnam in 111 BC. In a recent article, historian Keith Taylor said it best: "[T]he mantra about Vietnam having suffered during a thousand years of Chinese domination and then spending the next thousand years resisting Chinese aggression expresses one of the most entrenched yet most erroneous doctrines of Vietnamese nationalism."[4] All of these textbooks retell the stories of Vietnamese rebel heroes in detail but give only a passing nod to the reality that the Vietnamese accepted Chinese rule more often than not. Vietnam's most famous military leaders, such as the Trưng Sisters, Triệu Ẩu, Ngô Quyền, Trần Hưng Đạo and Lê Lợi, appear in these accounts as a lineage of heroes leading inevitably towards Hồ Chí Minh's 1945 proclamation of the August Revolution[5]—an event that in Herring's words "marked yet another milestone in Vietnam's centuries-old struggle against foreign domination."[6]

These historians obscure the Vietnamese past in two major ways: First, they do not allow for cooperation between China and Vietnam, such as the presence of a large Chinese army whose Song loyalist troops played a major role in Trần Hưng Đạo's victories over the Mongols in 1287–8. Second, this teleological version of the Vietnamese past limits itself to a single legitimate version of Vietnameseness at the expense of obscuring a distinct southern identity and polity with roots hundreds of years old. In most cases, Sino-Vietnamese relations were neither wholly positive nor adversarial; Vietnamese elites were most often divided in their views on China's role in their country. For every example of armed resistance to China, the historical record reveals another instance of cooperation with China by other groups of Vietnamese. For example, during one of Vietnam's many civil wars in the 1520s, both the ruling Lê house and the rebel Mặc sought assistance from the Ming Dynasty. Again in the 1880s, the Nguyễn ruler sought and obtained direct Chinese military intervention from the Qing Dynasty's youthful emperor Guangxu in an effort to turn back invading French forces.[7] The Qing troops arrived in strength, much as Chinese troops had stood with the Trần some six hundred years before, but in this case could not overcome the invaders. During the First Indochina War with France, Hồ Chí Minh, like other Vietnamese elites before, requested extensive Chinese economic and military aid in April of 1950.

Chinese military aid and direct participation continued until the Second Indochina War ended in 1975. A total of 320,000 Chinese troops served in Vietnam between 1965 and 1970, continuing a trend that had begun in 1950, when Chinese officers had been temporarily forced to assume some leadership roles in the inexperienced People's Army of Vietnam (PAVN). Much as Song Dynasty officers had stood with the Trần against the Mongols, the Chinese People's Liberation Army (PLA) played a substantial role in the victory over France and, later, the United States and the Republic of Vietnam. China also sent hundreds of thousands of weapons and millions of rounds of ammunition to its allies in North Vietnam.[8] Paradoxically, at the same time as Hanoi relied on extensive Chinese assistance, its historians were rewriting the history of Vietnam to allow only for hostile relationships with foreign powers. The imagined history of resistance played a central role in Hanoi's justification of its war aims against the United States and the RVN and in morale-building efforts. Accordingly, Chinese troops, though serving openly in PLA uniforms and with PLA equipment in some cases, were ordered to avoid any interactions with the people of North Vietnam, so as to better preserve the government's position that it fought alone in a nationalist revolution against foreign invaders. Though international participation and aid were critical to the war effort in the North, most accounts

VIETNAM DIVIDED

Figure 1.1 Statue of Trần Hưng Đạo, downtown Saigon, 1968. Monument to the Vietnamese hero who led the Vietnamese to major victories over the Mongols, 1287–8, and a key figure in the accepted version of Vietnam's resistance to Chinese rule.

Slide: vas037761, no date, William E. LeGro Collection, The Vietnam Archive, Texas Tech University.

19

of the war in English fail to frame the war in its true context; both North and South Vietnam were heavily dependent on outside aid and participation in the Indochina Wars. Likewise, civil war in Vietnam was every bit as common as was resistance and cooperation with foreign powers. In some important ways, the events of the 1950s and 1960s were based in the history of the civil wars of the sixteenth and seventeenth centuries. In order to help students better understand the complexity of these wars, we must place both the DRV and the Republic of Vietnam in the context of the Vietnamese past.

General accounts and textbooks, excepting Mark Moyar's *Triumph Forsaken*, locate the birth of the Republic of Vietnam entirely in the 1950s, and pose the southern state as a foreign creation and an illegitimate entity. George Herring's *America's Longest War* exemplifies this point of view by titling his chapter on South Vietnam's early development, "Our Offspring: Nation Building in South Vietnam, 1954–1961." George Moss takes a similar stance in *Vietnam: An American Ordeal*, where his third chapter, "An Experiment in Nation Building," takes a similar line, ignoring both the significance of the longer past and twentieth-century non-communist nationalism in favor of the idea that the United States somehow created South Vietnam in the context of the Cold War. However, in the field of Vietnamese studies, Keith Taylor, Li Tana, Philip Taylor, Yang Baoyun, Patricia Pelley, Edward Miller, Võ Văn Sen, and Claudine Ang have successfully challenged and overturned the Hanoi-centered teleology of resistance-driven history and replaced it with a more nuanced version that includes a distinct southern narrative, and a better sense of localized identities that had emerged before and during the colonial period that proved irreconcilable with Vietnamese communist rule.[9]

By and large, military historians have yet to incorporate alternative visions of Vietnamese history, and have thereby perpetuated an inaccurate general narrative that falls into line with Hanoi's master narrative, constructed during the 1950s to serve the needs of the Communist Party. Patricia Pelley has identified a process whereby wartime official historians in the North constructed a self-serving narrative,

> locating the origins of the national capital in Hanoi in the year 1010, the commemoration washed away the imprecision of the past; it glossed over the complications of historical geography and completely erased the political dynamics that normally had limited the government's reach. Moreover the commemorative literature proclaimed, since its founding in 1010 Hanoi had been the single legitimate center of authority, the source of centralized rule, and the country's cultural and economic hub.[10]

The resulting narrative identifies Hanoi as the only legitimate center of Vietnamese power and the epicenter of Vietnam's culture and economy, while denying the historical legacy that lay in the foundations of the Republic of Vietnam in the 1950s.

THE REPUBLIC OF VIETNAM'S ROOTS: THE SOUTH BEFORE 1860

In addition to global Cold War alignments, the Second Indochina War was also a war between distinct Vietnamese conceptions of that country, one centered on Hanoi and the other, one that grew up along with Saigon, a younger and radically different version. A unique southern identity grew out of Saigon's status as an economic gateway, and an ideology developed through that distinction. Saigon was by nature and history a capitalist market city, which makes it different from Vietnam's northern cities in several important ways. Saigon was a part of the formation of "the southern version of being Vietnamese" that originated with Nguyễn Hoàng's decision in 1600 to create a separate southern principality. His decision inaugurated a period of Nguyễn lordship of the South that lasted until 1788, which, in Keith Taylor's, words operated in "relative freedom from the Vietnamese past."[11] Whereas the northern Trịnh state in the seventeenth and eighteenth centuries remained bound to traditional institutions, particularly neo-Confucian views and suspicion toward foreigners, the South adopted a more cosmopolitan outlook. The South was "home to a multi-ethnic, ever changing population" that, as scholar Philip Taylor has pointed out, unlike the North, had a society "open to the exchange of people, objects and ideas."[12] The South under the Nguyễn lords was both culturally and literally divided from North Vietnam behind thirty miles of heavily defended border fortifications studded with over a thousand cannon, "a network [of walls] between the sea and the mountains in the basin of the Nhật Lệ river at Đồng Hới."[13] People in Nguyễn territory interacted with highland peoples—Khmers, Chams, Japanese, Chinese, and even some Europeans—in commercial and social exchanges that produced a society more prosperous and open than Đàng Ngoài, the northern state.

From its inception around 1698, Saigon was both a "first-rate trade center, which attracted crowds of foreign merchant navigators," and a place with a higher degree of personal freedom, leading some Vietnamese scholars to make an "analogy with the American Far West."[14] Indeed, as in the American West, firearms were an important part of the sixteenth-century southern Vietnamese economy. However, the analogy does not capture the full degree of separation between these two independent Vietnamese polities. Both northern and southern Vietnamese states engaged foreigners to supplement their arsenals, but the Nguyễn in the South, also called Cochinchina or Đàng Trong, proved to be the more successful in doing so, perhaps because their need for technology was greater. They had to be ready to turn back an invasion from the north at any time and did so many times with success, so southern traders kept an open attitude for reasons of economy and security, as well as a general cultural inclination towards openness and internationalism. In the North, visiting traders such as Samuel Baron found business difficult and both the northern economy and the reception of foreign visitors wanting:

> their domestick trade consists in rice, salt fish, and other sustenance; little raw and wrought silk for their own wear. They likewise drive a commerce with bowes and ai, though with no great profit, by reason of high expenses and large presents to the Eunuchs, who command

the avenues; nor do the Chinese that pass those ways fare better, being often exacted upon, and sometimes stripp'd of all they have by the ravenous Mandereens. And since it is one of the policies of the court not to make the subjects rich, lest they should be proud and ambitious, and aspire to greater matters than the king connives at those disorders, and oppresses them with heavy taxes and impositions; and should he know that any persons were to exceed the ordinary mean of a private subject, they would incur the danger of losing all, on some pretence or other; which Is a great discouragement to the industrious and necessitates them to bury their wealth, having no means to improve it . . . As for foreign traders, a new-comer suffers, besides hard usage in his buying and selling, a thousand inconveniences; and no certain rates on merchandizes imported or exported being imposed, the insatiable mandareens cause the ships to be rummages, and take what commodities may likely yield a price at their own rates, using the kings name to cloak their griping and villainous extortions; and for all this there is no remedy but patience.[15]

In order to hold back the threat of the much larger infantry of the Trịnh to the north, numerous cannon were mounted on the walls at Đồng Hới and later around the palace at Hue and in a series of coastal fortifications, mainly to preserve the South from invasion by the North. The Nguyễn sought to preserve a separate polity that, by either necessity or inclination, had markedly different attitudes about the world and the way to interact with foreign powers. Economic requirements of the state played an important role in trade, and one of the Nguyễn lords' imperatives was to maintain their military strength. Visitors to southern Vietnam found that military goods usually played a role in negotiations for trade rights.[16] Seventeenth-century southern Vietnam differed from the North in several important ways. A good part of that prosperity went to maintaining Cochinchina's military edge over its rivals. Visitors repeatedly recognized Cochinchinese expertise with firearms, and some European visitors admitted that even their own forces paled next to them.[17] Writing around 1620, Christoforo Borri discovered that European ships gave Cochinchinese gunners a wide berth, as the Cochinchinese were deadly accurate gunners.[18] The South developed remarkable military skills and trade networks because it wanted to keep the northerners out of its affairs entirely, and instead develop a state that was part of the open, fluid world of island Southeast Asia rather than the more staid Sinic world that included the northern Vietnamese state. Additionally, the blend of international participation and military commerce served as a precedent for the RVN's alliances in the 1954–75 war.

In 1695, Thomas Bowyear met with Cochinchinese officials seeking a trade agreement for his employer, the British East India Company; while negotiating with a Nguyễn high mandarin, the English merchant discovered that an important condition for reaching terms was the ability to supply cannon to the Nguyễn. Bowyear also noted that trade at Fai-Fo (Hội An) included Chinese ships bringing in saltpeter from Ning-Po, lead from Siam, and additional saltpeter from Batavia.[19] In 1642, Fransisco, a Japanese translator for Dutch traders in

Cochinchina, also noted the importance of gunpowder in trade there; he noted that saltpeter and lead came in from Siam, while sulfur came from Japan, Laos, or China.[20] The Nguyễn, according to Christoforo Borri, who resided in Cochinchina between 1616 and 1621, also imported a large quantity of Japanese swords, well known for their high quality.[21] The Dutch also offered three cannon along with 5,265 guilders in their trade and peace agreement with the Nguyễn in 1651.[22] War was an important business for the Cochinchinese, and foreign military technologies and advisers played an important role in it. The southerners made cannon a principal demand in foreign trade because these weapons had many times been the reason for victory in repelling Trịnh invasions and in the conquest of Cham and Cambodian lands.

Fortifications played a large role in the preservation of Đàng Trong, most notably the walls at Đồng Hới that divided South from North—a network of structures eighteen kilometers in length and six meters high that ran west to east from the mountains of the Annamite Cordillera to the East Sea.[23] The most accurate account, written by Cadière in 1906, tells of a series of wooden and earth barricades augmented with cannon, a full network of defensive walls designed to provide multiple lines of defense to keep the northerners out of the South.[24] Nguyễn fortifications also employed Western concepts well into the nineteenth century and reflected the designs of famed engineers such as Sebastian Vauban. Yet the Nguyễn began to fortify far earlier with the help of Europeans, such as the Portuguese engineer João da Cruz. Begun in 1631 at the suggestion of Đào Duy Từ, the defensive walls served as the principal barrier to Trịnh invasions and played an important role in turning the final battles of 1672 in favor of the Nguyễn.[25] The Trịnh, according to historian Victor Lieberman, "hurled up to 180,000 land troops at a time in seven major offensives—all unsuccessful—from 1627–1672."[26] Nguyễn cannon played a major role in these victories. In July 1643, three Dutch warships allied with the Trịnh were engaged and defeated by Nguyễn galleys, which used their guns to sink one Dutch ship and kill the captain of another.[27]

Alexander De Rhodes also commended the Cochinchinese navy and additionally noted that the Nguyễn had six hundred war elephants and at least six thousand well-trained musketeers.[28] The most important aspect of the Nguyễn military, though, was its artillery. The firearms technologies the Vietnamese acquired first from the Chinese and later from Europeans became vital to the survival of Đàng Trong. The defensive fortifications that held back the Trịnh would have been futile if not manned by a professional force and replete with cannon. Many of the "twelve hundred cannons, all made of bronze" the Nguyễn kept were placed on the defensive fortifications, making them a formidable obstacle to any attacker.[29] Cannon were such a high priority for the Nguyễn that they built a foundry near Hue and employed foreigners such as João da Cruz to direct the production of guns in the seventeenth century.[30] This tradition continued into the Nguyễn Dynasty (1802–83), when foreign advisers from neighboring Asian nations and the West played an important role in the military affairs of the Vietnamese state and in the society as a whole.[31] The South had accordingly developed a far more open attitude towards foreigners in comparison to the xenophobic and more regimented North. This international flavor was also apparent in the economic development of the South. Between

1598 and 1788, military independence and a different notion of economy and society colored the South in ways that made it difficult to envision it as being part of one state with the North.

By 1700, Saigon had already developed a philosophy based on a market economy and what Philip Taylor has called a "different sense of Vietnamese identity rooted in the social, cultural, and physical environment of the new southern state."[32] Major General Nguyễn Duy Hinh summarized this phenomenon:

> As Vietnamese territory grew in length, communication became difficult and the differences deepened between the North and South . . . By force of protracted separation the traditions and customs originating in the Northern heartland became relaxed in the free and pioneer spirit of the frontier. Contact with, and borrowing from, Indian civilization through the intermediary of the Chams and Khmers also brought about significant alterations in the heavily-Chinese influenced culture of the North. Time and isolation finally combined to accentuate these changes in the South.[33]

This first era of war between two independent Vietnamese states presaged the conflict to come in the 1950s. Though conflict between the two regions was interrupted by the rule of the Nguyễn over the entire country from 1802 to 1860, essential cultural differences had been established that neither the Southern rule of the entire country nor French colonialism could entirely suppress. To the contrary, discriminatory French colonial policies facilitated the preservation of a unique Southern culture and society based on these same ideas of internationalism and relative freedom.

COLONIAL SOUTH VIETNAM, 1862–1954

During the colonial era (1862–1954), Saigon was, in Philip Taylor's words, "more amenable to the type of economic programs favored in the course of French imperial expansion," through which Saigon and its surroundings "experienced the greatest impact of capitalism, commercialization, urbanization and a bustling traffic in new intellectual movements."[34] Saigon had become a "forest of masts" by the late eighteenth century and had a population already convinced of the value of trade and of a market-based society.

Between 1859 and 1954, French city planners built Saigon into a city that elevated its commercial bent to a new scale, and also added new ideological elements to the already unique Vietnamese city. Having learned about French society through education and colonial government propaganda, Vietnamese in Saigon became familiar with and understood French political notions such as democracy. French capitalism simply reinforced earlier southern Vietnamese notions of the free market that characterized Saigon. Additionally, France brought new conceptions of modernity and a more international attitude that resonated with Saigon's historical development under the Nguyễn. By the early twentieth century, Saigon was known for "publicized debates, political movements, symbolic events, and the charismatic intellectual and political figures of the city."[35] Scholar Shawn McHale has pointed out the existence of a livelier and "more dynamic" public sphere in Saigon that was the most open in all of colonial Vietnam.[36] From Constitutionalists to Asia's only Trotskyites, Saigon seethed with political ferment influenced by the colonial experience and the political ideas France had brought in.

Over ninety years of direct French rule, unlike the "protectorate" regime established by the French elsewhere among the Vietnamese, Saigon and its surroundings experienced an "engagement with the wider capitalist world . . . more intense than in any other part of the country."[37] Because France allowed Saigon a higher degree of freedom, Saigonese scholars and political leaders "assimilated certain bourgeois democratic notions, along with western methods of industrial and scientific development," which reinforced ideas that had characterized the city since its founding.[38] Saigonese could desire capitalism and the individual freedoms that France propounded in the *mission civilitrice* (civilizing mission); being exposed to French rhetoric of development and freedom as it existed in the metropole meant that such things were possible, even if not in Vietnam under French rule. Many urban southerners thus accepted French notions of commerce and individual freedom, based on ideas antithetical to the Marxist-Leninist worldview that came to dominate North Vietnam. The Republic of Vietnam, contrary to historical consensus, was for many Vietnamese an opportunity to maintain the historical character of Saigon, and thereby southern Vietnam, as a place where capitalism and a free society, rather than communism, was the most plausible version of a modern future. The colonial period and its administrative differences served to strengthen the cultural and economic separation that began in 1598; though in a peculiar and diffuse manner, the South remained politically distinct under French rule, an important precursor for another era of civil war between rival groups of Vietnamese with international support. However, at the same time, the French strengthening of an earlier administrative division into three regions (south, center, and north) also influenced new tensions between Central and South Vietnam. When the war broke out between North and South Vietnam in 1959, this was not a historical anomaly, but instead the product of both Cold War concerns and, more importantly, centuries of cultural, economic, and political divergence.

A NEW SOUTHERN STATE, 1954–75

Incorporating the regional history of South Vietnam into twentieth-century events allows us to see a firmer indigenous basis for the evolution of the First Republic of Vietnam in the 1950s. In Đàng Trong we find an economic, social, and military basis for a non-communist state with international ties and foreign military support. We can also find reasons for the lack of strong support for the Việt Minh in the South. By understanding that some people in the South had constructed a society whose economics and culture were rooted in a market economy and interaction with foreign, even Western, powers, who were comparatively international in nature, and who looked far more favorably on the presence of foreigners than was true in the North, we can understand that there were grounds for the continuance of these cultural and other differences. People in the southern state, Đàng Trong, long ago began to develop a society that could not be easily reconciled with Vietnamese communism, or to the rule of any northern regime, never having been so ruled. This markedly different southern society further differentiated itself under French rule, as the South's capitalist and internationalist stance only grew.

By the time the once-abdicated emperor Bảo Đại returned to preside over the French-sponsored Associated State of Vietnam in 1949, South Vietnam had begun to synthesize centuries of independent development with newer anticommunist sentiments. South Vietnamese generals Trần Định Thọ and Nguyễn Duy Hinh identified Bảo Đại as the rallying point for those opposed to the Việt Minh or alienated by their oppressive tactics.[39] Việt Minh terrorism and oppression of religious elements and political opposition swelled the ranks of those who sought an alternative Vietnamese state. Nearly 1 million northern refugees left their property behind and migrated to the South, becoming both a blessing and a problem for those trying to develop an independent South. Yet clearly, South Vietnam was no creation of the United States or the French, but rather the chaotic, if consistent, product of centuries of distinct social developments featuring a markedly different attitude toward foreigners and a history of military alliances and interactions that was incompatible with the staid and ethnocentric rule of the communists in the North; refugees from the North and other groups angered by the communists found in the South a place with a history that resonated with their desire to be freer and more independent than Hanoi would allow. Southern Vietnam had existed as an alternative to Northern rule for centuries before finally falling under Hanoi's control for the first time on April 30, 1975.

In addition to the Northern refugees, a number of native Southerners from a variety of religious and political backgrounds welcomed a non-communist state in the South in the 1950s. Buoyed by the aforementioned social and cultural history that separated them from the spartan, puritanical, and sometimes oppressive ways of the Vietnamese Communist Party's rule, groups of Vietnamese who sought an alternative path to a modern nation-state free from colonial trappings coalesced around the new prime minister, Ngô Đình Diệm. Soon to become the first president of the Republic of Vietnam, Diệm's career as written by English-language scholars serves as a microcosm for scholarship on South Vietnam generally.

A key part of the argument for South Vietnam's illegitimacy has centered on Diệm's political career. He has typically been painted as a tyrannical and inept leader on the one hand, and an American puppet on the other. Only recently have scholars taken a serious look at the first president of South Vietnam, and the portrait that has emerged through extensive archival research including French and Vietnamese language sources is far different. Much like the idea that South Vietnamese independence had no logical or historical basis, accepted ideas about Ngô Đình Diệm have proven far off the mark. Edward Miller's groundbreaking work on Diệm, based on extensive work in Vietnamese and French archives, reveals a competent and capable leader with far broader support than had previously been stated.

Diệm also came to power through his own abilities, as Miller has concluded; he

> secured the premiership through a combination of good fortune and careful coordination of his activities with those of his supporters in Indochina. Since Diệm was neither dependent on American support nor following US directives prior to June 1954, there is no reason to assume that he suddenly became reliant on American officials for guidance after that date. Having come to power mainly through his own efforts and those of his brothers, Diệm was not inclined to defer to Americans on matters of policy and political strategy.[40]

The South Vietnamese leader was the product of his own hard work, and his rise to power came in the context of his legitimacy as a rival to Hồ Chí Minh and his substantial support (though less than that of his rival by 1954) among Vietnamese people. He was indebted to foreign power no more than was Hồ Chí Minh. South Vietnam was home to many political and social ideas that were incompatible to those of the communists; instead of importing Marxism, the South chose other Western political ideas to guide its course in second half of the twentieth century. Diệm was the leader most capable of preserving a non-communist polity and maintaining foreign relations beneficial to the Republic of Vietnam in the 1950s. By coordinating and harnessing the various non-communist forces in the South, Diệm's leadership conferred political legitimacy on an independent state that rested on centuries of social and cultural differentiation from the North.

Though critics frequently bemoaned the lack of political freedom in the South, the southern government was a relative haven for individual rights and freedom of expression. While no opposition of any kind was brooked in Hanoi, Saigon's reporters, in contrast to the single-party totalitarian government in the North, enjoyed a remarkable degree of freedom. Reporters known to write stories detrimental to the government, such as David Halberstam, Merton Perry, and Neil Sheehan, were allowed to remain in the country and continue writing stories for years after they began to write pieces highly critical of the RVN leadership and military. More substantially, even during elevated levels of combat the South Vietnamese held regular elections for offices from the smallest hamlet up to the upper house of the legislature. Opposition candidates, except for communists, were allowed to run and take their seats when they ran; for example, the frequently militant An Quảng Buddhists had protested against the government for years, and were at times suspected of supporting the enemy. Nonetheless, the An Quảng party ran candidates in elections with the approval of the Nguyễn Văn Thiệu government (1967–75) and were allowed a prominent role in the government in the early 1970s; for example, the An Quảng took sixteen of twenty-four contested lower-house seats in the August 1971 elections.[41]

Hamlet, district, provincial, and national elections beginning in 1967 gave the South Vietnamese people far more say in their country's affairs than was possible in North Vietnam.

Likewise, Southerners continued to enjoy relatively more personal and political freedom than those living under communist rule, a centuries-old tradition by the time of the Republic of Vietnam. Excepting communists, few were excluded from public life, and censorship was mild compared to the total control of information that characterized Hanoi's administration. Many Vietnamese people had long been aware of a marked difference in the quality of life in the South over the North. Ever since widespread purges of ideological opposition began in the North in 1946–7, the communists had driven many out of their camp and confirmed what many others thought of them to begin with. In the 1960s and early 1970s, the nearly 1 million people who abandoned their lives to flee south in 1954 found themselves living in a freer society where they had some voice, however small.

Nguyễn Văn Thiệu's gradual political and social reforms may have been less than ideal, but compared to the fate of those above the seventeenth parallel, life in the South was noticeably better. When given a choice between communist rule and the Republic of Vietnam, people consistently chose the latter. In 1954, 1968, 1972, and 1975, refugees streamed into areas controlled by the South Vietnamese and away from areas occupied by the communists. When the war visited destruction on the South, the people fled to other areas under the RVN, rather

Figure 1.2
President Nguyên Văn Thiệu, March 1969.

Photograph: VA000115, Jackson Bosley Collection, The Vietnam Archive, Texas Tech University.

than welcoming Hanoi's troops or moving to areas under communist control. Consistent, if incomplete, efforts to improve the lives of the people by the RVN and the program of terrorism pursued by the communists against the population of the South combined to ensure that a viable percentage of the South Vietnamese population preferred President Thiệu's government to any practical alternative.

Beyond steady political progress, the southern government claimed a number of social and economic accomplishments. Urbanization progressed as a product of the war, which drove civilians into towns and cities from unsafe and less prosperous areas. By 1972 the South was 43 percent urban, compared to 15 percent in 1960.[42] The population also grew despite the ravages of war; from having approximately 10 million inhabitants in 1954, the RVN had become home to nearly 20 million people by 1974. Though the income per capita in the South was only two hundred dollars a year in 1971, this figure was equal to that in neighboring Thailand; it was nearly twice the average income of India and 25 percent higher than the average for China. Under the Communist Party, Vietnam did not reach that level again until 1993–4, even without adjusting for inflation. The RVN's economy was, like its political culture, steadily improving despite conditions of war.

Rice production and fishing increased annually through 1972, and the general economic trends remained steady through the war years despite widespread destruction by communist artillery, rockets, and acts of sabotage. Though the South remained highly dependent on foreign aid, it was making annual progress on its heavy imbalance of exports and imports. Oil exploration was under way, and industries were being developed to take the place of foreign aid in the long term. At the same time, the RVN was making progress toward future economic development through general and technical education. Primary and secondary student enrollment more than doubled between 1963 and 1972, while university enrollment more than quadrupled from 1961 to 1971. Technical and professional education at the postgraduate levels showed similar high increases between 1961 and 1971, nearly tripling enrollments in that period. On the whole, the RVN leadership was making efforts to improve the society and economy of the South; when considered alongside the higher degree of political freedom and freedom of expression, the Republic of Vietnam offered a compelling alternative to the totalitarian, regimented society of the North.

Critics often present a depiction of the RVN marred by corruption, scandals, and political unrest without realizing that these facets of South Vietnam were also problems in the North, and that in the South they were also the ironic product of a society that allowed its citizens to criticize their government and allowed people to generally pursue their self-interest and to express themselves publicly within boundaries set by the state of war. To call Hanoi's near-complete control over both public and private affairs an acceptable alternative is questionable. Saigon's leaders struggled with many challenges; they fought a protracted war against a larger country backed by two world superpowers while trying to reconcile disparate but determined non-communist elements under a fledgling democracy. Slowly but surely the RVN was improving the lot of its people, such as when Thiệu's vice-president, Trần Văn Hương, undertook nationwide programs to attack corruption head-on in the 1970s. The greatest and most formidable obstacle to the process of developing a strong independent South was not historical, political, or social, but military in nature.

Only when villages were free from acts of terrorism, sabotage, and PAVN rockets, mortar and artillery rounds could the RVN build a prosperous state that offered the people real benefits. Without a powerfully armed modern military, South Vietnam could not hope to defeat the PAVN, which had undertaken serious modernization programs with extensive Chinese support since the 1950s. Until the Republic of Vietnam's armed forces could match communist regulars weapon for weapon, their ability to defend their population and develop their society was dependent upon the United States' better equipped and fully modernized military to act as a counterweight to the rapidly improving and externally supplied and supported PAVN, and also on the competence of RVN officials in making the case for military aid with good military performance and planning. The RVN's greatest failing was its inability to build a comprehensible argument for its existence outside of a Cold War anticommunist stance. Had the South found a way to employ its unique history in service of its nationalist cause, rather than allowing Hanoi alone to utilize its narrative of Vietnamese history to spur its soldiers on, the RVN might have found a way to justify its war in compelling terms to both its people and its allies.

DISCUSSION QUESTIONS

1. What series of assumptions have dominated the recent narrative of Vietnamese history?
2. In what important ways did the southern part of Vietnam historically differ from the northern part of Vietnam?
3. Why did French colonialism arguably affect the region around Saigon more than the region around Hanoi?
4. What are the important schools of thought regarding the career of Ngô Đình Diệm?
5. Was South Vietnam a viable state during the period of US involvement in the Vietnam War?

SUGGESTED READING

Li Tana, *Nguyễn Cochinchina: Southern Vietnam in the Seventeenth and Eighteenth Centuries*. Ithaca, NY: Cornell Southeast Asia Program Publications, 1998.

Nhung Tuyet Tran and Anthony Reid, eds. *Vietnam: Borderless Histories*. Madison, WI: University of Wisconsin Press, 2006.

Pelley, Patricia. *Postcolonial Vietnam: New Histories of the National Past*. Raleigh-Durham, NC: Duke University Press, 2002.

Qiang Zhai, *China and the Vietnam Wars, 1950–1975*. Chapel Hill, NC, University of North Carolina Press, 2000.

NOTES

1. James M. Carter, *Inventing Vietnam: The United States and State Building, 1954–1968* (Cambridge: Cambridge University Press, 2008). Carter's bibliography consists entirely of English-language materials and ignores Vietnamese points of view on the war and the nature of the South Vietnamese state. This type of scholarship regrettably remains the norm for study of the Vietnam War despite the existence of extensive materials in both English and other languages that relate a variety of Vietnamese viewpoints.
2. George Donelson Moss, *Vietnam: An American Ordeal*, 5th ed. (New York: Prentice-Hall, 2006), 7.
3. Mark Moyar, *Triumph Forsaken* (Cambridge: Cambridge University Press, 2006), 3.
4. Keith W. Taylor, "A Vietnamese War," *Historically Speaking: The Bulletin of the Historical Society* 9 (3) (November/December 2007), 32.
5. Vietnam was first occupied by the Chinese Han Dynasty in 111 BC. The Trưng Sisters led an unsuccessful rebellion against Chinese rule between AD 39 and AD 43. Another female leader emerged in AD 248, when Triệu Ẩu led another abortive uprising. In the thirteenth century, General Trần Hưng Đạo directed a series of major victories over the invading Mongols, who had proved invincible before reaching Vietnam; however, it is rarely mentioned that he did so with the aid of large numbers of Chinese troops under his command. Lê Lợi is one of Vietnam's most famous rulers, as he came to power in late 1427 after leading the overthrow of the Ming Dynasty's brief reoccupation of Vietnam in the fifteenth century.
6. George Herring, *America's Longest War*, 4th ed. (New York: McGraw-Hill, 2002), 3.
7. The Manchurian Qing ("Pure") Dynasty ruled China from 1644 to 1911 and was often involved in Vietnamese affairs.
8. Historian Qiang Zhai's *China and the Vietnam Wars, 1950–1975* (Chapel Hill, NC: University of North Carolina Press, 2000) is a particularly valuable source of information on Chinese participation in the Indochina wars.
9. Keith Taylor's "Surface Orientations in Vietnam: Beyond Histories of Nation and Region," *Journal of Asian Studies* 57, 4 (November 1998), 749–78 successfully introduced the concept of non-national understandings of the Vietnamese past in 1998, which led to further works questioning the official narrative of history originating with Hanoi's historians. Li Tana's invaluable work on the unique cultural and political historical trajectory of the South appeared in her *Nguyễn Cochinchina: Southern Vietnam in the Seventeenth and Eighteenth Centuries* (Ithaca, NY: Cornell Southeast Asia Program Press, 1998). Tana's work built on Yang Baoyun's *Contribution à l'histoire de la principauté des Nguyen au Vietnam Meridional (1600–1775)* (Geneva: Editions Olizane, 1992). Philip Taylor's work on South Vietnamese identity in the modern era provides a sound foundation for future study of regional differences in modern Vietnamese history. Edward Miller's forthcoming monograph on Ngô Đình Diệm incorporates the aforementioned scholars' work into the study of the 1950s and 1960s. Claudine Ang's work on the use of history in the Republic of Vietnam in her Master's thesis at the National University of Singapore reveals that RVN leaders were well aware of the distinct history of the South and tried to make use of it, but also accepted many of the same problematic narratives that colored the Hanoi version of the Vietnamese past. Collectively, these scholars have overturned a Hanoi-centered historical teleology that Patricia Pelley has successfully deconstructed in *Postcolonial Vietnam: New Histories of the National Past* (Raleigh-Durham, NC: Duke University Press, 2002).
10. Pelley, *Postcolonial Vietnam*, 243.

11. Keith Taylor, "Nguyễn Hoàng and the Beginning of Southward Expansion," in Anthony Reid, ed., *Southeast Asia in the Modern Era* (Ithaca, NY: Cornell University Press, 1993), 45, 64.
12. Philip Taylor, *Fragments of the Present: Searching for Modernity in Vietnam's South* (Honolulu: University of Hawai'i Press, 2001), 8.
13. Keith Taylor, "Surface Orientations in Vietnam: Beyond Histories of Nation and Region," *Journal of Asian Studies* 57, 4 (November 1998), 960.
14. Nguyễn Khắc Viện and Huu Ngoc, *From Saigon to Ho Chi Minh City: A Path of 300 Years* (Hanoi: Gioi Publishers, 1998), 2–3.
15. Olga Dror and K. W. Taylor, *Views of Seventeenth-Century Vietnam: Christoforo Borri on Cochinchina and Samuel Baron on Tonkin* (Ithaca, NY: Cornell University Southeast Asia Press, 2006), 210.
16. Christoforo Borri, "Cochinchina." Translated into English from Borri's presentation to the pope by Robert Ashley (London: Robert Ashley, 1633), 64. Manuscript held by Cornell University Kroch Asia Rare Books Collection.
17. Thomas Bowyear, "Bowyear's Narrative," in Alistair Lamb, *The Mandarin Road to Old Hue: Narratives of Anglo-Vietnamese Diplomacy from the 17th Century to the Eve of the French Conquest* (Hamden, CT: Archon Books, 1970), 51.
18. Borri, "Cochinchina," 64.
19. Ibid., 52–3.
20. "Declaration of the Situation of Quinam Kingdom by Fransisco, 1642." In Li Tana and Anthony Reid, eds., *Southern Vietnam under the Nguyen: Documents of the Economic History of Cochinchina (Dang Trong) 1602–1777*. Data Papers Series, Sources for the Economic History of Southeast Asia no. 3 (Singapore: Institute of Southeast Asian Studies, 1993), 31.
21. Christoforo Borri, "Cochinchina," 63.
22. "Treaty from the Willem Verstegen Mission to the Court of Nguyen Phuc Lan, November 1651." In Tana and Reid, eds., *Southern Vietnam*, 35.
23. Lê Thánh Khôi, *Le Viet-Nam: Histoire et civilisation* (Paris: Éditions de Minuit, 1955), 247.
24. M. L. Cadière, "Le Mur de Đồng Hớ'i: Étude sur l'établissement des Nguyễn en Cochinchine," *Bulletin Française d'Extrême-Orient* 6 (1906), 138–40.
25. Yang Baoyun, *Contribution à l'histoire de la principauté des Nguyen au Vietnam Méridional (1600–1775)* (Geneva: Éditions Olizane, 1992), 108.
26. Victor Lieberman, *Strange Parallels: Southeast Asia in Global Context c.800–1830* (Cambridge: Cambridge University Press, 2003), 400.
27. Thomas Bowyear, "Narrative," 53.
28. Alexander De Rhodes, *Divers voyages de la Chine et autres royaumes de l'Orient: avec le retour de l'autheur en Europe, par la Perse et l'Arménie / le tout divisé en trois parties* (Paris: Christophe Lournel, 1681), 162.
29. Pierre Poivre, "Voyage," in Tana and Reid, eds., *Southern Vietnam*, 71.
30. Pierre-Yves Manguin, *Les Portugais sur les cités du Vietnam et du Campa* (Paris: École Française d'Extrême-Orient, 1972), 204–5.
31. Wynn Wilcox, "Transnationalism and multiethnicity in the early Nguyễn Ánh Gia Long Period," in Tran and Reid, *Việt Nam: Borderless Histories* (Madison, WI: University of Wisconsin Press, 2006), 197–8.
32. Li Tana, *Nguyễn Cochinchina: Southern Vietnam in the Seventeenth and Eighteenth Centuries* (Ithaca, NY: Cornell Southeast Asia Program Press, 1998), 99.
33. Tran Dinh Tho and Nguyễn Duy Hinh, *Indochina Monographs*, "The South Vietnamese Society" (Washington, DC: US Army Center of Military History, 1983), 73.
34. Philip Taylor, *Fragments of the Present*, 17.
35. Ibid.
36. Shawn F. McHale, *Print and Power: Confucianism, Communism and Buddhism in the Making of Modern Vietnam* (Honolulu: University of Hawai'i Press, 2004), 16.
37. Philip Taylor, *Fragments of the Present*, 6.
38. Viên and Ngọc, *From Saigon to Ho Chi Minh City*, 46.
39. Tho and Hinh, "The South Vietnamese Society," 17.

40. Edward Miller, "Vision, Power and Agency: The Ascent of Ngô Đình Diệm, 1945–54," *Journal of Southeast Asian Studies*, 35 (3) (October 2004), 457.
41. Southeast Asia Analysis Report August–October 1971, Center of Military History, Thayer Papers, 35.
42. Statistics on population, education, economy, and society drawn from Dr. Phan Quang Dan, *The Republic of Vietnam's Environment and People* (Saigon, 1975), 133–64, 348–55.

TIMELINE EVENTS

September 1945 – Ho Chi Minh declares Vietnamese independence from French colonialism

November 1946 – Beginning of French war in Indochina (First Indochina War)

1949 – Creation of the State of Vietnam and the "Bao Dai solution"

May 1950 – United States pledges military and economic aid to France for war in Indochina

1954 – The Battle of Dien Bien Phu and the Geneva Convention

1957 – President Ngo Dinh Diem of South Vietnam visits the United States

1960 – Establishment of the National Liberation Front (NLF)

January 1963 – The Battle of Ap Bac

November 1963 – Ngo Dinh Diem deposed by military coup

August 1964 – Tonkin Gulf Incident

November 1964 – Lyndon Johnson elected president

March 1965 – Introduction of American combat troops to South Vietnam

Chapter 2

Historians and the origins of the Vietnam War

Matthew Masur

> **CHAPTER SUMMARY**
>
> This chapter examines some of the most important books on the Vietnam War published in the past decade (1999–2009). In some ways, recent historiography continues the trends established in the initial accounts of the war. The works discussed in this chapter attempt to answer a basic question: How and why did the United States intervene in Vietnam? The chapter shows the continued importance of the "orthodox versus revisionist" debate in Vietnam War historiography. However, it does not simply repeat the work of earlier historians. Through the use of diverse (often international) source material and theoretical innovations in the study of history, its author offers a new perspective on the war.

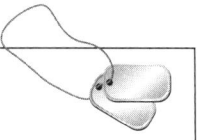

The historiography of the Vietnam War is typically described in terms of orthodoxy and revisionism. In the case of Vietnam, "orthodox" historians view the conflict as a mistake or, commonly, a "tragedy." Misunderstanding conditions in South Vietnam and overzealously wedded to containment, the United States committed itself to maintaining a non-communist South Vietnam at any cost. Once committed, the United States adopted military tactics that were as ineffective as they were brutal. The entire enterprise was doomed to failure.

Revisionist historians also tend to view the Vietnam War as a tragedy, but for other reasons. For them, the war was a legitimate and necessary stand against communist tyranny. American civilian leadership refused to adopt the military strategy to win the war. They succumbed to a vocal minority in the antiwar movement and lost the will to fight. In the process, the United States turned its back on the people of South Vietnam.

The simplified orthodox/revisionist dichotomy has become a sort of orthodoxy itself; almost every overview of Vietnam War historiography uses this template (and this chapter is no exception). Yet we must remember that the complexity of the Vietnam War has produced an equally complex historiography. Both the orthodox and the revisionist schools house a diverse set of scholars who produce diverse—and often conflicting—scholarship. Moreover, even at the height of the orthodox/revisionist debates of the 1970s, many historians did not fit neatly into these two categories. Some explored topics outside of the questions that typically animated the orthodox/revisionist debate: Why did the United States go to Vietnam and why did it lose?

This chapter compares several important studies of the Vietnam War published within the past decade: Mark Bradley's *Imagining Vietnam and America*, Seth Jacobs' *America's Miracle Man in Vietnam*, Mark Lawrence's *Assuming the Burden*, Fredrik Logevall's *Choosing War*, and Mark Moyar's *Triumph Forsaken*.[1] These works incorporate the dominant trends in diplomatic history over the past few decades, such as exploring the international dimensions of the conflict and the intersections of culture and foreign relations. They also have much in common with previous historians of the war. Although the authors came of age after the war was over (or when it was in its final years), they passionately defend or critique American policies in Vietnam. And like their predecessors, they focus on a central question in the historiography: How did the United States get involved in Vietnam? In doing so, the authors focus on the period up to 1965, thus ignoring the peak years of American involvement. This focus reinforces the conclusion that the outcome of the war was preordained, or at least overwhelmingly likely. For many current and past historians, the steps toward Americanization are more important than the story of the war itself.

In *Choosing War*, Fredrik Logevall explores the decisions that Americanized the Vietnam War during the late-Kennedy and early-Johnson administrations. While primarily domestic in focus, *Choosing War* also describes the international atmosphere in which these decisions were made and the international repercussions of American actions. In *Assuming the Burden*, Mark Lawrence describes the development of French, American, and British cooperation in opposing the Viet Minh in the late 1940s. Lawrence's balanced account of the major Western actors internationalizes the history of the conflict in Vietnam. Mark Bradley's *Imagining Vietnam and America* internationalizes the conflict in a different way: by exploring the roles of the Vietnamese themselves. He mostly eschews diplomatic decision making, exploring instead the cultural components of Vietnamese–American relations in the first half of the twentieth century. In *America's Miracle Man in Vietnam*, Seth Jacobs also demonstrates the importance of culture—in this case, race and religion—in understanding America's commitment to Ngo Dinh Diem and South Vietnam. Mark Moyar's *Triumph Forsaken* is in some regards the most traditional approach to Vietnam, though in a nod to internationalism he incorporates some Vietnamese sources to strengthen his argument. It warrants inclusion here because its unabashed revisionist thesis, more than any of the other works under consideration, challenges the existing scholarship on the war.

All history is to some degree presentist: it is the product of the time in which it was written. The initial accounts of the Vietnam War, some written before the war even ended, reflected the social, political, and cultural divisions of the 1960s and 1970s. Journalists in Saigon and officials in Washington wrote some of the most widely read accounts of the Vietnam conflict. Many of the historians who wrote on the war had some direct involvement in the conflict. George Kahin was an early critic of the war. William Duiker, David Anderson, and Harry Summers all served in Vietnam in some capacity.[2] This does not diminish the value of these earlier studies. Rather, it illustrates the obvious: the initial histories of the Vietnam War were written at a time when the war still had a certain immediacy.

If recent scholarship is any indication, the passage of time has not tempered the immediacy of the Vietnam War. While the war itself is more distant, the issues it raises are strikingly current: American hubris, failure to understand a foreign enemy, public opinion during wartime, constraints on the military. One could conclude that Iraq and Afghanistan have politicized current writing on the Vietnam War, but this misses the point. These topics stimulate debate because they are fundamental. Like any important historical topic, the Vietnam War spawned a contentious historiography because the war involved the issues that are most important to Americans.

THE YEAR OF DECISION

In *Choosing War*, Fredrik Logevall acknowledges the continuing resonance of the Vietnam War. He starts the book by noting that "a quarter of a century has passed since [the Vietnam War] ended for the United States, but it is still with us."[3] Logevall admits that he was surprised at his own emotional response when writing about the Vietnam War. He was distant from the war both temporally and geographically: a native of Sweden, he was born in 1963. When he started studying the Vietnam War, he explains, he had no "irreducible existential stake" in the subject.[4] Nevertheless, his research led him to a disturbing conclusion: the Vietnam War was not only a tragedy, but it was one that the United States *chose* and therefore could have avoided.

Logevall departs from recent historiographical trends by focusing on the period immediately preceding the introduction of American ground troops to Vietnam in April 1965. Many historians have chosen to look further into the past to find the roots of America's commitment to Vietnam. Instead, Logevall examines the months from August 1963 to February 1965, a period that he dubs "the Long 1964." It was "the most important [period] in the entire thirty-year American involvement in Vietnam, the period in which the Second Indochina War began in earnest."[5] For Logevall, "the Long 1964" was ripe with contingency. The United States was not on an inevitable course toward intervention and had realistic opportunities to change course. Logevall thus places responsibility for Vietnam squarely on the Johnson administration, to some degree absolving Eisenhower and Truman of the central role they have played in many recent studies.

Choosing War is a scathing indictment of the officials who dragged the United States into the war in Vietnam. He begins his account in August 1963, when Charles de Gaulle called for an end to outside interference in Vietnam's political affairs. France was not alone in favoring a negotiated settlement to the nascent conflict in Vietnam: so too did influential voices in Moscow, London, Beijing, and even Hanoi. In the United States, some of Kennedy's advisers—Chester Bowles, Averill Harriman, John Kenneth Galbraith—supported the nebulous concept of "neutralization" in South Vietnam. Kennedy, Logevall asserts, still had freedom to maneuver in Vietnam. Ngo Dinh Diem and Ngo Dinh Nhu's increasingly antagonistic behavior, especially during the Buddhist crisis of 1963, provided the perfect cover to pursue an exit strategy. Instead, Kennedy reiterated America's commitment to a non-communist South Vietnam. Thus, "the summer of 1963 constituted one of the great missed opportunities to prevent the tragedy that was the Vietnam War."[6] It would not be the last.

When Johnson became president in late 1963, he, too, faced a decision: increase America's commitment or pursue withdrawal. With the military and political situation in South Vietnam deteriorating, a political solution should have been attractive. France, the United Kingdom, Beijing, Hanoi, and the NLF were receptive to a Geneva-type agreement, but Johnson balked. Logevall dismisses the standard argument that Johnson was boxed in by political pressure. "What is most striking," he notes, "is how few individuals and publications in the spring of 1964 were willing to go on record favoring escalation in Vietnam."[7] Politicians, academics, and journalists expressed growing doubts about America's role in Vietnam. The danger for Johnson was not the political cost of withdrawal. It was that he "could not count on the American people or the vast majority of America's allies to support the war effort."[8] In mid-1964, support for an international peace agreement increased. Johnson chose instead to escalate, seeing negotiations as "a nightmare destination, to be avoided at any cost." As a result, "the summer of 1964 was like the summer of 1963, a time of missed opportunity for a political solution to the conflict."[9]

Johnson's best opportunity for disengagement came after the election of 1964, a three-month period that Logevall "ranks as supreme in importance" during America's twenty-five-year venture in Vietnam.[10] Johnson had defeated Goldwater in a landslide and enjoyed large majorities in both houses of Congress. The American public was largely skeptical about full-scale commitment to Vietnam. America's international rivals and allies continued to hope for a political solution to the crisis. But Johnson forged ahead. In February the United States launched another series of reprisal strikes on North Vietnam. The next month the United States initiated Rolling Thunder, a sustained bombing campaign, and introduced the first ground troops to South Vietnam. According to Logevall, "it was then that the hopes for an early diplomatic solution all but ended . . . [and] the last chance to prevent another full-scale war in Indochina had passed."[11]

The last chapter of *Choosing War* provides a succinct and clear summary of Logevall's main arguments and their implications. Logevall argues that the United States had realistic opportunities to disengage from Vietnam during the "Long 1964" that ran from August 1963 to early 1965. This assertion contradicts earlier writers, who argued that a host of factors

Figure 2.1 President Dwight D. Eisenhower and Secretary of State John Foster Dulles (from left) greet South Vietnam's President Ngo Dinh Diem at Washington National Airport, May 8, 1957.

ARC identifier 542189; local identifier 342-AF-18302USAF. Item from Record Group 342: Records of US Air Force Commands, Activities, and Organizations, 1900–2000. Courtesy of The National Archives.

made American intervention nearly inevitable: concerns about American credibility, Lyndon Johnson's political calculations, the public's commitment to anti-communism. Logevall disagrees that the decision for intervention was "overdetermined." Political leaders, he writes, "always had considerable freedom about which way to go in the war. They always possessed a real choice."[12] Logevall is especially troubled because the insurmountable obstacles to American success in Vietnam, and the possibility for a different course of action, were apparent at the time. In contrast to Arthur Schlesinger's description of Vietnam as a "tragedy without villains," Logevall impeaches the morality of the men who dragged the United States to war.[13]

Logevall believes there is plenty of blame to go around. Those who had doubts about the war, such as George Ball and many Democratic Congressmen, created a "permissive context" by muting their criticisms or, in Ball's case, accepting the role as the administration's token devil's advocate.[14] But the real responsibility rests with Robert McNamara, Dean Rusk,

McGeorge Bundy, and Lyndon Johnson himself—the four individuals who consistently refused to countenance a political settlement in Vietnam. Of these, Johnson carries the biggest burden, and not just because the buck stops with the president. The decisions during the "Long 1964" carried Johnson's imprint more than anyone else's. Vietnam was, quite simply, "Lyndon Johnson's War."[15]

Logevall also asks a troubling question: If Johnson had such real opportunities for withdrawal, why did he choose war? He was not, Logevall insists, a warmonger, a president who relished the possibility of America's deepening involvement in Vietnam. Nevertheless, he chose such a path. Like his key advisers, Johnson was obsessed with *credibility*. But for Johnson the credibility at stake was not America's, nor the Democratic Party's. It was his personal credibility and the fear of humiliation that fueled his decisions.[16]

Logevall argues that Kennedy might have found a way out of Vietnam if he had not been assassinated in November 1963. Logevall is not convinced that Kennedy, at the time of his death, had decided to withdraw American troops from Vietnam. Kennedy harbored doubts about the prospects for success in Vietnam, but he was also responsible for escalating US involvement. He probably hoped to keep his options open, postponing his decision for a later date. Nevertheless, Kennedy was less enthralled by his hawkish advisers than Johnson was; he was a more sophisticated student of international affairs, and he would have had greater political cover than Johnson. Most importantly, Kennedy was not afflicted with Johnson's paralyzing fear of humiliation.

THE VIETNAM WAR IN AN INTERNATIONAL PERSPECTIVE

Mark Lawrence's *Assuming the Burden* is a logical companion to Logevall's *Choosing War*. The two authors both earned their doctorates at Yale University, separated by less than a decade. Their books are award-winning studies of the Vietnam War. Like Logevall, Lawrence provides a detailed look at American policymakers, though he mostly bypasses the men at the top in favor of the "obscure bureaucrats . . . who counted most in recasting Indochina as a Cold War crisis."[17] Although Logevall's *Choosing War* is more focused on American decision making, he calls for "viewing the war in its international context." Lawrence obliges, conducting research at the Truman library, the British National Archives (formerly Public Record Office) in Kew, and the French colonial archive in Aix-en-Provence. His narrative jumps seamlessly from Washington to London to Paris to Hanoi. Indeed, *Assuming the Burden* is as much a history of Franco-Anglo-American relations as it is a book on America's journey toward intervention in Vietnam.

But *Assuming the Burden* is more than simply an "internationalized" history of America's road to Vietnam. Incorporating analytical models from other disciplines, Lawrence argues that the Franco-Anglo-American opposition to a communist Vietnam rested on a constructed version of Vietnamese and Cold War politics. In Lawrence's analysis this constructed reality was as meaningful and influential as any "objective" reality on the ground in Vietnam. In making this argument Lawrence demonstrates how a historian can blend the traditional and the modern in diplomatic history. Lawrence's work is synthetic: he applies the approaches of cultural historians to the questions at the heart of diplomatic history. The result is fresh and persuasive.

Lawrence describes the path that led the United States to support France in its war against the Viet Minh. After World War II, France and the United Kingdom hoped to re-establish order in Southeast Asia. This necessitated restoring French control over Indochina. American officials, however, were conflicted about the future of the region. Some policymakers, whom Lawrence labels "liberals," supported trusteeship leading to eventual independence for Indochina. "Conservative" policymakers, by contrast, believed that French colonial control was the best guarantor of stability. President Franklin Roosevelt was a leading supporter of trusteeship, but his death in 1945, combined with growing fears of communist expansion in 1946, ensured that the United States would not oppose French recolonization in Indochina. Still, the United States was reluctant to actively assist the French, instead settling on a policy of neutrality.

American neutrality was an incomplete victory for France. American passivity was clearly preferred to outright hostility, but the French still hoped to win active American support for their endeavors. When hostilities between France and the Viet Minh erupted in late 1946, France felt confident that it could prevail without enthusiastic support from its allies. As the war continued, however, the French came to realize that US aid was more crucial than ever.

France was able to secure American support in 1949 by offering a modicum of autonomy to Vietnam under the leadership of former emperor Bao Dai. The "Bao Dai solution," as it was known, alleviated American reservations about fighting a war in defense of communism. French officials were able to convince the United States that Bao Dai could siphon nationalist support from the Viet Minh and forestall communist advances in Southeast Asia. In the heightened Cold War climate of the late 1940s, and amid growing insurgencies in Southeast Asia, the United States was receptive to these arguments.

American support for the Bao Dai solution rested on a reappraisal of the political acumen of the Vietnamese people. In the waning years of World War II, some American officials were optimistic about eventual Vietnamese independence because of the "intelligence, cultural sophistication, and vigor" of the native population.[18] By 1949 the United States could only justify its support for the Bao Dai solution if its policymakers believed that the Vietnamese people would fall in line behind the former emperor. American officials resolved this dilemma by revising their earlier assessments. Rather than political sophisticates, the Vietnamese were "apolitical and ignorant of political ideologies except insofar as they affected their ability to subsist on the land." The Vietnamese, therefore, "would willingly throw their support behind Bao Dai if they were confident that he would win."[19] The Bao Dai solution allowed the United States, France, and Great Britain to finally find common ground in their approaches to Vietnam. This, according to Lawrence, made "the 1948–1949 period one of the most important spans in the history of Vietnam's wars after 1945."[20]

Logevall says historians should resist the temptation to "draw a straight line between the Truman Doctrine and the landing of the Marines at Danang."[21] Lawrence does not exactly violate this command, but his description of the path to Vietnam might strike Logevall as overly deterministic. "To understand the American war," Lawrence declares, "it is vitally necessary to understand what transpired in the years leading up to 1950."[22] In the years after World War II the United States went from seeing Vietnam as a marginal or peripheral concern to believing that it was a key part of the struggle against international communism. The completion of this transformation was the "landmark moment" when the United States offered financial and military support for France's efforts to defeat the Viet Minh and preserve its colony.[23]

Lawrence asserts that these early decisions are crucial to understanding the subsequent actions of American policymakers. "The decision to throw American aid behind the French war," he notes, "marked the first definitive American step toward deep embroilment in Indochina affairs, the start of a long series of moves that would lead the administration of Lyndon Johnson to commit U.S. ground forces to Vietnam fifteen years later."[24] Eisenhower's, Kennedy's, and Johnson's actions in the decade after Geneva were based on a "set of assumptions that . . . departed little from the ideas laid in place in 1950."[25] According to Lawrence, "[i]t would be going too far to argue that patterns of thinking established in the early Cold War years made a U.S.–Vietnamese war inevitable. Yet the pattern is unmistakable: basic ideas conceived in the late 1940s had remarkable staying power."[26] American officials in the 1960s may have had real choices, as Logevall argues, but they were burdened by the decisions their predecessors had made fifteen years earlier. Like Logevall, Lawrence laments America's missed opportunity, albeit in a much earlier period. From 1944 to 1950 "the Truman administration squandered the considerable leverage it held over France to force a better outcome to the Indochina problem."[27]

Lawrence convincingly argues that the decision to back the French has relevance beyond America's eventual intervention in Vietnam. In supporting the French, the United States compromised its commitment to liberalism while still espousing the importance of liberal institutions. Throughout the Cold War, the United States would repeat this pattern in other Third World countries: Guatemala, Indonesia, Ethiopia, and the Dominican Republic. In all of these cases, as in Vietnam, the United States chose to secure American geostrategic and economic objectives at the expense of true liberal reform.

Mark Bradley's *Imagining Vietnam and America* helps to correct an obvious flaw in the historiography of the Vietnam War. Even as historians have internationalized the conflict, they have generally focused on the United States and its Western allies, with a small group of historians examining the role of the Soviet Union and China in the conflict. The Vietnamese themselves are largely absent from these works. Those historians who want to explore the actions of Vietnamese politicians, intellectual figures, or military planners are often forced to rely on limited materials in English or French. As a result, historians are left with an incomplete picture of the very people who influenced the course toward war and were most affected by its outcome.

Bradley's approach allows—indeed, requires—the Vietnamese to have a voice in the story of the Vietnam War. *Imagining Vietnam and America* is a perfect example of a book on the Vietnam

War that bridges the gap between diplomatic history and area studies. Mark Bradley's dissertation advisers at Harvard included Ernest May and Hue-Tam Ho Tai, leaders in the fields of diplomatic and Vietnamese history respectively. In completing his study he conducted research at numerous libraries and archives in the United States, France, and Britain. In addition, he used an extensive collection of primary and secondary sources to reveal the Vietnamese perspectives on the war. These included documents housed at the National Archives Center 1 in Hanoi, personal interviews, published primary sources, and dozens of periodicals.

Most historians, Bradley argues, trace the roots of America's intervention in Vietnam to the "almost axiomatic starting point" of the late 1940s.[28] They emphasize the adoption of containment as the guiding principle in US foreign policy and the application of containment doctrine to events in Indochina. According to this dominant narrative, geostrategic considerations in the late 1940s and early 1950s set the United States on the path toward intervention in Vietnam. America's deepening involvement in Vietnam, according to these studies, "can *only* be understood in relation to the Cold War."[29] Bradley, by contrast, argues that American–Vietnamese relations in the first half of the twentieth century continued to exert an influence over the two countries in the 1950s and after.

Bradley finds that successive generations of Vietnamese nationalists looked to the United States as a model for their anti-colonial efforts. Phan Chu Trinh and other early-twentieth-century Vietnamese intellectuals, influenced by social Darwinism but steeped in neo-Confucianism, saw the United States as a model of reform and social evolution. The subsequent generation of Vietnamese nationalists, including Ho Chi Minh, emerged in the interwar years and adopted a more radical approach to Vietnamese independence. But they, too, imagined an America that could provide a model for Vietnam. They admired America's revolutionary heritage and "the voluntarist capacities of the Americans to exert their will to overcome historical circumstances."[30] They fused their view of American voluntarism with a continued attachment to Confucian virtue and a growing commitment to Maoist internationalism and Marxism-Leninism to create a "powerful, if sometimes contradictory" model for national independence.[31]

The United States, too, held particular beliefs about Vietnam and the Vietnamese. These views were informed by travel narratives, consular reports, and French depictions of the Vietnamese in the first decades of the twentieth century. Together, these sources created an image of Vietnam as backward, politically unsophisticated, and unprepared for independence.

These imagined versions of one another affected Vietnamese–American relations during World War II and in the immediate postwar years. Vietnamese nationalists reached out to the United States for support in their quest for independence. The United States, influenced by earlier attitudes toward Vietnam and concerned about the possibility of Chinese influence in the region, refused to support Vietnamese nationalism. Instead, the United States accepted, and then actively supported, a return to French control. Bradley concludes that "the largely imagined Vietnam and America that were constructed during the interwar and World War II periods fundamentally shaped the contours of the postcolonial Vietnamese state and its place in the articulation of post-1945 international order."[32]

Adding Vietnamese voices and shifting the timeline does more than simply augment earlier studies of the Vietnam War. Bradley reframes the conflict, situating it within the narratives of "colonialism, race, modernism, and postcolonial state making." His use of Vietnamese sources is both a cause and a consequence of this approach. Bradley's work is especially valuable because it is not solely—or even primarily—a study of the Vietnam War. *Imagining Vietnam and America* shows that a transnational approach can help "transcend the traditional Cold War narrative and the premise of American exceptionalism that have guided much of past scholarship" in the twentieth century.[33]

ASSESSING THE PRESIDENCY OF NGO DINH DIEM

In *America's Miracle Man in Vietnam*, Seth Jacobs begins with a question that animates much of the scholarship on the war: Why did the United States commit its blood and treasure to an area that was neither economically nor strategically important? Earlier orthodox historians answered this question by exploring the mindset of American policymakers. Blinded by a Manichean worldview and wholeheartedly committed to containment, American officials in the 1950s concluded that *all* parts of the world were strategically or economically important. Failing to hold the line against communism anywhere would upset the liberal economic order or, worse, damage American credibility. Therefore, the United States needed to demonstrate its resolve in Vietnam. Jacobs endorses this view, but it leads him to ask a different question: Why did the United States throw its weight behind Ngo Dinh Diem rather than some other anticommunist Vietnamese nationalist? This is a critical question, Jacobs argues, because America's decision to back Diem was "the crossover point from advice and support to cobelligerency in a Vietnamese civil war." It was, quite simply, "the essential precondition for the ensuing measures that led to the defeat and humiliation of the United States."[34]

Why, then, did the United States throw its support behind Diem? In retrospect, this decision seems irrational. By objective standards, Diem was hardly the best choice to be America's man in Vietnam: he was Catholic, fluent in French, dogmatic, rigid, and authoritarian. But, as Jacobs argues, policy decisions are always informed by ideology, and ideology is an outgrowth of culture. America's support for Diem was a reflection of the ideas, beliefs, and assumptions that permeated American society in the 1950s.

In order to explore the nexus of diplomatic and cultural history, Jacobs relies on a diverse collection of sources. He is at home in the National Archives in College Park, Maryland, or the Eisenhower Library in Abilene, Kansas. Eisenhower, John Foster Dulles, J. Lawton Collins, Edward Lansdale, and the American Friends of Vietnam all play prominent roles in his narrative. But Jacobs is equally comfortable with the sources of the cultural historian: the novels of James Michener, Broadway musicals, *Reader's Digest*, and Hollywood films. Some historians make a token effort to inject culture into diplomatic history (or vice versa). These studies can seem half-hearted or disjointed. *America's Miracle Man in Vietnam*, however, combines culture and diplomacy without sacrificing either approach.

Figure 2.2 President Lyndon B. Johnson meeting with Joint Chiefs of Staff around a picnic table on the L.B.J. Ranch front lawn, December 22, 1964. Clockwise from L.B.J.: President Johnson, Secretary of Defense Robert McNamara, Maj. Gen. Chester Clifton, Gen. Curtis LeMay, Gen. Earle Wheeler, Dep. Secretary of Defense Cyrus Vance, Gen. Harold Johnson, Adm. David McDonald, Gen. Wallace Greene.

Serial no.: W522-13a Yoichi R. Okamoto. Courtesy of the Lyndon B. Johnson Library and Museum, NARA.

According to Jacobs, the powerful categories of race and religion influenced American views of Asia in the 1950s. The early Cold War coincided with a religious revival in the United States. Jacobs points to Billy Graham's massive religious rallies, the advent of "Dial-A-Prayer," and the popularity of religious epics like *The Ten Commandments* as evidence that the decade represented the "Third Great Awakening" in American history. The religiosity of the decade was public, demonstrative, and conspicuous. It was also inextricably linked to the Cold War. Religious faith distinguished Americans from their godless Soviet counterparts. In Jacobs' estimation, "the conflict with international communism was in essence a holy war."[35]

Like religion, racial attitudes shaped America's understanding of the Cold War. In the 1950s, American popular culture was replete with "Orientalist" imagery of Asia and Asians. Hollywood films, popular fiction, and Broadway musicals all depicted Asians as childlike and passive. This dangerous combination made Asians especially susceptible to communist domination. Mark Bradley argues that American "Orientalist" thinking affected US policy toward Vietnam. After the division of Vietnam at Geneva, the United States worried that Ngo Dinh Diem, the emerging political leader in the South, embodied the worst qualities of the Vietnamese: venal and politically immature.

In *America's Miracle Man in Vietnam*, Seth Jacobs takes the opposite view. He agrees that Orientalist thinking shaped America's view of Vietnam and Ngo Dinh Diem in the 1950s. He also suggested a solution: American support for strong, even authoritarian, rulers who could help shepherd Asians into the family of free world nations. Thus, the Orientalism of American officials led them to support Diem, whom they saw as being unlike other Vietnamese. In the religious and racial atmosphere of the 1950s, the Catholic Ngo Dinh Diem was the logical choice—indeed, the only choice—to lead South Vietnam.

Jacobs's challenge is connecting the dots between generalized cultural attitudes and the actions of American policymakers. It would be convenient if American policymakers announced that their support for Diem was based on racial and religious considerations. They did not, although some of Diem's most fervent American supporters, including John Foster Dulles, Mike Mansfield, and John W. O'Daniel, came close. Instead, Jacobs identifies the main ideological components of 1950s America. He then demonstrates that American policymakers shared these cultural attitudes. Whether or not they were *influenced* by the culture or simply reflected the pervasive beliefs, their actions cannot be divorced from their ideological context.

Probably the most controversial recent book on Vietnam is Mark Moyar's *Triumph Forsaken*. Moyar initially intended to write a synthetic overview of the war, but he was troubled to find numerous flaws and omissions in the existing scholarship. He noticed that orthodox interpretations of the war were unquestioningly perpetuated while revisionist ones were ignored, dismissed, or marginalized. Moyar decided to write an overview of the war, revisiting the primary sources instead of relying on the orthodox secondary works that dominate the literature. In doing so, he reached many of the same conclusions of earlier revisionist historians. But Moyar is careful to separate *Triumph Forsaken* from existing revisionist historiography, noting that it "contains many new interpretations and challenges many orthodox interpretations that have hitherto gone unchallenged."[36]

Moyar lays out a relentless and audacious assault on the most dearly held orthodox views of the Vietnam War, beginning with his depictions of Ho Chi Minh and Ngo Dinh Diem. Orthodox accounts have sometimes mythologized "Uncle Ho" as a selfless and virtuous patriot clad in rubber sandals and worn-out military fatigues. Conversely, they dismiss Ngo Dinh Diem as stubborn, aloof, and ineffective—a mandarin and a Catholic who was out of touch with the people of South Vietnam. In these accounts, Ho's popularity and Diem's unpopularity are natural, expected, and inevitable.

Moyar inverts this conventional view. He revives the argument that Ho Chi Minh was a communist first and a nationalist second, pointing to his "single-minded and unswerving dedication to one objective: the imposition of [a] Communist government of Vietnam and the rest of the world". Diem, by contrast, was fiercely nationalistic and a "very wise and effective leader."[37] In *Triumph Forsaken* he is also a man of the people who helps his father plow the fields and volunteers to wash dishes at the seminary. As president, he slept on a cot and "ate a simple peasant's breakfast."[38] What other observers have seen as flaws become virtues to Moyar. Yes, Diem did wear a white sharkskin suit, but this was actually a sign of his austerity: at the time, he owned only two outfits!

Moyar's lionization of Diem extends to his actions as president. By the end of the 1950s, Diem had established political stability and he had overseen a successful land reform program. The combination of a growing insurgency and some high-profile political opposition caused setbacks for Diem in 1960 and 1961, the two worst years of his presidency. In 1962, however, Diem regained the initiative, thanks in large part to American military aid and the implementation of the strategic hamlet program. Although some historians have questioned the effectiveness of the strategic hamlet program, Moyar believes it was instrumental in giving the South Vietnamese the upper hand against National Liberation Front (NLF) insurgents in 1962. The people of South Vietnam, recognizing these many accomplishments, "had a high opinion of Diem."[39]

Some of the most vociferous critiques of Ngo Dinh Diem focus on the Battle of Ap Bac in January 1963 and his response to the Buddhist crisis in the spring and summer of the same year. These two events, many historians conclude, highlight the military and political ineffectiveness of the South Vietnamese government. Such assessments could not be further from the truth, according to Moyar. The Battle of Ap Bac was not the story of an outnumbered and under-equipped group of NLF fighters defeating a South Vietnamese army unit plagued by low morale and insubordination. In this David-versus-Goliath clash, it was the NLF who had the upper hand. In spite of long odds, the South Vietnamese army inflicted a strategic defeat on the insurgents.

The Buddhist protests that erupted in May 1963 are similarly misunderstood. Rather than an impromptu demonstration against Diem's religious intolerance, the protests were manufactured by communist sympathizers in the Buddhist movement who wanted to bring down the regime. The ringleader of the Buddhist protests was Thich Tri Quang, who Moyar suspects was a communist agent. Diem's attacks on Buddhist agitators did not alienate the population of South Vietnam. On the contrary, "the Vietnamese tended to look favorably on a government that suppressed public demonstrations, so long as they themselves were not the demonstrators and the crackdowns were carried out effectively."[40]

The Battle of Ap Bac and the Buddhist crisis were not signs of South Vietnam's military weakness or Diem's unpopularity. Rather, they were evidence of the harmful influence of a few credulous and naïve journalists. Neil Sheehan and David Halberstam incorrectly described the battle of Ap Bac as a defeat largely because they relied on information from the embittered American military adviser John Paul Vann. In the case of the Buddhist crisis, "[f]anatical Buddhists and covert Communists had made great headway in misleading both the American press and elements of the U.S. government into believing that the Saigon government was committing religious oppression."[41] These factually inaccurate reports were quite effective. By the summer of 1963 some American officials were recommending that Diem be removed from office if he refused to step down of his own accord.

Moyar's other unconventional conclusion is that the US–South Vietnamese alliance was generally quite successful in fighting the insurgency. Contemporary journalists and subsequent historians emphasized the strength of the NLF and the shakiness of the Southern government, but Moyar rejects these characterizations. At the time of Diem's death, the counterinsurgency efforts were "thriving."[42] Even the NLF and the North Vietnamese, Moyar argues, realized that they were fighting a losing battle in the South. It was only after Diem's death, and North Vietnam's expanded assistance to the insurgency, that conditions deteriorated in South Vietnam.

Like Logevall, Moyar is willing to explore intriguing counterfactuals about the Vietnam War. Somewhat surprisingly, he believes that if it had not been for the coup against Diem in 1963, the United States probably would not have had to commit large numbers of ground forces to Vietnam. In fact, he determines that South Vietnam might have survived without *any* American ground troops. Contrary to Logevall, Moyar believes that Kennedy would have continued to increase America's involvement in Vietnam as the circumstances dictated in 1964 and 1965.

Moyar, a proponent of the domino theory, also speculates about the consequences for Asia if the United States had refused to intervene in South Vietnam in 1965. "High was the probability," he concludes, "that the fall of Vietnam in 1965 would have knocked over many dominoes in Southeast Asia."[43]

One of Moyar's more controversial arguments is that South Vietnam needed a strong, authoritarian political figure who could win over the southern population by establishing order and eliminating opposition. To defend this position, Moyar relies on some rather broad generalizations about Vietnamese political culture. "From the beginning of their history," he states, "the Vietnamese people had always been very inclined to support whichever political faction appeared strongest."[44] This historic tendency survived into the 1960s, when the Vietnamese, "[l]ike their ancestors . . . almost invariably threw their support to the strongest" faction.[45] Diem's landslide in 1955 reflected "the people's lack of interest in democratic procedures and their willingness to follow the dictates of the government."[46] The peasants did not care about "ideology or democracy, but military power and good leadership."[47] Powerful leaders were the norm in Vietnam, where "the strongman was venerated" and "softness" led to a loss of prestige.[48] American policymakers failed to recognize these traits and therefore pursued inappropriate and ineffective political strategies in South Vietnam.

Unfortunately, Moyar offers little evidence to support his broad assertions about the immutable and essential characteristics of the Vietnamese people. What were the roots of such beliefs? Did such beliefs transcend religious, geographic, class, and ethnic lines? How did the Vietnamese define terms such as "power," "strength," "softness," "democracy," and "good leadership"? Did French colonial rule alter Vietnamese attitudes, either by introducing foreign political concepts or by fostering anti-colonial nationalism? These questions provide a perfect opportunity to use the tools of the cultural historian to strengthen a work of diplomatic history. Unfortunately, Moyar does not engage these issues with any depth, offering broad and unequivocal statements in place of analytical rigor.

Figure 2.3 *President Kennedy confers with General Maxwell Taylor and Secretary of Defense Robert McNamara in the cabinet room, 25 January 1963.*

Photograph by Robert Knudsen in the John F. Kennedy Presidential Library and Museum, Boston.

Triumph Forsaken directly challenges many of the assertions of the other authors discussed in this chapter. It is hard to believe that Moyar and Seth Jacobs are both describing Ngo Dinh Diem, so divergent are their assessments. And where Jacobs takes American policymakers to task for relying on an authoritarian despot, Moyar argues the opposite: the United States consistently erred in trying to force Diem (and subsequent South Vietnamese leaders) to liberalize their regimes. Similarly, Logevall depicts Lyndon Johnson as a hawkish president who aggressively Americanized the war. Moyar takes Johnson to task for failing to be *more* hawkish and for applying American force gradually.

Moyar's propensity for hyperbole lends an air of drama to his writing. If Tri Quang was a communist agent, "it was one of the most ingenious and effective uses of covert action in history."[49] Ho Chi Minh's failure to kill Diem when he had the chance was "the biggest mistake he ever made."[50] The US decision to support the coup against Diem was "by far the worst American mistake of the Vietnam War."[51] David Halberstam did "more harm to the interests of the United States than any other journalist in American history."[52] The coup against Diem was "one of the worst debacles in the history of American foreign relations."[53] Such unambiguous declarations are unlikely to sway Vietnam scholars who are already skeptical of the revisionist position. They also suggest that Moyar may be guilty of the very flaw that he attributes to David Halberstam and Neil Sheehan: a "tendency to turn everything into black versus white."[54] A more nuanced approach, while less entertaining, might be more convincing.

Triumph Forsaken has ignited a passionate debate about American involvement in Vietnam. Some historians and members of the public have welcomed Moyar's book as a needed corrective to the orthodox lionization of Ho Chi Minh and the NLF as nationalist freedom fighters. They have applauded Moyar for his academic approach to a topic that has sometimes been the subject of polemics. *Triumph Forsaken* was published by an academic press (Cambridge), includes copious notes, and relies on an impressive array of sources. Moyar boasts degrees from Yale and Cambridge and he has taught at several respected colleges and universities.

For Moyar, *Triumph Forsaken* is not just good history; it also addresses a basic problem in American higher education. The paucity of revisionist scholarship can be traced to a "harmful trend at American universities whereby haughty derision and ostracism are used against those whose work calls into question the reigning ideological orthodoxy, stifling debate and leading to defects and gaps in scholarship."[55] Indeed, Moyar, a professor at the Marine Corps University in Quantico, has found academia generally unwelcoming for people with revisionist—read conservative—viewpoints.[56]

But *Triumph Forsaken* has also prompted a wave of negative responses. Some historians see the book as a poor effort to repackage revisionist claims that were unconvincing the first time around. Experts on the history of Vietnam have cast doubt on Moyar's understanding of Vietnamese history and culture. At times the debate between Moyar and his critics has moved beyond the typical academic back-and-forth. At least one prominent historian has questioned Moyar's use of sources; Moyar, on his part, has questioned the objectivity and motives of his critics.[57] The contentiousness of this debate suggests a combination of legitimate intellectual disagreements and clashing personalities. It also shows that the Vietnam War continues to incite passions among historians and the public at large.

At the end of *Choosing War*, Fredrik Logevall warns that "America's avoidable debacle in Vietnam . . . could happen again." The "central lesson of the war" is that the "continued primacy of the executive branch in foreign affairs—and within that branch a few individuals, to the exclusion of the bureaucracy—together with the eternal temptation of politicians to emphasize short-term personal advantage over long-term national interests ensures that the potential" for another Vietnam exists. America's responsibility is to protect against the "permissive context" that could lead to such a "disastrous policy."[58] Logevall could not have known how prophetic these words were. With the outbreak of wars in Afghanistan and Iraq in the early 2000s, historians and commentators alike looked to Vietnam for "lessons" that could be applied to current conflicts.

But even without these military conflicts, interest in the Vietnam War will likely remain high. *Triumph Forsaken* and the controversy it sparked help to show why Vietnam has such a hold on Americans. During the 1960s the American debate over the Vietnam War was about fundamental values. Was the United States fighting selflessly for freedom and democracy against the forces of autocracy? Were opponents of the war treasonous? Or was the United States fighting to perpetuate a racist, imperialistic system? Was the government trying to suppress free speech and loyal dissent? These questions, or variations on them, are as powerful today as they were four decades ago. And as long as these questions remain important to Americans, the scholarship on Vietnam will remain passionate, vibrant, and contentious.

DISCUSSION QUESTIONS

1. How do "orthodox" and "revisionist" historians differ in their interpretations of the Vietnam War?
2. Why are historiographical debates about the Vietnam War still so heated?
3. According to recent studies, what were the critical periods or decisions that led to America's intervention in Vietnam?
4. How do historians view the presidency of Ngo Dinh Diem?
5. Are there similarities between the origins of the Vietnam War and the Iraq War?

SUGGESTED READING

Berman, Larry. *No Peace, No Honor: Nixon, Kissinger, and Betrayal in Vietnam*. New York: The Free Press, 2001.

Divine, Robert A. "Vietnam Reconsidered." *Diplomatic History* 12 (1) (January 1988): 79–93.

Duiker, William J. *Ho Chi Minh: A Life*. New York: Hyperion, 2000.

Hess, Gary R. "The Unending Debate: Historians and the Vietnam War." In *America in the World: The Historiography of American Foreign Relations since 1941*, edited by Michael J. Hogan. Cambridge: Cambridge University Press, 1995.

"Interchange: Legacies of the Vietnam War." *Journal of American History* 93 (2) (September 2006): 452–90.

McMaster, H. R. *Dereliction of Duty: Lyndon Johnson, Robert McNamara, the Joint Chiefs of Staff, and the Lies that Led to Vietnam*. New York: Harper Perennial, 1998.

Miller, Edward. "War Stories: The Taylor–Buzzanco Debate and How We Think about the Vietnam War." *Journal of Vietnamese Studies* 1 (1–2) (February/August 2006): 453–84.

"A Roundtable on Mark Moyar's *Triumph Forsaken: The Vietnam War, 1954–1965*." *Passport: The Newsletter of the Society for Historians of American Foreign Relations* 38 (3) (December 2007): 5–22.

Ruane, Kevin. "Putting America in Its Place? Recent Writing on the Vietnam Wars." *Journal of Contemporary History* 37 (1) (January 2002): 115–28.

"*Triumph Forsaken* Roundtable Review." H-DIPLO 8 (7) (2007), http://www.h-net.org/~diplo/roundtables/PDF/TriumphForsaken-Roundtable.pdf.

NOTES

1. Mark Bradley, *Imagining Vietnam and America: The Making of Postcolonial Vietnam, 1919–1950* (Chapel Hill, NC: University of North Carolina Press, 2000); Seth Jacobs, *America's Miracle Man in Vietnam: Ngo Dinh Diem, Religion, Race, and U.S. Intervention in Southeast Asia* (Durham, NC: Duke University Press, 2004); Mark Atwood Lawrence, *Assuming the Burden: Europe and the American Commitment to War in Vietnam* (Berkeley: University of California Press, 2005); Fredrik Logevall, *Choosing War: The Lost Chance for Peace and the Escalation of the War in Vietnam* (Berkeley: University of California Press, 1999); Mark Moyar, *Triumph Forsaken: The Vietnam War, 1954–1965* (Cambridge: Cambridge University Press, 2006).
2. Leslie H. Gelb and Richard K. Betts, *The Irony of Vietnam: The System Worked* (Washington: Brookings Institution, 1979); David Halberstam, *The Making of a Quagmire: America and Vietnam during the Kennedy Era* (New York: Random House, 1965); Stanley Karnow, *Vietnam: A History* (New York: The Viking Press, 1983); Arthur M. Schlesinger Jr., *The Bitter Heritage: Vietnam and American Democracy, 1941–1966* (Boston: Houghton Mifflin, 1966).
3. Logevall, *Choosing War*, xiii.
4. Ibid., xxiv.
5. Ibid., xiii.
6. Ibid., 5.
7. Ibid , 135.
8. Ibid., 154.
9. Ibid., 191.
10. Ibid., 405.
11. Ibid., 335.
12. Ibid., xvii.
13. Arthur M. Schlesinger Jr., *The Bitter Heritage*, 32.
14. Logevall, *Choosing War*, 400.
15. Ibid., 390.
16. Ibid., 389.
17. Lawrence, *Assuming the Burden*, 7.
18. Ibid., 51.
19. Ibid., 257.

20. Ibid., 233.
21. Logevall, *Choosing War*, 385.
22. Lawrence, *Assuming the Burden*, 280.
23. Ibid., 2.
24. Ibid., 3.
25. Ibid., 280.
26. Ibid., 3.
27. Ibid., 286.
28. Bradley, *Imagining Vietnam and America*, 7.
29. Ibid., 178 (emphasis in original).
30. Ibid., 34.
31. Ibid., 44.
32. Ibid., 7.
33. Ibid., 8.
34. Jacobs, *America's Miracle Man*, 3.
35. Ibid., 60.
36. Moyar, *Triumph Forsaken*, xiii.
37. Ibid., xiv.
38. Ibid., 12.
39. Ibid., xv.
40. Ibid., 216.
41. Ibid., 228.
42. Ibid., 274.
43. Ibid., 388.
44. Ibid., 16.
45. Ibid., 93.
46. Ibid., 55.
47. Ibid., 158.
48. Ibid., 316.
49. Ibid., 218.
50. Ibid., 18.
51. Ibid., xvii.
52. Ibid., 170.
53. Ibid., 275.
54. Ibid., 171.
55. Ibid., xii.
56. Gary Shapiro, "Mark Moyar, Historian of Vietnam, Finds Academe Hostile to a Hawk." *New York Sun*, April 30, 2007, http://www.nysun.com/new-york/mark-moyar-historian-of-vietnam-finds-academe/53422/.
57. See, for example, "*Triumph Forsaken* Roundtable Review," H-DIPLO 8 (7) (2007), http://www.h-net.org/~diplo/roundtables/PDF/TriumphForsaken-Roundtable.pdf and "A Roundtable on Mark Moyar's *Triumph Forsaken: The Vietnam War, 1954–1965*," in *Passport: The Newsletter of the Society for Historians of American Foreign Relations* 38 (3) (December 2007): 5–22.
58. Logevall, *Choosing War*, 412–13.

TIMELINE EVENTS

April 28, 1956 – US Military Assistance and Advisory Group (MAAG) takes over the training of South Vietnamese armed forces

February 8, 1962 – MAAG becomes the US Military Assistance Command, Vietnam (MACV)

November 1, 1963 – South Vietnamese president Ngo Dinh Diem is overthrown in a coup

June 20, 1964 – General William Westmoreland takes over MACV

January 31, 1968 – Tet Offensive begins

June 10, 1968 – Westmoreland replaced by General Creighton Abrams

July 25, 1969 – Policy of Vietnamization announced by President Nixon

April–June 1970 – US/Army of the Republic of Vietnam invasion of Cambodia

February–March 1971 – Operation Lam Son 719

March–April 1972 – Easter Offensive

January 1975 – North Vietnamese forces overrun Phuoc Long Province

April 8–21, 1975 – Battle of Xuan Loc

April 30, 1975 – Fall of Saigon

Chapter 3

The "other" Vietnam War

Andrew Wiest

CHAPTER SUMMARY

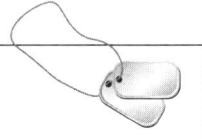

The popular historical understanding of the Vietnam War in the United States is that the conflict was a uniquely American tragedy in which US forces won all of the battles but still lost the war amid a collapse of national will on the home front. In this dominant historical narrative the Vietnamese themselves are often wholly absent or shunted aside. However, a full understanding of America's failed crusade in Vietnam *must* investigate the strengths and weaknesses of the South Vietnamese state and military. While Americans could and did win battlefield victories, only South Vietnam could have transformed those victories into a situation of strategic sustainability. Understanding South Vietnam, then, is critical to understanding why the American war there failed.

An ongoing American fascination with the Vietnam War is evident in a myriad of cultural signposts, ranging from movies like *Forrest Gump* to the lines of solemn visitors at the Vietnam Veterans Memorial to college classrooms packed with students eager to learn about their parents' war. The answers to why Americans remain fixated on what was a small and distant war are many, but all center on the same uncomfortable question: How did the United States, history's greatest superpower and a nation that had long stood as a beacon of hope, lose a war to a third-rate power like North Vietnam, while it also lost its soul in a cultural catharsis made up of protests, war crimes trials, and assassinations?[1]

The arbiters of America's past, whether they be film directors, novelists, historians or reporters, have provided a dizzying array of potential answers, some controversial and others taken as dogma, to explain American failure in the Vietnam War. President Lyndon Johnson was too distracted by his Great Society and micromanaged the war. The American media turned the nation against the war. American society was too fractured and its will was too weak. General William Westmoreland never really understood the war that was his to command. The US military relied on overly traditional tactics. The US military did not rely enough on traditional tactics. The power of the US Air Force was never truly unleashed. Airpower was used too indiscriminately. The ignominious roll call is, indeed, quite long, leaving no shortage of villainous characters contending for the leading part in the American morality play that is the history of the Vietnam War.

Much of the historical and cultural debate concerning the failure of the American war in Vietnam, though, is complicated by the very fact that its participants all too often view the conflict simply as an *American* war. Arguably perpetuating the fatal flaw of the US military effort in Vietnam, the American popular and historical consciousness regularly omits the Vietnamese from the story of their own war. What for Americans was arguably part of a much wider geopolitical chess match was for Vietnam a brutal civil war that fractured the nation along ethnic, social, religious, geographic, and economic fault lines, the roots of which extended well beyond the transitory motivations and concerns of the Cold War. While popular portrayal concedes that the conflict in Vietnam can be dated back to 1945 and the reimposition of French colonialism, actually the struggle can be seen as a part of a broader Vietnamese dynamic of South versus North competition that extends back at least as far as the 1500s. Viewing such a complex conflict only from the perspective of its final foreign interloper is overly simplistic. A full understanding of the Vietnam War, and of America's failed crusade, requires coming to terms with Vietnam's Vietnam War.

To complicate matters further, the only Vietnamese who seem to register in the American public consciousness, and who receive coverage in most popular accounts of the war, are America's enemies—Victor Charlie: the cunning VC and the hard-bitten warriors of North Vietnam. Allowing time for and praise of enemy forces in Vietnam makes perfect historical sense, for facing such stalwart adversaries—the inheritors of a martial tradition that had bested everyone from the Mongols to the Chinese—makes America's failure in its Vietnamese adventure somehow more palatable. By comparison, America's allies, the South Vietnamese, receive little notice and have become very nearly historically invisible. When not totally ignored in Western accounts of the conflict, the South Vietnamese usually receive only damning reference as a collection of cowards and incompetents who served a fatally flawed government that had little connection to Vietnam's glorious past. In the popular historical mind, then, geopolitical fate forced the United States to back the wrong horse in the Vietnam War, setting the stage for all that followed in America's great tragedy.

In recent years, though, Western scholars have devoted an increased level of academic scrutiny to South Vietnam that has begun to reshape the history of the conflict. While the new history admits that South Vietnam and its military were flawed instruments, it maintains that the South had a deep connection to Vietnam's past and was not simply predisposed to failure. Even the briefest of accounts of the South Vietnamese experience of war draws a picture that is uncomfortably at odds with the popular understanding of America's conflict in Southeast Asia. As part of an imperfect alliance and in the service of a flawed state, the South Vietnamese fought for twenty years at the cost of 200,000 military and at least 400,000 civilian dead. After the fall of Saigon, millions chose to flee to face an uncertain future abroad as refugees rather than to live under the rule of their brothers from the North. It seems, then, that many in South Vietnam fought long and hard for their own independence and were unwilling to accept defeat.

The emerging twin historical themes that the war in Vietnam was not simply an American war abroad and that South Vietnam was more than just a victim of history greatly complicate the standard intellectual framework that buttresses the American understanding of the conflict. If South Vietnam and its military, the Army of the Republic of Vietnam (ARVN), were more than a historical parody peopled by cardboard cutout officers and men, why is it not reserved for the descendants of the North Vietnamese to wonder at the nature of their eventual defeat? Perhaps South Vietnam and the ARVN have served as the excuse for America's lost war for too long, and it is time to consider more fully America's role in the defeat of a nation that actually did have a chance to survive.[2]

The Vietnam War stands as the quintessential "limited war," with President Lyndon Johnson famously choosing not to invade North Vietnam in a conscious effort to stop the conflict from flaring into a global conflagration. There would be no American tanks rolling into Hanoi to seal ultimate victory. Instead, success in the Vietnam War hinged on the continued survival of South Vietnam, a goal that American troops alone could not achieve. In the end, South Vietnam had to be capable of and worthy of its own survival. A full accounting of America's failed crusade in Vietnam, then, *must* involve an investigation of the nexus point of the war: the flawed US–South Vietnamese alliance. Only by putting a more human face on ARVN and by understanding both its complexities and its often uneasy relationship with its American sponsors can historians truly begin to understand the nature of that troubled institution—and thus the nature of the Vietnam War.

A FLAWED BEGINNING

Conceived in the wake of the Geneva Accords of 1954, South Vietnam was a nation born amid conflict, with its president, Ngo Dinh Diem, fighting for his own survival against powerful internal political enemies while also facing the specter of war with the communist North and its popular leader, Ho Chi Minh. Scrambling to save America's client state from collapse, the 342-man-strong Military Assistance and Advisory Group, Vietnam (MAAG),[3] initially under Lieutenant General John O'Daniel and then Lieutenant General Samuel Williams, had to build the ARVN effectively from scratch. Making matters worse, the only military tools to hand were the remnants of the defeated indigenous defenders of French colonialism, the Vietnamese

National Army (VNA). Creating the ARVN from such raw materials was fraught with danger, tainting the ARVN with a link to the colonial past and creating a Francophile ARVN leadership that arguably had limited loyalty to the new state. But war with the communists seemed close at hand, and MAAG had to prepare for the coming conflict in great haste.

Still smarting from the recent experience of the Korean War, US military advisers rushed to create ARVN as a conventional force ready to face an invasion from North Vietnam. However, the leadership of the fledgling South Vietnamese military, all of whom had fought against the Viet Minh as part of the VNA for years, disagreed with MAAG's design for the ARVN, countering that South Vietnam was more likely to face an insurgency than an invasion and contending that the ARVN should be constructed as a more lithe force based on maneuverability and sustainability within the Vietnamese cultural system.[4] In his memoir of the period, a frustrated General Tran Van Don lamented that such arguments "fell on deaf ears."[5] The Americans, though, did not relent and eventually settled on creating an ARVN of seven standardized infantry divisions whose task it was to stand against a North Vietnamese invasion long enough for American forces to arrive on the scene to save the day, as they had in Korea.

President Ngo Dinh Diem agonized over the decision to create an American-style army in South Vietnam and recognized that his own generals held a different vision for the army, but by 1956 domestic needs and the promise of American funding overrode his own generals' arguments. The United States chose, with Diem's approval, to create a mirror image of the American military in South Vietnam, and labored to construct an ARVN built on the primacy of conventional firepower and lavish logistical support. However, the American plan ran considerable risk, for South Vietnam, a developing nation, could not hope to support the considerable logistic, armament and training needs of such a military on its own.

Amid the furor of establishing both a national will and the institutions of government, the fragile construct of South Vietnam had great difficulty in meeting the challenge posed by also fielding a Western-style military. Reliant on labor-intensive wet rice agriculture for their survival, the peasants of South Vietnam saw little reason to abandon their work in the fields and the care of their families to join the military of the nascent state. Unable to rely on volunteerism to supply the military with manpower, South Vietnam turned to a draft system that was riddled with abuses, including serial draft dodging and payment of draft substitutes, to provide 65 percent of the army's total troop levels, making it one of the most heavily conscripted armies in history. Amazingly, ARVN still fought long and hard, and one study indicated that if the United States had mobilized the same proportion of its adult male population, it would have sent 8 million men per year to Vietnam.[6]

Exacerbating the already considerable difficulties, MAAG's reliance on conventional operations resulted in a Westernized ARVN that stood apart from its people and from the nation's own martial past. Promising counterinsurgency techniques based on small units of territorial forces raised on the local level and tied intrinsically to the people were ignored in favor of standard Western tactics of attrition for the next twelve years. To MAAG a possible insurgency was only a diversion that threatened to take attention away from a Korean-style

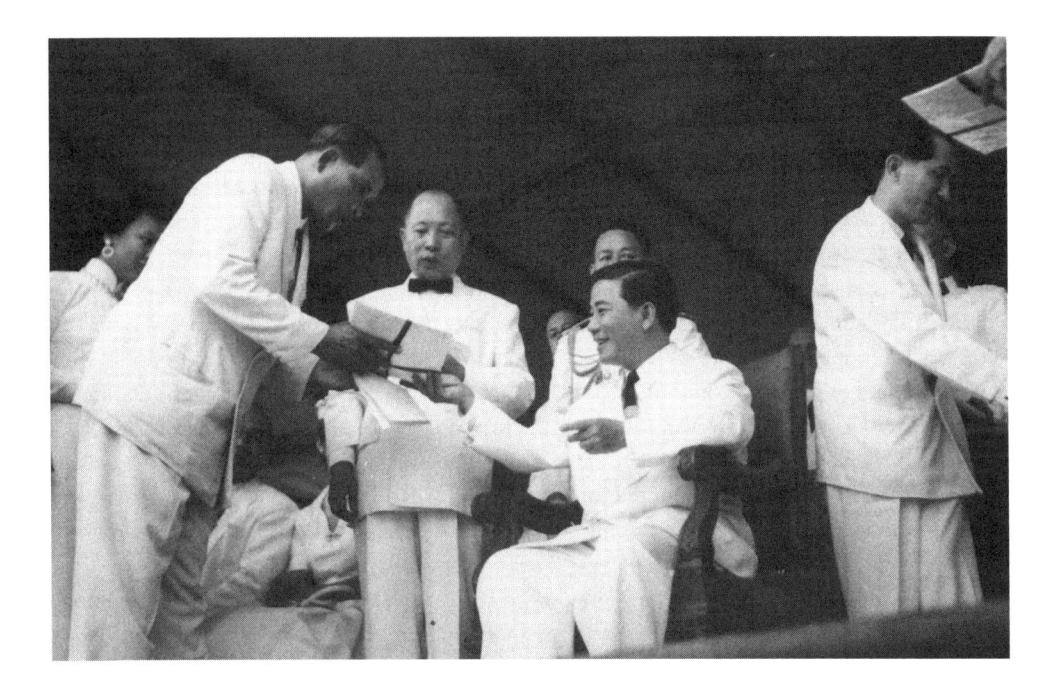

Figure 3.1 *President Ngo Dinh Diem (1956) of South Vietnam, a controversial figure who agonized over the decision to create an "American-style" military in South Vietnam.*

Photograph VA041128, January 1956, Ogden Williams Collection, The Vietnam Archive, Texas Tech University.

communist invasion. In 1955 Diem had railed against the American's traditionalist approach to the conflict, telling Williams, "We should start Guerrilla Warfare of our own. . . . The Army does not understand, as it sees only the classic military solution."[7] Thus, MAAG restructured the ARVN quickly, in an American mold, and readied it for a conventional war that never came.[8] In the words of ARVN Lieutenant General Ngo Quang Truong:

> When fighting finally broke out, it did not take the form of a conventional, Korean-style invasion. It rather began as a brush-fire war fought with subversive activities and guerrilla tactics away from urban centers. Waged day and night, this small war gradually gained in tempo, nipping away at the secure fabric of rural areas. In the face of the growing insurgency, ARVN units found themselves ill-fitted to fight this type of war for which they had not been trained.[9]

With the lion's share of nation building in South Vietnam dedicated to defense, as in so many fledgling nations, the ARVN quickly became the most important tool at the government's disposal. Making matters worse, many ARVN leaders, with only limited loyalty to the newfound state, turned to political games of power brokering and graft rather than to the business of readying for war with North Vietnam. For his part, Diem came to value political loyalty from his military commanders over bravery and combat effectiveness. For the remainder of the conflict, the leadership of the ARVN became intertwined with the state, and the line between politics and the military became so blurred that no regime in Saigon could survive without military support, which made the ARVN synonymous with the government.[10] The ARVN was and remained both the main power base of the South Vietnamese government and its governing apparatus, a system rife with potential political liabilities.[11]

Perhaps not unexpectedly, the South Vietnamese state did not perform as well as its American sponsors had hoped, and in 1960 it fell victim to a growing Viet Cong (VC) insurgency. After an initial round of stunning communist gains, though, the ARVN was able to hold the conflict in an uneasy state of stasis. However, following the assassination of Ngo Dinh Diem in 1963, in a plot that at the very least had tacit American support, South Vietnam disintegrated into chaos as a parade of ARVN leaders competed for ultimate control of the state. Amid the anarchy, the ARVN's war against the Viet Cong ground to a halt, and South Vietnam teetered on the brink of collapse.

Convinced that the ARVN was no longer combat ready, General William Westmoreland, commander, United States Military Assistance Command, Vietnam (which had taken over from MAAG as America's involvement in the war deepened), pressed for the commitment of American ground forces to save the situation. As the advisers to Lyndon Johnson debated Westmoreland's request, only Maxwell Taylor, then ambassador to Vietnam, objected, stating that an infusion of American forces into the war "would simply encourage the South Vietnamese armed forces to let the United States carry the full burden of the war . . . [and]would raise the specter of French colonialism and encourage a majority of the population to turn against the United States." Regardless of Taylor's warnings, distracted by its own political battles and the domestic Great Society program, the Johnson White House made the fateful decision to begin the American ground war in Vietnam in earnest.[12]

The arrival of American combat troops, concurrent with the rise of a much more stable South Vietnamese government under the leadership of Nguyen Van Thieu and Nguyen Kao Ky, had an immediate tactical effect as US forces fought the Viet Cong to a standstill. While most within the ARVN welcomed the American intervention, the relationship was not one of equals and signaled a dangerous shift in the ongoing conflict. As American forces took over many of the combat responsibilities, the ARVN became spectators instead of participants in what should have been its war.[13]

Supremely confident in their ability, incoming US forces essentially pushed the ARVN to one side in an attempt to destroy the communist threat single-handedly. As Maxwell Taylor later reflected, "We never really paid attention to the ARVN Army. We didn't give a damn about them."[14]

Although American forces famously "won all of the battles" of the conflict, the policy of attempting to win the war *for* South Vietnam proved to be shortsighted. In part because of limits placed on the use of military force for geopolitical reasons, a corresponding escalation of the conflict by the North Vietnamese, and the stalwart nature of the Viet Cong insurgency, the Americans could not hope to win by traditional methods of warfare alone. The best hope for success instead lay in a symbiosis of US and ARVN efforts and the creation of a South Vietnam that was capable of ensuring its own survival.

For nearly the first five years of the conflict, though, ARVN would serve only as a combat adjunct to its mighty American ally as the United States vainly sought to win a conventional military victory in Vietnam. Only in 1969, after America had tired of and begun its withdrawal from its war, did the military emphasis begin to shift back toward creating an ARVN that could survive on its own. But by then it was too late.

General Ngo Quang Troung put the situation succinctly:

> Entering the war with the posture and disposition of a fire brigade, the Americans rushed about to save the Vietnamese house from destruction but took little interest in caring for the victims. Only after they realized that the victims, too, should be made firefighters to save their own houses, did Americans set about to really care for them. Valuable time was lost, and by the time the victims could get onto their feet and began to move forward a few steps after recovery, the fire brigade was called back to the home station.[15]

THE TET OFFENSIVE

Books, movies, and documentaries abound that chronicle the American experience in battle during the Vietnam War. While these studies often minutely dissect US strategic and tactical moves and motivations, most simply omit the ARVN from their calculations. While it is true that the Americans shunted the ARVN aside in a fatally bifurcated strategy that entailed the United States and South Vietnamese fighting two separate wars in the same country, the ARVN in fact played a role, whether large or small, in every major American operation in the Vietnam War. In the years devoted to prosecution of Westmoreland's attritional strategy, roughly 1965–8, the ARVN, though sadly often as something of an afterthought, invariably fought alongside its American allies and prosecuted its own independent series of campaigns. Although the quality of ARVN units varied widely, from the wonderfully good to the tragically bad, in general the ARVN acquitted itself well in battle, better than many Americans had dared to hope. Knowing the strengths and weaknesses of how the ARVN functioned in combat is critical to a fuller understanding of how the wider conflict unfolded. Even a cursory look at the ARVN's role in one of the most important "American" battles of the war, the Tet Offensive, demonstrates the importance of writing the South Vietnamese into the tactical history of their war.

Americans rightly understand the Tet Offensive of 1968 to be perhaps the single pivotal moment in the Vietnam War. After luring US forces into the Vietnamese hinterlands in 1967, and after a massive buildup of troops that went almost unnoticed by American military intelligence, on January 31, 1968 the Viet Cong attacked virtually every urban area in South Vietnam, focusing their efforts on Saigon and the old Vietnamese imperial capital of Hue. After the initial shock of battle, the standard version of the Tet story contends, the Americans reacted quickly, resulting in heavy, and often bitter, fighting. Fatally, the VC, a nimble force that usually relied on guerrilla tactics, had chosen to stand toe to toe with the might of US firepower. In most cities the VC attacks failed utterly, and only in Hue did communist forces take and hold ground for any length of time. Across the length and breadth of South Vietnam the VC paid a fearsome butcher's bill for its mistake, losing an estimated 58,000 soldiers from its force of 84,000 dedicated to the battle.

Although American forces had won a signature victory over a determined foe, tactical success was somehow lost amid the implosion of American national will. Potentially biased media coverage blended with tumultuous events on the American home front to sap public support for the war, leaving painful pictures that told the story of a war gone awry: vivid images including Westmoreland's pre-Tet confident prediction made in November 1967 that "We have reached an important point when the end begins to come into view. . . . The enemy's hopes are bankrupt";[16] scenes of bitter fighting in the US embassy compound in Saigon; famed CBS anchorman Walter Cronkite declaring that the war could not be won; Lyndon Johnson, worn down and beaten by years of war, declining to run again for the presidency; American cities on fire; and riots in Chicago during the Democratic National Convention. Historical and popular attention has focused on this most central moment of the uniquely American tragedy that was the Vietnam War—attention that seeks to explain how such an overwhelming tactical victory actually led to eventual defeat.

In analyzing the fascinating American context of the Tet Offensive, though, much Vietnam War scholarship has left a rather glaring hole in the understanding of Tet's place in the wider conflict. Although the VC and North Vietnamese Army (NVA) often play leading roles as the story's protagonists, the ARVN and the South Vietnamese population are often consigned to the footnotes and sidebars of the history of the offensive and its aftermath. The popular historical view, however, is flawed, for in most ways the Tet Offensive was a fratricidal affair aimed at destroying the ARVN and provoking an uprising to oust the Americans. The VC and NVA realized that they could not defeat the Americans in battle; their plan had been to lure US forces away from the cities and then attack and destroy the political and military structure of South Vietnam to present the mighty Americans with a fait accompli. The communists believed that, since the South Vietnamese and ARVN were unwitting stooges of American capitalism, the corrupt state and its puppet military would fall quickly when sorely pressed. The Tet Offensive, then, in many ways did not even directly involve the Americans and must be understood as Vietnamese in context.

At the strategic level the most significant developments of the Tet Offensive were that the South Vietnamese population did not rise up, and that instead of crumbling, the ARVN fought bravely—more bravely than the Americans dared hope, leaving the VC and NVA to suffer severe losses at the hands of US and ARVN firepower. Driven from the cities, and with the VC smashed

THE "OTHER" VIETNAM WAR

as an effective fighting force, the communists surrendered land that had been under their control for years. Apart from the physical losses suffered during Tet, the ambivalence of the South Vietnamese population forced the communists to consider the nearly unthinkable possibility that the people of South Vietnam were something more than unwitting American puppets. Both their combat losses and the realization that South Vietnam was more resilient than they had ever imagined led the communists to several conclusions. The war would be longer and more difficult than even they had imagined, and, with the loss of so many VC cadres, would also become increasingly more conventional in nature, thus playing to the strengths of the US and ARVN forces.

THE ARVN AND THE BATTLE FOR HUE

The popular historical understanding of the Tet Offensive is also flawed in a tactical sense, because most accounts simply omit the ARVN from the story. While fighting raged across South Vietnam, the epicenter of the Tet Offensive focused on the imperial capital of Hue. The communists realized that raising their banner aloft above the seat of Vietnamese emperors would inherit for the VC the mantle of Vietnam's glorious nationalistic past, while demonstrating the impotence of ARVN and US forces and the moral bankruptcy of the Saigon regime. Accordingly, the communists dedicated two entire regiments to the task of seizing Hue, which resulted in the most ferocious fighting of the entire Tet Offensive, involving a bitter month-long battle in which American and ARVN forces had to fight a street-by-street urban battle to evict the communists from the imperial city.

The story of the struggle for Hue is comparatively well known in the United States. After the fall of much of the lightly defended city, the US Marines reacted by devoting more and more force to the urban maelstrom, slowly grinding away at the tenacious VC resistance. However, the popular historical accounts of the fighting in Hue generally omit the role of the ARVN in the battle. At the furthest extreme, Keith Nolan's *Battle for Hue* rarely mentions the ARVN at all and relegates it to a role of "mopping up behind the Marines," while accusing the ARVN of "moving from house to house in organized looting parties."[17] In the struggle to retake Hue it is beyond doubt that the US Marines demonstrated the individual bravery and unit battle prowess that has marked the members of the United States Marine Corps as the finest infantry in the world. The Americans gave of themselves selflessly and indeed fought an epic battle in Hue, losing 147 killed in action.[18]

However, the Americans were not the focus of the battle. The VC wanted to destroy the ARVN and to capture Vietnam's imperial capital. In a much less heralded struggle that received little of the glaring press coverage that chronicled the Marines' every move and has received little historical coverage since, it was actually the ARVN that undertook most of the fighting in Hue, especially in the Imperial Citadel, besting the vaunted VC in a long and bitter series of battles.

At the outset of the struggle, only the Hac Bao (rapid reaction) company and the Headquarters Company of the ARVN 1st Division stood between the attacking VC and NVA and their goal of seizing the Hue Citadel. In bitter, often hand-to-hand fighting the embattled defenders held out in the 1st Division headquarters, retaining a bridgehead in the walled city. Over the next days, ARVN units fought their way to the citadel through a series of NVA blocking positions and ambushes, to the aid of the stranded 1st Division headquarters. Once reinforcements began to arrive in the city, the commander of the 1st Division, General Ngo Quang Truong, quickly launched a counterattack. However, the NVA and VC, well supplied and having created a maze of interlocking defenses from the buildings of the city and the walls and towers of the citadel itself, fought with desperation.

Figure 3.2 *Hue City from the air during Tet. An aerial view of the southeastern portion of the Hue Citadel during the Tet Offensive.*

Photograph VA035396, June 24, 1968, Peter Braestrup Collection, The Vietnam Archive, Texas Tech University.

Lacking the heavy organic fire support that typified American units, the ARVN slogged forward for nearly a month in some of the most difficult fighting of the war, struggling from ruined building to ruined building. On February 24, ARVN troops hoisted the South Vietnamese flag above the shattered remains of the ancient Vietnamese capital, signifying victory in one of the most important battles of the entire war. During the fighting for Hue, ARVN forces lost 357 killed in action and inflicted an astounding 2,642 battle deaths on the NVA and VC forces.[19] That the US Marines fought hard and well in Hue is beyond doubt. However, the popular view of the battle as an American struggle with a bit of perfunctory ARVN aid is invalid.

The Vietnam War was fought as part of an alliance, with American and other free world forces acting in tandem with the ARVN amid a Vietnamese war. Indeed, since American forces chose not to invade North Vietnam, or even Cambodia and Laos, sustained success rested with an ARVN that was capable of fighting and winning its own war. Analyzing how ARVN fitted into the American alliance is critical to understanding the ebb and flow of the war as a whole. ARVN was there for every battle in Vietnam, but its strengths and weaknesses, its victories and defeats, are usually absent from the history books. The flawed prevailing public perception of the Tet Offensive makes clear the fact that our understanding of the Vietnam War will remain incomplete until the ARVN is written into its own story. The Tet Offensive was, at its heart, a Vietnamese battle, and a full analysis of its place within the dynamics of the Vietnam War must include the complete Vietnamese perspective.

AN UNREPORTED WAR

Americans steadily lost interest in their failing overseas adventure in the wake of the cataclysm of the Tet Offensive. Although there were certainly bouts of renewed public angst over the war, especially surrounding the fighting for Hamburger Hill in 1969 and the Cambodian incursion of 1970, which led to the shootings at Kent State, the slow drawdown of the conflict by President Richard Nixon succeeded in dampening the controversy over, and public interest in, the Vietnam War. Tragically, much of the American polity, as it tired of the war, turned its attention to other matters. Somehow, the American war ended with Tet, and everything following was an anticlimax, even as the fighting in Vietnam raged for another seven years.

The popular historical perception of the war in Vietnam has mirrored the distorted public perception of the time. While historians and journalists lavish attention on the war prior to Tet, the period after 1968 often receives only cursory coverage and remains something of a fallow historical field. Stanley Karnow's Pulitzer Prize-winning *Vietnam: A History* stands as perhaps the leading example; although the massive work weighs in at nearly 700 pages, Karnow devotes only 92 pages to the years following the Tet Offensive. What if histories of World War II essentially ended with the Battle of El Alamein or the Battle of Midway? The picture, though, is not as gloomy as it first appears, for several historians are working to chronicle the final years of the Vietnam War, but it will take some time for their work to permeate the public consciousness.

One critically important reason that the second half of the United States' war in Vietnam resonates little with Americans is that the war was becoming less and less American in nature. Faced with a mounting political liability on the home front, Nixon began the process of withdrawing American forces from Vietnam, a scheme dubbed "Vietnamization." For their part, the South Vietnamese were mystified by American actions in the wake of Tet. The Viet Cong had been bested in battle, and was being driven back into its highland sanctuaries. To the ARVN, then, the post-Tet period seemed to be the logical time to strike against an enemy that seemed to be reeling from defeat. Instead, America, for reasons related to events taking place far from the battlefield, began to disengage from the conflict. Although few South Vietnamese could believe the nightmare scenario that America, after the investment of so much blood and treasure, would quit the war entirely, such would be the case. While America's Vietnam tragedy was ending, however, South Vietnam's national tragedy was only just beginning.

While the ARVN had fought well as an adjunct to US forces under the American rubric of the Vietnam War, its success had come at a steep price. With little control over strategy, ARVN leaders ceded most military planning to their American allies. In addition, the ARVN had constant access, through the American advisory system, to massive US firepower and logistic support, which ensured tactical victory in battle. However, the ARVN quickly became dependent upon American leadership and firepower support instead of developing its own capabilities. As a result, South Vietnam found itself wedded to a conventional style of war that alone it could not economically or socially ever hope to support.[20] The flaws and dependencies of ARVN remained safely hidden beneath the surface, as long as it acted in its comfortable

Figure 3.3 American advisers and Army of the Republic of Vietnam troops: Australian adviser Max Kelly and US adviser Harvey Zimmerle with ARVN soldiers while on patrol in 1969.

Courtesy of Harvey Zimmerle and Andrew Wiest.

role as an adjunct to the powerful Americans. However, America was disengaging from the Vietnam War, leaving the ARVN to its fate. Major Tom Jaco, who served as a US adviser to the ARVN 54th Regiment, put the situation best when he remarked:

> The ARVN [in 1970] was dependent on the United States–dependent on advisory groups, dependent on support; air support, fire support, medical support . . . we could teach them how to call upon that support, but if it was not there to be called it would not do them a heck of a lot of good.[21]

The first true test of the ARVN's ability to stand on its own came in the Lam Son 719 invasion of Laos, designed to cut the Ho Chi Minh Trail, in 1971. In an operation that receives little notice in the West, in February 17,000 of the ARVN's best forces, aided by prodigious amounts of US air support, struck toward the Laotian village and communist logistics hub of Tchepone, expecting minimal resistance. However, instead of retreating, the North Vietnamese chose to stand and fight. As a result, the ARVN forces, without the aid of American ground forces or even of US advisers, found themselves facing an estimated 60,000 enemy defenders.

At the outset, the communists struggled to react to the point of the ARVN attack and worked mainly to gather and reposition their forces, which allowed the ARVN operation to begin well, with a mixed force of armor and infantry advancing on the ground augmented by helicopter-borne assaults on its flanks. Soon, though, the ARVN forward movement bogged down amid a crisis of command. Finding themselves tasked with tactical planning duties that heretofore had been reserved for the Americans, the ARVN operational leadership failed, amid constant politically motivated intervention from South Vietnam's president, Nguyen Van Thieu. Owing to the failures of command, ARVN armor sat stationary and unused as ARVN infantry units, isolated in firebases on the highest hilltops flanking the armored advance, began to be surrounded and destroyed by the gathering enemy force. Tom Jaco, who witnessed events at ARVN's forward command post at Khe Sanh, was stunned to find a situation with "more political intrigue than you can ever imagine." As the armor sat in place "without a clue," Jaco watched in horror as "command and control fell apart," sacrificing the lives of brave ARVN soldiers to ineptitude and political infighting.[22]

On the battlefield, ARVN soldiers acquitted themselves well and fought with a grim tenacity while exacting a heavy toll on their NVA attackers. However, ARVN units, as they had been trained to do so often in the past, exhibited a marked tendency to remain reliant on American airpower instead of maneuver in dealing with the gathering NVA. As a consequence, many ARVN units found themselves cut off, and dependent on American airpower for their very survival. Without their American advisers, who had long served as the conduit to US airpower, the ARVN forces were at a fatal disadvantage. Colonel Benjamin Harrison, who served as senior adviser to the 1st ARVN Division, put the human cost paid by the ARVN by fighting without its advisers into stark perspective:

The ARVN could scream and cry, but by not having their advisers with them they could not transmit the true nature of the situation across to the Air Force as well as their adviser would have. . . . [In situations which] normally a US adviser would have raised all kinds of hell . . . [the ARVN often could not get their point across and] got their asses shot off by the NVA and couldn't get any tactical air support.[23]

After shaking off the command malaise, ARVN forces achieved a token occupation of Tchepone before engaging in a fighting withdrawal from Laos under tremendous enemy pressure, which saw several ARVN units obliterated. Although Lam Son 719 tragically fell short of expectations, in some ways the invasion of Laos actually represented what was good and right about the ARVN, which after years of being sidelined was able to extemporize an operation outside its national borders in an area where the NVA held virtually every advantage. During the fighting the ARVN, aided by the might of US airpower, also forced the NVA to pay a fearsome butcher's bill for the retention of their base areas in Laos, doing great damage to the Laotian logistics network and inflicting some 13,000 battle deaths on the NVA.

Figure 3.4 Army of the Republic of Vietnam troops on operations near the Laotian border in 1969. Courtesy of Harvey Zimmerle and Andrew Wiest.

In Lam Son 719, though, ARVN units suffered nearly 8,000 total casualties and an estimated 3,800 killed in action, representing a loss rate of 45 percent of the total force allocated to the operation. In support of Lam Son 719, United States forces lost more than 100 helicopters and seven fixed-wing aircraft. That the operation had started with such high hopes but bogged down under the weight of ARVN's own command problems and tactical inefficiency was especially galling to American and Vietnamese observers alike. While the operation proved that ARVN had great potential, its multiple command failings and the resiliency of the NVA indicated that the ARVN was not yet ready to shoulder the burden of war alone.

Immediately after the conclusion of Operation Lam Son 719, President Nixon proclaimed, "Tonight I can report that Vietnamization has succeeded." He then announced an acceleration of the US troop withdrawal process, with an additional 100,000 troops slated to return to the United States by November 1971, and promised his war-weary constituents that "American involvement in Vietnam was coming to an end."[24] The complex military legacy of the ARVN's performance in Laos, demonstrating at once both great potential and critical dependencies, nearly faded from view amid the bright light of political expediency, for regardless of the overall ability of the ARVN to survive, America was quitting South Vietnam.

THE EASTER OFFENSIVE

Spread increasingly thin, the ARVN scrambled to cover for the quickened pace of the withdrawal of forces by its mighty ally. In addition, after having marginalized ARVN for so long, US forces belatedly began a crash course in readying the South Vietnamese to face the war on their own. However, the North Vietnamese, who rapidly recovered from their grievous losses in Laos, decided to disrupt allied planning. With few American forces in Vietnam, and before the South could transform its armed forces, the North gambled on an attempt to achieve an ultimate military victory instead of being forced to settle for a less cathartic end to the conflict through ongoing negotiations in Paris. On the morning of March 30, 1972, North Vietnam committed nearly its entire combat force—fourteen divisions, twenty-six separate regiments, and supporting armor and artillery units—into an invasion of South Vietnam dubbed the Easter Offensive.

The three-pronged operation, with attacks aimed at An Loc in the south, Kontum in the Central Highlands, and Hue and Da Nang in the north, took the form of conventional frontal assaults against thinly held ARVN defensive lines. Caught unawares in positions not designed to face such an attack, ARVN forces fell back quickly on all three fronts. Although there were moments of near-panic and military disarray, when well led, ARVN soldiers fought hard against the invaders. However, the ARVN again demonstrated ineptitude at the highest levels, involving presidential interference in the battle, multiple command inefficiencies, and outright failure to obey orders on the part of politically powerful ARVN generals.

Stung by the reverses, the South Vietnamese reshuffled their command structure, purged some of the worst ARVN offenders, and rushed reinforcements to the affected areas. While the higher echelons of ARVN remained imperfect, for the neglect of nearly twenty years cannot be undone amid a single crisis, the ARVN responded well to its sternest test. After its initial failures, it regrouped and held firm against repeated NVA assaults outside Hue, Kontum, and especially in a bitter seventy-day urban battle at An Loc. Once the crisis had passed, and the NVA tide had broken against the ARVN's new defenses, the South Vietnamese launched counter-attacks in all three major operational areas. The fighting was most prolonged south of the Demilitarized Zone, where by July ARVN forces had pushed the NVA out of much of its territorial gains, resulting in a fierce, often hand-to-hand struggle for Quang Tri City.

In many ways the struggle across South Vietnam during the Easter Offensive, one of the largest and most important battles of the entire war, represented the ARVN at its best and served to vindicate American strategy in the Vietnam War. Although no American ground forces had taken part in the battle, unlike in Laos, during the Easter Offensive the ARVN worked with its US advisers and their link to lavish American airpower. The ARVN had never been meant to stand on its own; it had always functioned as part of an alliance with the United States. With access to American know-how and firepower, in the Easter Offensive the ARVN stood firm and repulsed an all-out attack by the NVA. The fighting had been difficult, with South Vietnam losing 8,000 killed in action and 3,500 missing, while the NVA suffered as many as 40,000 killed out of a total of 200,000 committed to battle.[25]

General Creighton Abrams, commander of US forces in Vietnam, was quite frank in his estimation of the ARVN's performance during the Easter Offensive, and remarked at the time:

> There's been some poor performances. But there <u>always</u> have been poor performances in war—in war or anything else. And I think that there always will be. . . . Some poor performances are not going to lose it. It's the <u>good</u> performances that are going to win it. . . . But—I <u>doubt</u> the fabric of this thing could have been held together without U.S. air. But the thing that had to happen before that is the Vietnamese, some numbers of them, <u>had</u> to stand and fight. If they didn't do that, <u>ten times</u> the air we've got wouldn't have stopped them. So—with <u>all</u> the screwups that have occurred, <u>and</u> with all the bad perform-ances that have occurred—they've been there, we wouldn't be where we are this morning if some numbers of the Vietnamese hadn't decided to stand and fight. . . . And the reason, the <u>first</u> reason, is that the Vietnamese . . . have decided by god they've gone far enough and they're going to fight if they get some kind of chance.[26]

The invasion of Laos and the Easter Offensive make clear that the ARVN was still a flawed instrument, one not yet ready to fight a war as complex and brutal as that in Vietnam on its own. However, in those battles the ARVN had functioned well as part of the rubric of the American-defined war in Vietnam, in which the ARVN was meant to fight alongside a First World ally. Its command inefficiencies notwithstanding, with American support and firepower, which had long been the fundamental determinant of the conflict, in the Easter Offensive the ARVN had fought the vaunted NVA to a standstill. The system of combining ARVN manpower with American know-how and firepower was working. But even as the Easter Offensive drew to a close in the summer of 1972, the entire war stood on the brink of a fundamental change. With its effort to achieve military victory in tatters, and suffering from the heaviest bombing of the entire war, North Vietnam agreed to Nixon's peace overtures in negotiations that gave the communists very nearly everything they wanted. As a result, in early 1973 the United States made good its exit from the war in an agreement that left communist forces in place in South Vietnam, even as American forces withdrew completely. American money, American advisers, and American firepower were gone, but the NVA and its sources of external support remained.

No matter the grand claims that Nixon made on behalf of Vietnamization, the ARVN was not yet ready to prosecute the war alone—and the outcome after 1973 was inevitable. The ARVN had been created as a mirror image of the United States' armed forces, the military of a First World nation that could not be supported by the tattered economy of a Third World nation. Lavishly strong on paper, the ARVN would fight on, but ironically in many ways proved not to be Vietnamese enough in structure and form to withstand the American withdrawal and the eventual stripping of funding that followed.[27] Once the United States left the conflict completely, the ARVN faced a war not of its own creation in which it had always played a strictly subsidiary role, and its doom quickly became clear.

CONCLUSION

South Vietnam was not a perfect nation; its leadership was often inept and ham-fisted. Graft and corruption were rife. The nation never provided its people with an adequate political rationale for their service, or even simple rural security. However, South Vietnam and the ARVN were not the bumbling, hapless cowards of American popular imagery. Instead, South Vietnam and its military were vibrant and complex institutions involved in a life or death struggle that was at once part of a civil war and part of a clash of global superpowers. Far from being simply an American war, the struggle in Vietnam can only be understood in a multinational context, with South Vietnam and the ARVN at its core. Existing at an uncomfortable nexus point where geopolitical fault lines intersected with the needs of nation building amid a time of war, the ARVN balanced precariously between life as an American-inspired force and the realities of fighting a brutal Vietnamese war. The obvious tensions imposed by the ARVN's position were great and eventually proved to be overwhelming.

Harry Summers begins his famous work *On Strategy* with a quotation from his own experience as part of the Four-Party Joint Military Team in Hanoi after the fall of Saigon in 1975. Summers remarked to his North Vietnamese counterpart, "'You know you never defeated us on the battlefield.' . . . The North Vietnamese colonel pondered this remark for a moment.

'That may be so,' he replied, 'but it is also irrelevant.'"[28] While Summers meant his remark, in part, to support his own thesis that the United States should have hewn more to the aggressive application of conventional force in the Vietnam War, the wisdom expressed by that North Vietnamese colonel sheds valuable light on Vietnam as a civil war. For all of its military might and stunning tactical successes, the United States failed to achieve its primary aim of an independent South Vietnam. Indeed, no number of American battlefield victories could ever have achieved that goal, for only the South Vietnamese could have transformed tactical success into strategic sustainability. Understanding the American failure in Vietnam, then, must include an analysis of South Vietnam itself and the complex relationship between the ARVN and its American sponsors. Especially given the ongoing American efforts in Iraq and Afghanistan, and with the prospect that modern warfare is trending more toward insurgencies and nation building and away from "traditional" modes of state-to-state conflict, understanding the failed dynamics of the US–South Vietnamese relationship becomes even more urgent.

DISCUSSION QUESTIONS

1. Why has Western scholarship failed to take adequate note of South Vietnam in what was a Vietnamese war?
2. What flaws were there in the creation of ARVN?
3. Why should the Tet Offensive be seen as more Vietnamese in nature?
4. How was the process of Vietnamization flawed?
5. Did the ARVN actually have a chance to survive?

SUGGESTED READING

Brigham, Robert. *ARVN: Life and Death in the South Vietnamese Army*. Lawrence: University Press of Kansas, 2006.
Catton, Philip E. *Diem's Final Failure: Prelude to America's War in Vietnam*. Lawrence: University Press of Kansas, 2002.
Krepinevich, Andrew. *The Army and Vietnam*. Baltimore: Johns Hopkins University Press, 1986.
McMaster, H. R. *Dereliction of Duty: Lyndon Johnson, Robert McNamara, the Joint Chiefs of Staff and the Lies That Led to Vietnam*. New York: Harper, 1997.
Moyar, Mark. *Triumph Forsaken: The Vietnam War, 1954–1965*. Cambridge: Cambridge University Press, 2006.
Tran Van Don, *Our Endless War: Inside Vietnam*. San Raphael, CA: Presidio Press, 1978.
Wiest, Andrew. *Vietnam's Forgotten Army: Heroism and Betrayal in the ARVN*. New York: New York University Press, 2008.
Willbanks, James. *The Battle of An Loc*. Bloomington: Indiana University Press, 2005.

THE "OTHER" VIETNAM WAR

Willbanks, James. *Abandoning Vietnam: How America Left and South Vietnam Lost Its War*. Lawrence: University Press of Kansas, 2004.

NOTES

1. This section of the chapter appeared in an earlier form in my foreword for Lam Quang Thi's *Hell in An Loc* (Denton, TX: University of North Texas Press, 2009) and is reprinted with the kind permission of the University of North Texas Press.
2. Portions of this chapter have been revised from my account of ARVN entitled *Vietnam's Forgotten Army: Heroism and Betrayal in the ARVN* (New York: New York University Press, 2007) and are reprinted with the kind permission of New York University Press.
3. Ronald H. Spector, *United States Army in Vietnam. Advice and Support: The Early Years, 1941–1960* (Washington, DC: Center of Military History, 1983), 256.
4. Thomas R. Cantwell, "The Army of South Vietnam: A Military and Political History, 1955–1975" (PhD diss., University of New South Wales, 1989), 16. Also see Tran Van Don, *Our Endless War: Inside Vietnam* (San Raphael, CA: Presidio Press, 1978), 171.
5. Don, *Our Endless War*, 149; Robert Brigham, *ARVN: Life and Death in the South Vietnamese Army* (Lawrence: University Press of Kansas, 2006), 5.
6. Brigham, *ARVN*, 5–7, 11.
7. Arguably, conventional war did come to South Vietnam with the Easter Offensive of 1972. By that time, though, the fundamental reality of the ARVN had been long set. Philip E. Catton, *Diem's Final Failure: Prelude to America's War in Vietnam* (Lawrence: University Press of Kansas, 2002), 87.
8. John A. Nagl, *Learning to Eat Soup with a Knife: Counterinsurgency Lessons from Malaya and Vietnam* (Chicago: University of Chicago Press, paperback edition 2005), 120.
9. Lt. Gen. Ngo Quang Truong, *Territorial Forces*, Indochina Monographs (Washington, DC: Center of Military History, 1980), 25.
10. Cantwell, "The Army of South Vietnam," 23.
11. Arnold Isaacs, *Without Honor: Defeat in Vietnam and Cambodia* (Baltimore: Johns Hopkins University Press, 1983), 102.
12. H. R. McMaster, *Dereliction of Duty: Lyndon Johnson, Robert McNamara, the Joints Chiefs of Staff and the Lies That Led to Vietnam* (New York: Harper, 1997), 204–5.
13. Cantwell, "The Army of South Vietnam," 247.
14. Andrew Krepinevich, *The Army and Vietnam* (Baltimore: Johns Hopkins University Press, 1986), 196.
15. Lt. Gen. Ngo Quang Truong, *RVNAF and US Operational Cooperation and Coordination*, Indochina Monographs (Washington, DC: Center of Military History, 1980), 172.
16. James H. Willbanks, "The Battle for Hue, 1968," in *Block by Block: The Challenges of Urban Operations*, ed. William Robertson and Lawrence Yates (Fort Leavenworth, KS: US Army Command and General Staff College Press, 2003), 123. Also see James H. Willbanks, *The Tet Offensive; A Concise History* (New York: Columbia University Press, 2006).
17. Keith Nolan, *Battle for Hue, Tet, 1968* (Novato: Presidio, 1983), 87.
18. Ibid., 185.
19. Department of the Army, 45th Military History Detachment, "The Battle of Hue, 19 March 1968," 14.
20. Truong, *RVNAF and US Operational Cooperation*, 164.
21. Author's interview with Major Tom Jaco.
22. Ibid.
23. Author's interview with Colonel Benjamin Harrison.
24. James Willbanks, *Abandoning Vietnam: How America Left and South Vietnam Lost Its War* (Lawrence: University Press of Kansas, 2004), 115.

25. Lewis Sorley, *A Better War: The Unexamined Victories and Final Tragedy of America's Last Years in Vietnam* (New York: Harcourt, 1999), 339.
26. Lewis Sorley, ed., *Vietnam Chronicles: The Abrams Tapes, 1968–1972* (Lubbock: Texas Tech University Press, 2004), 825–6. Emphasis in the original.
27. Isaacs, *Without Honor*, 129.
28. Harry G. Summers, *On Strategy: A Critical Analysis of the Vietnam War* (New York: Dell, 1984), 21.

TIMELINE EVENTS

1942 – Women's Army Auxiliary Corps (WAAC) established

1943 – WAAC absorbed into regular army and renamed Women's Army Corps (WAC)

1948 – President Harry Truman signs into law the Women's Armed Services Integration Act, which makes women permanent members of the armed services, subject to military authority and eligible for veterans' benefits.

1965 – Two WAC officers arrive in Saigon to help establish the South Vietnam's Women's Armed Forces Corps (WAFC); the first battalions of US combat troops land at Da Nang

1968 – WAC detachment moves from Saigon to Long Binh, where the United States Army Vietnam (USARV) is headquartered

1969 – President Richard Nixon begins the withdrawal of US combat troops from South Vietnam

1971 – US Army does away with the WAC advisory position to the WAFC

1972 – WAC detachment at Long Binh closed; remaining WACs transferred to Saigon

1973 – The US Defense Department ends the Vietnam War draft; the armed services begin to aim recruitment campaigns at women in hopes of filling the ranks of an all-volunteer military

1978 – President Jimmy Carter signs a bill dissolving the Women's Army Corps and fully integrating women into the Army

Chapter 4

The Women's Army Corps goes to Vietnam

Heather Stur

> **CHAPTER SUMMARY**
>
> In 1942 the United States Army established the Women's Army Auxiliary Corps (WAAC) to offer women temporary military employment during World War II. The WAAC was renamed the Women's Army Corps (WAC) in 1943, and through the WAC, American women served tours of duty overseas during World War II, the Korean War, and the Vietnam War. The WAC was dissolved in 1978, and the Army set out to integrate servicewomen fully into its ranks. This chapter focuses on the experiences of WACs in Vietnam, and it explores the ways in which ideas about appropriate gender roles shaped the WAC image. It also examines the disconnect between the image of Army women and the realities of war.

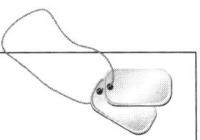

Several months before US combat troops landed at Da Nang in South Vietnam in March 1965, two Women's Army Corps (WAC) officers arrived in Saigon to advise on the development of a training center for the Women's Armed Forces Corps (WAFC), the South Vietnamese counterpart to the WAC. WAFC personnel worked primarily in secretarial roles to assist the Army of the Republic of Vietnam (ARVN) in its various clerical needs. Some WAFCs also worked as nurses and in "welfare service," taking care of dependents who traveled with ARVN soldiers. WAFCs, like WACs, were not trained in combat, but those employed in the welfare service stayed near combat zones with troops, thus performing "the most dangerous assign-ments in the corps."[1] Most WAFCs came from middle-class backgrounds, for a Military Assistance Command Vietnam (MACV) memo about the Vietnamese women's corps observed that "most report for duty in the flowing Vietnamese *ao dai*,"[2] typical middle-class attire.[3] Although the US Army had invited one WAC, Major Anna Marie Doering, to work in the office

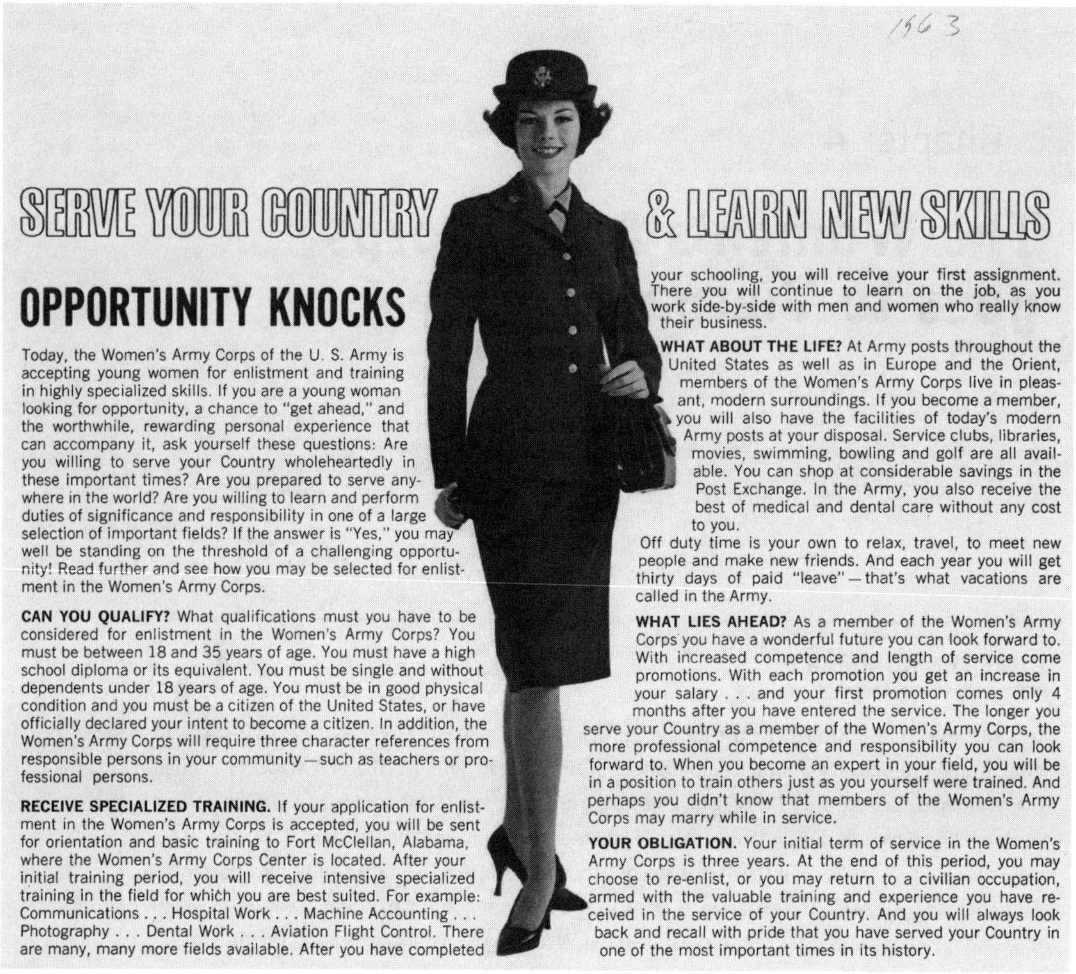

Figure 4.1 a *"Opportunity Awaits You in the Women's Army Corps."*

Washington, DC: US Government Printing Office, 1963. National Archives Record Group 319. Records of the Army Staff, Women's Army Corps, 1945–78.

of its Military Assistance Advisory Group (MAAG) in Saigon in 1962, it was not until 1965 that WACs went to Vietnam with a specific mission.

In his request for military women to come to Saigon, Brigadier General Ben Sternberg, personnel officer for US forces in Vietnam, asked for a captain or major who was well versed in WAC policies and who was "extremely intelligent, an extrovert and beautiful."[4] Colonel Emily Gorman, WAC director, responded to Sternberg with a letter in which she wrote, "the combination of brains and beauty is of course common in the WAC."[5] Major Kathleen I. Wilkes and Sergeant 1st Class Betty L. Adams met Sternberg's criteria, and in January 1965 they went to Saigon and worked with Major Tran Cam Huong, director of the WAFC, to develop a training program for Vietnamese women enlistees. As part of the program, fifty-one Vietnamese

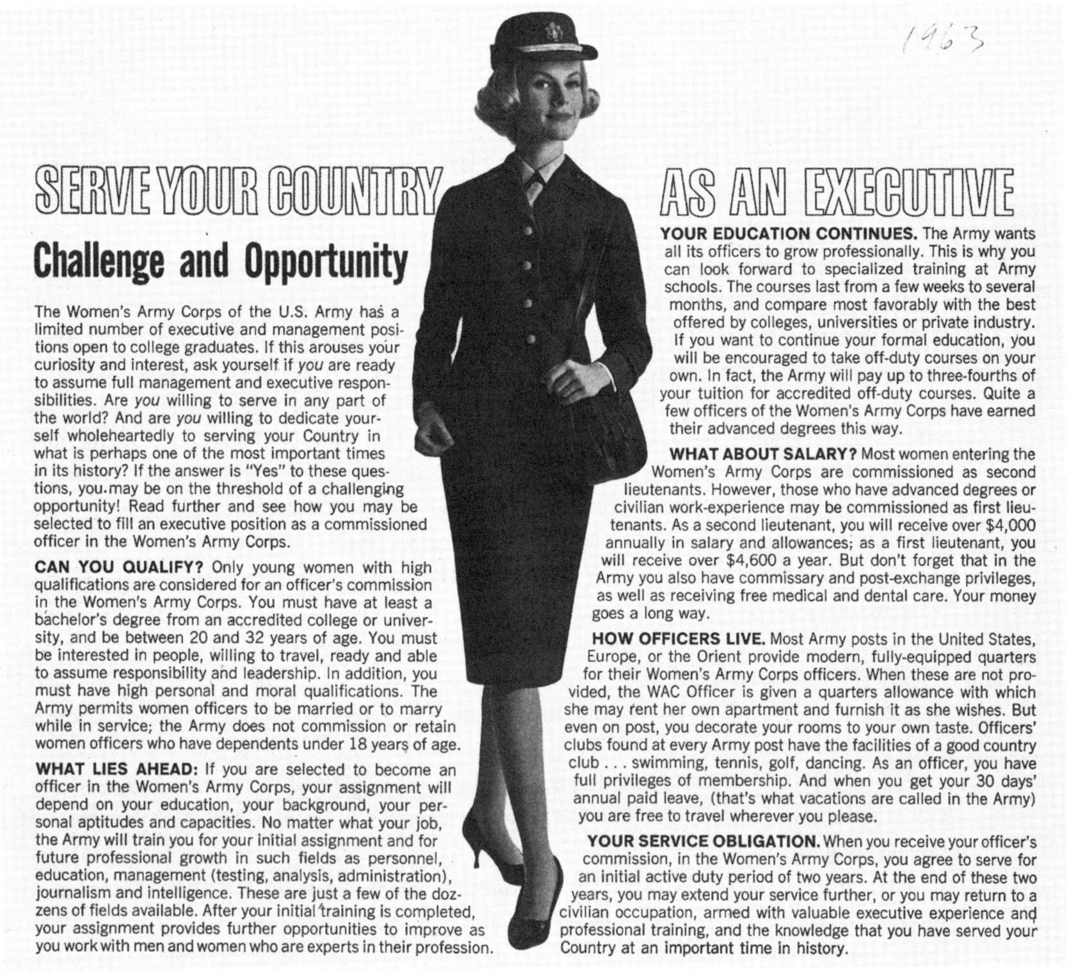

Figure 4.1 b "Opportunity Awaits You in the Women's Army Corps."

women completed advanced training in the United States with the Women's Army Corps at the WAC headquarters at Fort McClellan, Alabama.[6] In order to be eligible for officer training, WAFC recruits had to pass a test demonstrating that they had the equivalent of a US 11th grade education. All other recruits needed the equivalent of a US junior high school degree.

The WAC's early connection with WAFC demonstrates a cross-cultural sharing between the US Army and the ARVN about what roles were appropriate for women in wartime. Controversies over the appearance and duties of WACs highlight the gender tensions that brewed in the United States and followed American women and men to Vietnam. A look at the Women's Army Corps in Vietnam highlights one of the ways in which gender constructions were defined during the Vietnam War.

Newspaper articles, recruitment brochures, and official and unofficial conversations about the Corps attempted to define the women in it, but the realities of war sometimes rendered the definitions irrelevant. Still, concerns about "femininity" and attitudes about who belonged in a war zone influenced the experiences of WACs who served in Vietnam. Although relatively few American women served in Vietnam compared to the number of men who served, ideas about and images of women were staples of the war, symbolizing the home front, enforcing beliefs about US troops' masculine power, and revealing the disconnect between the ideals of Cold War domesticity and the realities of the social changes taking place in the United States.

American women served in all branches of the US armed forces in Vietnam, but WACs numbered the second largest group of American military women to serve, following nurses. Estimates indicated that approximately 6,300 military nurses served in Vietnam, more than 5,000 of whom were members of the Army Nurse Corps.[7] Although women in both military and civilian capacities have been nurses for troops throughout US history, the deployment of military women for other duties is relatively new, beginning with the creation of the Women's Army Auxiliary Corps (WAAC) during World War II. Founded in 1942, the WAAC was designed to be a temporary branch of the Army to be opened in times of national emergency. The WAAC was absorbed into the Army and renamed the Women's Army Corps (WAC) in 1943, and in 1948 President Harry Truman signed into law the Women's Armed Services Integration Act, which made women permanent members of the armed forces, subject to military authority and entitled to veterans' benefits such as the GI Bill. The law prohibited women from serving in combat units, and it limited the number of women in each military branch to 2 percent of the branch's total membership.[8]

Critics feared the WAAC would upset the gender construction that defined men as the protectors and women as the beings who needed men to protect them. The concerns did not apply as much to nurses because the care-giving aspect of nursing fitted with the idea of women as nurturers. Nursing was work that was socially acceptable for women to do. Therefore, in order to assuage critics the Army emphasized the "femininity" of WACs.[9] After the passage of the Women's Armed Services Integration Act in 1948, military publicity and recruitment efforts sought to portray WACs as traditionally feminine. Concerns about the WAC image continued into the Vietnam War era.

Throughout the course of the Vietnam War, about 700 WACs worked "in country" as stenographers, typists, clerks, air traffic controllers, cartographers, reporters, and photographers. Some women worked in communications and military intelligence, while others processed casualty reports and paperwork related to troop movements. In general they worked in offices, and none of them were armed for combat. The WAC detachment was stationed at Tan Son Nhut Air Base until the end of 1968, when it moved to new barracks at Long Binh. In Vietnam, though, defining separate men's and women's spheres was difficult because there were no combat lines. The guerrilla rules of the Vietnam War did not set battle lines, and any space was fair game for an attack. Therefore, even though the US military did not allow American women to participate in combat, in Vietnam women found themselves dodging bullets and shrapnel, escaping grenades and bombs, and diving into barracks alongside men. Yet clothing, hairstyles, makeup, and ideas about what spaces were appropriate for women and men to operate in served to reinforce gender stereotypes.

COLD WAR CONCERNS ABOUT GENDER AND SEXUALITY

Cold War era concerns about sexuality and gender roles undoubtedly shaped debates about how WACs should look and act. Scholarship on women's participation in the workforce continues to debunk the notion of the 1950s middle-class woman as housewife. The culture of consumption that marked post-World War II American life meant that many families needed two incomes to buy the homes, cars, and appliances that defined the "good life." By 1960, more than 30 percent of married women worked outside the home for wages. As more women graduated from college, and the birth control pill changed ideas about sex and childbearing, some women chose to delay marriage and build their careers instead. Additionally, the shift from an industrial to a service market created jobs that were culturally constructed as women's work. As Alice Echols has written, as women continued to move into the workforce, ideas about domesticity and women's proper place in US society became more entrenched as the social norm.[10]

Sexuality had been placed on trial in the midst of the paranoia of McCarthyism that swept the United States in the early 1950s. The hunt for homosexuals in public and private institutions, coupled with rigid definitions of men's and women's social roles, further demonized homosexuality. Regarding concerns about lesbianism, Donna Penn argues that "lesbians were labeled deviant to the degree that they symbolized, represented, and actualized lives that defied strict gender distinctions during a period of profound anxiety regarding gender roles and the postwar restoration and maintenance of 'normal' family life."

In particular, "mannish" women—lesbians who appeared to model themselves as men in dress, hairstyle, and demeanor—became the obsession of social scientists, doctors, psychologists, and educators in the 1950s and 1960s, and "masculine appearance became the yardstick against which lesbianism was measured." During those decades, notions of heterosexuality included the "social responsibilities associated with the heterosexual way of life, most importantly marriage and family." Thus, studies of lesbians determined that women who lived a lesbian lifestyle—one in which they derived sexual, economic, and emotional support from other women—did so to shirk the duties of marriage and motherhood. Experts blamed parents for not providing their daughters with clear models of the proper roles men and women play in the context of the family. The movement of women into the workforce during World War II and their continued presence in wage-earning jobs outside the home blurred ideas about gender roles. The most hysterical concerns about lesbians expressed a belief that if more and more women refused the roles of wife and mother, the upset of gender roles eventually would lead to "the destruction of the human race, albeit a white, middle-class race" because women would fail to reproduce.[11]

The studies concluded that one of the clearest indications of a lesbian's rejection of "traditional" gender roles was her appearance and behavior, and thus additional research efforts aimed to understand masculine tendencies in women. A 1955 study in which researchers asked subjects about their childhoods concluded that, as young girls, lesbians preferred "sports, fighting, and male clothing" to dolls and "feminine occupations." The same study called lesbianism a "flight from femininity" and charted physical characteristics such as hair, body type, and voice to explain what at that time was considered a condition of gender inversion. In 1965, sociologists studying female prisoners in Frontera, California, argued that the masculine appearance rendered lesbians deviant, and thus masculine women at the prison were told to "grow their hair longer, even report to the cosmetology department to wave or curl it, thereby reducing the overt manifestations of homosexuality." A woman "whose hair is crew cut and whose dress and mannerisms are strongly masculine" was considered deviant. This separated

Figure 4.2 "Meet Today's WAC Officer."

Washington, DC: US Government Printing Office, 1966. National Archives Record Group 319. Records of the Army Staff, Women's Army Corps, 1945–78.

"true homosexuals" from women who engaged in "homosexual behavior" only while in prison. The thought was that if women could be persuaded to enjoy "feminine" pursuits and appearance, they could be conditioned to normalize gender roles.[12]

In this context, concerns over the appearance and actions of Army women became much more serious. When the WAC's predecessor, the Women's Army Auxiliary Corps, was founded during World War II, critics worried that it would encourage mannishness in its members and become a haven for lesbians.[13] That image, combined with the sexual politics of the Cold War era, made the Women's Army Corps a prime target for criticism and persecution. Therefore, the emphasis on uniform style, the use of cosmetics, and the demeanor of WACs likely was rooted in concerns about public opinion about the Corps. However, women who served in Vietnam learned that domestic social conventions often were impractical—if not downright absurd—in the context of war.

WACS AND THE COLD WAR

After World War II and into the mid-1950s, WAC recruitment and re-enlistment dropped steadily. In June 1950 more than 59 percent of WACs re-enlisted, but four years later the number had fallen to about 24 percent.[14] The publication in 1957 of *Womanpower*, a book by the National Manpower Council (NMC), influenced the Army in its decision to increase WAC recruitment by identifying jobs that could be done by women as well as men.[15] Susan Hartmann has noted that the NMC, along with the Commission on the Education of Women (CEW), advocated for the use of women in employment outside the home to advance national security in the early Cold War world. While acknowledging that employment "must not detract from the importance of their roles as wives and mothers," the NMC and CEW argued that women could help "to expand our industry to new heights, to assist our allies, and to maintain a military force strong enough to deter aggression [and] to build a base for full-scale mobilization."[16] Advances in technology as part of the "space race" also helped create jobs for WACs because Army studies concluded that women were capable of working with electronics and other types of technology.[17]

Foreign relations also boosted both the perceived need for women in the military and enlistment. In the summer of 1961, East German troops built the Berlin Wall, dividing Berlin in two and effectively sealing off East Germany from West Germany. President Kennedy responded by calling for military mobilization, and the Army included the WAC in its buildup. In August 1961, WAC recruitment saw a record 1,052 recruits for one month, in contrast with the previous record of 800, and of the 100 reserve units activated in October 1961, 16 included WACs. A WAC historian attributed the enlistment increase to "the tense situation in Berlin, a rise in unemployment, socio-economic patterns in the United States, and a surge of patriotism following the inauguration of President John F. Kennedy in January 1961." During the "Berlin crisis" the WAC reached its highest enrollment, more than 11,000 members, since World War II.[18]

Discussions about sending WAC battalions to Vietnam occurred as the United States deepened its commitment to South Vietnam in the mid-1960s. A Defense Department study group concluded in August 1966 that all branches of the armed services should increase women's membership by up to 73 percent and recommended that they station more women personnel overseas. In response, the Army called for a 38 percent increase in WACs, the Navy requested a 20 percent increase in Women Accepted for Voluntary Emergency Service (WAVES), and the Air Force called for a 60 percent increase in its Women in the Air Force (WAF) program enlistees along with a 33 percent increase in officers. The Marines capped its number of women at 1 percent of total Marine Corps strength. By 1965 about twenty WACs were stationed in Saigon.[19]

As WAC officers worked with Vietnamese women in the WAFC, General William Westmoreland, at the time the commanding general of MACV, asked the Women's Army Corps to send a few more officers, as well as some enlisted women trained as stenographers, to work on his staff in Vietnam. In 1965 the first battalions of US combat troops arrived in Vietnam, and as the number of fighting men escalated, so did the number of military women. In April 1966, Westmoreland ordered that a WAC detachment—a unit of troops deployed for a specific mission—of fifty enlisted women trained as clerk-typists be organized and sent to Vietnam. Captain Peggy E. Ready commanded the first WAC detachment deployed to Vietnam. The Army commissioned the building of barracks for the women at Tan Son Nhut Air Base, US military headquarters, about three miles outside Saigon. By the end of the year, sixty women had orders to report for duty in Vietnam.[20]

"I REALLY WANTED TO DO SOMETHING"

An assortment of factors motivated American women to join the Women's Army Corps. An anti–Vietnam War rally in Berkeley, California, inspired Linda McClenahan to enlist in the Corps in 1968. She was a senior in high school, and on the day she made her decision the bus she rode home from school was rerouted owing to an antiwar demonstration that had erupted into a riot. Through the bus window she saw a police car on fire, and at that moment she knew she had to go to Vietnam to learn the truth about the American war effort there. And she figured she might have an adventure as well.

Like the boys who grew up watching Westerns and aspiring to be gunfighters in the image of John Wayne, McClenahan admired Annie Oakley and other strong-willed, independent female characters featured in Westerns. "Women of strength were always my heroes. . . . I mean, Miss Kitty on *Gunsmoke*, this woman was an independent businesswoman, very successful, and a tough lady. . . . Calamity Jane, Annie Oakley. I had an Annie Oakley air rifle." She loved Patricia Neal's character in *In Harm's Way*—a nurse, and John Wayne's girlfriend, on the day the Japanese attacked Pearl Harbor. McClenahan as a young girl saw the character as a strong woman who had no regrets about the life she lived. "There was something about her that was so worldly and

Figure 4.3 Untitled Women's Army Corps recruitment pamphlet, 1959.

National Archives Record Group 319. Records of the Army Staff, Women's Army Corps, 1945–78.

so wise," McClenahan said. But, she added, "you only see the glory in those movies. You don't see the gory, only the glory." Beyond her pop-culture heroines, McClenahan believed she had a duty to serve her country. And so she went, accompanied by her reluctant father, to the Army recruiting office in Berkeley to sign up for Vietnam. She served at the US Army Vietnam (USARV) Communications Center at Long Binh from November 1969 through November 1970, where she processed reports from units in the field. "A lot of classified information went out of our offices," she said.

> Troop movements, surveillance reports, and every casualty report from Vietnam went out through our office. I often would tell the combat troops that I knew more about the battles they were in than they did because we were getting pieces from all over the place.[21]

She and one other WAC were the only women in her office, and they worked with forty to fifty men on each shift.[22]

Karen Offut also needed her reluctant parents' permission to join the Women's Army Corps at age nineteen. The way she saw it, it was unfair that young men had to fight while she stayed home. "I just didn't see any differentiation between the men and the women as opposed to why should someone be putting their life on the line and not me just because I happened to be female," said Offut, who worked as a stenographer in Long Binh and Saigon. "I didn't know anything about women's lib. I just knew that it didn't seem right for me not to go."[23] Marilyn Roth had joined the Women's Army Corps in 1964 and was discharged in 1967, but she re-enlisted sixty days later so that she could go to Vietnam. It sounded like an adventure. She said she was not like the other Jewish girls she grew up with in Brooklyn. "Jewish women don't join the Army. [But] I couldn't afford to go to college or marry a doctor or a lawyer, so I decided to join the army," Roth said. "I felt I'd get to travel, I'd get an education, and get experience, which my friends back in New York have never experienced." Like most other WACs, Roth was stationed at Long Binh, where she worked in intelligence, writing encoded messages for helicopter pilots.[24]

Achieving the post of WAC detachment commander in Vietnam was the high point of Nancy Jurgevich's career. She arrived at Long Binh in October 1968 and managed about 100 women who were doing jobs in communications, engineering, intelligence, and logistics. She noted that most of the women stationed there were in their early twenties, and they were dedicated both to their jobs and to the US mission in Vietnam "at a time when many Americans were turning their back on the United States." Jurgevich viewed ensuring the health and safety of the WACs she oversaw as her primary responsibility in Vietnam, and she admired their professionalism and strength. During her tour of duty, Jurgevich had the opportunity to take a unit of WACs to visit the WAFC Vietnam Women's Training Center in Saigon, and she experienced a strong sense of camaraderie among the American and Vietnamese women.[25]

For some African American servicewomen the Vietnam War had intruded directly into their families and communities. Black servicemen comprised about 11 percent of US troops in Vietnam, but they made up about 13 percent of those killed there.[26] It was in 1967 that

Elizabeth Allen enlisted in the Army, and while men all over the country clung to college and graduate school in order to avoid the draft, Allen took her Master's degree in nursing from Ohio State University, enlisted in the Army, and asked for an assignment to Vietnam. Her decision had nothing to do with love for her country, a belief in US foreign policy, or a desire to see for herself what was happening in Southeast Asia. Allen, a captain with the Army Nurse Corps, was thinking about black soldiers when she volunteered to go to the war.

> I knew African Americans were most likely to end up in battle units, in the death units, and I really wanted to do something. There are extremely few minority folks in health care. A lot of aides, but in terms of professional folks, very few. I needed to go. I made a quick decision on my own.

Her hospital in Pleiku was the first American hospital bombed during the Tet Offensive.[27] Every night, the hospital got hit by incoming fire, but the nurses kept working. "Men's lives were dependent on me, and my being scared was not useful," Allen said. "You had these guys with massive wounds. . . . I had to protect [them]. I had to make sure [they] didn't bleed or choke to death. I had to make sure if a mortar hit, the shrapnel didn't hit [them] again."[28]

When Marie Rodgers enlisted in the Army in 1952, she hoped to escape the racism of Jim Crow Alabama. She worked her way up to the rank of colonel in the Army Nurse Corps and spent her first overseas tour of duty in Korea. In 1967 she volunteered for an assignment in Vietnam because she wanted to be closer to combat. Stationed at the Twenty-fourth Evacuation Hospital at Long Binh, Rodgers managed the operating room, and that year the hospital received its first Meritorious Unit Citation. Rodgers later earned a Bronze Star commending her management of her unit while under fire.

Like Rodgers, Air Force Captain Juanita Forbes found professional advancement in military service in Vietnam. She was one of 350 Air Force nurses who rode with Military Airlift Command flights on medical evacuation missions. Forbes directed an Aeromedical Evacuation (Air Evac) team of two nurses who were women and three medical technicians who were white male sergeants.[29] With a black woman supervising white men, the team challenged gender and racial conventions of the time. In the 1960s it would have been unheard of in parts of the United States for a black woman to administer a group that included white men. Captain Olivia Theriot, another African American nurse who served with Forbes, stated that she fostered good relations between men and women by treating "the med techs like men, not like lower-ranking men."[30] The reasons American women joined the Army to serve in Vietnam were diverse, but a number of common themes ran through the images and perceptions of WACs and their military function.

"SHARE THE ARMY ADVENTURE"

Army recruitment brochures that targeted women during this time of escalation are interesting examples of the type of femininity the military constructed for female enlistees. In many cases the picture of the Women's Army Corps was an attractive young white woman with perfectly coiffed blonde hair, and the typical tour of duty sent women to "romantic" destinations abroad where attractive young white servicemen waited for them. One brochure touted "the facilities of today's Army posts," including "service clubs, libraries, movies, swimming, bowling, and golf."[31] Another brochure listed "glamour" as one of the perks of joining the military.[32] Recruitment materials did describe the career opportunities available to military women in fields such as communications, technology, finance, and intelligence. A pamphlet aimed at officer candidates noted that a struggle against inequality motivated some women to join the military while still perpetuating gender stereotypes and divisions—"some accept a commission for the challenge of a man-size job, some for equality of sex and/or race." In a subtle way, it acknowledged gender and race inequalities even though it enforced images and ideas that fueled the disparities.

Some brochures also assumed that potential recruits were interested in men. A recruitment pamphlet for officer candidates explained that members of the Women's Army Corps "have a busier social life than ever before! That's because you'll have the opportunity to meet and work side-by-side with the young men in the Army." It went on to encourage WACs to marry, highlighting the matchmaking qualities of military life. Women officers, the brochure asserted, "will continue to meet and get to know people of your own background and interests. So it's likely, then, that you may meet your future husband at some point in your Army career—as so many WAC officers do."[33] Rather than acting as an agent for social change for American women seeking to move beyond middle-class, heterosexual gender roles, the Army enforced the gender definitions.

Clothing played a significant role in defining women. Marilyn Roth remembers that military women not in uniform had to wear a dress, nylon stockings, and high heels in Vietnam. Women could wear pants if going to or participating in a sporting event, but otherwise dresses and skirts were the rule. She says:

> It was the military's way of saying, "You're in the Army, you're not boys, you're not men. We want you to dress like ladies." That's what we were called—ladies. We weren't called soldiers, we were called ladies and we were treated as ladies. You had to wear nail polish, you had to wear makeup, you had to wear lipstick, you had to be just perfect.[34]

Concerns about WACs maintaining a feminine appearance caused Colonel Elizabeth Hoisington's mood to shift quickly from proud to angry when she opened the January 1, 1969, issue of the *Observer*, the official newspaper of the US military command in South Vietnam. The issue featured a tribute to American military women serving in Vietnam, and Hoisington, director of the Women's Army Corps (WAC), undoubtedly had looked forward to the publicity. But the photographs accompanying the article upset her, for they showed corps members in "the unflattering women's field uniforms"—fatigues and combat boots—rather than the Army Green Cord, a polyester and cotton outfit consisting of a skirt and top. Even worse, to Hoisington's mind, was that the paper had published the photos alongside pictures of nurses in white dresses, members of the Women's Air Force in "skirted summer uniforms," and a civilian woman employee in a sundress. In response, Hoisington wrote a letter to Major Gloria Olson of the WAC Public Information Division in Vietnam expressing her dismay at the photographs and the image she feared they portrayed of WAC troops. She worried that parents, whose permission was required for high school graduates to enlist, would get the wrong idea about women's service in Vietnam. "They do not like to envision their daughter in terms of the rough, tough environment conveyed by the field uniform," Hoisington wrote. In her opinion, pictures of "WACs in these trousered uniforms" would hurt recruitment efforts. Only nurses, she wrote, could be photographed in work uniforms without harming recruiting because the public understood the role of the nurse in a war zone.[35]

The controversy over the *Observer* photos was not the first time Hoisington had taken issue with the appearance of WACs stationed in Vietnam. In early 1967 she exchanged letters with Major Shirley Heinze of the WAC Career Branch regarding efforts to ensure WACs maintained a "feminine appearance at all times." At that time, the particular problem was combat boots. Hoisington, stationed stateside in Washington, DC, argued that WACs should wear service shoes—low-heeled black pumps. Heinze explained that "boots are highly desirable for field wear since they offer maximum protection from snakes, mosquitoes, and undesirable terrain and conditions which prevail here."[36] But Hoisington was not easily swayed, and it was not until 1969, after the Tet Offensive, a survey of WACs in Vietnam and a number of discussions, that combat boots became an official part of Army women's uniforms.[37]

Embedded in the conflicts over the appearance of military women in Vietnam were beliefs and assumptions about gender roles, specifically how women should look and act in a war zone, a place mainstream US culture had defined as a masculine realm. The reality was, American women *did* serve in "the rough, tough environment" of the Vietnam War. Military rules prohibited them from joining combat units, but fighting happened all around them, and American women were potential casualties even though they were not members of combat units. In the midst of the Tet Offensive, Captain Joanne Murphy wrote to Colonel Hoisington to tell her that rocket fire hit Long Binh's ammo dump, causing "two spectacular explosions." The attack occurred in the middle of the night, about one o'clock in the morning, and "bounced some women out of their beds." Though probably shocking the first few times, such wake-up calls became somewhat routine, and the women of Long Binh mastered the art of sleepwalking into fatigues and helmets in the middle of the night "quickly, quietly, and assuredly without hesitation or question."[38]

As the war raged and fighting intensified, WAC leaders worried that sending women to Vietnam would lose favor in the eyes of the American public. In February 1969, Lieutenant

Colonel Lorraine Rossi, overseeing the WACs still stationed at Tan Son Nhut, tried to reassure Hoisington that the Army women generally were safe. "I imagine the news coverage at home once again has most of Vietnam in ruins from mortar and rocket attacks," Rossi wrote. "There has been activity in the last few days, but it has been scattered and relatively little damage has resulted." Rocket attacks on Saigon were concentrated in the downtown area, and since Tan Son Nhut was a few miles from the city, it had been spared any major damage. Military leaders instructed personnel at Tan Son Nhut to stay close to their work sites and the barracks, and not stray from the base. Mortar and rocket rounds also hit the US base at Long Binh, but the WACs stationed there escaped major injury. "One girl received a bruise, but very minor," Rossi wrote. On her mind as she apprised Hoisington of the situation in Vietnam were the parents of the women serving there. "I know it is difficult to reassure parents, and you must get queries, but the quarters are all well-guarded, and the men are most protective of the women," she wrote. "Of course, there is always the possibility of a terrorist attack or a direct hit on a building, but the chances are slim, and as I write to my parents, I feel as safe (if not safer) here than I did in Washington DC."[39] By the end of 1970, Hoisington's concern for the safety of WACs in Vietnam led her to ask that Army women not be assigned to posts other than Long Binh and Saigon.[40]

There was no separate "woman's space" in the war, nothing to shield women from battles—or from dust, humidity, or hard rain. The clashes also indicated a disconnect between the Women's Army Corps brass in Washington and the enlisted women and officers stationed in Vietnam. WAC leaders in Washington such as Hoisington made and enforced rules and regulations governing what uniforms WACs should wear and what image they should exude. Colonel Hoisington, at least, expected WACs to be "ladies," and quarrels over what women stationed in Vietnam should and should not wear led to a wardrobe poll of enlisted women serving in Indochina. By June 1969 Hoisington was "still waging war to get our women out of those awful field uniforms and into the Army Green Cords," (also called the Class A uniform).[41] Later that month, Captain Joanne Murphy, commanding officer of the WACs in Vietnam, sent a memo to the WAC brass regarding the uniform issue. It listed several points for discussion, among them two that indicated an awareness of disparities between the way the military regarded women and men respectively in Vietnam. Enlisted men wore fatigues and boots in Vietnam.

The memo then went on to list some facts of life in Vietnam that made the Class A uniform impractical. The post exchange at Long Binh, where the WAC detachment was located at the time, carried scant supplies of girdles, garter belts, hosiery, and slips—all required because the women's uniform included a skirt, not slacks, and the women had to wear pantyhose. Pumps, particularly the heels on them, did not hold up well pounding the gravel roads and sinking into muddy spots, but there were no shoe repair shops on or near the base. The memo also noted that washers and dryers at the base often broke down, and several were completely unusable. It also blamed Vietnamese maids for ruining uniforms when they ironed them on the wrong setting. Finally, the memo reminded readers that attacks sometimes occurred during on-duty hours, meaning that WACs could have to "hit the dirt"—gravel, concrete, actual dirt, depending on where they were—in their dress uniform.[42]

As the lengthy memo continued, it revealed the absurdity of requiring military women to wear pumps, skirts, and hose in an environment where the temperature often exceeded 100 degrees Fahrenheit and featured oppressive humidity, where helicopters regularly created gusts of dirt and dust during takeoff and landing, and where heavy rains made puddles of mud the rule rather than the exception. Appealing to the femininity issue, the memo argued that sweaty blouses and skirts stained reddish-brown from dust would create "an unkempt and unsightly appearance." Furthermore, "the women will present an unladylike appearance when getting into/out of jeeps and scouts in their fairly form fitting skirts." Lastly, women walking to the mess hall or other places on base often were "splashed with mud by passing vehicles during the rainy season."[43] Murphy knew that in Vietnam, mud and sweat wiped away the kind of femininity Colonel Hoisington wanted WACs to exhibit.

Beyond the unrealistic nature of the Class A uniform requirement in Vietnam, what bothered some enlisted women even more was the attitude that WACs should be morale boosters for male troops. The memo stated that there were "a substantial number of individuals" who believed that the Army Green Cord would "improve the image of the WAC" and "improve the morale of the men." In a survey of enlisted women conducted on the post, one woman responded to the point about improving men's morale by writing, "What about our morale? We'd like to see men in khakis (instead of fatigues)." Another woman responded, "I came to help out. If I had known I was coming to improve the morale of men, I wouldn't have come." One woman wrote, "Being feminine doesn't mean wearing a dress." On the subject of femininity, a respondent stated, "there is hardly any doubt that the WACs here are aware that a small part of their femininity has been sacrificed. But then, are we here to satisfy the desires of the male ego which prefers women in dresses, or are we here to do a job?" Another continued, "Now I'm sure the Army didn't send the WACs over here for the mere purpose of 'prettying' up an office or for the morale of the men!" She went on the promise that "the women will be feminine and ladylike in whatever uniform they wear." An office worker wrote that

> I work in an office that is unbearable with the window closed and almost cloudy with dust when it's open. Just sit in front of the detachment and watch the dust fly in from the road. Our fatigues, while not particularly attractive or stylish, are serviceable, reasonably comfortable, and suitable for this area.

Wondering when the Army would consider the women's morale, she added, "I think the guys would prefer a smile to a skirt." Stating the obvious, one woman wrote, "I think we look just as feminine with our fatigues on as we do with our Class A. If they can't see that we are ladies, then they need glasses."[44]

Captain Murphy's memo summed up the feelings of the women by arguing that focusing on the morale of the men would harm the morale of the women in Vietnam.[45] Yet even after enlisted women voiced their opinions through the uniform survey, women and men among the military brass continued to speak disparagingly of women in fatigues. In a letter to Hoisington in December 1968, Major Charlotte Clark mentioned that she had met a Colonel Sullivan, the commanding officer of Special Troops in Vietnam. He told her that "the girls look cute in their breeches." But Clark wrote to Hoisington, "I'm afraid he has yet to see the ones who look anything but cute."[46] In 1968, though, in light of the Tet Offensive and the subsequent increase in fighting in Saigon as well as in the countryside, the Army approved a new women's uniform consisting of lightweight fatigues, a baseball-style cap, and black boots.[47]

"ARE WE HERE TO SATISFY THE DESIRES OF THE MALE EGO?"

As if to counter any doubts about the femininity of WACs, military newspapers and magazines published in Vietnam generally portrayed their "womanly" qualities. The June 1969 issue of *Army Digest*, a magazine that billed itself "the official magazine of the Department of the Army" and was published by the US Government Printing Office, featured an article about the Women's Army Corps. It included a sidebar about efforts to incorporate a course called "Personal Standards and Social Concepts" into the WAC curriculum. According to the report, the class was "a charm course—how to feel, be, and look your best; how to be feminine and a soldier, too." The sidebar quoted Major Ruth G. Kuhl, the "attractive redhead" who spearheaded the effort to add the course to the curriculum, as saying that "we're soldiers to be sure, but we're women, too. We should take more advantage of our advantage." The piece noted that the class included "instruction in personal hygiene, basic etiquette, personal conduct, spending money, makeup, how to sit and walk, fashion basics—in short, all the things necessary to insure that the girls are watched when the music is played." The accompanying photo featured a woman in an Army dress uniform applying eye shadow.[48] The photograph of a smiling young white woman named Lynn Kussman graced a page in a 1971 issue of *Pacific Stars and Stripes* that featured an article entitled "Long Binh Wacs Provide a Study in Women's Lib."

Praising the WACs, a male major told the newspaper that "the young woman who works in my office does twice as much work as the guys. Besides that, she's a lot better looking." As for GIs who reported to women officers, one told *Stars and Stripes*, "If you're low man on the totem pole, you're going to have to work for somebody, right? So why not have somebody who's pretty to look at while she is chewing you out?" The article described Captain Marjorie Johnson as "the pretty detachment commander," and the caption under Kussman's photo read that Kussman's "big smile . . . helps brighten up her office."

Describing her encounters with men on arrival at Long Binh, Priscilla Moseby told the paper a story that rang with a bit of youthful innocence. "The guys sure make you feel wanted," she said. "The first day that I arrived at the detachment, I walked to the PX [post exchange], about two blocks away, and before I got there I had received four ride offers, requests for nine dates,

Pacific Stars & Stripes 5 Nov 71

Long Binh Wacs Provide A Study in Women's Lib

By S. SGT. FRANK MADISON

LONG BINH, Vietnam (Special) — Pallas Athene has gone to war, and like everything else she does, she is doing it with class and style.

Pallas Athene is the patron goddess of women soldiers, and is depicted on the brass of the Women's Army Corps.

"Pallas Athene is also the goddess of victory," one WAC captain quipped. "Maybe if we had gotten here sooner. . . ."

The WAC is represented in Vietnam by an approximately 70 women at Long Binh. They fill mostly clerical and administrative slots at various commands around the post, an arrangement that seems to suit everybody just fine.

Most units fortunate enough to have a WAC working for them feel that the WACs are worth their weight in mink stoles. "The young woman who works in my office does twice as much work as the guys," a major said. "Besides that, she's a lot better looking."

The women who come to Vietnam are screened for ability, attitude and stability. And they are all volunteers. Most have at least a year's service prior to Vietnam, and all must be at least specialist 4. Add to that the fact that a lot of them extend, sometimes as much as two full tours. The additional job training makes for improvement.

Most of the women here are at least specialist 5, and there is a liberal sprinkling of noncommissioned officers. Which means women are actually the bosses in quite a few offices.

Strangely enough, except for a few chauvinists who quickly find new jobs, most men don't object at all. "I'm the supervisor of five men," Spec. 5 Brenda Burk said, "and I only had trouble once. He was kind of new, so the other guys took him outside and had a long talk with him. I don't know what they said to him, but I never had any more trouble."

A GI working at the hospital explained it this way, "If you're low man on the totem pole, you're going to have to work for somebody, right? So why not have somebody who's pretty to look at while she is chewing you out?"

Capt. Majorie Johnson, the pretty detachment commander, feels there is not a stabler, more mature group of women anywhere in the world. "Maybe it is because of our common bond, but all of the girls get along great. And disciplinary problems are almost non-existent."

What's it like to be a WAC in Vietnam?

"Well, one thing for sure," Spec. 4 Priscilla Moseby said, "the guys sure make you feel wanted. The first day that I arrived at the detachment, I walked to the PX, about two blocks away, and before I got there I had received four ride offers, requests for nine dates, and three proposals of marriage."

"Our living conditions have to be among the best in Vietnam," Spec. 6 Joyce Oakes said. That was a common feeling among the women soldiers. Their area looks more like a summer resort than a billeting area in a combat zone. There are trees and well manicured lawns, air-conditioned barracks and a reception area where the women may receive guests.

Most of the detachment has never seen a shot fired in anger, but a few of the veterans were here during the 1968 Tet offensive.

S. Sgt. Rose Jackson was one of those. "The worst part was having to wear a helmet all of the time. Oh, there were a few rocket attacks, and the bus that I was riding once got hit by machine gun fire, but those helmets were heavy."

Even though many of the women do extend, most are glad when their tour is over. S. Sgt. Audrey Bergstresser expressed the sentiments of most of the girls when she said, "I wouldn't trade the experience that I have had for a million dollars. This has been one of the most interesting years of my life, but I am glad to be going home."

A big smile from Spec. 5 Lynn Kussman helps brighten up her office. (USA)

Figure 4.4 "Long Binh Wacs Provide a Study in Women's Lib," Pacific Stars and Stripes, November 5, 1971

National Archives Record Group 319. Records of the Army Staff, Women's Army Corps, 1945–78.

and three proposals of marriage." The average age of enlisted men in Vietnam was about 19, so it is easy to imagine the hormonal rush that coursed through the veins of young, heterosexual men who had been away from women for a while. Undoubtedly, some of the focus on pretty faces and disarming smiles spoke to that. But the article ended with a reminder that military women were stationed in a war zone, and it made the obsession with WACs' appearance frivolous, even dangerous. Staff Sergeant Rose Jackson was stationed in Long Binh during the Tet Offensive, and while she disliked wearing her helmet, she realized its lifesaving power after being caught in the crossfire. "There were a few rocket attacks, and the bus that I was riding on once got hit by machine gun fire, but those helmets were heavy," she said.[49]

Lynn Kussman, the smiling face in the *Stars and Stripes* article, also made the pages of *Army Times* in its "WAC of the Week" feature. The first thing the article did was describe her appearance. Calling her "the best thing to ever happen to a set of jungle fatigues," the report's opening paragraph contended that "petite Lynn Kussman would brighten any office anywhere, and at the Military Personnel Directorate, Long Binh, where she performs as a clerk, she is particularly illuminating." The story went on to explain that "although only 4-feet, 11-inches tall, our bright-eyed gal of the week performs a man-sized job." The statement implies that Kussman was able to execute her military duties *despite* her gender, as though any wartime military job, even one behind a desk, naturally was a man's job. At first glance, the article seems complimentary of Kussman's abilities and work in Vietnam. But by stressing that her stature was something she overcame in order to do her job, the article assumes that in an ideal situation a man would occupy her position.[50]

When *Army Times* featured Susie Carter as its "WAC of the Week," it went so far as to include her "measurements"—the size of her chest, waist, and hips—in the profile. It also provided her height and weight, and it judged her "good-figured." The story offered a brief character sketch of Carter, an African American enlisted woman, describing her as "our happy-go-lucky dazzler," "personable and attractive," "young lovely," "young personality miss," and "vivacious." Although the piece mentioned Carter's job as a clerk at Long Binh and the volunteer work she did at a hospital and an orphanage in Vietnam, it read like a cross between a personals ad and a beauty pageant biography. She enjoyed horseback riding, swimming, acting, dancing, and modeling, the article reported. It also expressed a surprised revelation that Carter once had been a "tomboy" who enjoyed baseball, basketball, and football.[51] To judge by the tone of the article, Carter's credibility stemmed from her potential for attracting men, not from her educational or employment credentials. It painted a picture of the ideal military woman as one whose pretty face and perky demeanor gave purpose to her presence in the war zone of Vietnam.

Figure 4.5 "Wac of the Week: One of 85 in 'Nam," Army Times, *November 10, 1971.*

National Archives Record Group 319. Records of the Army Staff, Women's Army Corps, 1945–78.

CONCLUSION: "AN INTERESTING EXPERIENCE"

As part of President Richard Nixon's "Vietnamization" plan, US troops gradually began withdrawing from Vietnam in 1969. The military downsizing meant that WACs went home, too, and in 1971 the US Army did away with the WAC advisory position to WAFC.[52] In September 1972 the WAC detachment at Long Binh closed. The Army relocated remaining WACs back to Tan Son Nhut, where the majority of those making up the shrinking US presence were stationed. Periodically, Saigon went off-limits to American personnel because of unrest, but other than that, life for WACs in the waning moments of the Vietnam War was calm. Sometimes, calm turned into boring. Lieutenant Colonel Jebb wrote to Captain Bennett:

> Life continues at the daily deadly pace, each day following the last with a sameness that is incredible. I think that anybody who extends more than once over here has a serious problem they are afraid to face back in the world of reality. Even once is too much in my estimation.

But in retrospect, Jebb would not have passed up her chance to serve in Vietnam. "I wouldn't have missed this for the world," she wrote at the end of her letter to Bennett.[53] As she left the WAC detachment at Long Binh, Major Dolores Hubik summed up the Vietnam War in one sentence: "It has been an interesting experience."[54]

WACs had a variety of responses to their tours of duty in Vietnam. During the war, Nancy Jurgevich met WACs who "were outstanding, dedicated, and extremely motivated," and she spoke with women "who say it was a very important time in their life, and they will always treasure that." Years after Marilyn Roth returned home from Vietnam, she wished she could afford to make a trip back to see what had happened since the war. Karen Offut had been eager to serve in Vietnam, but the experience haunted her for years after. She suffered nightmares and depression, and she had three children born with cancer and other illnesses, which she attributed to having been exposed to Agent Orange.[55] Linda McClenahan also struggled to come to terms with her experiences in Vietnam. Civilian life seemed insignificant, and she had trouble relating to family and friends. Like Offut, McClenahan had nightmares, and she also battled alcoholism. It was not until she joined a support group for women Vietnam veterans that she was able to begin to make peace with the war.[56] The range of responses by women vets is another example of the complexity of the Vietnam War.

The story of the WACs in Vietnam illustrates both the gender ideals that informed the deployment of American military men and women to the war and the incompatibility of some of those regulations with the realities of the war zone. Even as gender relations began to shift in the United States in the 1960s, WAC leaders attempted to enforce Cold War standards of femininity among the Corps' ranks. Recruitment materials portrayed enlistment in the WAC as a means through which women could have it all—a career and access to scores of eligible men. The Vietnam War was poised on the fault line between Cold War domesticity and the backlash against the "feminine mystique," and the WAC tried to walk the fissure, offering educational and career opportunities for women while maintaining the acceptable gender roles of the time. After the draft ended in 1973, all four branches of the US armed services launched major recruitment campaigns aimed at women in order to ensure that the ranks would be filled. Once held up as an exclusively masculine institution, in the mid-1970s the military recreated itself as an institution where women as well as men could get an education and learn job skills. In 1978, President Jimmy Carter signed a bill dissolving the Women's Army Corps and fully integrating women into the Army.[57] However, although American women have become increasingly more visible in the armed forces in the years since Vietnam, attitudes toward women soldiers still are in flux among Americans and the military. The story of Private Jessica Lynch, whose unit was ambushed early in the Iraq War, is an example of the ambivalence toward women in the military. As journalist Susan Faludi has written, the media portrayed Lynch's ordeal as "a tale of a maiden in need of rescue," despite the fact that she was only one of six soldiers, two of them female and four male, captured in the attack.

DISCUSSION QUESTIONS

1. Why did American women join the Women's Army Corps during the Vietnam War era? Describe the similarities and differences among the various reasons.
2. What image of the WACs did Colonel Elizabeth Hoisington try to construct? How did Hoisington's concerns reflect the ways in which many Americans thought about gender roles during that time? How were WACs portrayed in military magazines?
3. How were WACs' experiences in Vietnam different from the WAC image that recruitment brochures and directives from the brass painted?

SUGGESTED READING

Bartimus, Tad, Denby Fawcett, Jurate Kazickas, Edith Lederer, Ann Bryan Mariano, Anne Morrissy Merick, Laura Palmer, Kate Webb, and Tracy Wood. *War Torn: Stories of War from the Women Reporters Who Covered Vietnam.* New York: Random House, 2002.

Gruhzit-Hoyt, Olga. *A Time Remembered: American Women in the Vietnam War.* Novato, CA: Presidio Press, 1999.

Hornung, Jan. *Angels in Vietnam: Women Who Served.* San Jose, CA: Writers Club Press.

Norman, Elizabeth M. *Women at War: The Story of Fifty Military Nurses Who Served in Vietnam.* Philadelphia: University of Pennsylvania Press, 1990.

Steinman, Ron. *Women in Vietnam.* New York: TV Books, 2000.

Turner, Karen Gottschang. *Even the Women Must Fight: Memories of War from North Vietnam.* New York: John Wiley, 1998.

Walker, Keith. *A Piece of My Heart: The Stories of Twenty-six American Women Who Served in Vietnam.* New York: Ballantine Books, 1985.

NOTES

1. Memo, "Women's Armed Forces Corps," Office of Information, US Military Assistance Command Vietnam, November 12, 1966, National Archives Record Group 319—Records of the Army Staff, Women's Army Corps, 1945–78 [hereafter NARA RG 319].
2. Ibid., "Women's Armed Forces Corps."
3. Harvey H. Smith et al., *Area Handbook for South Vietnam* (Washington, DC: US Government Printing Office, 1967), 138.
4. Letter from Brigadier General Ben Sternberg to Colonel Emily Gorman, November 17, 1964, NARA RG 319.
5. Letter from Colonel Emily Gorman to Brigadier General Ben Sternberg, November 23, 1964, NARA RG 319.
6. Bettie J. Morden, *The Women's Army Corps, 1945–1978* (Washington, DC: Center of Military History, United States Army, 1990), 217.

7. Owing to incomplete record-keeping, the exact number of US military nurses who served in Vietnam is unknown. Scholarly works on the experiences of American nurses in Vietnam include Elizabeth M. Norman, *Women at War: The Story of Fifty Military Nurses Who Served in Vietnam* (Philadelphia: University of Pennsylvania Press, 1990); Winnie Smith, *American Daughter Gone to War: On the Front Lines with an Army Nurse in Vietnam* (New York: Morrow, 1992); Kara Dixon Vuic, "'Officer. Nurse. Woman.': Defining Gender and the U.S. Army Nurse Corps in the Vietnam War," Ph.D. dissertation, History, Indiana University, 2006; ibid., "'Officer. Nurse. Woman.': Army Nurse Corps Recruitment for the Vietnam War," *Nursing History Review* 14 (2006): 111–59.
8. Morden, *The Women's Army Corps*, 48.
9. For a comprehensive analysis of the Women's Army Auxiliary Corps and subsequent Women's Army Corps, see Leisa D. Meyer, *Creating G.I. Jane: Sexuality and Power in the Women's Army Corps during World War II* (New York: Columbia University Press, 1996).
10. Alice Echols, "Women's Liberation and Sixties Radicalism," in *Major Problems in American History since 1945*, ed. Robert Griffith and Paula Baker (Boston: Houghton Mifflin Company, 2001), 402–3.
11. Donna Penn, "The Meanings of Lesbianism in Postwar America," in *Gender and American History since 1890*, ed. Barbara Melosh (London: Routledge, 1993), 106–24.
12. Ibid., 116
13. Meyer, *Creating G.I. Jane*, 51–70, 148–78
14. Morden, *The Women's Army Corps*, 137–42.
15. Ibid., 165.
16. Susan Hartmann, "Women's Employment and the Domestic Ideal in the Early Cold War Years," in *Not June Cleaver: Women and Gender in Postwar America, 1945–1960*, ed. Joanne Meyerowitz (Philadelphia: Temple University Press, 1994), 84–100.
17. Morden, *The Women's Army Corps*, 168.
18. Ibid., 173–9.
19. Ibid., 217–23.
20. "WACs in Vietnam (1962–1972)," NARA RG 319.
21. Interview with Linda McClenahan, Racine, Wisconsin, December 12, 2005.
22. Ibid.
23. Ron Steinman, *Women in Vietnam: The Oral History* (New York: TV Books, 2000), 256.
24. Ibid., 224.
25. Ibid., 233–8
26. Yvonne Latty, ed., *We Were There: Voices of African American Veterans from World War II to the War in Iraq* (New York: Amistad, 2004), xvi.
27. Ibid., 91–8.
28. Ibid., 95.
29. "Samaritans on Wings: Black Nurse in Vietnam," *Ebony*, May 1970, 60–6.
30. Ibid., 66.
31. "Opportunity Awaits You in the Women's Army Corps" (Washington, DC: US Government Printing Office, 1963), NARA RG 319.
32. "For You: An Officer's Career in the Armed Forces" (Washington, DC: US Government Printing Office, no date), NARA RG 319.
33. Ibid.
34. Ibid., 228–9.
35. Letter from Col. Elizabeth Hoisington to Maj. Gloria Olson, January 1, 1969, NARA RG 319.
36. Letter from Maj. Shirley Heinze to Col. Elizabeth Hoisington, March 4, 1967, NARA RG 319.
37. Morden, *The Women's Army Corps*, plate 34.
38. Letter from Capt. Joanne Murphy to Col. Elizabeth Hoisington, February 24, 1968, NARA RG 319.
39. Letter from Lt. Lorraine Rossi to Col. Elizabeth Hoisington, February 25, 1969, NARA RG 319.
40. Letter from Col. Elizabeth Hoisington to Lt. Col. Margaret Jebb, November 3, 1970, NARA RG 319.
41. Letter from Col. Elizabeth Hoisington to Maj. Charlotte Clark, June 3, 1969, NARA RG 319.
42. Memo: "Wearing Class A Uniform—WAC Personnel," June 26, 1968, NARA RG 319.

43. Ibid.
44. "Individual Responses to Uniform Survey," NARA RG 319.
45. Memo: "Wearing Class A Uniform—WAC Personnel."
46. Letter from Maj. Charlotte Clark to Col. Elizabeth Hoisington, December 17, 1968, NARA RG 319.
47. Morden, *The Women's Army Corps*, 244, 472.
48. "Women on the Go," *Army Digest*, June 1969, 43, NARA RG 319.
49. "Long Binh WACs Provide a Study in Women's Lib," *Pacific Stars and Stripes,* November 5, 1971, NARA RG 319.
50. "One of 85 in 'Nam," *Army Times*, November 10, 1971, NARA RG 319.
51. "Model Vietnam Vet," *Army Times*, September 30, 1970, NARA RG 319.
52. Letter from Col. Edward H. Metzger, Chief, Personnel Advisory Division, U.S. Military Assistance Command Vietnam, to Col. Tran Cam Huong, Director, WAFC, November 17, 1971, NARA RG 319.
53. Letter from Lt. Col. Margaret Jebb to Capt. Joanne Murphy, August 10, 1970, NARA RG 319.
54. Letter from Maj. Dolores Hubik to Lt. Col. Alice Long, September 16, 1972, NARA RG 319.
55. Steinman, *Women in Vietnam*, 223–40, 266–9.
56. Keith Walker, *A Piece of My Heart: The Stories of Twenty-six American Women Who Served in Vietnam* (Novato, CA: Presidio Press, 1985), 26–7.
57. Jeanne Holm, *Women in the Military: An Unfinished Revolution* (Novato, CA: Presidio Press, 1982), 260–88.

TIMELINE EVENTS

February 1965 – Malcolm X assassinated

August 1965 – Watts riots

October 1966 – Black Panther Party formed

April 1967 – Stokely Carmichael coins phrase "black power"

April 1967 – Martin Luther King "A Time to Break Silence" speech denounces war in Vietnam

May 1967 – Panthers protest for gun rights at California state capitol

October 1967 – Huey Newton wounded and charged with killing a police office

March 1968 – Eldridge Cleaver publishes *Soul on Ice*

January 1969 – Black Panther Party free breakfast program begins

September 1969 – Chicago branch of Black Panther Party opens free medical clinic

May 1970 – Creation of National Committee to Combat Fascism

Chapter 5

The Black Panthers and the Vietnam War

Curtis Austin

CHAPTER SUMMARY

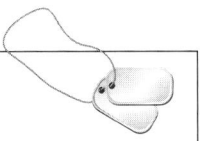

This chapter highlights Vietnam-era race relations by looking through the prism of the Black Panther Party, an organization founded in Oakland, California, in 1966, whose stated goals included defending black communities from police brutality and murder, developing self-reliance among blacks, and creating programs to serve the various social needs of African Americans. This chapter will not repeat previous scholarship concerning the role of black soldiers in Vietnam—that they served on the front lines at rates disproportionate to their number in the general population, that racial turmoil and discrimination were rampant on bases throughout Vietnam, and that blacks were dishonorably discharged at higher rates than whites, among many other racially inequitable statistics. What it does do, however, is show that black participation in Vietnam was critical to the political maturity of many blacks throughout the United States. In time, the Vietnam War came to represent a crucial turning point in how many blacks viewed themselves and the world around them.

The Vietnam War transformed many blacks from apolitical country bumpkins to sophisticated and politicized practitioners of social engineering. Even the city slickers, slick as they were, did not escape this transformation. The Vietnam War succeeded in fashioning thousands of black soldiers into a force that contributed to the expansion of the black freedom struggle, popularly called the civil rights movement, then increasingly identified as the black pride movement, and later known as the Black Power movement. Untold numbers of returning veterans offered their skills and dedication to what they saw as a necessary push toward black liberation. New Yorker Francisco Torres, who volunteered for the war and served in the elite 101st Airborne, explained that "[w]e went over there blind, with our eyes closed, but when we came back our eyes were opened." Torres, who had once worked as a VISTA (Volunteers in Service to America) volunteer, began to re-examine his own political awareness during the war. Having participated in numerous firefights in the Central Highlands and at places like the infamous "Hamburger Hill," he experienced a literal trial by fire and immediately joined the Black Panther Party upon his discharge from the Army.[1]

Arriving on the scene as part of the rapidly spreading Black Power movement, Vietnam veterans added the element of calculated action to an already advanced movement whose hallmark was armed self-reliance. Indeed, in response to black military capabilities on the home front, state and local governments, with major infusions of cash, training, and materials from the federal government, created SWAT (Special Weapons and Tactics) teams in urban areas throughout the United States. Most of those chosen to join this elite group of law enforcement officers had also done tours of duty in Vietnam. It would not be long before these opposing sides clashed in a war that left dozens dead on both sides, hundreds wounded, just as many incarcerated, and uncounted numbers left suffering from the same post-traumatic stress as that experienced by those who fought in the Mekong Delta, My Lai, Hue, Da Nang, and so many other locales. This story then, illuminates how Vietnam helped contribute to the origins and development of a new black man, one who proudly joined his forebears in taking a stand to fight and die for his freedom and the freedom of his people; and not since Vietnam has a war had such an impact on race relations, not only inside the United States but across the globe.

ORIGINS OF THE BLACK PANTHER PARTY

In 1954 the Vietnamese defeated the French at Dien Bien Phu, and that same year the US Supreme Court unanimously ruled in *Brown v. Board of Education* that segregation in public accommodations, especially schools, was unconstitutional. This ruling opened the floodgates of civil rights activity, which until that point had been a hardly noticed trickle barely commented upon by mainstream media. Blacks began to feel that they could assert their rights to free speech, to assembly, to vote, and to bear arms. In a span of five years after *Brown*, blacks had organized a nationwide movement aimed at removing the vestiges of Jim Crow segregation and discrimination and at improving the life chances of all poor and oppressed peoples. This movement, primarily led by young people, was growing strongly by 1963, and the United States could tell the world that the Civil Rights Act of 1964 and the Voting Rights Act of 1965 stood as proof that its way of life, as opposed to that of communism, was the most desirable.

While these gains represented tremendous social improvements on paper, few blacks could say that their lives had materially changed by this point. Most blacks in the South still could not vote. In both the North and the South, segregation remained intact in many places despite the federal law against it. Almost no schools were integrated by 1965 and only a small number of blacks attended college. Police brutality toward, and murder of, blacks continued to rise, while high unemployment rates, lack of access to decent health care, and poor housing wreaked havoc on the lives of black families. It is into this strange mix of progress and pain, love and hate, law and lawlessness that blacks began to re-evaluate their citizenship rights and responsibilities.

This was especially the case when it came to black soldiers who either served or had the potential to serve in Vietnam. Human rights activist and former Nation of Islam spokesman Malcolm X could be heard on street corners in New York telling blacks not to fight in the jungles of Vietnam, but instead to lay down their lives in the streets and on the back roads of America. He admonished blacks that they bled only when whites told them to bleed. Referencing the black soldiers' role in American wars, Malcolm noted that blacks were afraid to bleed for their own people:

> As long as the white man sent you to Korea, you bled. He sent you to Germany, you bled. He sent you to the South Pacific to fight the Japanese, you bled. You bleed for white people, but when it comes time to seeing your own churches being bombed, and little black girls murdered, you haven't got no blood. You bleed for the white man . . . but when it comes to someone blowing up four little black girls in a church, you haven't got no blood."[2]

He argued that real men would not let such atrocities happen without an appropriate response.

Many blacks took Malcolm X's sentiments to heart and decided to move on his recommendations. Huey Newton and Bobby Seale were two of the people in this category. Taking advantage of the increasingly militant wave of protest sweeping the country, they formed the Black Panther Party (BPP) and immediately attracted recruits with its insistence on approaching the race problem with an eye-for-an-eye philosophy. There could be no action, however, without a clear program to guide the organization.

Subsequently, Newton and Seale, now Minister of Defense and chairman of the BPP respectively, set out to put their mission in writing. After consulting with hundreds of Oakland residents, the Panther leaders in October 1966 drew up a mission statement. They called this document the *Ten Point Program: What We Want, What We Believe*. Their program demanded the following: the right of black communities to determine their own destinies; full employment; equal economic opportunities; decent housing and education; the exemption of blacks from the military; an end to police brutality and murder of black people; fair trials; the release of all black men from federal, state, and local jails; social justice; and land, bread, and peace. They explained that their major political objective was to have "a United Nations supervised plebiscite to be held throughout" the African American community "for the purpose of determining the will of black people as to their national destiny."[3]

The Panthers' attempts to implement these goals provoked a level of calculated political violence by police authorities heretofore unseen in the United States. As Lawrence Lader pointed out in *Power on the Left*, the Panthers "designated themselves an armed agency to protect the community, to put the police on notice that if a black were mistreated or a home invaded without legal warrant, black protest would be backed up with bullets."[4] In other words, the group set out not to placate whites or even to gain respect in the minds of liberals, who often supported black demands for change, but to win black freedom in any way it could. Unlike other protest groups of the period, the BPP had little tolerance for any position not consistent with the immediate and total liberation of black and other oppressed people. This unwillingness to compromise or equivocate not only gave it a reputation as having "the baddest niggas on the scene," according to one former Panther, but also attracted recruits.[5] With the Vietnam War raging and blow-by-blow accounts appearing on the evening news, Panther efforts paid off.

In addition to its founders, the Black Panther Party's members at this time included Sherman and Reginald Forte, Bobby Hutton, and Elbert Howard. Hoping for the opportunity to demonstrate to the community that their philosophy and tactics helped advance the cause of black liberation, they held political education classes daily in an attempt to bring ideological uniformity to the group. They also had sessions where they learned how to break down, clean, and reassemble weapons, to fire them, and to handle them safely. Newton wrote, "a number of people who [he] knew had just come from Vietnam, and they helped train [the Panthers] in weaponry." Oakland resident John Sloane, who had been in the military, gave the group its first lessons on "field stripping and shooting," according to Seale.[6]

The BPP wanted it known that its actions were well within the laws of a city, a state, and the nation. This insistence on exercising human rights to life, liberty, and happiness, like the Vietnamese, pitted the members of the Black Panther Party for Self-Defense against the most powerful government on earth. That they could not win in a firefight was beside the point. They simply wanted to demonstrate their desire to enjoy their Second Amendment rights to bear arms; this was diametrically opposed to a social system that required a degraded, brutalized underclass as a cheap source of labor. In addition, they hoped to infuse a sense of fearlessness into the general black population. They believed if black fear of white authority were overcome, then blacks as a whole could begin to address some of the more pressing issues they faced. Many members of the Black Panther Party who had served in Vietnam were crucial in instilling these ideas into their fellow party members. Bobby Seale, the party's co-founder, who had once served in the Air Force, delivered his most famous recruitment speech at the state capitol in Sacramento when the group went to protest a proposed law that would strip them of their right to bear arms.

After taking a contingent of about thirty Panthers and community residents to Sacramento, Seale unknowingly led the contingent onto the Assembly floor and in the process caused a huge stir. After things settled down, he was able to read what Newton had written and termed Executive Mandate Number One. The message explained the reason the Panthers had come to Sacramento. Seale spoke of the impending Mulford Act, which sought to disarm citizens at the same time that "racist police agencies throughout the country are intensifying the terror, brutality, murder and repression of black people." The message delineated what the Panthers described as the murderous violence that the American government had perpetrated against non-white people such as the Japanese, Native Americans, and Vietnamese. He then compared this violence abroad to the violence that whites had perpetrated against blacks, whether they had been participants in the non-violent quest for equal rights and justice or not. "As the aggression of the racist American government escalates in Vietnam," he read, "the police agencies in America escalate the repression of black people throughout the ghettoes of America. Vicious police dogs, cattle prods, and increased patrols have become familiar sights in black communities." Noting that local governments had demonstrated no inclination to halt this brutality, Seale concluded his statement by providing the rationale for armed self-defense. Blacks would be destroyed, he said, if whites were allowed to continue terrorizing them with impunity. According to the statement, the pending Mulford Act brought "the hour of doom one step nearer."[7]

While this incident did little to stop the passage of this bill into law, the Panthers' act of bravado, coupled with the fact that it was televised and shown on news outlets throughout the nation, encouraged thousands to join the organization. Almost overnight the BPP went from a local group consisting of about thirty members to a national, and later international, organization with more than ten thousand members and chapters, branches, and affiliates throughout the United States, Europe, Asia, the Middle East, and the Americas. The violence that so permeated Vietnam had begun to be duplicated in locales across the globe. Indeed, Panther members often used Vietnam as a way to recruit new members and to encourage aggression on the part of blacks. This tactic was especially the case when it came to the speeches of Panther Minister of Information, Eldridge Cleaver.

RECRUITING BLACK VETERANS FOR THE BPP

Eldridge Cleaver, who had become famous after writing the book *Soul on Ice* in prison, urged black soldiers in Vietnam to come home and fight for black freedom "against the very same pigs who have you over there doing their dirty work for them." "Your people need you," he said, "and your military skills—to help us take our freedom and stop these racist pigs from committing genocide upon us, as they have been doing for the past 400 years." He then told the black soldiers in Vietnam that "you niggers have your minds all messed up about Black organizations or you wouldn't be the flunkies for the White organization—the U.S.A.—for whom you have picked up the gun." He wondered aloud whether they could "dig niggers, brothers and sisters off the block, who have said later for the pigs and have picked up guns in Babylon" to bring about freedom from "the racist yoke of the white man." Cleaver wanted these soldiers to understand that they were "either part of the solution or part of the problem" and that they were "desperately" needed before it got "too late."[8]

Maintaining this position, he urged black soldiers not "to carry out the same dirty work against us, in the name of 'Law and Order' that they carried out against the Vietnamese people." Constantly appealing for their aid, Cleaver counseled his black brethren to "either quit the army now, or start destroying it from the inside." "Anything else," he said, "is a compromise and a form of treason against your own people." Lest his words be misunderstood, he unequivocally told them to "stop killing the Vietnamese people" and "start killing the racist pigs who are over there with you giving you orders." In case they still did not get his drift, he advised that they "kill General Abrams and his staff, all his officers. Sabotage supplies and equipment or turn them over to the Vietnamese people." Cleaver believed that if these steps were taken, then blacks could enjoy "freedom and liberation in our lifetime" and "leave behind us a decent world for our children to live in."[9] In effect, by using statements like this one, Cleaver helped assure an alarmed federal government's use of overwhelming force against the BPP.

Viewing the black struggle in America as an integral part of all the liberation struggles taking place around the globe, Cleaver hoped to impress upon his audience the urgency of the matter. He explained to them that "this is the moment in history that our people have been working, praying, fighting and dying for. Now, while the whole world is rising up with arms against our oppressors, we must make a decisive move for our freedom." "If we miss this chance," he said, "this golden opportunity, who knows when we will get another chance?"[10] Undoubtedly, Cleaver held fast to the notion that the United States could not successfully fight wars and skirmishes abroad while at the same time dealing with guerrilla activity on the home front. The problem with this line of reasoning, however, was that most blacks failed to see the utility in the Panthers' position. The ones who agreed left Vietnam and joined the movement for black liberation. Not a few of these returning soldiers joined the Black Panther Party and used their military skills to help secure black liberation.

In an effort to draw attention to their cause, the Panthers made an unsuccessful attempt to disrupt American forces in Vietnam by encouraging insubordination. They claimed that US aggression in Vietnam was no different than police aggression in the ghettos. Agreeing with the Panthers, many black soldiers, at home and abroad, engaged in political agitation. Dwight Rawls, a former Marine stationed in Germany in 1968, told one journalist that "you'll find a black pride overseas as strong as any place back home." According to former Panthers and *The Black Panther*, a number of black soldiers, even while they served abroad, sought membership in the BPP. Not only did these individuals join overseas support groups for the BPP, but many of them joined the party when they returned from their tours of duty.[11] This trend mirrored the one that emerged after World War II more than two decades earlier. Black men learned in war what the streets and plantations could never teach them: military discipline and marksmanship. The pride instilled in a person once he or she learns the art of personal self-defense cannot be overestimated here. The black willingness to put life, family, and possessions on the line after learning that oppression in a foreign land mirrored one's own seemed for some a small price to pay for the freedom that awaited.

The contributions these individuals made to the party were immeasurable. Like other members, they used their skills to serve and protect the black community. Their knowledge of armed self-defense ensured, for the most part, that party members knew how to handle themselves in crisis situations. Their willingness to confront external violence with violence of their own meant that the black movement had shifted to a higher stage of development, something that had to occur if the high cost of freedom were to be paid. That this stage had been

Figure 5.1
Support for the Black Panther Party and opposition to America's involvement in Vietnam came from a variety of sources.

Yellow Peril, Oakland, California, 1969.

Courtesy of Roz Payne.

in the incubation period for decades, with flurries of growth in various cities in the North and South, indicated that the strategy of armed self-reliance had won an increased number of supporters. The BPP's open recruitment of men with professional military skills became necessary if the party was going to continue to grow and to champion Malcolm X's philosophy of freedom by any means necessary. With the war in Vietnam monopolizing people's lives as much as their television screens, and with black unemployment and poverty increasing while whites as a whole experienced economic growth, the Panthers' task of accomplishing such a goal was made much easier.

Men like Thomas Jolly and Thomas McCreary in New York City, Malik Rahim in New Orleans, and Geronimo (Ji Jaga) Pratt in Los Angeles were but a few of the people who left fighting in the jungles of Vietnam to resume fighting in the alleys, roads, and streets of the

United States. Still others, like Bobby Seale, Elbert Howard of Oakland, and George Edwards of New Haven, who all did peacetime duty in the Air Force, emerged from the military with the willingness to donate their skills to the black struggle for self-determination. While the number of those with military experience is not ascertainable, it is certain that each chapter had several of these veterans. With thirty-two chapters across the country at the BPP's height, the number is at least in the low hundreds. That there could have been as many as five times that number is borne out by oral histories of Panther members.[12] What is more important than the numbers, however, is the contribution these individuals made to the party.

The activities of the BPP, along with that of other militant, dissident, and mostly white radicals, concerned the United States government enough to prompt open Senate hearings on the question of the alleged subversion of the armed forces, especially those stationed in Southeast Asia. Claude Pepper of Florida, chairman of the Committee on Internal Security, explained that the hearings "were initiated in part due to the plethora of rather sensational press accounts of desertion and disorder within the military." He added that "'fragging' style murders of officers and NCOs, deliberate sabotage of military equipment, and a general picture of mass alienation by American servicemen represented the overall theme" of those press accounts. Such issues as "Vietnam, civil rights, and racial discrimination," continued Pepper, "have been highly exploited" by "various Marxist groups" and "subversive elements" like the BPP.[13]

Leaders of the armed forces, therefore, became increasingly suspicious of the BPP. The US government demonstrated its concern with the BPP when one of the committee members inquired of a high-ranking Army officer whether he felt there had been "any effect upon the soldiers" in "connection with a letter from Eldridge Cleaver urging them to go to Vietnam and kill General Abrams and his staff" and "Black Panther urgings to 'turn your guns' on commanding officers." Although the officer answered that he did not know, the question was well founded since Dr. Robert Landeen, an Army psychiatrist, asserted that "black radicals" were one of the groups who "quickly resorted to fragging," a term meaning to "threaten, intimidate or kill the NCO with a fragmentation grenade."[14] One GI stated that "these whites think that every time colored guys get together, well he's Panther."[15] They may have held this misconception because the Panthers, in numerous ways, made it known that they were recruiting army personnel.

THE BPP AND THE COMMUNIST WORLD

While in exile, having fled the Oakland police, Eldridge Cleaver made a two-week visit to North Vietnam, where, in a radio broadcast from Hanoi, he urged "black GI's to desert, commit sabotage, and rip-off the commander of the U.S. forces in South Vietnam." In addition, party founder Huey Newton offered the National Liberation Front and the Provisional Revolutionary Government of South Vietnam (Viet Cong) "an undetermined number of troops" in their "fight against American imperialism." While the deputy commander of the Viet Cong in South Vietnam turned down this "concrete assistance," he advised the BPP that its "persistent and ever-developing struggle is the most active support to our resistance against U.S. aggression."[16] This offer of troops hardly seemed plausible, since by this point the Panthers were experiencing extreme difficulty in keeping people in the party. Nevertheless, the Panthers continued to press for an international attack against racism and oppression.

In an overture to their allies abroad, the Panthers made foreign contacts with the North Koreans and the Chinese. In 1969, Cleaver visited North Korea to address the North Korean Conference of Journalists and to set up ties with the North Korean government. After this visit, both the North Korean and the Chinese governments "joined in public expressions of sympathy for black Americans and the Black Panther Party in particular." A congressional investigation of the group revealed that the governments of North Korea and China "concurred with the Panthers that the United States was the world's public enemy number one as a result of its imperialistic foreign policy and fascist domestic programs." A North Korean radio broadcast declared that the people of North Korea "expressed solidarity with the Panthers and will actively support and encourage their struggle." In 1970, North Korean premier Kim Il Sung sent a telegram to the Panthers expressing his personal wishes "for the Panthers' success in their just struggle to abolish . . . racial discrimination and win liberty and emancipation." On September 23, 1970, a Chinese international broadcast deplored the US government's treatment of the party and expressed its support for the group. According to Senate testimony, while Cleaver visited North Korea, "the regime designated 18 August 1970, as an international day of solidarity with the black people of the United States."[17]

A VIETNAM VETERAN HEEDS THE CALL

These gestures went a long way to encourage Panther recruitment and heighten the level of revolutionary violence. Fortunately for the Panthers, they could rely on returning Vietnam veterans to replenish their ranks. Nowhere was this strategy more evident than in the case of Elmer Ji Jaga Pratt, commonly referred to as "Geronimo" or simply "G." "G" became active in the Los Angeles BPP after he took an early discharge from the Army in exchange for two tours of duty in Vietnam, Cambodia, and Laos. He explained that his Army service did not result from any feelings of patriotism, but from the mandates of his "elders," who instructed him to join the service to acquire the skills needed to properly conduct the coming war for black liberation. Whether this is true or not, it is clear that the ex-officer used his Army training in the service of the black struggle. Not long after his release, Pratt, like many veterans, took advantage of his GI Bill benefits. These benefits allowed him to enroll at the University of California at Los Angeles through the High Potential Equal Opportunity Program (HIPOT), originally designed to aid lower-class inner-city residents in attending college. Though the name of this program fits well with Panther culture, it emerged as a direct result of the 1965 Watts riots. Not long after his entry into the program, Pratt became acquainted with John Huggins and Alprentice

"Bunchy" Carter, the latter of whom "nurtured a close personal friendship, and recruited [him] into the Party during the fall [of 1968]."[18] Interested in Pratt because he supported the Black Power movement, the Panthers likely recruited the ex-soldier because of his extensive military training. In addition to being a paratrooper, he was highly trained "in light weapons and irregular warfare." During his tours of duty in Southeast Asia, Pratt "participated in a series of highly classified missions, garnering some eighteen combat decorations—including the Silver Star, Bronze Star (for valor), the Vietnamese Cross of Gallantry and the Purple Heart." These achievements seem more outstanding when one considers that the Louisiana native, who joined the Army in 1965 as a seventeen-year-old, accomplished them before he reached his twenty-first birthday. Pratt's subsequent disenchantment with the war, along with his increasing aversion to the rapidly deteriorating racial crisis in the United States, therefore made him a likely target for Panther recruiters.[19]

After establishing close ties with various members of the national hierarchy as a result of his work on Minister of Information Eldridge Cleaver's 1968 presidential campaign and on the party's Free Breakfast For Children program, Pratt gradually began to assert his influence in southern California. In their study of the FBI's treatment of radical groups, Ward Churchill and Jim Vander Wall point out that Pratt's "effective" political work throughout 1968 garnered him this coveted position. Some of this work included instructing fellow Panthers in the science of office and building secuity and physical training. The untimely murder of Los Angeles Panther leader "Bunchy" Carter catapulted Pratt into his leadership position in the Los Angeles chapter. Someone "discovered that Carter had left an audio tape (prepared for such an eventuality) designating the ex-GI his successor as head of the LA-BPP." After this series of events, the FBI began to target the newly installed Panther leader in many of its special counter-intelligence operations under the program name COINTELPRO.[20]

A SEARCH-AND-DESTROY MISSION INSIDE AMERICA

Designated a Key Black Extremist (KBE) and placed in the FBI's National Security Index, Pratt subsequently became "an individual to be eliminated by local police action." In a memo to G. C. Moore, Charles Brennan, former head of the FBI's Domestic Intelligence Division, explained that the bureau implemented the KBE program to keep track of "key leaders or activists" who insist on violent revolution in the United States. Subsequently, FBI headquarters disseminated a long list of guidelines and "measures to be taken" against KBEs to "all field offices." Not only were these individuals included in Priority I of the Security Index and placed in the newly created Black Nationalist Photograph Album (BNPA), but the government also monitored their financial investments, income tax returns, bank accounts, and safe deposit boxes. FBI headquarters required its field offices to submit reports on all KBEs "every ninety days." It also urged them to employ "initiative and imagination in order that the desired results are achieved." Based on a "total war" philosophy, somewhat similar to the effort being undertaken in Vietnam, the FBI's KBE program led the agency to embrace the most extreme measures in neutralizing BPP leaders. One observer noted that "within eight months, three of the top KBE cases were permanently closed." He explained that "Fred Bennet, Black Panther Coordinator of the East Oakland branch office, Samuel Napier, distribution manager for the Black Panther newspaper; and George Jackson, Black Panther Field Marshal and coordinator of the San Quentin branch, had been assassinated."[21] Once again the US government confirmed its faith in the kill-the-head-and-the-body-will-die philosophy.

The "inevitable consequence" of Pratt's becoming a KBE "was that the new LA-BPP [leader] was placed under intensely close surveillance by the FBI and subjected to a series of unfounded but serious arrests."[22] Between April and June 1969 the Los Angeles Police Department arrested Pratt at least three times. In early April the authorities charged him with possessing an explosive while driving. The charge brought no conviction because the police failed to produce the alleged evidence of a pipe bomb and blasting caps. Later in the month, on April 23, LAPD officers arrested Pratt and four other party members, one of whom turned out to be an FBI informant, for the kidnapping of fellow Panther Ollie Taylor. A Los Angeles jury acquitted him of this charge in April 1971. In June the police arrested Pratt and other party members for the murder of fellow Panther Frank Diggs, whose body had surfaced the previous December in an isolated area south of the Watts community. After this harassment the police almost immediately dropped the charges.[23] According to Pratt, the police arrested him primarily to foil a Panther rally and community fundraiser to be held the following day.[24]

In keeping with its official goal, however, the FBI's desire to eliminate Pratt became even more urgent when the Panther began to play an increasingly active role in the Black Liberation Army (BLA), later named the Afro-American Liberation Army (AALA). This organization derived some of its membership from Black Panthers who, for any number of reasons, were driven "underground." For the most part these members hid out in several cities throughout the country to avoid arrest on real or fabricated criminal charges.[25] After joining this "underground" organization, their primary duty was to engage the police and other government agencies in guerrilla war. One BLA member noted that the group wanted to take "the war to the enemy instead of waiting for the enemy to bring the war to us." One member described the newly formed group as being a decentralized guerrilla army made up of small units "knowledgeable of the particular area in which they operate." He added that one had to be serious about revolution to be admitted. For Pratt, the BLA had a real Pan-African connection because

> it recognizes our connectedness with Africa, in terms of the history of how Africans were torn away from their homelands and how we, as descendants of those brought to North America as slaves, are joining, gun in hand, with our comrades, the descendants of those who were left behind to suffer under colonial and neo-colonial domination.[26]

In particular, the FBI, the Department of Defense, and other federal agencies sought to stop Pratt and his comrades before they seriously damaged the American infrastructure or, worse, attracted significant public support for their activities. Pratt's neutralization therefore became increasingly important. FBI headquarters then assigned more agents to follow his movements. This assignment took them on a wild and exciting journey.

Pratt described how, in August 1970, the BLA assigned him to organize guerrilla units throughout the United States. He added that this program enjoyed success from the start because the young and impoverished blacks he encountered seemed eager to join the Panthers' cause. Pratt noted that "these individuals made ideal revolutionaries because their lives on the street had taught them the art of adaptation and survival."[27] The willingness of blacks to join such a radical organization is testament to the extent of deprivation and oppression experienced on the streets and in the backwoods of America.

Pratt insisted that "one of the main reasons the pigs have been keen on me is that I trained Special Forces at Fort Bragg and endured three wars (four now)." Because of his training and experience, Pratt insisted that racist and imperialist actions were easily understood and countered once one understood the general laws of warfare. He went on to write that when the army released him, "guys were being offered high-paying jobs—including myself—by the CIA." Pratt claimed that his love for the street life ("pimping and the rest") saved him.[28]

In 1971 the authorities falsely charged and convicted Pratt of the 1969 robbery and murder of Caroline Olsen, a teacher in Santa Monica, California. Julius Butler, the now infamous agent provocateur, provided the crucial evidence that convicted him. Butler claimed that Pratt had confessed to him not only that he murdered the woman, shot her husband, and robbed them of eighteen dollars, but also that he had replaced the gun's barrel to avoid detection.[29] Not that Pratt would have divulged this information to someone he agreed with, but by this point the Panther leader thoroughly distrusted Butler and is not likely to have provided this information.

The Bureau, of course, knew of Pratt's innocence. It had the BPP under heavy surveillance. As a result, FBI agents had recorded the proceedings of a BPP central committee meeting in Oakland at the same time as the murder took place. From this surveillance the FBI knew of Pratt's presence at the meeting. Pratt's team of lawyers, led by the once famous but recently deceased Johnnie Cochran, subpoenaed these FBI documents. Pratt's defense team discovered during the trial that the tapes on which these proceedings had been recorded, as well phone taps of calls Pratt made from Oakland to Los Angeles on the day of the murder, were conveniently lost. Thus, Pratt's alibi went unsubstantiated. Months earlier, Pratt and a newly freed Newton had serious personal and ideological disagreements, and, as a result, Newton expelled Pratt. Pratt's expulsion stemmed from his close associations with Cleaver. The FBI knew of this split and capitalized on it by charging Pratt with a two-year-old unsolved murder. With the help of a well-placed informant, the charges stuck.[30] The government's timing proved perfect in this situation. FBI officials knew of the split and hatred between the two factions and rested on their confidence that Newton was not going to allow anyone present at the meeting to testify on Pratt's behalf. As a result, Pratt went to jail for nearly thirty years for a crime the federal government and local prosecutors knew he did not commit. Before he went to jail, however, Pratt and some of his former army buddies helped organize the Panther presence in the bayous of Louisiana.

VIETNAM VETERANS AND THE PANTHERS IN NEW ORLEANS

The prevalence of police brutality in New Orleans, along with widespread poverty, unemployment, and rampant discrimination, provided fertile soil for the Panthers. In May 1970, Victor Hudson, Harold Holmes, and New Orleans native Stephen Greene set up a National Committee to Combat Fascism (NCCF) in New Orleans. As in the establishment of other southern chapters, Geronimo Pratt (Ji Jaga) employed his military skills in helping the new organization prepare to go to work. New Orleans's deputy superintendent of police, Louis J. Sirgo, later provided the Senate with a detailed description of how the office operated. There were about "eight persons who are the hard core members" and "an office staff of volunteers, including females, consisting of about 40 young people," he recounted. Noting that the NCCF had "a military type setup," the deputy superintendent pointed out that the group designated an armed "officer of the day" to monitor everyone who came in and out of the office. This individual was also responsible for monitoring all police radio calls.[31]

Because of the widespread police attacks on Panther offices throughout the country, it became customary for existing chapters and newly established BPP affiliates to reinforce offices with sandbags, gun-port holes, and escape tunnels beneath their offices. Pratt (Ji Jaga) supervised much of this reinforcement throughout the nation. In a February 1998 speech in Jackson, Mississippi, he explained that he and a number of cohorts traveled around the country teaching fellow Panthers these "survival techniques." Panther Minister of Culture Emory Douglas pointed out that "G was responsible for saving a lot of lives by doing this—that's why they [the police and federal government] wanted him off the streets."[32]

This sandbagging activity on the part of the New Orleans NCCF garnered it an eviction from its original location, and it subsequently moved near the notorious Desire Project, a federal housing development with some 10,000 residents. Sirgo noted that "this is an impoverished area with high crime rate and boundaries such as a drainage canal and railroad tracks which tend to isolate the area from the rest of the community." Set off like a city within a city, the project's location, according to one newspaper, is in

> an area where few buses, and no taxis come after dark; of few shops; little police protection and minimal sanitation; of not a single newsstand; of two schools so closely fenced with wire that local children cannot play in the schoolyards after school lets out.

This move turned out to be a positive one for the NCCF because, as Sirgo noted, "its membership grew to about 300 persons, mostly young people, many female." He also noted that in addition to fortifying its new headquarters with sandbags and gun-port holes in the front and rear doors, the group also "placed wire over the windows . . . to prevent gas grenades from being thrown in."[33]

After setting up its headquarters, the NCCF followed BPP guidelines and instituted weekly political education classes, set up a breakfast program, sold the party paper, put up posters around headquarters and on buildings and telephone poles throughout the area, and engaged in other necessary office work. The Panthers, by providing protection to the elderly and others from robbers and by clearing the community of drug dealers, transformed the Desire Project from one of the most dangerous places in the city to one of the safest. Malik Rahim, Vietnam veteran and one of the Panther leaders in New Orleans, recalled that "rapes and break-ins also went down" after the group's arrival. As in other locales, the Panthers believed they had to get violent with those who insisted on bringing violence into the black community. "Once we let them know that that type of activity would not be appreciated," Rahim remembered, "they usually got the point and left or did their dirt elsewhere." "Of course," he added, "there were those who thought they were bad or did not take us seriously so we had to show them." Rahim noted that "showing them" sometimes included a good beating. In the most extreme cases, some robbers and drug dealers were shot or shot at and then run out of the community.[34]

As this activity continued into 1970, the Panthers simultaneously engaged in the first major incident with the New Orleans Police Department (NOPD). Officer Raymond Reed, raised in the Desire Project area, arrested two NCCF representatives for placing Panther posters on public property. Sirgo noted that prior to the NCCF organizing in the city, Reed had been "very effective in making arrests of wanted subjects from the area," which likely made him suspect to many residents. NCCF members learned from community residents that Reed customarily harassed the local citizenry. Subsequently, NCCF members painted signs on buildings and distributed leaflets advocating the killing of Officer Reed.[35] One of those leaflets proclaimed that Reed needed to be exposed because he was a "bootlicker, puppet, and nigger pig" who pretended to protect and serve the black community. Claiming that Reed and "his White racist components of the N.O. Pig Department are nothing but tools and fools to be used to terrorize the black community and keep Niggers intact [sic]," the leaflet informed readers that Reed had "openly showed his hand by unjustly brutalizing brothers on the block and dressing it up by making them look like criminals and he the victim." It further noted that since Reed was a traitor, he deserved "DEATH." In an effort to ensure that everybody knew that the men who joined the party were men indeed, the leaflet labeled the black officer a cowardly "Faggot" and said that he was "just like any other Pig and he can bleed." For his crimes against black people, the leaflet said that Reed had to be "brought to justice." So that no one was mistaken about the justice he was to receive, it added that "he has no choice but to die with the Pigs." Its architect concluded by calling for "All power to the people" and "DEATH TO RAYMOND REED."[36] This brazen declaration of war against a member of the New Orleans Police Department, a department widely known for its brutality and corruption, signaled the beginning of a serious confrontation between these two groups.

Deputy Superintendent Sirgo told Congress that shortly after the flyer went up, "Officer Reed and his partner [Orticke] were patrolling near the NCCF headquarters when their patrol car came under fire." Shattered glass showered Reed's face and upper body. Despite being wounded, the other officer succeeded in driving the two of them to the hospital. Describing the battle that ensued as "a reign of terror in the Desire area" and explaining that they heard gunfire throughout the night, Sirgo testified that "the automobile which the two undercover officers were using was set afire and driven into a canal." He described how "other automobiles were wrecked and burned and used as roadblocks at major intersections leading to the NCCF headquarters." The deputy superintendent noted that the party made its national scope clear when the BPP's "public information officer received a telephone call from UPI" stating that the group's "Oakland chapter issued a release saying that the Black Panther headquarters in New Orleans was under siege by the New Orleans Police Department."[37]

In his Senate testimony a year later, Sirgo explained how in early September 1970 the NOPD began to prepare arrest warrants for those responsible for the infiltrators' beatings and search warrants for NCCF headquarters. He reported that he and his coworkers spent the night's remaining hours preparing a task force since they "were aware of the amount of arms and ammunition located in the headquarters." At the central lock-up before the raid, one black policeman told a reporter that what they were about to do was "a job" and that "somebody had to do it." A convoy of police buses and cruisers, accompanied by carloads of newsmen, then made its way through the downtown rush hour traffic and onto Interstate Ten. When the first officers arrived in the Desire area around 8:00 a.m., heavy gunfire met them before they came within 300 yards of the building. "My God, it sounds like a war," one policeman exclaimed as "automatic rifle and machine gun fire punctuated the early morning stillness." Along to provide aid and support to the NOPD were the Louisiana State Police and members of the Jefferson Parish Sheriff's Office.[38]

In unequivocal terms, Sirgo exclaimed that "armed combat and open warfare had come to the city of New Orleans." The Panthers used "high powered rifles, automatic weapons, and handguns in their battle against the authorities," noted the *Times-Picayune*. There was a lapse of about four hours "until shooting began again . . . when police attempted to force their way into the two-story building housing the Panthers." According to the police, all they wanted to do was "serve search and arrest warrants on the Panthers."[39] They brought their newly purchased armored tank along just in case the Panthers refused to surrender. Malik Rahim, who took part in the two-day gun battle, explained that it was a very scary time, but that the Panthers had to defend themselves and their offices. He remembered crawling around the headquarters checking to see if everybody was all right and thinking that "surely a lot of us had been killed because that damned tank out there was rocking those walls." To his surprise, people all over the office who had taken up their prearranged positions yelled out "we alright in here!!" in response to his question, "anybody dead in there?" Explaining that the walls in their office had been reinforced with layers and layers of sandbags, he noted that "we surrendered because we had proven our point": blacks could defend themselves, maintain their dignity, and live like real men and women if they only tried. The police, however, thought it was the teargas canisters that forced "the revolutionaries to surrender." Sirgo noted that "small-arms fire continued from other locations in the Desire area."[40]

This subsequent shooting could have come from Panthers who had fled to other buildings or from members of the community who supported the BPP. For example, after the Panthers were finally cleared out of the building, "[a] large bottle and rock-throwing crowd gathered and began pushing and shouting" and lifting "clinched fists, a sign indicating support of the Panthers," according to the *Times-Picayune*. The paper added that "the crowd managed to force police officers across a drainage canal bridge on nearby Higgins Blvd. The officers were finally withdrawn at 12:10 p.m."[41] Still others provided medical aid, protection, and shelter for the severely wounded Steve Green, one of the primary people the police had sought to arrest. Additional evidence indicating that it might have been community residents doing some of the shooting is that many blacks told reporters that they regarded the raid and Panther defense of their office as "the first heroic chapter in the life of the New Orleans chapter." According to the *New York Times*, "others went to the headquarters the following day to get it together for reopening." The paper went on to say that "the nearby community is heavily armed to protect the Panthers."[42]

In November 1970 the police again attempted to evict the Panthers from their Desire headquarters, given to them "by the people," according to NCCF spokesman Harold Holmes. This time, "hundreds of angry Negroes blocked the armored tank, many shouted profanities," noted the *Times Picayune*. When the police, armed with riot guns and wearing bullet-proof vests, urged the people to move out of the area for their "own safety," the group replied in unison, "More power to the people" and began throwing bottles at newsmen who watched the fracas from the side of the Community Center.[43] After a five-hour standoff the police withdrew. Undoubtedly some community members had become fed up with their deplorable living conditions and police maltreatment of New Orleans blacks.

What is amazing about the shootout is that only one person died; he happened to be neither a Panther nor a policeman. The police did, however, effect more than a dozen arrests. They booked and charged with attempted murder three women and twelve men, all but one between the ages of seventeen and twenty-two. The police also charged a fourteen-year-old boy. According to the *Times Picayune*, federal agents of the Alcohol Tobacco and Firearms (ATF) division of the Treasury Department "also filed complaints against the 16 for violating the Federal Gun Control Act," as the police had "confiscated 11 shotguns, two revolvers, an M-1 rifle, a training rifle, and a Bowie knife."[44] Had the Panthers not been trained and prepared for this eventuality, many lives might have been lost. Had men recently returned from Vietnam not joined their cause, many lives might have been lost.

CONCLUSION

The Black Panther Party engaged in many more gun battles with law enforcement, but the point is that they likely would not have done so if the violence of Vietnam had not permeated American popular culture at the time. Their ability to recruit those who had expertise and military-style discipline meant that they would enjoy some success. Nevertheless, like the Viet Cong, they were never able to match the military might of the US government and as a result fell victim to death, incarceration, exile, and post-traumatic stress.

Their efforts, however, were not all in vain. The BPP served hundreds of thousands of poor people across the country nutritious free breakfasts. They provided free health care for thousands as well. Their insistence on decent education for all people led to the creation of black and ethnic studies programs across the nation. Finally, their presence ensured that black pride remained an integral part of black life for the next several decades. Returning soldiers from Vietnam played no small part in this drama. Indeed, it can be argued that were it not for the Vietnam War and the veterans it produced, the BPP might well have been a flash in the pan and gone unnoticed by most Americans.

DISCUSSION QUESTIONS

1. What was the purpose and mission of the Black Panther Party?
2. What strategies and arguments did the Black Panther Party use to recruit black veterans?
3. What roles did black veterans play in the Black Panther Party?
4. How did the Black Panther Party identify itself as part of an international revolution?
5. What were the essential elements of the confrontations between the Black Panther Party and various law enforcement agencies?

SUGGESTED READING

Arend, Orissa. *Showdown in Desire: The Black Panthers Take a Stand in New Orleans*. Fayetteville, AK: University of Arkansas Press, 2009.

Austin, Curtis J. *Up Against the Wall: Violence in the Making and Unmaking of the Black Panther Party*. Fayetteville, AK: University of Arkansas Press, 2006.

Black, Samuel W. *Soul Soldiers: African Americans and the Vietnam Era*. Pittsburgh, PA: Senator John Heinz Pittsburgh Regional History Center, 2006.

Graham, Herman III. *The Brothers' Vietnam War: Black Power, Manhood and the Military Experience*. Gainesville, FL: University Press of Florida, 2003.

Newton, Huey P. *War against the Panthers: A Study of Repression in America*. New York: Harlem River Press, 1996.

Olsen, Jack. *Last Man Standing: The Tragedy and Triumph of Geronimo Pratt*. New York: Doubleday, 2000.

Pearson, Hugh. *Shadow of the Panther: Huey Newton and the Price of Black Power in America*. Reading, MA: Perseus Books, 1994.

Westheider, James. *The African American Experience in Vietnam*. Lanham, MD: Rowan & Littlefield, 2008.

NOTES

1. Francisco Torres, telephone interview with author, May 12, 2009.
2. "The Black Revolution Requires Bloodshed," http://www.marxists.org/reference/archive/malcolm-x/index.htm (accessed May 17, 2009).
3. Huey Newton, *War against the Panthers: A Study of Repression in America* (New York: Harlem River Press, 1996), 119–22.
4. Lawrence Lader, *Power on the Left: American Radical Movements since 1946* (New York: Norton, 1979), 218.
5. Eddie Thibideaux, interview with author, cassette recording, January 10, 1996, Oakland, CA.
6. Huey Newton, interview, in Henry Hampton and Steve Fayer with Sarah Flynn, *Voices of Freedom: An Oral History of the Civil Rights Movement from the 1950s through the 1980s* (New York: Bantam Books, 1990), 361; Bobby Seale, *Seize the Time: The Story of the Black Panther Party and Huey P. Newton* (1970 reprint; Black Classic Press: Baltimore, 1991), 85, 78.
7. Seale, *Seize the Time*, 161–2.
8. Eldridge Cleaver, "To My Black Brothers in Viet Nam," open letter, January 4, 1970, in Black Panther Party File, State Historical Society of Wisconsin, Madison, Wisconsin.
9. Ibid.
10. Ibid.
11. *New York Times*, January 21, 1971; Eddie Thibideaux, interview with author, January 10, 1996; Emory Douglas, interview by author, cassette recording, August 10, 1997, Oakland, California; *The Black Panther*, September 20, 1969.
12. Malik Rahim, interview with author, tape recording, New Orleans, Louisiana, August 8, 2002; Thomas McCreary, interview with author; Emory Douglas, interview by author, August 10, 1997; Elbert Howard, interview with author, cassette recording, July 19, 2003, Memphis, Tennessee; Ronald Freeman, interview with author, cassette recording, February 24, 2003, Hattiesburg, Mississippi.
13. United States House of Representatives, Committee on Internal Security, *Investigation of Attempts to Subvert the United States Armed Services*, part 2 (Washington, DC: US Government Printing Office, 1972), 6977–8; see also Eugene Linden, "The Demoralization of an Army: Fragging and Other-Withdrawal Attempts," *Saturday Review*, January 8, 1972, 12–17, 55.
14. Linden, "Demoralization of an Army," 13–17.
15. Washington Post, *Army in Anguish* (Washington, DC: Pocket Books, 1972), 38.
16. *The Black Panther*, August 29, 1970; January 9, 1971.
17. United States Congress. House Committee on Internal Security Hearings on the Black Panther Party. *Gun Barrel Politics: The Black Panther Party, 1966–1971*. 92nd Congress, 1st session. Washington, DC: United States Government Printing Office, 1971.
18. Geronimo Pratt, "Political Prisoners," lecture given at Anderson United Methodist Church, Jackson, Mississippi, February 21, 1998, in possession of author. Hereafter referred to as "Pratt Lecture."
19. Ibid.
20. Ward Churchill and Jim Vander Wall, *Agents of Repression: The FBI's Secret Wars against the Black Panther Party and the American Indian Movement* (Cambridge, MA: South End Press, 2002), 79.
21. United States Senate. Final Report of the Select Committee to Study Governmental Operations with Respect to Intelligence Activities. *Books I, II, and III*. 94th Congress, 2nd Session. Washington, DC: United States Government Printing Office, 1972.
22. Churchill and Wall, *Agents of Repression*, 79.
23. Ibid., 81. The authors noted that Diggs was Butler's immediate superior in the party and might have figured out the agent's true identity, "and could have easily suffered his execution style fate as a result." Still no one has been prosecuted for Diggs's murder.
24. Geronimo Pratt, "L.A. Shootout Before and After," in *Humanity, Freedom, and Peace* (Los Angeles: Revolutionary Peoples Communication Network, no date), 4; Malik Rahim of the New Orleans chapter explained that "Chuckie," the guy from New York who helped set up the Panther chapter in the Crescent City, was one of these fugitives.

25. David Hilliard and Lewis Cole, *This Side of Glory: The Autobiography of David Hilliard and the Story of the Black Panther Party* (Boston: Little Brown, 1993), 299–300.
26. "Interview with L.A. P.O.W.'s," Geronimo Pratt, interview by Revolutionary Peoples Communications Network (RPCN), in *Humanity, Freedom, and Peace*, 8; anonymous Panther, interview by Lee Lew-Lee in *All Power to the People: The Story of the Black Panther Party* (San Francisco: Peoples Press, 1970).
27. "Interview with L.A. P.O.W.'s," 8–10, in *Humanity, Freedom, and Peace*. In his autobiography, Hilliard claims that he and Geronimo came up with the idea that "members in trouble with the law" could be "put on ice" down south since no white person in Rockville or Jackson would ever notice them. He added that in the meantime, the members "could hone their military skills" in relative obscurity; Hilliard and Cole, *This Side of Glory*, 299.
28. "Interview with L.A. P.O.W.'s," 10.
29. *New York Times*, July 20, 1997, Y-10.
30. Emory Douglas, interview by author, August 10, 1997; Cleaver, interview in *All Power to the People*; *Los Angeles Times*, July 20, 1997.
31. United States Senate, Hearings before the Subcommittee to Investigate the Administration of the Internal Security Act and other Internal Security Laws of the Committee on the Judiciary, *Assaults on Law Enforcement Officers*, 91st Cong., 2nd sess. (Washington, DC: US Government Printing Office, 1970), 96–8. Hereafter referred to as *Assaults on Law Enforcement Officers*; see United States, Bureau of the Census, *New Orleans Public Attitudes about Crime* (Washington, DC: Department of Justice, Law Enforcement Assistance Administration, *National Criminal Justice Information and Statistics*: US Government Printing Office, 1980); Jeryl Shaw and Michael Austin, interview by author, cassette recording, New Orleans, Louisiana, August 22, 1997.
32. "Pratt Lecture." Emory Douglas, interview by author, August 10, 1997.
33. *Assaults on Law Enforcement Officers*, 100–1; newspaper clipping of a *New York Times* article, no title, no date, found in Facts on Film archive at Cook Memorial Library, University of Southern Mississippi.
34. Malik Rahim, interview with author, August 8, 2002.
35. *Assaults on Law Enforcement Officers*, 101.
36. Ibid., 102; emphasis in original.
37. Ibid., 108.
38. "11 Are Shot; 16 Arrested: Police, Black Panthers Clash Anew near Project Tuesday Night," New Orleans *Times Picayune*, September 16, 1970. According to this paper, "many people left the area in an exodus remindful of wartime refugees. Some people carried duffle bags and suitcases packed with belongings. Police, however, limited what they could carry to small items only."
39. Ibid.
40. Ibid. On at least two occasions, hundreds, if not thousands, of Desire Project residents used their bodies as human shields to prevent the authorities from storming the BPP headquarters. Only after police had begun to work with local priests from Tulane University were they able to penetrate Panther defenses. Ingeniously, the police dressed as priests, thereby making it possible for them to walk through the projects unmolested. Upon reaching the door of the Panther office, they were immediately detected by a female Panther, who screamed "pigs" when she noticed a shotgun protruding from the coat of one of the officers. This incident brought about the last shootout between these combatants.
41. Ibid. For a similar situation in Detroit, see "Seeking Killer of Ambushed Comrade: Angry Cops Hold Fire in Black Panther Siege," *National Observer*, no date, Facts on Film archive, Cook Memorial Library.
42. Paul Delaney, "New Orleans Blacks Say They Shelter a Wounded Panther," *New York Times*, September 20, 1970. Because of the extreme hatred of the police in the Desire Project area, ostensibly created by Panther agitation, this same article noted that "the police stopped nighttime patrols inside the 12-block housing project, patrolling only the periphery."
43. Don Hughes and Danny Thomas, "Truce Ends Tense Day," New Orleans *Times Picayune*, November 20, 1970. See also "Black Militants Refuse to Give Up Building They Took Over," *Birmingham News*, November 19, 1970.
44. "11 Are Shot; 16 Arrested: Police, Black Panthers Clash Anew near Project Tuesday Night." New Orleans *Times Picayune*, September 16, 1970.

TIMELINE EVENTS

March 24, 1965 – the first "teach-in" on the war is held at the University of Michigan

April 15, 1967 – National Mobilization Committee to End War in Vietnam ("Mobe") demonstrations, including a draft-card burning in Central Park

May and November 1967 – Sweden holds International War Crimes Tribunal hearings

June 1, 1967 – Vietnam Veterans Against the War (VVAW) is formed

April 3, 1968 – Draft-card turn-in demonstration held nationwide

May and June 1969 – Names of the war dead are read at the Capitol in Washington, DC

November 13, 1969 – The My Lai massacre is revealed to the public

May 4, 1970 – Four students killed at Kent State University

May 14, 1970 – Two female black students killed and twelve black students wounded by 300 state trooper bullets fired into a dormitory at Jackson State University

January 31 – February 2, 1971 – VVAW's Winter Soldier Investigation is held in Detroit, Michigan

March 13, 1971 – *Free the Army*, Jane Fonda's effort to bring "political vaudeville" to US troops, debuts at the Haymarket GI Coffeehouse near Fort Bragg, North Carolina

June 13, 1971 – Pentagon Papers published by the *New York Times*

July 1972 – Jane Fonda visits Hanoi

November 7, 1973 – War Powers Act passed by Congress

1974 – Release of two anti-war documentaries: *Hearts and Minds*, directed by Peter Davis, and *Introduction to the Enemy*, produced by the Indochina Peace Campaign

Chapter 6

Patriots for peace
People-to-people diplomacy and the anti-war movement

Amy Scott

> **CHAPTER SUMMARY**
>
> As the arms race escalated, Cold War Americans lived in the shadow of the atomic bomb. For some Americans, nuclear fears and the growth of a national security state, as well as America's involvement in Southeast Asia, generated activism for peace abroad and justice at home. This peace movement was not limited to student activists who opposed the draft and the war in Vietnam. In fact, liberal internationalists, radical pacifists, and religious-minded dissenters not only opposed the war in Vietnam but sought to create a world based on democratic principles and international justice. In many instances these groups practiced what some call people-to-people diplomacy or citizens' diplomacy, and their legacy became part of the municipal diplomacy of the late Cold War era.

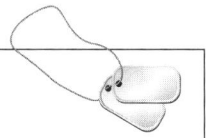

During the early Cold War period, two primary groups of peace activists, liberal internationalists and radical pacifists, worked to develop peaceful alternatives to escalating Cold War confrontations. Liberal internationalists created organizations such as the United World Federalists, the Federation of Atomic Scientists, and the World Citizen Movement in hopes of preventing superpower conflict and nuclear war through collective security and world government. Radical pacifists, on the other hand, believed that an individual was first responsible to his or her conscience. Some pacifists were also socialists, who saw peace work as part of a larger movement for social reform. Others were influenced by theologians' revision of the just law theory of war to fit the nuclear age; fewer and fewer religious leaders and peace activists were willing to grant the assumption of justice to the state and permit the state's decisions to stand for all individual consciences. Instead, groups such as the Catholic Workers emphasized

"Christian personalism," and argued that "a nation's decision to declare war was the ultimate question to be faced by the individual."[1] Pope John XXIII condemned nationalism and the arms race and encouraged individuals to "observe, judge, and act."[2] Trappist monk Thomas Merton called for "nuclear pacifism" and argued that individual peacemakers, not the state, were responsible for matters of war and peace.

In concert with their political and moral beliefs, radical pacifists took action to encourage a peaceful foreign policy. They urged total non-cooperation with policies such as the draft, which they believed kept America on a war footing, and eventually they moved beyond non-cooperation to civil disobedience. In 1956, radical pacifists led by A. J. Muste were arrested for refusing to participate in Civil Defense air raid drills in Manhattan. Radical Quakers served time in prison for sailing their ship, *The Golden Rule*, into a nuclear testing site in the Pacific Ocean in 1958. The Committee for Nonviolent Action sponsored a peace walk from San Francisco to Moscow, and protestors from the Committee for a Sane Nuclear Policy (SANE) and Women Strike for Peace (WSP) picketed public fallout shelters and held vigils in front of the Atomic Energy Commission in New York.

Even as these diverse strains of the peace movement joined forces and created new organizations to oppose atmospheric nuclear testing, they were deeply influenced by the tactics of non-violent civil disobedience with which African American activists were waging a campaign for racial justice in the American South. Cold War peace activists were also in tune with the New Left politics that was emerging on university campuses. After the nuclear test ban treaty of 1963 and the election of President Johnson in 1964, peace activists began to turn their attention to the growing conflict in Indochina.

STUDENT RADICALISM AND THE ANTI-WAR MOVEMENT

As the 1960s dawned, American politics was defined by political liberalism. Sixties liberals, who inherited a politics shaped by the Great Depression, World War II, and the Cold War, eschewed ideologically driven politics for viable—but not always just—political solutions. Presidents John F. Kennedy and Lyndon B. Johnson used their position at the center of American politics to steer the economy toward greater affluence, suggest institutionally directed social reforms, and contain international communism. After 1960, liberals sought to apply their "fusion of expert knowledge and democratic progressivism" to halt the encroachment of communism in Southeast Asia.[3] As "technocrats in search of humane public policy," they imagined that they could separate Vietnamese civilians from communist guerrillas by relocating them to developing, democratic hamlets. President Johnson even talked of a massive development project on the Mekong River "to dwarf even our own TVA [Tennessee Valley Authority]."[4]

Civil rights activists, students, and pacifists who questioned American involvement in Vietnam began to expose a darker side of establishment liberalism, and especially of technocratic liberal internationalism. To achieve its objectives in Vietnam the United States was using overwhelming military force, and by 1965 many Americans had concluded that the technocratic war was destroying Vietnam and ruining America's reputation worldwide. As historian David Burner writes, "Whatever the moral shortcomings of the communists, and they were large, they were nearly buried from sight beneath the flare and pounding of American bombs."[5]

By 1965 the student New Left, working primarily through the national organization Students for a Democratic Society (SDS), began to shine a light on the consequences of liberal internationalism in Southeast Asia. This multi-issue student reform movement did not, however, originate in opposition to the Vietnam War. It was based on three generational realities: (1) the desire for new cultural values and participatory democracy that might counter the deadening influence of blinding consumerism and dehumanizing bureaucracies; (2) outrage at liberals' moderation on social reform; and (3) opposition to a Cold War foreign policy that "contemplated, as a matter of publicly stated planning, a nuclear exchange with the Soviet Union in which an estimated 130 million Americans would die."[6] The New Left believed that only sweeping social change brought about by participatory democracy would assuage their cultural anxieties. They found meaning in political action and, eventually, in cultural experimentation. Confident that their ideas were more righteous and democratic than those of technocratic Washington bureaucrats, movement activists stepped into the political cracks opened by the conflicts over racial justice and the Americanization of the war in Vietnam. Consequently, they forced a full and open discussion about American politics and the nation's purpose in the world.

Most powerfully, in 1965 the New Left, already radicalized by civil rights actions in the South, applied its critique of liberal hypocrisy to the war in Vietnam. Only ten days after President Johnson explained America's intentions in Vietnam, SDS president Paul Potter addressed a large crowd of protesters at the 1965 Easter March on Washington, DC. The New Left anti-warrior sharply criticized the architects of the nation's war policies and lambasted an undemocratic, dehumanizing "system" that allowed liberals to place the concerns of humanity a distant third, after misguided Cold War policies and corporate interests. Potter proclaimed that the conduct of the war "depends on the construction of a system of premises and thinking that insulates the President and his advisors thoroughly and completely from the human consequences of the decisions they make." He continued:

> I do not believe that the President or Mr. Rusk or Mr. McNamara or even McGeorge Bundy are particularly evil men. If asked to throw napalm on the back of a ten-year-old child they would shrink in horror—but their decisions have led to mutilation and death of thousands and thousands of people. What kind of system is it that allows good men to make those kinds of decisions?[7]

After 1965, anti-war activists held mass rallies in major cities and on campuses across the nation. They also encouraged draft resistance and draft evasion. The move toward resistance exemplified activists' frustrations with the government's widening of the war in Vietnam in the face of mass protest, and they were determined to provoke a confrontation through civil disobedience. On October 15, 1965, Catholic Worker David Miller became the first to burn his draft card after Congress criminalized the act and made it punishable by a $10,000 fine and/or five years in federal prison. Students who resented that their universities were cooperating with and even supporting the war effort also criticized the class bias in the Selective Service System's (SSS) "Manpower Channeling"—the government's plan to use student and occupational deferments to "channel" young men into careers that contributed to the defense effort in "patriotic service to the Nation." In response, David Harris and Lennie Heller formed The Resistance. By giving up their deferments, returning their draft cards, refusing induction, and going to prison, massive numbers of draft resisters would "deny the government the troops with which to wage the war."[8] At the very least, they intended to clog the criminal courts and create bureaucratic headaches that would either stop the war or shut down the government. On October 16, 1967, during "Stop the Draft Week," over 1,000 men returned draft cards, and by the end of the war 600,000 men had violated the Selective Service laws. Only 3 percent of draft resisters' cases were prosecuted.

During the 1960s the rise of ecumenicalism—a movement for cooperation and better understanding between different religious traditions—also led peace activists to emphasize human solidarity over nationalism and patriotism; there were, peacemakers maintained, human reasons for opposing war such as sanity, justice, and love. As Thomas Merton wrote in "Taking Sides in Vietnam," "The side I take is, then, the side of the people who are sick of war and want peace in order to rebuild their country."[9] Of his friend Thich Nhat Hanh, a Vietnamese Buddhist monk and well-known peace activist, Merton wrote:

> I have more in common with Nhat than I have with many Americans, and I do not hesitate to say it. It is vitally important that such bonds be admitted. They are the bonds of a new solidarity and a new brotherhood which is beginning to be evident on all the five continents and which cuts across all political, religious, and cultural lines.[10]

Two Catholic priests, the brothers Daniel and Philip Berrigan—both of whom had attended Thomas Merton's seminar "Spiritual Roots of Protest"—embraced the goal of human solidarity and intensified draft resistance. On October 27, 1967, Philip Berrigan and three companions poured animal blood on draft records in a Baltimore induction center. On May 17, 1968 the Berrigans and seven others raided a draft board in Catonsville, Maryland. After restraining the receptionist the group hauled 400 draft files to the parking lot and set them ablaze with a homemade napalm bomb. The decision to symbolically ignite the files with napalm followed Daniel Berrigan's journey to Vietnam to meet with the Hanoi government and secure the release of three American prisoners of war. Berrigan was deeply moved by the destruction that he witnessed. He labeled Vietnam "the land of burning children" and declared that "to have seen the truth has its price attached."[11] The federal court found the Catonsville Nine guilty of destruction of federal property and violation of the Selective Service Act, and they were sentenced to an average of two and a half years in prison. Presbyterian minister and member of the nation's most influential ecumenical organization Clergy and Laity Concerned About Vietnam (CALCAV) Robert McAfee decried "the grotesque moralities that have been erected in this country: we give medals to men who drop napalm on civilians in SE Asia, but imprison men who drop napalm on pieces of paper in the southeast United States."[12]

Activists like the draft resisters believed they were standing up to the morally unconscionable actions of the United States in Vietnam, and many believed they could persuade other Americans to join them. For many radicals, however, political protest had become detached from persuasion by October 1967. Radicals, determined to "bring the war home," aimed instead at disruption. Following a mass gathering of 100,000 at the Lincoln Memorial, 35,000 protesters crossed the Arlington Memorial Bridge, and the most radical among them began a thirty-two-hour occupation on the plaza of the Pentagon. Their presence, although most were peaceful, was provocative: Abbie Hoffman and his wife donned Uncle Sam hats and had sex in front of National Guardsmen, protesters urinated in unison on the wall of the Pentagon, one young man placed flowers in the barrel of a National Guardsmen's rifle, and Alan Ginsberg led the crowd in chants of "om" in an attempt to "levitate" the Pentagon and exorcise its war demons. Eventually, paratroopers of the 82nd Division marched into the crowd to break up the festival atmosphere and disperse the protesters; US marshals followed, "cracking heads, bashing skulls."[13] In 1968 the protesters would once again battle the police on the streets of Chicago.

CONNECTING THE WAR TO JUSTICE MOVEMENTS AT HOME

As black radicals embraced a liberation politics that understood the African American freedom struggle as part of a worldwide revolution against imperialism, activists such as Student Nonviolent Coordinating Committee (SNCC) leader Stokely Carmichael labeled liberals amoral hypocrites and branded the war in Vietnam an imperialistic venture. In 1966, SNCC urged blacks to resist the draft and stand in solidarity with Vietnamese revolutionaries. Carmichael quipped that the draft was "white people sending black people to make war on yellow people in order to defend the land they stole from red people."[14]

Radicals also criticized Martin Luther King Jr.—the nation's foremost advocate of non-violent disobedience and winner of the Nobel Peace Prize—for holding his tongue on the brutal war that was raging in Vietnam. King had privately opposed the war since 1964 because it drained resources from Great Society reform programs. Liberals in Washington had long urged African American leaders not to publicly criticize President Johnson's war policies lest the president withdraw his support from the civil rights movement. King had managed to hold together a left–liberal civil rights coalition through the mid-1960s. But as black power activists recast their movement as a global liberation struggle against white imperialism and a fight for independent black political power, he realized that his coalition was splintering. He understood that black youth, outraged by violent attacks on civil rights activists in the South

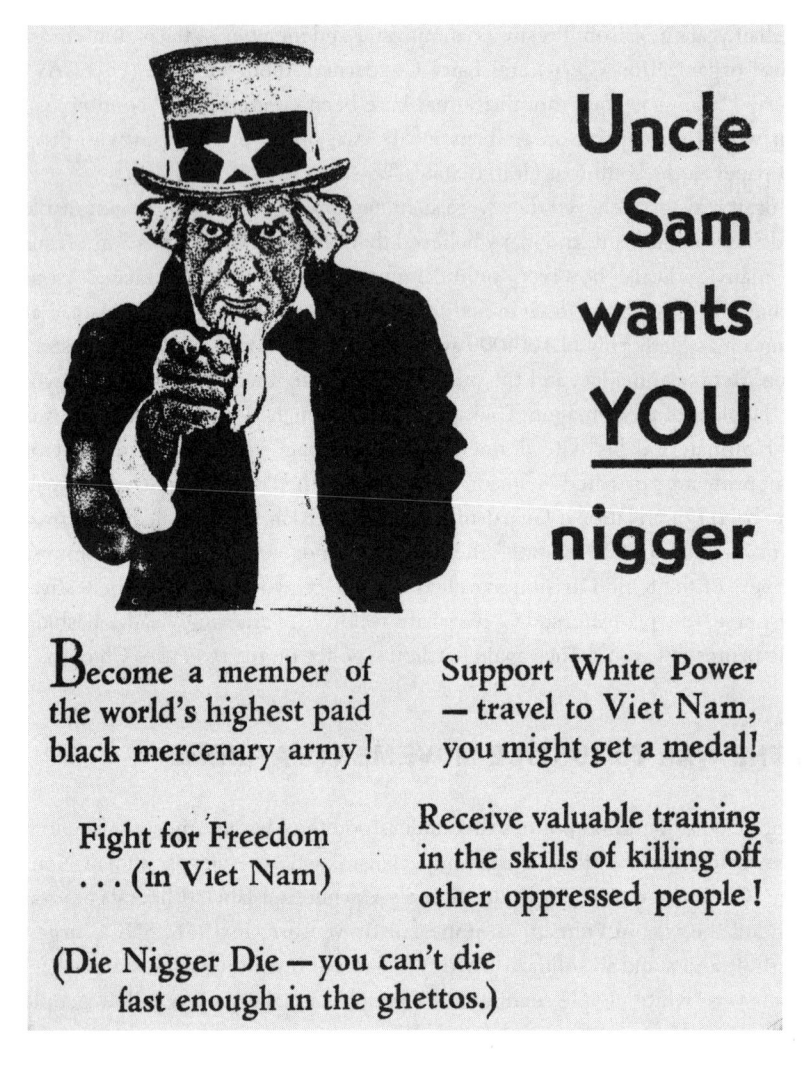

Figure 6.1
US poster regarding the recruitment of black soldiers to fight in Vietnam, 1967.

Courtesy of the Anti-Vietnam War Movement papers of Jack Askins at the University of Warwick Library.

> Uncle Sam wants YOU nigger
>
> Become a member of the world's highest paid black mercenary army!
>
> Support White Power — travel to Viet Nam, you might get a medal!
>
> Fight for Freedom ... (in Viet Nam)
>
> Receive valuable training in the skills of killing off other oppressed people!
>
> (Die Nigger Die — you can't die fast enough in the ghettos.)

and the intractable problems of poverty, educational inequality, and police brutality that plagued urban America, were moving away from a non-violent path to social justice. But rather than making race-specific demands, King began to expose the roots of poverty and racial injustice, and he too began to think about the international dimensions of justice.

In January 1967, King viewed a *Ramparts* magazine color-photo essay on Vietnamese children who had been disfigured by napalm bombs. He was horrified, and he decided to come out forcefully against the war. On April 4, 1967, King delivered a powerful speech at the Riverside Church in Manhattan in which he explained why the work of social justice must include stopping the war in Vietnam. "Every man of humane convictions must decide on the protest that best suits his convictions," King preached, "but we must all protest." King chastised the American government as "the greatest purveyor of violence in the world today." His speech was also an effort to humanize the Vietnamese. The Vietnamese, he said,

> languish under our bombs and consider us—not their fellow Vietnamese—the real enemy. . . . They watch as we poison their water, as we kill a million acres of their crops. They must weep as the bulldozers destroy their precious trees. They wander into the hospitals, with at least twenty casualties from American firepower for each Vietcong-inflicted injury. So far we may have killed a million of them—mostly children.

Anticipating that many would label him an unpatriotic communist sympathizer, King, similarly to other religious leaders such as Thomas Merton and Thich Nhat Hanh, declared that opposing the war was not a question of "national allegiance" but a matter of morality and human solidarity. "It is clear to me," King said, "that there will be no meaningful solution there until some attempt is made to know them and their broken cries." Showing that black radicals were not the only activists who cared about the freedom of people in the developing world, King argued for alternatives to the broken policies of liberal internationalism: "All over the globe men are revolting against old systems of exploitation and oppression, and out of the wombs of a frail world, new systems of justice and equality are being born." As he encouraged Americans to step outside of the logic of the Cold War, King concluded, "We in the West must support these revolutions. . . . We must find new ways to speak for peace in Vietnam and justice throughout the developing world—a world that borders on our doors."[15] As we shall see in the next section, travelers to Vietnam were already in the process of doing just that.

Chicano activists also called for opposition to the war, arguing that Mexican Americans and the Vietnamese shared a history of colonial oppression and racial inequality. While their fathers had fought in World War II and Korea to prove their loyalty and gain respect, Chicano youth did not see military service in Vietnam as a path to citizenship and equality.[16] To them, patriotism and Americanism did not reside in wartime service, but in citizenship rights that permitted cultural differences. In her movement's publication, *El Grito del Norte*, Chicano activist and publisher Elizabeth "Bettita" Martinez linked the Chicano fight for equality and cultural freedom to revolutions in Latin America and Cuba. In a special 1970 issue she reported directly from Hanoi. Her article, "Lo que ve en Vietnam" ("What I Saw in Vietnam") expressed a common sentiment among Chicano activists: the same powerful people who permitted the dehumanizing treatment of Mexican American farmworkers, displaced Hispano villagers in northern New Mexico, and allowed police brutality against barrio youth were also perpetrating daily atrocities against Vietnamese peasants through pacification programs and fragmentation bombs. "The history of the war in Vietnam began because of the land," wrote Martinez. "Many years ago, the peasants lost their lands to the large landowners, the latter very powerful men (just like what happened to our ancestors)."[17] Luis Valdez, founder of the farmworkers' guerrilla theater troupe El Teatro Campesino, also found common ground with the Vietnamese: "How can we let the enemy rob us of our humanity with a little racism and police brutality? Compared to the Vietnamese, our life at the hands of the gringo has been an afternoon stroll set to accordion music."[18]

DON LUCE AND THE INTERNATIONAL VOLUNTARY SERVICE

While protesters were expressing dissent in America's streets and expressing commonality with the Vietnamese based on racial oppression at home, some activists were taking their protests abroad. By mid-century, many American peace activists had begun to see "the whole world as their arena of action and discourse."[19] As American involvement in Vietnam grew, activists who joined organizations such as the International Voluntary Service and the Peace Corps, and religious organizations such as the World Council of Churches, began to develop models for global organizing that prioritized concepts of world citizenship and human solidarity over national allegiances. Given these different priorities, activists abroad would inevitably clash with the Cold War aims of establishment liberals.

The political transformation experienced by Don Luce, who worked for the International Voluntary Service (IVS) in Vietnam from 1958 to 1967, demonstrates how global humanitarian workers became anti-war activists. When Luce arrived in South Vietnam in 1958, he supported the domino theory and shared President Dwight Eisenhower's determination to prevent the nation from falling to the communists. IVS was a private organization but it received government contracts for agricultural work in the Vietnamese countryside as well as educational programs in urban and rural areas that furthered the American government's goal of containing communism in South Vietnam. The organization was so successful that Sargent Shriver used it as a model for the Peace Corps Program in 1961.

American youth who wanted to live abroad and do humanitarian work volunteered for IVS, and the Selective Service channeled conscientious objectors into the program. As Luce learned the Vietnamese language, grew accustomed to the culture, and began to talk with Vietnamese friends and students, his understanding of the conflict departed from the official justifications for American military action in Vietnam. For instance, it was impossible to assist farmers when bombs and defoliants were destroying crops and land. How could IVS schools function when most of their students had been drafted into the South Vietnamese Army? What should IVS do about the imprisonment and torture of political dissidents in South Vietnam? Was IVS complicit in the destruction of Vietnamese life and land if its volunteers cared for refugees who had been uprooted by the US declaration of "free-fire zones"? When IVS was placed under the control of the US military in 1966, Luce and other IVS workers objected forcefully. They told the American ambassador to Vietnam, Ellsworth Bunker, "Our work is to help people, not to kill them."[20] Like many of his co-volunteers, Luce was increasingly sympathetic to the Vietnamese. His loyalties were divided, and his definition of patriotism was changing. He would later recall, "The name of the game in social change is the restructuring of relationships, but you can't restructure a relationship as long as you remain completely loyal to one side."[21] By 1967, Luce had moved to a total rejection of America's actions in Vietnam. He resigned as IVS director and, along with fifty IVS volunteers, signed an open letter to President Johnson calling on the president to negotiate with the National Liberal Front, to stop bombing villages and defoliating the countryside, and to stop producing refugees through the creation of strategic hamlets and free-fire zones.

Luce remained in Vietnam as a civilian dissident, professor, and humanitarian worker for the World Council of Churches. He helped students at the Saigon College of Agriculture publicize the imprisonment and torture of political dissidents by the Saigon regime. In 1970, Luce led a congressional delegation to the prison on Con Son Island, where the delegates gazed in horror on student protesters, Buddhist monks, and communist revolutionaries who wasted away in 5-foot by 9-foot subterranean concrete "tiger cages," their feet shackled to an iron bar on the floor. As prisoners begged for water and told the visitors that guards had thrown lime on them, urinated on them, and fed them rice mixed with sand, congressional aid Tom Harkin snapped photographs. The exposé on Con Son hit the American press that summer, embarrassing the administration and resulting in the transfer of 180 men and 300 women from Con Son.

Luce was asked to leave Vietnam after revealing that the United States had awarded a contract for 264 additional tiger cages to a Houston company, so he took his activism to the small cities of America. Realizing that most Americans knew very little about the Vietnamese, he organized the "Indochina Mobile Education Project." For three years he traveled the country, showing films and photos and giving lectures on Vietnamese culture, history, and everyday life. Like others who had met the Vietnamese face to face and changed their positions on the war, Luce hoped that once Americans had learned about the Vietnamese, it would become "much easier to understand that when you bombed villages and created strategic hamlets, moved people off their farms, that they were going to get angry, and that the whole process was counter-productive."[22]

THE AMERICAN FRIEND SERVICES COMMITTEE IN SOUTH VIETNAM

By 1966, popular magazines such as the *Ladies Home Journal* had printed eyewitness accounts that exposed the military's use of napalm on Vietnamese civilians. Napalm was an inextinguishable jellied gasoline that stuck to human skin and continued to burn into the bone; if it did not burn its victims to death, it left them severely disfigured. As Americans learned of such atrocities, outrage at the war reached beyond the New Left politics of university students and into the suburbs and boardrooms of the nation. In northern California, women blocked trucks loaded with napalm bombs for seven hours. Others boycotted Saran Wrap, a popular kitchen product that was made by Dow Chemical, the foremost producer of napalm in the United States. In an early example of municipal diplomacy the Residents of Redwood City, California, petitioned their local government to block the production of napalm in their city. In response, the *Palo Alto Times* editorialized scornfully that allowing people to weigh in on issues of national security at the local level was fraught with danger:

> To place on a municipal ballot decisions on military and foreign policy is to invite chaos. If all cities in the United States were to decide for themselves whether to permit the manufacture of military aircraft, bombs, rifles, grenades, rockets, torpedoes and other war material, they would wreck our armed forces. If all of them were to arrogate to themselves decisions on foreign policy, they would wreck the national government.[23]

A few activists moved to South Vietnam to help civilians. In 1966, Quaker activists and members of the American Friends Service Committee David and Mary Stickney began working in Quang Ngai province to aid Vietnam's refugee population. There were an estimated 1,000,000 refugees at the time. The Stickneys established a day-care center and offered classes in nutrition and home sewing. Outraged by the use of napalm and fragmentation bombs on civilians in Vietnam, they also opened a physical therapy clinic to treat the wounded. Roger Marshall, a prosthetics specialist at the clinic, described working with Vietnamese bombing victims as a harrowing experience that was like "looking through a hole into Hell." He wrote of his first day in the clinic:

> There seemed to be shattered bodies everywhere. I stepped across stretchers on the floor and saw two women with severe back wounds suckling their babies. An old man had been shot in the throat. There was every conceivable wound one could think of to be seen. Flesh and bones had been ripped by shrapnel or cannon fire.[24]

Such personal encounters with human suffering of wounded and dying Vietnamese, shorn of ideological discourse and focused on individual tragedy, strengthened activists' determination to end the war. Dot Weller, a physical therapist at the Quang Ngai rehabilitation center, was outraged by her daily encounter with injured civilians. She demanded to know, "What are we saving them from that could be any worse than what they endure now??!!"[25]

TRAVELING TO NORTH VIETNAM

In July 1965, ten Women Strike for Peace (WSP) activists traveled to Indonesia to meet with women from the North Vietnam Peace Committee and the National Liberation Front. WSP member Dagmar Wilson recalled:

> In spite of the fact that our country was in a war with Vietnam, we said, "The women of America will get together with the women of Vietnam and we will discuss what we can do to stop our countries from fighting each other."[26]

This "peaceful confrontation" was the first time that American women had listened to Vietnamese women talk about what it was like to endure American bombing raids, right down to a detailed description of the difficult task of pulling shards of metal and tiny pellets from the mangled bodies of civilians wounded by fragmentation bombs. Contrary to anti-war activists who were calling for an immediate cease-fire and negotiations on all sides, the WSP activists returned to the United States convinced that the North Vietnamese would not negotiate for peace until the United States agreed to stop bombing North Vietnam and withdraw troops from the South.

Despite the federal government's efforts to link activists with international communism and to prevent them from expressing dissent in Vietnam by manipulating passport laws, by the end of the war three hundred Americans had gone to see for themselves what was happening in North Vietnam.[27] By 1969 the Vietnam Peace Committee hosted about one group of Americans per month. Most who traveled to Vietnam believed that not only had the highly trained experts in the State Department made poor decisions about the war in Vietnam, but they had also lied to the American people about the war. Americans were paying a high price in blood, treasure, and national reputation; the war was damaging Vietnam's environment, killing innocent people, and turning millions into refugees. Activists were convinced that policymakers' immoral actions rendered illegitimate their authority to represent the people of the United States to the world. They intended to talk to Vietnamese leaders and meet the Vietnamese people face to face.[28]

American travelers journeyed to Vietnam as patriots for peace, claiming that the actions of the government did not represent peace-loving Americans and with the idea that they might contribute to a peaceful solution to the conflict. As Shelly Thurber, a student at Sarah Lawrence College, explained, "At least the people of Vietnam will know that, though thousands of Americans have poured into their country to make war, some came who wished to stand for peace."[29]

Perhaps one of the most instructive records that we have of an activist's journey to Vietnam is the journal of Carol McEldowney, an SDS activist and community organizer who traveled to Hanoi after attending the 1967 Bratislava peace conference in Czechoslovakia. A graduate of the University of Michigan, McEldowney had been active in SDS since 1963. Local organizing was McEldowney's passion, and she did not intend "to get carried away by the romanticism of internationalism." Rather, she traveled to Vietnam because she believed that "as long as we are going to work to change America, we must be more aware of the rest of the world and where the U.S. fits in."[30] She understood the need to "read between the lines" of "hack presentations" and "DRV propaganda," but McEldowney wanted to learn the truth about the war in Vietnam and return home with "concrete evidence" to explain her anti-war position.[31]

Like many Americans, President Johnson accused the travelers of giving aid and comfort to the enemy. In 1967 he instructed the FBI, "I want someone to carefully look at who leaves this country, where they go, why they are going, and if they're going to Hanoi, how are we going to keep them from getting back into this country."[32] McEldowney's group of six New Leftists and four reporters departed from Prague in an old Russian bomber that had been converted into a passenger plane and touched down in Beirut, Bombay, Rangoon, and Phnom Penh before boarding a weekly International Control Commission flight to Hanoi. American warplanes controlled the skies over Hanoi, and passenger planes had an "open window" of only a few hours daily to land in Hanoi. Flights were often turned back because of imminent bombardment.[33]

McEldowney's group spent nineteen busy days in North Vietnam. As was typical for American peace activists who journeyed to North Vietnam, they met with the Vietnamese Peace Committee, the Hanoi Committee for the Investigation of War Crimes, cabinet officials, the mayor of Hanoi, and worker representatives. They viewed exhibits at the Museum of the Revolution and the Museum of the Vietnamese People's Army. They visited mobile factories and hospitals and toured a "hatred house" in the village of Phu Xa. The "hatred house," constructed on the site where a family of eight was killed in their home, featured mementos of village life prior to the bombing situated alongside pieces of detonated American bombs. The symbolism of the "hatred house" was clear: the monument was "a constant reminder of what happened and what perhaps might happen again if people don't resist successfully."[34] The group also visited a weapons exhibit, where they got an up-close look at the kinds of bombs that Americans were dropping on North Vietnam—including those banned by international law such as herbicides, napalm, white phosphorus, magnesium bombs, and fragmentation bombs. Finally, the peace activists met with three American POWs whom the North Vietnamese planned to release to them.

Almost all of the travelers tried to understand and convey what life was like for the people who were living under US bombardment. Appealing to the humanitarian sensibilities of their fellow Americans, travelers described and documented, in photographs and in their writing, human carnage, bombed-out villages, defoliated fields, and cities devoid of children. Jon Christopher Koch, who traveled to Vietnam with the Du Bois Club, tried to put a face on the enemy by describing victims of US air raids:

> a ten-year old boy who had lost his leg above the knee when he was caught in his school yard by a strafing plane; a twenty-eight-year-old woman, seven months pregnant, caught on the highway during a raid, who had her back broken; a twenty-seven-year-old young man whose insides were torn out by bullets as he was working in the fields.

"The villagers," Koch wrote, "do not forget these victims."[35] Americans also learned that it made little difference to the Vietnamese if civilian bombings were "accidental."

Activists also discovered that the history and culture of Vietnam—rooted in a legacy of colonialism and revolution—were more instructive than American Cold War logic in understanding the war aims of the North Vietnamese and National Liberation Front. As Americans learned when they visited Hanoi's museums, the Vietnamese believed the conflict with the United States was the last battle in a long war of nationalist struggle. If Americans understood the war within the context of Vietnamese history rather than trying to reduce conditions in Southeast Asia to a technocrat's theory of falling dominoes, they might conclude that the Vietnamese people were fighting for the freedom to define their own future. As McEldowney observed, "Vietnam now suffers greatly as the object of the American war. What happens there is the result of American success or failure; very little regard is paid to the strength of the Vietnamese as their own agents."[36] Peace activists were frequently told by their hosts that America, not North Vietnam, had lost site of its mission and purpose in the world and risked isolating itself in world opinion. "The image of America will never again be the image of revolution, freedom and democracy," said a South Vietnamese Buddhist leader, "but the image of violence and militarism." Most travelers to Vietnam were doing their best to prevent this prediction from becoming a reality.[37]

The innovation and determination of the North Vietnamese in their struggle for independence, and the sacrifices that they made as they devoted themselves to a total war effort, also impressed American visitors. Rural factories and mobile hospitals testified to North Vietnamese innovation. McEldowney visited one such factory.

> We walked into what appeared to be thatched huts, to find humming (heavy) machines, sunk in cement, going full force. Modern equipment, in the middle of the countryside, with production moving along smoothly. I don't know what my image had been of an "evacuated factory" but this was not it![38]

Travelers reported that despite the overwhelming firepower of the United States Air Force, the US air war was not stopping the Vietnamese war effort. McEldowney observed, "But what is evident is the repeatedness and thoroughness of the U.S. attacks, not their success in stopping transport and communication."[39] To emphasize that the North Vietnamese had no intentions of surrendering, travelers also repeated a tale which they generally attributed to Ho Chi Minh: "A bandit comes into your home, steals half your property, kills half your family, and then says, 'Let's negotiate.' Do you sit down at the table with him or kick him out first? This is the mood of Vietnam today."[40] Travelers' observations and narratives kept alive a discourse that held out the possibility of victory for the North Vietnamese and defeat for the United States.

Finally, after surveying the war-torn landscape of Vietnam, Americans were generally surprised that the North Vietnamese could treat them pacifically and refer to them as friends. The fact that the Vietnamese were not devoured by hatred toward Americans earned them hero status in the eyes of American activists. Luis Valdez praised the dignity, "human love," and "positive spirit" of the Vietnamese, comparing their ability to welcome Americans even as the United States was raining bombs all around to the non-violence of Cesar Chavez. In "Pensamiento Serpentino," Valdez lauded the solidarity that was developing between the North Vietnamese and American peace activists:

> And what did Uncle Ho say? Well, that despite the bombings, mines, biological warfare, blood spilled in the nation's rice paddies, the Vietnamese people continue to embrace the people of North America, for they do not blame the Americans because only their

government is responsible. Nixon (may God forgive him). LBJ (may God forgive him). They are not the United States.[41]

Not all went to Vietnam simply to witness the destruction, put a face on the enemy, and return home. Some, like radical Quakers, went to deliver humanitarian aid. In 1965, after the US Treasury Department denied the American Friends Service Committee a license to ship medical supplies and pharmaceuticals to North Vietnam, activists formed A Quaker Action Group. The group notified the White House of its intentions to send aid directly to North Vietnam, stating, "If it has become the national interest of the United States to bleed the Vietnamese to death then surely the least we can do is put our government on notice that Friends are in the business of giving transfusions."[42] The group sent medicine and cash to activists in Canada, where Canadian Quakers loaded the materials onto a Soviet ship which sailed from Montreal to Haiphong Harbor. By 1967 the Quaker underground operation was sending about $1,000 per week in aid to the North Vietnamese. The "Quaker Navy" also made three humanitarian voyages to Vietnam on a private vessel. A crew of five Quakers packed the *Phoenix* with $30,000 worth of medical supplies and sailed from Tokyo to Haiphong Harbor to deliver the goods.

During the Vietnam War, people-to-people diplomacy became one means by which activists who were frustrated with what appeared to be the government's unbending position on the war could demand the right to participate in the nation's ability to wage war and to criticize its methods of warfare.

CITIZEN DIPLOMACY ON THE RIGHT

Anti-war activists were not the only Americans who acted outside of official state channels to try to alter policy on Vietnam. Many Americans held "peaceniks" in great disdain and resented the fact that their compatriots traveled to enemy territory and returned to depict the Viet Cong as "heroes."[43] Marine combat veteran Bart Bonner believed that US leaders "had betrayed their word of honor" by signing a peace treaty with North Vietnam. Bonner believed that the government had turned its back on the sacrifices of American fighting men and destroyed the South Vietnamese people's only hope for freedom. He founded the Veterans and Volunteers for Vietnam to recruit mercenaries to fight for South Vietnam during the final days of the Nguyen Van Thieu regime. After 1975 the organization, renamed Veterans and Volunteers for Freedom, served as a clearinghouse providing information on how mercenary soldiers could join the fight against communism in Angola and Zambia.[44]

Special forces veteran Robert K. Brown was also active in the Veterans and Volunteers for Freedom. He engaged in citizen diplomacy on the right of the political spectrum, using his magazine, *Soldier of Fortune*, to publicize opportunities for mercenaries who wanted to take up arms against communist revolutionaries around the globe. Brown also sponsored Giang Bang

La, his former interpreter in Vietnam—who "was wounded three times and otherwise distinguished himself fighting communists"—allowing the war refugee to move his family to Boulder, Colorado. And for the armchair mercenary who wanted to stick his politics in the face of a liberal peacenik, Brown's magazine offered bumper stickers that read, "Peace through Superior Firepower."[45]

PEACE IS PATRIOTIC: TOM HAYDEN AND JANE FONDA

Travel to Vietnam slowed after 1972, and mass anti-war resistance weakened with draft reform and the withdrawal of American troops, but leaders continued to work to stop the bombing of North Vietnam, publicize the imprisonment and torture of political dissidents in South Vietnam, and establish humanitarian projects to rebuild the country. The Indochina Peace Campaign (IPC), founded by two activists who had taken multiple trips to North Vietnam, was the most effective anti-war organization from 1972 to 1975.

For years, anti-war activists had maintained that radical dissent in a time of war was the highest form of patriotism. They had taken their dissent to the streets, but by 1972 many felt that most Americans opposed the war after seven years of sometimes chaotic protest, and there were positive signs that a majority of congressmen might finally be susceptible to public pressure to end the war. One of the SDS founders, Tom Hayden, explained:

> At the height of the war and the urban riots, those of us looking for change faced a closed political system and it was logical to carry our dissent into the streets. By doing so we opened a crack in the system, and having opened it, it is now hardly surprising for us to enter.[46]

In 1972, Tom Hayden and Jane Fonda organized the Indochina Peace Campaign with the intention of impacting the upcoming presidential election and, consequently, US involvement in Vietnam. Hayden had been teaching university classes on Vietnam, and Fonda had recently returned from a controversial trip to Hanoi. Both had collected materials, including photographs and films, on their trips to Vietnam which they would use to educate Americans about the nation's history and culture and the consequences of the war on everyday life. Like travelers before them, they hoped educational enlightenment would result in a change in national conscience and a wider political base for opposing the war.

The IPC's first action consisted of an eight-week speaking tour of the northeastern states to register voters for presidential candidate George McGovern and bring the anti-war movement into the mainstream. They averaged four presentations per day and visited ninety-five cities. According to IPC organizer Jack Nicholl, the educational strategy was more effective than street protests: "We found that when people actually came to understand the history of Vietnam . . . it was a big leap forward in their understanding of why the war had to end."[47] By eschewing radical slogans and political theater and presenting well-evidenced explanations for

Figure 6.2 *Actress Jane Fonda and North Vietnamese soldiers and peasants near Hanoi in July 1972. Fonda, seated on an anti-aircraft gun, went there to "encourage" North Vietnamese soldiers fighting against "American Imperialist airraiders." Congress investigated her activities and travels for potential treason, but Fonda was never charged with the crime.*

AP Photo/Nihon Denpa News.

their anti-war position, Hayden and Fonda were also reclaiming the flag and crafting a rhetoric of patriotism for the anti-war movement. Opposing the war, Hayden told audiences, "does not mean condemning your country but means that it must be rescued and changed."[48] As part of its educational program, the IPC distributed 100,000 copies of an abridged version of the Pentagon Papers and sponsored the "International Days of Concern with Saigon's Political Prisoners" in 1973.

THE LEGACY OF PROTEST

Citizens' diplomacy during the Vietnam War produced a new model of political organizing for activists who were determined to "deal with life-and-death problems on a global scale."[49] After the Vietnam War ended in 1975, activists influenced by the peace and anti-war movements began to draw connections between foreign policy problems such as the nuclear arms race and local environmental issues. Many embarked on "goodwill tours" to the Soviet Union. By the early 1980s, municipal government became an additional organizational tool for citizen diplomats who were thinking globally and acting locally. In 1982, Earl Molander, a Portland State University professor, and his twin brother Roger, a former nuclear strategist for the National Security Council, used nuclear war gaming to "twin" 1,052 American and Soviet cities and asked nuclear freeze activists and religious organizations to "launch a first strike" by mailing "community portrait" peace packages to civilian leaders in the paired Soviet city.[50] The community of San Juan, Washington, explained its reasons for adopting a sister Soviet city: "The goal . . . is to reach out, on a community level and find common ground . . . under the clang of mayhem and missiles that goes on almost full-time between the Kremlin and the White House."[51]

Municipal diplomacy was not without critics. Some Americans saw subversive forces at work in their local sister cities projects. One Bellingham, Washington, resident feared that city twinning was "a diabolical scheme to persuade American citizens to provide the Soviet military with the vital information necessary to target the most important American cities with their ICBMs." City leaders who favored sending demographic data, descriptions of businesses and factories, and photographs of the surrounding countryside to the Soviets, he wrote, were "gullible victim[s]" of the Soviets.[52]

In cities on the coasts and university communities across the nation, activists linked the peace and environmental movements, and sometimes offered economic alternatives to the military industrial complex that undergirded the Cold War economy. For instance, in Los Angeles, thousands of citizens began to divert pension funds from military investments to "humane" investments, activists held vigils at the Nevada Test Site and blocked trains carrying nuclear warheads to military bases on the West Coast, and people in Boulder, Colorado, tried to shut down the Rocky Flats nuclear processing facility, declaring it a "global hazard; local threat."[53] By thinking globally and acting locally, peace and justice activists continued to expand on the ideological achievements and organizational accomplishments of anti-war activists, bringing the peace movement into the late Cold War era.

> ## DISCUSSION QUESTIONS
>
> 1. Discuss the strategies and methods used by anti-war activists to resist the draft.
> 2. Discuss the role religious groups played in the peace movement.
> 3. Explain the anti-war rhetoric and views of African American and Chicano activists.
> 4. What were the goals, messages, and contributions of anti-war activists who visited Vietnam?
> 5. What is people-to-people diplomacy?

SUGGESTED READING

Anderson, Terry. *The Movement and the Sixties: Protest in America from Greensboro to Wounded Knee.* New York: Oxford University Press, 1996.

Chatfield, Charles. "At the Hands of Historians: The Antiwar Movement of the Vietnam Era." *Peace and Change* 29 (3–4) (July 2004): 483–526.

Daum, Andreas W., Lloyd C. Gardner, and Wilfried Mausbach, eds. *America, the Vietnam War, and the World: Comparative and International Perspectives.* Cambridge: Cambridge University Press, 2003.

DeBenedetti, Charles. *An American Ordeal: The Antiwar Movement of the Vietnam era.* 1st ed. Syracuse, NY: Syracuse University Press, 1990.

Hershberger, Mary. *Jane Fonda's War: A Political Biography of an Antiwar Icon.* New York: New Press, 2005.

Hunt, Andrew. *The Turning: A History of Vietnam Veterans Against the War.* New York: New York University Press, 1999.

McEldowney, Carol. *Hanoi Journal, 1967.* Amherst: University of Massachusetts Press, 2007.

Maraniss, David. *They Marched into Sunlight: War and Peace, Vietnam and America, October 1967.* New York: Simon & Schuster, 2003.

Oglesby, Carl. *Ravens in the Storm: A Personal History of the 1960s Antiwar Movement.* 1st ed. New York: Scribner, 2008.

Oropeza, Lorena. *¡Raza si?! ¡Guerra no! Chicano Protest and Patriotism during the Viet Nam War Era.* Berkeley: University of California Press, 2005.

Small, Melvin. *Antiwarriors: The Vietnam War and the Battle for America's Hearts and Minds.* Wilmington, DE: Scholarly Resources, 2002.

NOTES

1. Patricia McNeal, *Harder than War: Catholic Peacemaking in Twentieth-Century America* (Brunswick, NJ: Rutgers University Press, 1991), 36.
2. Ibid., 96.
3. David Burner, *Making Peace with the 60s* (Princeton, NJ: Princeton University Press, 1996), 195.
4. Lyndon B. Johnson, "Peace without Conquest," April 7, 1965, *Public Papers of the President of the United States: Lyndon B. Johnson, 1965*, vol. 1 (Washington, DC: Government Printing Office, 1965), 394–8.
5. Ibid., 198.
6. Michael Flamm, *Debating the 1960s: Liberal, Conservative, and Radical Perspectives* (Lanham, MD: Rowman & Littlefield, 2008), 10.
7. Paul Potter, "Name the System! (April 17, 1965)," in *Debating the 1960s: Liberal, Conservative, and Radical Perspectives* (Lanham, MD: Rowman & Littlefield, 2008), 95.
8. Tom Wells, *The War Within: America's Battle over Vietnam* (Lincoln, NE: iUniverse, 2005), 125.
9. McNeal, *Harder than War*, 125.
10. Ibid.
11. Ibid., 193.
12. Michael Friedland, *Lift Up Your Voice Like a Trumpet: White Clergy and the Civil Rights and Antiwar Movements, 1954–73* (Chapel Hill: University of North Carolina Press, 1998), 208.
13. Terry Anderson, *The Sixties*, 3rd ed. (New York: Pearson Longman, 2007), 99.
14. Wells, *The War Within*, 124.
15. Martin Luther King Jr., "Declaration of Independence from the War in Vietnam," in *Against the War: Writings by Activists*, ed. Mary Susannah Robbins, revised ed. (New York: Rowman & Littlefield, 1999), 101–10.
16. George Mariscal (ed.), *Aztlan and Vietnam: Chicano and Chicana Experiences of the War* (Berkeley: University of California Press, 1999), 10.
17. Ibid., 6.
18. Luis Valdez, "Pensamiento serpentino," in Mariscal (ed.), *Aztlan and Vietnam*, 230–1.
19. John Boli and George M. Thomas, *Constructing World Culture: International Nongovernmental Organizations since 1875* (Stanford, CA: Stanford University Press, 1999), 14.
20. Wells, *The War Within*, 183.
21. Paul A. Rodell, "International Voluntary Services in Vietnam: War and the Birth of Activism, 1958–1967," *Peace and Change* 27 (2) (April 2002): 16.
22. Wells, *The War Within*, 531.
23. H. Bruce Franklin, "Burning Illusions," in Robbins (ed.), *Against the War*, 73.
24. Wells, *The War Within*, 165.
25. Ibid., 167.
26. Ibid., 49.
27. John Lofland, *Polite Protesters: The American Peace Movement of the 1980s* (Syracuse, NY: Syracuse University Press, 1993), 53. Lofland notes the difference between citizen diplomacy and "track two diplomacy": "Citizen diplomacy aimed to build a generalized kind of good will and understanding, while track two diplomacy aimed to achieve specific national accords through the use of amateur diplomats who had special relations to figures in governments or some special credibility with the public at large."
28. David Cortright, *Peace Works: The Citizen's Role in Ending the Cold War* (Boulder, CO: Westview Press), 12.
29. Mary Hershberger, *Traveling to Vietnam: American Peace Activists and the War* (Syracuse University Press, 1998), 58.
30. Carol McEldowney, *Hanoi Journal, 1967* (Amherst: University of Massachusetts Press, 2007), 18, 12.
31. Ibid., 58.

32. Wells, *The War Within*, 207.
33. Hershberger, *Traveling to Vietnam*, 24.
34. McEldowney, *Hanoi Journal*, 138.
35. Hershberger, *Traveling to Vietnam*, 26.
36. McEldowney, *Hanoi Journal*, xxx.
37. King, "Declaration of Independence," 106–7.
38. McEldowney, *Hanoi Journal*, 43.
39. Ibid., 61.
40. Hershberger, *Traveling to Vietnam*, 27.
41. Valdez, "Pensamiento serpentino," 230.
42. Hershberger, *Traveling to Vietnam*, 111.
43. Operation Plain Talk, *Tom Hayden, Jane Fonda, and the Campaign for Economic Democracy: A Special Insider's Report* (Cyprus, CA: Operation Plain Talk, 1981), 1.
44. Jay Mallin, *Merc: American Soldiers of Fortune* (Boulder, CO: Paladin, 1979), 138–40; "U.S. Vets Attempt to Fight for Saigon," *Soldier of Fortune*, Summer 1975, issue 1.
45. "Bob Brown Sponsors Vietnamese Family," *Soldier of Fortune*, September 1983, 16, 69.
46. Operation Plain Talk, *Tom Hayden, Jane Fonda, and the Campaign for Economic Democracy*, 1.
47. Wells, *The War Within*, 551.
48. Charles DeBenedetti, *An American Ordeal: The Antiwar Movement of the Vietnam Era*. 1st ed. (Syracuse, NY: Syracuse University Press), 338.
49. Betty Zisk, *The Politics of Transformation: Local Activism in the Peace and Environmental Movements* (Westport, CT: Praeger, 1992), 4.
50. Lofland, *Polite Protesters*, 54–5. The number 1,052 was supposedly the number of intercontinental ballistic missile silos in existence in 1982. Lofland estimates that 300 packages were mailed to Soviet cities.
51. Ibid., 56.
52. Ibid., 70.
53. Zisk, *The Politics of Transformation*, 24–5; Barbara Epstein, "The Politics of Moral Witness: Religion and Nonviolent Direct Action," in *Peace Action in the Eighties: Social Science Perspectives*, ed. Sam Marullo and John Lofland (New Brunswick, NJ: Rutgers University Press), 108.

TIMELINE EVENTS

Spring 1964 – University of California—Berkeley "Free Speech" Movement

August 1964 – Gulf of Tonkin Resolution –

1964 – 18,000 CO deferments granted

March 1965 – *United States v. Seeger* Supreme Court decision

1965 – Three hundred and forty draft evasion prosecutions

January 1968 – Beginning of the Tet Offensive

April 1968 – Martin Luther King Jr. assassinated

June 1968 – Robert F. Kennedy assassinated

January 1969 – Richard Nixon inaugurated and the "Vietnamization" policy begins

March, 1970 – Nixon authorizes the bombing of Cambodia

May 1970 – Four Kent State University students are shot to death by members of the Ohio National Guard during a protest at the US bombing of Cambodia

June 1970 – *Welsh v. United States* Supreme Court decision

1971 – Sixty-one conscientious objector deferments granted

1972 – Five thousand draft evasion prosecutions

January 1973   Conscription suspended

April 1975 – Conscription is discontinued

January 1977 – Newly inaugurated President Jimmy Carter declares an amnesty for Vietnam War draft evaders

1980 – Draft registration is resumed

Chapter 7

Vietnam and the conscientious objector experience

Philip Szmedra

CHAPTER SUMMARY

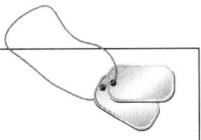

The Vietnam War era was a defining period for the cohort of men born directly after the end of World War II, members of the first wave of the baby-boom generation. The war increased political awareness and moral consciousness for many young people. For some young men, the way in which the necessity of war was perceived, as well as the reasons for going to war, changed. In this environment the number of men declaring themselves conscientious objectors (COs), opposed to war and their participation in it, greatly increased when compared to earlier American involvement in foreign wars. COs were men officially classified by the Federal Selective Service System as being exempt from military service on religious and/or moral grounds. This chapter describes the CO experience from initial declaration of CO intention and the process involved, the alternative aspects of CO life and living, the social and political environment that led thousands of young men to declare themselves COs, and finally the denouement, when, at the close of the war, men whose lives had been altered sought to move on. This chapter was influenced by my own experience as a CO, beginning with the declaration and petitioning process, through the granting of CO status in September 1970, and assignment to alternative service begun in January 1971 and completed in January 1973.

THE SETTING

From the Gulf of Tonkin Resolution in August 1964 to the ceasefire signed by the United States and the North Vietnamese in January 1973, more than 23 million men were draft-eligible. Of that number, 11 million served in the military and 2.6 million served in Vietnam. About 170,000 men were classified as conscientious objectors (COs) during the Vietnam era; 300,000 others were denied CO status. This compares with the 20,873 men who were granted non-combatant status by their draft boards during World War I in addition to the 4,000 men during that era who were members of the Quaker, Brethren, or Mennonite churches and traditionally exempted from military service. During World War II, 37,000 men were classified as COs by the Selective Service and an additional 43,000 served in the military as non-combatants; in 1964, 18,000 CO draft deferments were granted; in 1971, 61,000 were granted.[1] The significant increase in the numbers of men officially declaring and gaining CO status during this period reflects the turbulent social and political times that characterized the 1960s: the questioning of authority, and the unprecedented generational revolution that swept through American middle-class youth.

But beyond a generation declaring its independence, the Vietnam War aroused unprecedented anti-war behavior, including draft evasion. During the Vietnam War era about 600,000 men illegally evaded the draft, some by crossing the border into Canada. Two hundred thousand were formally accused of draft offenses. Draft evasion prosecutions increased from 340 in 1965 to 5,000 in 1972. At the height of the prosecutions, draft evasion cases comprised about 10 percent of all federal cases prosecuted.[2]

The Federal Selective Service System currently defines a CO as "someone who is opposed to serving in the armed forces and/or bearing arms on the grounds of moral or religious beliefs."[3] Until the Vietnam War era, only members of religious groups that held strong pacifist convictions were eligible to be granted CO status. The complexion of claiming CO status changed dramatically, however, after two landmark Supreme Court decisions: *United States v. Seeger* in 1965 and *Welsh v. United States* in 1970. Daniel Andrew Seeger, born in 1934, was raised as a Roman Catholic but claimed a self-styled agnosticism and had been morally influenced by Quaker pacifist thinking. Seeger was denied CO status in 1958 under the Military Draft Law of 1948 because his religious beliefs did not include a belief in a "supreme being." In 1960 he was ordered into the armed forces and after refusing induction into the Army was convicted of draft refusal and sentenced to one year and one day in prison.[4] Seeger appealed his conviction. The Court of Appeals reversed the trial court's decision, with the case eventually being brought before the Supreme Court.

In *United States v. Seeger*, Seeger claimed that the Universal Military Training and Service Act (UMTSA), which exempted people from military service if the type of religious training or belief received forbade participation in the military, was discriminatory against non-religious COs and discriminated between different types of religious beliefs. The court ruled that an individual claiming CO status did not have to identify himself as belonging to a class of beliefs that were officially sanctioned by the UMTSA. Individuals could now claim CO status if they held non-traditional monotheistic beliefs as long as their beliefs were not strictly personal and those beliefs served a function similar to that of traditional religious beliefs.

Elliott Ashton Welsh II was classified 1-A, or eligible to be drafted into the military, in December 1961. When ordered to report for a draft physical exam in 1964, Welsh stated that he was conscientiously opposed to participation in war in any form. But he had altered the Selective Service form (SSS Form 150) to exclude any reference to religious background training as his reason for claiming CO status. Instead, he claimed that the CO status requirement, based in part on belief in a supreme being, was an unconstitutional distinction between theistic and non-theistic religious beliefs.[5]

The court ruled in *Welsh v. United States* that CO status could be conferred on moral grounds rather than on strictly religious beliefs. The decision created a seismic shift in the way in which individual beliefs and convictions were to be viewed by the Selective Service and by local draft boards when considering a CO application. One could now claim a moral or ethical opposition to war. The Selective Service was to judge the depth of those beliefs on the basis of supporting documentation and, in many cases, one or more personal interviews before the local draft board.

By 1970 the demand for military conscripts to stock the ranks of combat divisions in Vietnam had waned, and yet CO deferments were increasing. After the Tet Offensive in the spring of 1968 it was apparent to both the political leadership in Washington and the American military command that a military victory over the armies of North Vietnam and the Viet Cong was unattainable, given the tactics of the North and the apparent sympathy for the Northern cause in much of the South Vietnamese population. After the inauguration of Richard Nixon in 1969 a policy of "Vietnamization" was implemented, in which US ground-force levels would be reduced, giving way to greater Army of the Republic of South Vietnam combat responsibility. Previously, American military strategists had planned American force reductions and withdrawal to coincide with decreased numbers of enemy troops in the South. Vietnamization rested on the assumption that no political settlement would be reached between the combatants and that fighting would continue.[6]

The timing and size of American troop withdrawals after 1970 were motivated by political considerations in the United States rather than strategic or tactical considerations in the theater of war. Meanwhile, the Selective Service was supplying the Army 50,000 conscripts each month, with more draft-age young men volunteering for the other uniformed services to avoid being drafted into the Army. The diminished military manpower need contributed to the precedent-setting *Welsh v. United States* decision and the loosening of the requirements for CO status.

THE VIETNAM WAR-ERA CONSCIENTIOUS OBJECTOR IN CONTEXT

While many COs based their beliefs on long-held and deeply felt convictions of pacifism and religious imperatives, many draft-eligible men declared their CO status as a direct reaction to, and in sympathy with, the revolutionary spirit that permeated the 1960s. Many draft-eligible men saw draft resistance as a natural extension of the anti-establishment ethos of youth. Those in the generation that came of age during the Vietnam War era were fortunate, if that is the word, in having an unpopular war to help shape their contrarian thinking and actions. Younger generations usually demonstrated their distinctiveness through music and clothing, more rarely through literature and art. The Vietnam War-era young had the war to help define who they were and what they believed. It was the war that defined an era and an age that was unique in American history and has had an immense influence on the American experience since.

The 1960s became "edgy" for American youth even before the large-scale involvement of the US military in Southeast Asia. The 1950s era of sweet and innocent rock and roll music effectively ended with the emergence and eventual dominance of British rockers such as the Beatles and the Rolling Stones. The music then morphed into the hard rock and acid rock drug-tinged culture. Hair became longer, skirts shorter, morals looser, and a collective fixation on the culture of youth much more pervasive. The 1960s banished the past and established the feel-good generation. To be young, aware, plugged in, and turned on meant everything. The establishment was to be viewed with suspicion; the elderly not to be trusted. A motto of the time was "Don't trust anyone over thirty."

Within this cultural whirlwind there evolved an effective political aspect. The "Free Speech" movement at the University of California–Berkeley beginning in 1964 gave birth to the student political activism that was to help define the decade. Berkeley students demanded the right to engage in on-campus political activities and to be able to express themselves freely on political issues. The movement was to be a bellwether of the seismic change in attitudes toward political activism on American college campuses. The young were to be more than human capital builders whiling away four years preparing themselves to smoothly integrate into a socioeconomic system that many viewed through a jaundiced eye. The technical abilities and moral maturation that one gained in the halls of the academy would now include the ability to react to and possibly influence political and social issues, including what many believed to be a morally wrong war.[7]

The war, in creating outrage among many college-aged young, became a medium for anti-establishment attitudes. Many men, influenced by the temper of the times, refused the expected role of bearing arms in the service of their country. For many, "My country, right or wrong" no longer applied.

More and more, the official rationale for involvement in Vietnam—arresting the spread of communism in Southeast Asia—was deemed lacking, first by college youth and then gradually by other sectors of American society. This questioning of moral imperatives led many young men to reject establishment expectations to do the right thing. Moral incertitude clouded any type of patriotic clarity, which made renunciation of the system the only choice remaining to a person of conscience.

From this cauldron of social turmoil arose the origins of conscientious objection on moral grounds. It also created cultural fissures between the better and less well educated because the better educated could use their education to delay or avoid military service.

VIETNAM AND THE CONSCIENTIOUS OBJECTOR EXPERIENCE

Figure 7.1 *The author with his mother and younger brother prior to his graduation from Penn State University, University Park, Pennsylvania, in June 1969. The white armband, worn by about 300 of the approximately 6,000 graduating seniors, was a planned demonstration by students who held anti-Vietnam War sentiments.*

Courtesy of Philip Szmedra.

CO status was heavily populated by the college educated. Many of these men were protected from the draft by their 2-S student deferments while enrolled in undergraduate and graduate school studies. Being draft-deferred for four to six years while pursuing a degree allowed time to contemplate the future and to develop an appreciation of life's possibilities. Upon finishing one's studies and losing the draft deferment it would take an unusual individual

Table 7.1 Classification of those potentially available for military service

Class	Category
1-A	Available for unrestricted military service.
1-A-O	Conscientious objector available for noncombatant military service only.
1-C	Member of the Armed Forces of the United States, the National Oceanic and Atmospheric Administration or the Public Health Service.
1-D-D	Deferment for certain members of a reserve component or student taking military training.
1-D-E	Exemption of certain members of a reserve component or student taking military training.
1-H	Registrants not subject to processing for induction
1-O	Conscientious objector to all military service. A registrant must establish to the satisfaction of the board that his request for exemption from combatant and noncombatant military training and service in the Armed Forces is based upon moral, ethical or religious beliefs which play a significant role in his life and that his objection to participation in war is not confined to a particular war.
1-O-S	Conscientious objector to all military service.
1-W	Conscientious objector ordered to perform alternative service.
1-Y	In case of war or national emergency only. Class discontinued in December 1971.
2-A	Registrant deferred in support of the national interest.
2-B	Registrant deferred because of occupation in a war industry.
2-D	Registrant deferred because of study preparing for the ministry.
2-S	Registrant deferred because of collegiate study.
3-A	Registrant deferred because of hardship to dependents.
3-A-S	Registrant deferred because of hardship to dependents (separated).
4-A	Registrant who has completed military service.
4-A-A	Registrant who has performed military service for a foreign nation.
4-B	Official deferred by law.
4-C	Alien or dual national.
4-D	Minister of religion.
4-F	Registrant not acceptable for military service. To be eligible for Class 4-F, a registrant must have been found not qualified for service in the Armed Forces by a Military Entrance Processing Station (MEPS) under the established physical, mental, or moral standards. The standards of physical fitness that would be used in a future draft would come from AR 40-501.
4-G	Registrant exempted from service because of the death of his parent or sibling while serving in the Armed Forces or whose parent or sibling is in a captured or missing in action status.
4-T	Treaty alien.
4-W	Registrant who has completed alternative service in lieu of induction.
5-A	Registrant who is over the age of liability (26) or if previously deferred (35)

Source: http://www.answers.com/topic/selective-service-system#Classifications (accessed May 5, 2009).

not to seek some way to avoid being involved in a "hot" war in which many contemporaries were being killed or maimed.

Further, the motivational level among college males toward their course of study was extremely high during the late 1960s since failing grades made more likely the possibility of being dismissed on academic grounds, which meant more than personal humiliation: it meant the loss of a 2-S deferment, a reclassification as 1-A, and being eligible for the draft. This was at a time when the war was being prosecuted in earnest and American casualties were at their highest. Similarly, the successful completion of one's course of studies also prompted a draft reclassification. This was the principal reason why many men during that period pursued graduate degrees: to lengthen the period of protection from the draft that they enjoyed with a 2-S deferment.

Men with high school diplomas or less had fewer prospects. In the past, many of these men had used the military as a way to develop technical skills that would make them more marketable after their military service. The war confounded their technical training aspirations as many were drafted into the infantry to serve as foot soldiers. They went into the military in numbers sufficient to allow college students to remain protected from conscription until they completed their degree.

Besides aggravating class resentment by the presumption of privilege based on educational achievement, the deferral system arguably sowed some of the seeds that germinated into the cultural wars that were to afflict the United States beginning in the 1970s. From the contented postwar prosperity of the 1950s, through the political and social upheavals of the 1960s, and finally to the fraying of the American fabric in the 1970s, American society had effectively polarized into camps that had either progressive or conservative attributes.

The Vietnam War was the cauldron from which these cultural divisions were distilled. Though the CO aspect was just a minor skirmish in the political and cultural battles that raged around American participation in the war, the issue contributed to the social friction between those content with the social and cultural status quo and others who felt "the edge" and desired a new social order.

QUESTIONING THE NOTION OF A JUST WAR

Upon gaining CO status one's draft classification was changed from 1-A, or draft eligible, to 1-O, or CO unwilling to do military service, and then to 1-W, assigned and working at an approved alternative service activity.[8]

There was generally no elation involved on receiving the decision of the draft board; there was no celebration. The journey to this point for many men was long and difficult.

The baby boomers grew up in the 1950s with comic books that dramatized the Korean War and World War II. They believed that the United States was protecting freedom, democracy, and national and individual self-determination from being overrun first by the Nazis and

Figure 7.2a, b
The author's draft cards indicating changes in draft status.

Courtesy of Philip Szmedra.

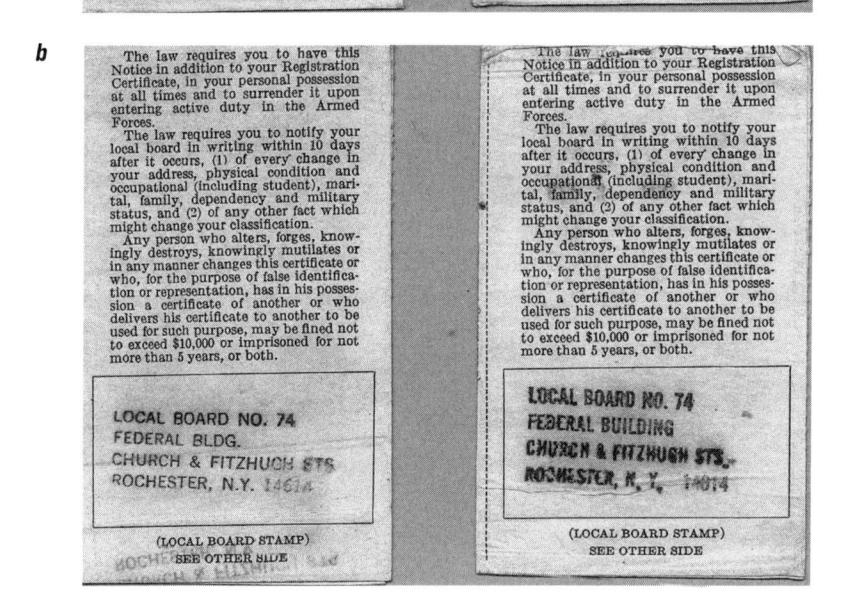

Japanese and then by the North Koreans and the Communist Chinese. These were wars worth fighting. The nation's actions in defense of American ideals were just and right, and to be judged in the light of patriotic duty. The nation had little alternative but to go to war if Americans' peaceful and peace-loving way of life were to be protected from the forces of subjugation and totalitarianism.

The Gulf of Tonkin Resolution in 1964 fueled a spirit of patriotic outrage at the temerity of a backward nation of rice farmers and fishermen challenging the military superiority of the United States. That outrage was adopted by the great majority of American young in the mid-1960s. The war had not yet devolved into the horrid, grinding, soul-emptying morass it was to become after the Tet Offensive in 1968. There was optimism that victory could be achieved with sufficient manpower and appropriate tactics that could counteract a rebel insurgency in the South and at the same time draw out the North Vietnamese army into set-piece battles of the kind the American military was most effective in fighting.

That was these men's attitude in 1965 as they went off to college or trade schools, to a job, or to the military. Though an uneasiness existed about the role of the United States in its overseas military adventures, the thought of questioning the reasons for US involvement or their potential personal role in it was beyond what they were capable of, intellectually and culturally. Both Daniel Seeger and Elliott Welsh were exceptional individuals willing to defend their right of conscience against participating in military service in spite of the patriotic tenor of the times. Their refusal to be inducted into the military established a legitimate framework and means by which thousands of draft-eligible men expressed their anti-war sentiments and their repugnance at this war in particular, though the notion of individuals determining which wars were just and in which they were willing to fight and which were not was expressly forbidden by the Supreme Court decisions easing CO requirements. Nevertheless, the notions of just and unjust war were never far from the moral calculus of the Vietnam War-era CO.

It took many years for the American public to turn against the American presence in Vietnam. After President Nixon's 1968 campaign promise of a plan to end the war, announced after his inaugural in 1969, the continued large-scale involvement of American forces and the apparent escalation of the conflict by the bombing of North Vietnamese supply lines in Cambodia in 1970, it was apparent that a sea change in American public opinion against the war had occurred. The shooting of four Kent State University students by Ohio National Guardsmen in May 1970 during a peaceful campus demonstration condemning the bombing of Cambodia seemed the final moral outrage that coalesced anti-war feeling across a wide spectrum of the American public.

THE PROCESS

Under the Selective Training and Service Act (STSA) of 1940, every American male upon reaching 18 years of age was required to register with the Selective Service System to create a pool of eligibles to man the military services. Later amendments passed after the beginning of World War II required registration for the draft by those aged from eighteen to sixty-five years of age, with men between eighteen and forty-five eligible for immediate induction.[9] The STSA also established the Selective Service System as an independent agency responsible for identifying and inducting young men into military service. On the expiration of the STSA the

US Congress passed the Selective Service Act of 1948, which required all men aged eighteen to twenty-six to register with the Selective Service System to maintain a pool of qualified individuals for potential conscription.

In the years between the end of the Korean War and the intensification of Vietnam, few men were drafted into the military, as the ranks of each service were adequately filled by volunteers. But as manpower needs increased and volunteer enlistments proved inadequate to supply the demand for soldiers, the Selective Service began calling into service conscripts to fully man the Army and, to a lesser extent, the Marine Corps.

The other uniformed services used few conscripts during the Vietnam War as volunteer numbers adequately supplied personnel needs. Volunteers for the Navy and Air Force were plentiful, as the thinking by the draft-eligible male was that serving in these branches minimized the possibility of being sent to Vietnam.[10] If one were unlucky enough to be sent to the theater of war as a Navy or Air Force enlistee, the likelihood of being involved in jungle combat was lower than for an Army draftee. The Marines were and continue to be a breed apart, attracting individuals with a desire for adventure and risk that assures their early involvement and engagement in any foreign escapade. Approximately 500,000 Marines served in Vietnam from 1962 through 1975. In 1968, Marines numbered 86,000 of the 501,000 American troops under Military Advisory Command Vietnam (MACV). About 20,000 men were conscripted into the Marine Corps during the Vietnam War.[11] The Army was the institution most reliant and dependent on the draft. Approximately 95 percent of all inductees during the Vietnam era served in the Army.[12]

Draft boards throughout the United States were ill prepared to handle the administrative consequences of the *Welsh v. United States* decision. The result was an extensive and lengthy process (involving initial declaration of CO status by the claimant to the eventual granting or rejecting of the CO declaration, which took many months, sometimes years). The timeline was dependent upon the caseload of the local draft board and the efficiency with which the caseload was processed. Personal appearances to argue one's case before the board were scheduled months in advance. The subsequent board decision arrived through the mail weeks or months later. During that time, potential COs lived in a state of suspended animation unsure of whether they were to prepare themselves for flight to Canada if their appeal was rejected if that was their leaning, submit to the siren song of the war underground and head for cities with a significant population of like-minded individuals such as San Francisco or New York, or optimistically begin to search for an alternative service job that would be far enough away from their hometown and sufficiently low-paying to be acceptable to the local draft board.[13] But the whirlwind that enveloped each draft-age male made even that final draft board decision anticlimactic—a denouement to a story that was both much too common and uniquely individual.

Vietnam-era draft-eligible men were the sons of what Tom Brokaw termed the "Greatest Generation."[14] Military service was a right of passage, an individual's contribution to maintaining a bulwark of liberty and freedom. For someone to deny that responsibility was to deny that an obligation to one's country existed. To pick and choose among wars one was willing to fight and those that were morally repugnant jeopardized the United States' status as a moral beacon willing to dedicate its blood and treasure to promote and protect freedom—freedom of the individual and the collective freedom to determine what a nation is and what it is to become.

But many young men decided that their repugnance toward this particular war was so great that their personal involvement in it would damage their own moral rectitude. By comparison, the decision of their fathers to fight was not as morally vexing. Few of these men had qualms about their involvement in war against Nazi Germany or Imperial Japan. The United States had been attacked; militaristic regimes claiming racial superiority had subjugated nations and were using genocide as a method to cleanse populations of what they deemed undesirables. America was threatened. The question of personal involvement held no moral ambiguities for most men. And in any case, the ability to express those misgivings was far more limited.

DECLARING CO STATUS

The declaration of CO status required obligatory forms to be submitted to the local draft board as well as testimonials in writing from individuals who had known the claimant during his young life and vouched for his unstinting moral rejection of war as a method to resolve disputes between nations or whose "moral, ethical, or religious beliefs would give them no rest or peace if they allowed themselves to become a part of an instrument of war."[15] The depth, fervency, and verity of the petitioner's beliefs, as demonstrated by his own witness as well as letters of support from parents, clergy, and others who were aware of the pacific values and deeds of the individual, would be evaluated by the members of his local draft board, who would ultimately decide the truthfulness of the claim and whether the individual was to be exempted from military service.

Besides the necessary documentation, a personal appearance before the board without the benefit of counsel was usually required. In many instances the awarding or denying of the petition for CO status was determined on the basis of the petitioner's responses to the questions posed by the board as well as the previously mentioned letters of reference from individuals who played a significant role in the petitioner's life that could attest to the sincerity of his CO claim. In most instances the skepticism of the board members to the petitioner's request was barely hidden. The general line and content of the questions reflected that fact. For instance: "How did these moral principles that underlie your CO claim come to be developed?" "Who were the people most influential to you in developing those principles?" "Are you against all wars or just this war?" "What organizations do you belong to that may have influenced your decision to claim CO status?" "What will you do if your CO petition is denied?" The responses were measured, reflecting the petitioner's best guess at what the board members expected to hear from one opposed to personal participation in war: that you had always been sensitive to the needs and sensibilities of others; that you had been greatly influenced by the religious precepts of faith, hope, and love of your fellow man; that war is an abomination and never just; and that your personal plans did not extend beyond this all-important draft-board meeting.

The local draft boards were made up of men who had fought in World War II and Korea, where moral uncertainty was a non-issue. If your country called, then your patriotic duty was to serve. This war was the responsibility of this generation just as previous wars were the responsibility of past generations. The draft board's general perception was that the individual standing before the board was attempting to evade the draft in which many others had been called and responded in the expected patriotic way. Any attempt at evasion, it was thought, had nothing to do with avoiding personal moral degradation but rather the foisting of patriotic responsibility on others.

The decision of the draft board was delivered to the petitioner through the mail accompanied by a newly issued draft card declaring the individual's petition either a failure, classifying him 1-A and eligible for the draft, or successful, issuing a 1-O classification, meaning "CO not willing to do alternative service in the military"— the latter being determined during the draft-board interview. Approximately 170,000 men were officially recognized as COs during the Vietnam War era.[16] If a 1-O was issued, the newly declared CO was allowed to search for appropriate alternative service employment with no general guidelines as to what was acceptable by the board. If the newly recognized CO was successful in finding employment, it was the local draft board members who ultimately determined whether the employment was appropriate.

THE REALITIES OF ALTERNATIVE SERVICE

Many newly declared COs found themselves assigned work at community hospitals engaged in jobs that during that era were essentially reserved for individuals who had not finished high school, a much more commonly encountered characteristic in the labor force during that time than it is today. The CO was left to decide whether his draft status should be part of his public persona. Confidentiality was a distinct advantage in regions of the country that harbored hostility toward those men who refused military service, most notably the South, from which historically was drawn a large percentage of those in the active military. The South had the highest rate of combat deaths in Vietnam: 31 per 100,000 of military-age men. The Northeast had the lowest rate, 23.5.[17] Further, in the more accepting Northeast, COs were typically seen as individuals of conscience rather than draft evaders and generally treated with respect. The CO was thus afforded a level of personal dignity that made alternative service for most a generally rewarding time.

One stipulation of alternative service was that work assignments had to be at least two hundred miles from the CO's permanent residence so that a hardship should be endured by the CO commensurate with what an Army draftee would experience by being inducted into the military, sent to basic training, and then being shipped overseas. Another *de facto* stipulation was that compensation for alternative service should be no more than the minimum wage, which in

February 1970 was $1.45 per hour. These requirements effectively deprived the successful CO of the ability to apply whatever level of training and skills he had developed during his formal education, be it high school or some form of higher education, and required the acceptance of a job normally reserved for the unskilled. For example, a typical alternative service assignment involved hospital orderly duties. An orderly's responsibilities encompassed all aspects of patient care, including the entire range of human needs from in-patient personal hygiene to ultimately post-mortem care. For many uninitiated COs, hospital work exposed them to the vicissitudes of life and death for the first time. In so doing, the hospital experience created a maturity in the CO as profound and tangible as military service.

The stipulations of alternative service deprived the country of the talents of this large group of males who were arguably above average in intellectual abilities and talent relative to the general population of their male cohorts and to those serving in the military. Eighty percent of men who served in the military during the Vietnam era came from poor and working-class backgrounds. The demographic was heavily blue-collar, low-income, and disproportionately minority.[18] As a result, the COs' contribution to the economic vitality of the United States during their years of alternative service was less than it could have been.[19] And more importantly for many COs, their life's direction would be forever altered by the experience, a justifiable rationale and consequence of refusing military service, as the lives of those who did serve in the military were also forever altered. There was justice in that consequence in the eyes of those who sat on the draft board committees making these decisions and also in the eyes of the general public who deemed a refusal to serve in the military as a punishable act.

Domestic resistance to the war through campus demonstrations, marches for peace, celebrity anti-war testimonials, and the like helped gradually to turn the tide of public sentiment away from the notion of prosecuting the war until some semblance of victory could be declared. But also, public sentiment was affected by the numbers and passion of those men who declared both officially and unofficially that they would not participate as combatants in the war. America had never experienced the magnitude of a renunciation of war by the men expected to fight in it that it did during the Vietnam era. Even in regions of the country with a strong militaristic tradition the sheer numbers of draft resisters created doubt among the "My country right or wrong" groups of the rightness of the war's prosecution. By the beginning of the 1970s the message from that side of the political spectrum was more and more to declare victory and leave. From the anti-war Left the message was "just leave and call it a lesson learned."

The bubbling pot of domestic politics was continuously salted by the issue of the draft and draft resistance. The continuation of the draft was one of those issues in the forefront of the national debate on the war that was perceived to be creating cultural and class hostilities. The Congress decided to make it a non-issue by suspending conscription in 1973. By then peace accords had been signed and the levels of manpower needed to oversee the US withdrawal from the country were reduced. The draft was halted, but not before 18,000 draftees had been killed in combat, accounting for about 30 percent of US combat deaths.[20]

CLASSIFYING THE TYPES OF CONSCIENTIOUS OBJECTORS

The Selective Service system categorized declared COs into two distinctive groups according to their willingness to wear a military uniform. Some men decided that they could serve as a CO in the military as a non-combatant, either as a medic or a corpsman in the combat branches of the military, or in some administrative function not requiring the carrying of arms. Two of the more prominent individuals in the former category were Desmond Doss during World War II and Thomas Bennett from the Vietnam era. Doss was a Seventh Day Adventist and refused to kill or carry a weapon into combat. He was the first CO to receive the Congressional Medal of Honor (CMH) for his heroic service during World War II as an Army medic on Okinawa in the Pacific theater. His name became a symbol of gallantry in the infantry division in which he served. Thomas Bennett was a deeply religious individual who enlisted in the Army as a CO and was trained as a field medic. He was awarded the CMH in February 1969 for his actions in the Central Highlands region of Vietnam during a firefight between North Vietnamese Army regulars and his unit.[21] COs who served in the military as non-combatants elicited mixed emotions from their fellow soldiers. While some admired the moral convictions that drove the uniformed CO to be in the field as a corpsman or medic, aiding the wounded without a weapon or refusing to use a weapon against the enemy, others felt more vulnerable by being short-handed in firepower by having a non-combatant in the combat group.

Some COs believed that non-combatant military service aided in the prosecution of the war by replacing someone who would be transferred to a combat role and contribute to the war effort. These individuals refused to participate in any way in the military. It was these COs who searched creatively for alternative service acceptable to their draft boards. Since no guidelines existed as to what was an acceptable alternative service post, many individuals relied on self-interpretation of the language of the Selective Service Act of 1940, which stated that alternative service was a job "deemed to make a meaningful contribution to the maintenance of the national health, safety, and interest." The alternative service guidelines are much more succinct today than they were during the Vietnam War.[22] The guidelines exist because of the confusion and perceived arbitrariness of the decisions by local draft boards determining what was and was not acceptable alternative service. Current examples of acceptable alternative service should conscription be reinstituted according to more recent revisions of the Selective Service Act include conservation, caring for the very young and the very old, educational projects, and health care.

There existed different degrees of anti-war emotion within the newly qualifying CO community—that is, those who could legally claim CO status after *Welsh v. United States*. The newly minted "*Welsh*-CO" came from a much more divergent religious and ethical background than did the religion-based CO. These dissimilarities were often expressed in their political activism or lack thereof. Religious-based COs were more likely to ally and involve themselves strongly with the anti-war movement, which was a necessary outgrowth of their pacific beliefs. They were members of anti-war groups that gave a meaningful structure to the anti-war movement and were the core of non-violent activism during the period. They believed that state violence could be confronted, condemned, and ultimately ended through peaceful protest and personal non-violence. The social pressure to end the war drew its energy from pacifist groups, to which other groups and individuals attached themselves to coalesce into arguably the largest and most influential anti-war movement in US history.

The *Welsh*-CO was more likely to be apolitical; anti-war and willing to demonstrate that feeling and commitment in organized demonstrations, but unwilling to consecrate his whole being to the anti-war movement. Many saw this period of their lives not as a defining moment—few young men have that level of self-awareness or perspective—but rather as another event in a tumultuous decade full of history. Rather than continuing to engage in that tumult, the process of CO declaration and recognition being sufficiently turbulent, many preferred to withdraw into quiet lives of alternative service. They sought the ability to find shelter from the months or years in which the CO essentially had no control over his destiny, a period of suspended animation in which his future hinged on decisions made by the generally unsympathetic members of the local Selective Service board, a period in which falling into a cynical and fatalistic attitude regarding life and its prospects was a very easy step to take. Establishing some semblance of normality was the ultimate gratification.

Normality involved integration into the life of his workplace and community and the acceptance of a postponement in the life for which he had intellectually prepared himself. For many COs this type of integration was not difficult at all. Time for a young man is a series of lazy meanderings from season to season with usually no pressing need to accomplish even intermediate life goals. There was always next week, next month, or next year. Time was a friend that comforted rather than oppressed. Most young men newly classified as COs were thankful for the respite from a turbulent period in their lives and anxious for a taste of normalcy.

RACE AND THE REALITY OF OBJECTION

In spite of the victories achieved through Supreme Court decisions outlawing segregation and assuring equal opportunity and equal access for African Americans, the fight for equality was still in its adolescence when the Vietnam War began heating up in earnest in 1965. The energies devoted to making civil rights a national imperative in the early 1960s under the leadership of Dr. Martin Luther King Jr. were now being dissipated by a nation newly focused on the battle to contain communism in Southeast Asia.

The American military, arguably a leader in offering equality of opportunity for the African American during that era, was siphoning many young blacks from communities that offered them little hope in improving their lot, toward opportunities where they would be judged on the basis of merit rather than skin color. For many, joining the military was a way to demonstrate an aspiration for self-improvement in an environment of relative meritocracy. By serving in the military, the young black man had the chance to earn a place at the American table, which many whites believed he had no right to aspire to.

Though leaders of the civil rights movement were critical of American involvement in the war and some were actively involved in the anti-war movement, the military still held a strong attraction to the young black male. Blacks enlisted, were drafted, and were represented in the military in the same proportions as their numbers in the general population.

However, few blacks declared themselves COs. Despite the great admiration that all African Americans had for Dr. Martin Luther King Jr., his non-violent civil disobedience approach to civil rights did not translate to the young black male as relevant when it came to the decision regarding military service. Dr. King's anti-Vietnam War stance and his attempts to focus African American energies on domestic issues of racial equality and poverty did little to persuade young black men to oppose the war as a matter of conscience.

One young black man who did claim CO status under unusual circumstances was James A. Daly. Born and bred in Brooklyn, New York, he enlisted in the Army in 1966 on the admonition of an Army recruiter that he would be able to claim CO status as an enlistee in the Regular Army. He was told that he would not have that ability if he were drafted, which was untrue. Fearing that his 1-A classification would cause his immediate induction, he enlisted. He believed his strict Seventh Day Adventist beliefs and total aversion to war and killing would be immediately recognized by the Army and he would be assigned training in a non-combatant role as a cook. His petitions for CO status were ignored and he eventually became a rifleman in the 196th Light Infantry Brigade stationed in Quang Tin province, South Vietnam. He was captured during a firefight with Viet Cong forces in January 1968 and held as a POW in prison camps in both South and North Vietnam. His story is unusual in that during his service in Vietnam prior to his capture he continued to proclaim his aversion to war and refused to use his weapon against the enemy. While in captivity he became a member of a POW group called the Peace Committee whose members were accused of collaboration with their North Vietnamese captors by other POWs and eventually by the US Army. Daly's case was unusual, however. Investigations into why more young black males did not claim CO status as a viable way to oppose the war and to engage in a method of civil disobedience that would align themselves with the tactics of the civil rights movement are lacking.[23]

Possibly the reality had more to do with the opportunities the military offered than those of objection. From the black perspective the military was much more a meritocracy than American society in general. For an African American the potential for self-improvement through technical training and other educational opportunities was greater in an organization that mandated equal opportunity and practiced *de jure* integration. Rebelling against this institution was essentially renouncing the only available access to self-improvement and integration into the larger American society that was available for the ordinary black male at the time. As a result, few renounced conscription and military service. This fact is surprising considering the temper of the 1960s, when challenges to authority, and certainly white authority, would have seemed the natural birthright of every black male.

Racial antagonisms existed in Vietnam among American troops, reflecting the racial divisions in wider American society. Black urban riots in Los Angeles, Detroit, Newark, and many other American cities during the 1960s fomented racial hostility among some white and black soldiers in Vietnam. The rise of Black Power and black pride resulting from the successes of the Civil Rights Movement was carried into the paddies and highlands of Vietnam and met aggressively on occasion. But this does not diminish the degree to which the American military provided the black soldier a way to be judged on his merits rather than the color of his skin.

THE EMPLOYMENT ENVIRONMENT

During the 1960s the draft-eligible male upon high school graduation knew exactly what his career choices were. Continuing his education either by going on to college or technical school assured a 2-S student deferment which prevented him from being placed into the draft pool until the completion of his studies. Attending seminary or other religious studies institutions for preparation as a priest, minister, or rabbi provided 2-D shelter from the draft. Moving into the labor force and attempting to find gainful long-term work was difficult, as potential employers inquired about draft status. High school graduation without the demonstrated intent of continuing studies transferred the young man into the 1-A pool—eligible to be drafted.

Few employers were willing to incur the expense of training an unskilled worker without the understanding that that employee would remain in the position for a worthwhile period. The draft-eligible male could not guarantee to his employer that he would not be removed from that job by the draft. In order for an employer to seriously consider an applicant, the individual was usually required to pledge to address his draft obligation in some way. This usually meant joining the Army Reserve or the National Guard. Subsequently, demand for available spots in those branches of the military was strong because of the low risk of a deployment to Vietnam. During the Vietnam era, however, one had to be politically well connected to land a spot in the Reserves or National Guard. It was during this time that former president George W. Bush became a pilot in the Texas Air National Guard and remained in the United States during his entire tour of duty. Other subsequently prominent individuals such as former president Bill Clinton and former vice president Dick Cheney used deferments to avoid military service. Clinton became an active anti-war and anti-draft advocate and demonstrator during his Rhodes Scholar years at Oxford University in England while being deferred from the draft because of his student status. Dick Cheney received five deferments between 1959 and 1967, when he was no longer eligible for the draft, four as a student and the final deferment for becoming a new father.[24]

Approximately 96,000 Vietnam-era COs successfully completed two years of alternative service, which was slightly more than half of the 170,000 men granted CO status.[25] Many COs who chose to do alternative service and had been offered jobs prior to their CO classification found on their return from their two-year obligation that those jobs no longer existed. As a result, many former COs were compelled to choose different career paths than the ones they had envisioned when their college careers began.

A domestic backlash existed against those men who chose CO status and alternative service. Hostility existed against those who chose to evade the draft through illegal means such as flight to Canada or becoming part of the anti-war underground. But those who chose to fulfill their military obligation through alternative service also carried the stigma of what was felt by many as an unpatriotic affront to the United States, its military, and the military's mission. Many COs were shunned on attempting to reintegrate into general society on completion of their alternative service. This led rationally to COs practicing a "don't ask, don't tell" approach during prospective employment interviews. But not disclosing their draft status always led to questions about those two years spent doing menial work, in many instances with a college degree. As a result, non-disclosure became guilt by omission and not a very effective method in attempting to place back on track a derailed career path.

When their alternative service obligation ended, many COs left for other cities to begin another life. Many men found that the only jobs open to them were very similar to the alternative service jobs that they had recently left. Many were forced to take those jobs until other prospects appeared. Of those COs who spent their alternative service in a hospital environment, many found the cocoon of hospital life enriching enough to persuade them to pursue registered nursing degrees or diplomas, or licensed practical nursing certificates. Some chose to become physician assistants, a relatively new health-care career at that time. Others continued with the work they had been assigned at the beginning of their CO service. They were young, independent from their families, reasonably comfortable in an existence that they had created in the midst of trying times, in general surrounded by friends, and proud of their alternative war experience. The problem inherent in that choice was that the dossier of job experience they were building suited them only for the particular work which they were doing. Many COs stayed in the work they were doing for years after their commitment had expired, until the point where ability and aspirations overcame the inertia of comfort and stability.

Other prospects involved graduate school and a movement once again out of the labor force to retrain for something new. The longer out of the labor force one could remain, the less relevant became the period of alternative service and the easier it would become to effectively begin with a clean slate. By the mid-1970s the CO who had done alternative service was looking to emerge into the post-Vietnam War period of his life. The country itself was anxious to call an end to the animosities created by conscription of men to fight in what had become America's first military defeat—so much so that in 1976, President Jimmy Carter declared an amnesty for men who had fled the country or who went underground to avoid the draft. Everyone wanted to turn the page and get on with their lives.

THE LEGACY OF THE VIETNAM WAR-ERA CONSCIENTIOUS OBJECTOR EXPERIENCE

The Vietnam War-era Supreme Court decisions that allowed a greater number of men to claim and be granted CO status legitimized the right to view war as a social aberration that required redressing. Previously it was the individual of conscience who refused to take up arms in a war effort who was perceived as the oddity and treated as the social aberration. Future wars would now require justification from an ethical and moral perspective rather than simply a geopolitical one. The CO experience during the Vietnam era legitimized that moral questioning. It allowed the non-pacifist to question the moral imperatives of sovereign belligerency and decide whether a war was just or simply an opportunistic adventure. Although the Supreme Court had determined that a CO could not pick and choose between what he perceived to be just and unjust wars, the sheer numbers of men who applied for CO status during the Vietnam era suggest that this is exactly what was happening. They determined that there was no good reason to fight this war and they were not willing to sacrifice themselves in its prosecution. They reflected the eventual feelings of an American populace that had determined that the Vietnam War was morally wrong and simply not worth the blood and treasure that were its costs.

Although anti-war movements had existed throughout the history of the United States, none had the breath of public support of the anti-Vietnam War movement. While not entirely due to the influence of COs, the vanguard of this thinking surely had to be the CO demonstrating his opposition to this war. They were the heroes of the left who made their position felt through a quiet earnestness that gave others the strength and heart to protest the war, and gave society an alternative perspective on war, on those who fought and those who chose not to fight. Moral certitude was no longer to be had, and the moral clarity that accompanies the will to war would henceforth be questioned.

DISCUSSION QUESTIONS

1. Describe the cultural environment that motivated hundreds of thousands of draft-eligible men to pursue CO status.
2. Why did many young people consider the Vietnam War unjust and one in which they were not willing to fight?
3. What were the moral and ethical differences facing the World War II-era soldier compared with the Vietnam War GI?
4. What were some of the issues involved in having a great many COs emerge from the "educated classes?"
5. How did COs influence the anti-Vietnam War movement?

SUGGESTED READING

Beam, Christopher Bear. *Invisible Warrior: A Conscientious Objector's Narrative of the Vietnam Era Journey.* Bloomington, IN: Xlibris, 2008.
Dickerson, James. *North to Canada: Men and Women against the Vietnam War.* Westport, CT: Praeger, 1999.
Elmer, Jerry. *Felon for Peace: The Memoir of a Vietnam-Era Draft Resister.* Nashville, TN: Vanderbilt University Press, 2005.
Foley, Michael S. *Confronting the War Machine: Draft Resistance during the Vietnam War.* Chapel Hill, NC: University of North Carolina Press 2003.
Hagan, John. *Northern Passage: American Vietnam War Resisters in Canada.* Cambridge, MA: Harvard University Press, 2001.
MacPherson, Myra. *Long Time Passing: Vietnam and the Haunted Generation.* Bloomington, IN: Indiana University Press, 2001.
Sherman, Ben. *Medic! The Story of a Conscientious Objector in the Vietnam War.* New York: Random House, 2002.
Solheim, Bruce O. *The Vietnam War Era: A Personal Journey.* Westport, CT: Greenwood, 2006.
Terry, Wallace. *Bloods: Black Veterans of the Vietnam War: An Oral History.* Toronto: Random House, 1984.

NOTES

1. John Mascari, "U.S. Conscientious Objectors in World War II," www.friendsjournal.org/u-s-conscientious-objectors-world-war-ii (accessed March 20, 2009).
2. James W. Tollefson, *The Strength Not to Fight: An Oral History of Conscientious Objectors of the Vietnam War* (New York: Little, Brown, 1993).
3. Selective Service System. Office of Public and Intergovernmental Affairs, www.sss.gov/FSConsobj.htm (accessed November 23, 2008).
4. "The Conscientious Non-believer," *Time*, January 31, 1964, www.time.com/time/magazine/article/0,9171,897121,00.html (accessed January 18, 2009).
5. *Elliott Ashton Welsh, II, Appellant, v. United States of America, Appellee*, United States Court of Appeals Ninth Circuit, 404 F.2d 1078, September 23, 1968, Rehearing Denied, January 31, 1969, http://cases.justia.com/us-court-of-appeals/F2/404/1078/225130/ (accessed January 18, 2009).
6. "Vietnamization: Lasting Effects on South Vietnam," www.studyworld.com/Vietnamization.htm (accessed January 20, 2009).
7. See, for instance, "Zen Koans and New Recruits," in James Miller, *Democracy Is in the Streets: From Port Huron to the Siege of Chicago* (New York: Simon & Schuster, 1987), 222–6.
8. An additional draft classification was 1-A-O, defined as being conscientiously opposed to training and military service requiring the use of arms but willing to serve in the military in a non-combat role.
9. J. Garry Clifford and Samuel R. Spencer, *First Peacetime Draft* (Lawrence, KS: University Press of Kansas, 1986).
10. Joshua D. Angrist, "The Draft Lottery and Voluntary Enlistment in the Vietnam Era," *Journal of the American Statistical Association*, 86 (1991): 584–95.
11. Charles D. Nelson, *U.S. Marine Riflemen in Vietnam 1965–73* (Oxford: Osprey Publishing, 1998).
12. Michael Useem, *Conscription, Protest and Social Conflict: The Life and Death of a Draft Resistance Movement* (New York: Wiley, 1973).

13. The war underground was a network of individuals providing safe houses for war resisters seeking to evade the draft and in general make their way to Canada to declare asylum. It also connotes radical groups such as the Weather Underground Organization, or Weathermen for short, which actively engaged in sometimes violent acts of war protest, including bombing and other forms of sabotage.
14. Tom Brokaw, *The Greatest Generation* (Random House, New York, 1998).
15. *Welsh v. United States* (398 U.S. 333 (1970); majority opinion of Justice Black.
16. The Peace Abbey Multi-Faith Retreat Center. The National Registry for Conscientious Objection, http://www.peaceabbey.org/confcenter/coregistry.htm (accessed January 19, 2009).
17. "The Veteran's Hour," Vietnam War statistics and exclusive photos, http://www.veteranshour.com/vietnam_war_statistics.htm (accessed October 5, 2008).
18. Joseph Bishop, "Marxist Lecturer Talks on Issues Surrounding Vietnam, Iraq Wars," http://media.www.mainecampus.com/media/storage/paper322/news/2005/11/07.shtml (accessed January 20, 2009). For more on class distinctions in the draft selection process, see James Fallows, "What Did You Do in the Class War, Daddy?" in *The Vietnam Reader*, ed. Walker Capps (London: Routledge, 1991).
19. My own experience is a case in point. I held a bachelor's degree in economics. After being granted CO status and a number of fruitless months of searching for an alternative service post, I was offered a job as a program representative for the Centers for Disease Control in Atlanta, working on the CDC syphilis eradication program in inter-city Atlanta. My offering of that work to my local draft board as alternative service was denied with no formal reason given. The draft board eventually secured a position for me as a nursing orderly at a large community hospital about 250 miles from my hometown.
20. "The Veteran's Hour" (accessed October 5, 2008).
21. Center of Military History, United States Army, Medal of Honor Recipients, World War II (A–F), www.history.army.mil/html/moh/WWII-a-f.html (accessed February 13, 2009).
22. The Selective Service System's "Alternative Service for Conscientious Objectors" is to be found at http://www.sss.gov/FactSheets/FSaltsvc.pdf (accessed September 28, 2008).
23. James Daly and Lee Bergman, *A Hero's Welcome* (New York: Bobbs-Merrill, 1975).
24. Katherine Seelye, "Cheney's Five Deferments during the Vietnam Era Emerge as a Campaign Issue," *New York Times* online, May 1, 2004 (accessed March 29, 2009).
25. James Quay, "Life, Liberty, and the Right to Protest," in Capps, ed., *The Vietnam Reader*, 205–12.

TIMELINE EVENTS

December 26, 1961 – George Fryett, first American POW of the Viet Cong

August 5, 1964 – Everett Alvarez, first American POW of North Vietnam

July 13, 1965 – Isaac Camacho, first successful escape

October 22, 1965 – Fred Cherry, first African American POW of North Vietnam

May 10, 1966 – Jeremiah Denton blinks "torture" in Morse code on television

July 6, 1966 – Hanoi March

Summer 1967 – Broadcast of *Pilots in Pajamas*

October 26, 1967 – John McCain captured

December 31, 1968 – James "Nick" Rowe escapes

February 16, 1969 – First Plantation releases

June 1969 – National League of Families formed

September 3, 1969 – Death of Ho Chi Minh

November 21, 1970 – Son Tay Raid

November–December 1970 – Creation of Camp Unity

February 12 – March 29, 1973 – Operation Homecoming

November 8, 1985 – Creation of the POW medal

Chapter 8

The American POW experience

Glenn Robins

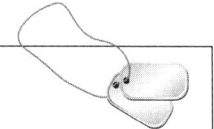

CHAPTER SUMMARY

By some official US government estimates there were slightly less than eight hundred American prisoners of war (POWs) during the Vietnam War, 1961–73. Although the Hanoi Hilton has dominated the popular historical perception of the POW experience in Vietnam, other Northern camps such as the Briarpatch and the Plantation provided unique elements to the POW stories. Similarly, the jungle camps of the South were smaller and held fewer prisoners than the northern camps and offered yet an additional dimension to the POW experience, one that has not been fully appreciated. Thus, the American POW experience has to be studied chronologically as well as geographically within the broader notion that there is no official or master POW narrative.

The first week of March 1965 bore witness to America's increased military involvement in the Vietnam War. On March 2, Operation Rolling Thunder commenced. Lasting three years and nine months, Rolling Thunder became the longest bombing campaign in American military history. On March 8 the first US combat units, the 9th Marine Expeditionary Brigade, arrived at Da Nang. At that time the communists of North Vietnam held three prisoners: Navy Lieutenant (j.g.) Everett Alvarez, who was shot down on August 5, 1964, during Operation Pierce Arrow, the retaliatory strikes for the Gulf of Tonkin incidents; Navy Lieutenant Commander Robert Shuman; and Lieutenant Hayden Lockhart, the first Air Force POW, who had been captured the day Rolling Thunder began. All three men would leave North Vietnam together, on February 12, 1973. Their stories stand in stark contrast to those of American prisoners held by the Viet Cong in South Vietnam, which had started more than three years before that fateful month of March 1965.

THE FIRST POWs OF THE SOUTH

On the day after Christmas 1961, Army Private George Fryett became the first American captured by the Viet Cong. A clerk in the office of the chief of staff at MACV (Military Assistance Command, Vietnam) in Saigon, Fryett, in search of some relaxation, had decided to visit a local swimming pool. While he was riding a bicycle to his destination, two Vietnamese cyclists ambushed him using hand grenades. Fryett suffered shrapnel wounds during the explosion and his attackers quickly subdued him. For the next six months, Fryett endured what has been described as "harsh but not brutal" treatment. "The Viet Cong beat him when he was uncooperative, fed him little, and several times forced him to dig his own grave." He escaped once but was immediately recaptured. The Viet Cong interrogated him, but appeared to follow no routine or system for information gathering. Abruptly, the Viet Cong released Fryett in late June 1962.[1]

Notwithstanding the favorable outcome to Fryett's captivity, the fate of Americans held by the Viet Cong between 1961 and 1964 was anything but predictable. Once prisoners were in enemy hands, the captors quickly prepared them for relocation to a secure prison site. A common practice implemented by the Viet Cong at the time of capture was to remove the prisoners' shoes, thereby exposing their tender bare feet to the coarse jungle terrain as a way of thwarting possible escape attempts. As part of the relocation process the captors often stopped in small villages to display the captured Americans publicly. Some prisoners have described these marches as relatively benign because they were not dragged behind farm animals and were not placed on trial for war crimes. On the basis of his own experience, Army Sergeant George Smith admitted that the villagers "were clearly upset and agitated" at the sight of the American prisoners, but the "closest they came to abuse was when an old woman in one village . . . started hitting" a fellow prisoner. A guard intervened and stopped the incident. Other prisoners did experience humiliating episodes during relocation, such as a group of three POWs who stopped in a small village, where the guards placed them "in the middle of a pigpen filled with pigs" and forced them to eat a meal before a crowd of mocking onlookers. In North Vietnam, staged propaganda scenes would be of a more elaborate nature.[2]

In contrast to the large, mainly urban detention centers of the North, the jungle prison camps of the South were small and typically held no more than six prisoners at a time. Less than a month after his capture, West Point graduate and Army Special Forces adviser Lieutenant "Nick" Rowe arrived at his "first formal prison camp." After being detained in several temporary camps in the Plain of Reeds, a Viet Cong stronghold west of Saigon, Rowe and his fellow prisoners moved southward on an arduous journey into the Ca Mau Peninsula. Their camp was situated in an area regulated by the tidal flow of the Gulf of Siam. At low tide, Rowe could observe a graveyard of "dead and rotting" tree trunks. A log dock and log walkway transported prisoners from an entry canal to the prison compound.

> To the right of the walkway was a small hut serving as a kitchen and mess hall. Just behind it was a storage hut which became Rocky's [Captain Humbert "Rocky" Versace's] first home.

Further down the walk, under the spreading leaves of a thicker clump of trees, were a series of four long, relatively narrow huts, built, as were all the huts, on posts, raising them above the water level. One, for the guards, was beside the walk and the other three were facing it on the other side of a crosswalk. The middle one of these was slightly higher than its companions and had open sides. The other two huts had barred walls and were obviously for prisoners. To the left of the walk, midway between the kitchen and first guard hut, was a single square hut with thatched walls as well as a roof. It was of better construction and housed the cadre.[3]

As for the individual prison cells or, more accurately, cages, they varied in size and construction. Most often constructed of bamboo and thatch, the height, width, and depth of cages could be 10 feet by 8 feet by 10 feet. Or they could be so small that a man only had room to sit up, not enough to stand. Sometimes caves were used as prison cells. When not in their cells, the prisoners had to battle a primitive environment, diseases, and malnutrition. The jungle itself could be a cruel tormentor. The leeches, snakes, fire ants, scorpions, and rats presented daily threats, but the swarms of mosquitoes, which could cover a man's hand or foot in a matter of seconds, exposed the POWs to several strains of malaria. The thick foliage of the massive trees created multiple canopies that concealed the camps from detection and shielded the prisoners from direct sunlight. Thus, during the monsoon seasons the POWs languished in damp or muddied conditions. Their diet consisted of not much more than three cups of rice per day— rice that was often rotting or contaminated with animal feces—and supplemented with manioc, an edible root high in starch content but low in nutritional value. Most of the prisoners developed severe cases of dysentery. Some men defecated fifty to one hundred times a day and were in such a weakened state that they were often unable to reach their jungle latrines. Thus, the camps became cesspools of human excrement. The primitive environment, diseases, and malnutrition contributed to extreme weight loss. During his one and a half years in captivity, Sergeant Isaac Camacho lost 60 pounds, going from 170 to 110 pounds. Sergeant Daniel Pitzer lost 75 pounds and testified that he returned to the United States "with a nutritional disease, permanent damage to my legs . . . and permanent damage from vitamin A deficiency to my right eye."[4]

Despite the poor physical condition of the POWs, the Viet Cong still subjected them to indoctrination sessions. In his memoir, *P.O.W.: Two Years with the Vietcong*, George Smith described the tenor and content of these sessions as well as his interactions with a political cadre member, identified simply as Man With Glasses. "Rather than interrogating me, Man With Glasses gave me a history lesson on Vietnam," Smith explained, "much like a lecture." Man With Glasses covered the French colonial period and the Vietnamese victory at Dien Bien Phu. He revealed a detailed understanding of the 1954 Geneva Accords, emphasizing the stipulations for free and supervised elections. Man With Glasses argued that the United States opposed elections because the Americans knew that Ho Chi Minh would win any election. To forestall the inevitable, the United States had installed the puppet regime of Ngo Dinh Diem, who Man

With Glasses claimed "had spent most of his time in New Jersey . . . while Vietnam was fighting the French." (Diem had in fact been in exile from 1950 until after Dien Bien Phu.) For someone like Smith, who expressed contempt for the US Army prior to his deployment to Vietnam and in his own words "had been captured while guarding Madame Nhu's [the wife of Diem's brother]

Figure 8.1 *American POWs: Edward R. Johnson RA 33510856 from Harrisburg PA, adviser with the 1st Battalion, 31st Regiment, 21st Infantry Division. Captured July 21, 1964, Luc Phi (the town of Vi Thanh) by Liberation Army. Daniel Pitzer, Sergeant RA 24457675.*

Photograph VA009188, no date, Douglas Pike Photograph Collection, The Vietnam Archive, Texas Tech University.

goddamned sugar mill—while her own soldiers in the mill hadn't fired a shot," Man With Glasses made a compelling case.[5]

Of the twenty-five Americans captured by the Viet Cong from December 1961 to December 1964, four of the five civilians died in captivity or were killed. Of the twenty-one servicemen, the Viet Cong released nine prior to 1967 and killed five; four died in captivity, and two escaped. The remaining POW of this initial group was Army Captain Floyd "Jim" Thompson. Captured by the Viet Cong on March 26, 1964, and later transferred to the North, Thompson's release did not come until March 16, 1973. His nearly nine years in captivity made him the longest-held prisoner of war in American military history.[6]

TORTURE ERA OF THE NORTH

No pilots were shot down over North Vietnam between Operation Pierce Arrow on August 5, 1964, and the beginning of Operation Rolling Thunder on March 2, 1965. The intensification of the bombing campaign naturally increased the number of American prisoners in North Vietnam. By the end of 1965, sixty-three airmen had been captured. In almost every instance the North Vietnamese had transported the POWs to Hanoi for initial processing. However, before completing their rendezvous with hell, the prisoners became part of North Vietnam's evolving propaganda campaign.[7]

One of the most common propaganda rituals was the public gauntlet. Historically, the gauntlet functioned as a type of prison initiation ritual in which the captors formed two lines and armed themselves with sticks, rocks, or assorted weapons. Then the captors forced the captives to run between the two lines, exposing themselves to physical harm. More than a mere exercise in intimidation, the gauntlet served the political purpose of unifying the North Vietnamese people in their war with the United States by publicly displaying those responsible for the bombing raids.

Local militia captured Navy pilot Lieutenant Commander Cole Black on June 21, 1966, making him the ninety-fifth shoot-down. "One elder of the village" impressed Black because "he seemed to command a great deal of respect," and when the elder approached Black, the other villagers backed away and cleared a path to the prisoner. "He looked at me," Black recalled, "and said in almost perfect English, 'war is hell.'" Eventually, the militia turned Black over to the regular army, but before the transfer was completed, a militiaman entered the room, held up Black's survival knife, and the other hand was held up and open. Black interpreted the gesture to mean that he was the fifth American captured by the village. After the exchange the villagers "had a big celebration" with a "big sack of rice" that they received as a reward for the captured airman. On the way to Hanoi the guards stopped twice to "display" the prisoner. On the first occasion, they stopped at a "woodsy place" and after a moment "marched back into the woods," turned around, and walked straight back to the original spot. The entire incident lasted only a few minutes, but when they returned, Black realized that four jeeps had been set up to provide lighting for a camera. He concluded that the North Vietnamese staged the scene in order "to show a picture of the young heroic Vietnamese boy and girl capturing the American air pirate. That was their means of making a piece of propaganda."[8]

As the North Vietnamese communists transitioned from the First to the Second Indochina War, they utilized a pragmatic Strategy of People's War that incorporated the new American adversary and linked the past with the present. According to Ho Chi Minh's biographer William Duiker, the "strategy offered useful lessons on how diplomacy and the techniques of psychological warfare could supplement revolutionary violence in countering the military advantages of a more powerful adversary."[9] Success in the Second Indochina War depended on the Communist Party's ability to garner the support of all North Vietnamese people, both military and civilian, and to cultivate military–civilian unity. Furthermore, as America's role in the war escalated, party leaders downplayed the importance of modern weapons and instead celebrated the "decisive role of man" in war.[10] These staged gauntlet episodes represented a valuable component of North Vietnam's internal or domestic propaganda program.

Virtually every early captive in the North has admitted that two keys to survival and resistance were the establishment of communication techniques and a chain of command system. With respect to prisoner communication, no one played a greater role than Air Force Captain Carlyle "Smitty" Harris. The sixth pilot captured in the North, on April 4, 1965, Harris arrived at the Hanoi Hilton the next day. As Harris recalled during a television interview after the release of all POWs,

> from the very beginning the North Vietnamese tried to prevent us from communicating with each other. They went to almost insane efforts to keep us from even seeing another American by putting up blinds and when we went out to pick up our food or dump our [waste] bucket there was no way we could see another American.

Joking that the Morse Code was not an option because "the only tools we had were our knuckles and a bare wall and it's really tough to send a dash with the knuckle," Harris explained the introduction of the "tap code," which he had picked up during survival training at Stead Air Force Base in Nevada.[11]

The tap code consisted of a 5 by 5 matrix of the alphabet minus the letter K, with C representing both C and K:

A	B	C	D	E
F	G	H	I	J
L	M	N	O	P
Q	R	S	T	U
V	W	X	Y	Z

> A prisoner could tap out or spell on the prison walls a message based on the arrangement of the letters in the matrix. The first tap or taps signified the location of the letter in the horizontal rows and the second signified the location in the vertical rows. For example, 2-3, 1-1, 4-2, 4-2, 4-3 spelled H—A—R—R—I—S.

The tap code could be transmitted by coughs, shuffling feet, or whisking brooms. Prisoners used the tap code to compile a list of names of all captives, to offer encouragement to one another, to announce policies, or simply to pass the time. The military's propensity to use acronyms and abbreviations facilitated communications. Most importantly, the tap code was used to inform prisoners about interrogation techniques and convey strategies for coping with torture. In addition to the tap code, POWs used a form of sign language to communicate, used cigarette ash, bamboo slivers, and toilet tissue as pen and paper, and scratched messages on the bottom of plates and cups. They even discovered that they "could talk directly through a brick and mortar wall eighteen or more inches thick" by pressing a "tin cup up against the wall" and covering their heads with blankets "to muffle" the conversation. In a bizarre twist of fate the Vietnamese policy of shuffling prisoners "from cell to cell and camp to camp," in an effort to disrupt group solidarity, actually spread vital information and communication techniques.[12]

Coinciding with the development of various forms of communication, the early shoot-downs in the North quickly formulated a chain of command, and four men stand out for their decisive leadership. In order of capture, they were Air Force Major Lawrence Guarino, Navy Commanders Jeremiah Denton and James Stockdale, and Air Force Lieutenant Colonel Robinson "Robbie" Risner. Following the dictates of the military Code of Conduct, the four men worked through the process of establishing who was the senior ranking officer (SRO) and "decided to base seniority on rank at the time of shootdown." During the years 1965–70, the SRO and his executive assistants interpreted the Code of Conduct and set the policies for resistance and responding to torture.[13]

One of the most common and most feared forms of torture used by the North Vietnamese was the so-called ropes treatment. Captors tightly bound the prisoner's arms behind his back and cinched the wrists and elbows together with rope or nylon cords from parachutes. The pressure from the ropes immediately began to cut off blood circulation in the arms and hands. Then, as Air Force Captain Konrad Trautman explained, the interrogators would

> take the strap and pull the arms up, up your back, to the back of your head . . . imagine this with both arms tied tight together—elbow to elbow, wrist to wrist—and then using the leverage of his feet planted between your shoulder blades, with both hands, he pulls with all his might, 'til your arms are up and back over your head, forcing your head down between your feet, where your legs are between iron bars.

These unnatural contortions obstructed the windpipe and impeded the breathing. The pain and lack of air made it "difficult to even maintain a bit of rationale," and nausea also set in, producing fits of the dry heaves. Sometimes, Trautman added, "after about 10 or 15 minutes" the pressure of the ropes was so tight that the upper body could become "numb." Breathing was "still difficult, but the pain is gone." Trautman called this interlude a strange "blessing." However, bringing a prisoner out of the ropes produced a sadistic irony because "the procedure works *completely* in reverse . . . the same pain coming out . . . as you did going in." Some POWs have remarked that the pain was more intense coming out of the ropes.[14]

Obviously, interrogators desired classified and non-classified military information such as unit locations, bombing targets, and aircraft capabilities. However, the North Vietnamese interrogators also utilized an institutionalized program of torture to obtain confessions to war crimes and autobiographical statements. In short, POWs were forced to admit that they were not prisoners of war but war criminals, to denounce South Vietnam as a puppet of the US imperialists, and acknowledge their receipt of humane and lenient treatment. "The North Vietnamese game plan was very simple," explained Navy Captain Jeremiah Denton, "they brought the full power of the system to bear on one objective: break our will." The

Figure 8.2 "The Vietnamese Rope Trick."

Page 79 of John McGrath, *Prisoner of War Six Years in Hanoi* (Annapolis, Maryland: Naval Institute Press, 1975).

Annapolis-educated aviator related the communist strategy to the Clausewitzian principle "war is an act of violence to break the enemy's will." Because of the "guilt" associated with compliance, Denton believed that any statement or admission "had high value for them . . . [and] the highest value was the destruction of our organization." The forced confessions and autobiographies also created a dilemma for POWs because of their apparent violation of the Code of Conduct. This dilemma cannot be understood adequately without placing it within the proper historical context.[15]

The Cold War hysteria generated by Senator Joseph McCarthy and the tarnished legacy of American POWs of the Korean War formed the context for the development of the military Code of Conduct. The number of American soldiers held in captivity, first under the supervision of the North Koreans and later by the Chinese, exceeded 7,000. Of that number, 2,700, or roughly 40 percent, died in captivity, the highest percentage of POW deaths in any American war. The high death rate, along with the decision of twenty-one Americans to refuse repatriation during the prisoner exchange program, generated concern regarding the performance of American POWs during the Korean War. Critics charged that the twenty-one defectors had been brainwashed during indoctrination sessions. They also charged that a disturbing number of POWs had been cooperative during indoctrination sessions and had expended little effort in attempting to escape, and explained the high death rate as a function of personal weakness. In assigning blame, critics argued that "the nation's homes, schools, and churches had failed" to instill in its young men the "traditional American values of patriotism" and masculine toughness.[16]

Although Department of Defense (DOD) studies subsequently found that the Korean War POWs had acquitted themselves well, concluding that most of the POW deaths were a consequence of brutal forced marches and extreme malnutrition, the myth of failure persisted. With the blessing of President Dwight D. Eisenhower, the DOD appointed an eleven-man committee that ultimately produced the Code of Conduct:

THE CODE OF CONDUCT

I

I am an American, fighting in the forces which guard my country and our way of life. I am prepared to give my life in their defense.

II

I will never surrender of my own free will. If in command, I will never surrender the members of my command while they still have the means to resist.

> **III**
> If I am captured, I will continue to resist by all means available. I will make every effort to escape and aid others to escape. I will accept neither parole nor special favors from the enemy.
>
> **IV**
> If I become a prisoner of war, I will keep faith with my fellow prisoners. I will give no information or take part in any action which might be harmful to my comrades. If I am senior, I will take command. If not, I will obey the lawful orders of those appointed over me, and will back them up in every way.
>
> **V**
> When questioned, should I become a prisoner of war, I am required to give only name, rank, service number, and date of birth. I will evade answering further questions to the utmost of my ability. I will make no oral or written statements disloyal to my country and its allies or harmful to their cause.
>
> **VI**
> I will never forget that I am an American, fighting for freedom, responsible for my actions, and dedicated to the principles which made my country free. I will trust in my God and in the United States of America.

If interpreted literally, the six articles would have set unrealistic expectations for American service personnel held in enemy hands. Thus, the SRO and his executive assistants formulated the standards for resistance and interpreted the Code of Conduct for all POWs.

One of the first decisions made by the senior officers concerned the acceptable responses to interrogation. To a man, former prisoners of war conceded that everyone had a breaking point. Moreover, any interrogator, given enough time and with no restrictions on interrogation methods, could extract a statement from a POW. Except for vital military information, senior officers instructed their fellow prisoners to resist to a point short of permanent bodily harm before making a statement. Following a confession, an interregnum would ensue and the seniors' policy was for the prisoner to "bounce back," a call to reclaim their honor and manhood and prepare to resist, to the utmost of their individual ability, the next round of interrogation.[17]

A more formalized and comprehensive strategy for resistance appeared in early 1967, known by the acronym BACK US:

B—Bowing. Do not bow in public, either under camera surveillance or where nonprison observers were present.
A—Air. Stay off the air. Make no broadcasts or recordings.
C—Crimes. Admit to no "crimes," avoid using the word in coerced confessions.
K—Kiss. Do not kiss the Vietnamese goodbye, meaning show no gratitude, upon release.
US—Unity over Self.

The mindset behind these instructions was not to appear submissive but rather to devise ways to exert resistance and non-compliance. Concepts A and C emphasized the need to avoid being part of the North Vietnamese propaganda program. Because of the constant shuffling of POWs, the BACK US program was disseminated throughout the North Vietnamese prison system. Despite the severity and inhumanity of the torture era, BACK US provided much-needed guidance and helped prisoners cope emotionally with the consequences of being tortured.[18]

Adherence to the Code of Conduct became even more difficult as the North Vietnamese failed to follow the dictates of the Geneva Convention. Following World War II the International Committee of the Red Cross (ICRC) drafted a new agreement to replace the 1929 Geneva Convention. Interestingly, the Korean War had commenced before any nation had ratified the 1949 agreement. Hence, the Vietnam War "presented the first test" of the new convention.[19]

Aside from the expectation of humane treatment and prohibitions against "physical mutilation" or "medical or scientific experiments of any kind" (Article 13), the 1949 Geneva Convention afforded prisoners of war a number of important protections. Accordingly, POWs were entitled to know the geographical location of their place of confinement (Article 23), and restrictions existed to preclude prisoners from being forcibly segregated from their fellow prisoners (Article 22). The convention required food and water rations sufficient to maintain proper nutritional health (Article 26). In addition, prisoners held the right to correspond with family members and register with an international prisoner agency within a week of captivity (Article 70). Finally, prisoners were authorized to select a representative who would speak on their behalf before prison officials and who carried the authority to make formal complaints regarding their treatment and conditions of their captivity (Articles 78–80).[20]

In addition, Articles 82–108 specifically covered the procedures and regulations for prosecuting prisoners of war for war crimes. The conventions required that prisoners of war receive at least three weeks' prior notice to any judicial proceeding, and be allowed qualified representation (Article 105). Also, POWs could appeal any ruling (Article 106). Even if a trial produced a guilty verdict, Article 85 specified that "prisoners of war prosecuted under the laws of the Detaining Power for acts committed prior to capture shall retain, even if convicted, the benefits of the present convention." Moreover, Article 89 provided that "in no case shall disciplinary punishments be inhuman, brutal or dangerous to the health of prisoners of war."[21]

Although the government of Ho Chi Minh ratified the 1949 Geneva Convention in 1957, Hanoi filed an important "reservation" at the time regarding its view of Article 85. The North Vietnamese position read:

> The Democratic Republic of Vietnam declares that prisoners of war prosecuted for and convicted of war crimes or crimes against humanity, in accordance with the principles established by the Nuremberg Tribunal, will not enjoy the benefits of the provisions of the present Convention as provided in Article 85.

The delegation representing the Soviet Union had submitted a similar objection at the diplomatic convention that drafted the original articles.[22] The precedents for the prosecution of war crimes established at Nuremberg, and also during the Tokyo war crimes trials, had a particular appeal to the North Vietnamese communists during the Vietnam conflict. Indeed, between September 1965 and July 1966 the government of Ho Chi Minh revealed its intention to place American prisoners of war on trial for war crimes. In addition to frequent broadcasts over Hanoi Radio, various news outlets reported that the North Vietnamese had notified the Egyptian foreign minister as well as Czechoslovakian diplomats of impending trials.

On July 6, 1966, fifty-two POWs (sixteen from a camp called the Briarpatch and another thirty-six from the Zoo) participated in what became known as the Hanoi March. Upon arriving in the Northern capital, the POWs quickly learned that unless they publicly renounced their role in the American military effort, they would be tried and executed as war criminals. Paired and handcuffed, the POWs formed two long columns; the distance between each pair was roughly ten feet. The guards then instructed the POWs to bow their heads as a sign of contrition and respect, and to march through a throng of Vietnamese people, some of whom had gathered in bleachers or reviewing stands. Uncertain as to what to expect, the Americans stood firm and held their heads high. Slowly but progressively, men, women, and even children filtered into the procession of prisoners; pandemonium ensued. Indeed, the crowd completely engulfed the two columns of prisoners, and the guards clearly lost control of the staged event. One POW was clubbed in the head, another in the groin; another was kicked in the testicles; and it appeared that several prisoners were on the verge of being beaten to death. In a panicked reaction the guards tried to shield the prisoners from the enraged mob.[23]

The POWs fought their way through a two-mile-long gauntlet that lasted for nearly an hour, escaping with their lives when they reached the safety of one of the city's stadiums. Amazingly, the international media had captured the entire ordeal, and for once world opinion worked against the North Vietnamese. From the floor of the US Senate the junior senator from New York, Robert F. Kennedy, made these remarks:

> I have dissented at many points from this war and its conduct. But I am at one with all Americans in regarding any reprisals against these young men and indirectly against their families, as an intolerable act—contrary to the laws of war, contrary to all past practices in this war, a plunge into barbarism which could serve the interest of no man and no nation.[24]

The North Vietnamese abandoned the idea of a war crimes tribunal, but the torture era continued.

Figure 8.3 *American POWs who participated in the Hanoi March were surrounded by hostile crowds and were punched, kicked, and cursed.*

BEYOND THE HILTON

The North Vietnamese operated a total of fifteen camps over the course of the war. Most of the camps were in Hanoi or just outside the city; however, there were several camps well beyond the capital's boundaries. Each camp, for various reasons, added new dimensions to the POW experience. In late August 1965 the North Vietnamese opened the Briarpatch, located some thirty-five miles west of Hanoi in a remote mountainous region near Xom Ap Lo. The following description of the Briarpatch is based on a study conducted in 1974 by thirty-five former Vietnam POWs while assigned to the Air War College at Maxwell Air Force Base. Perhaps the most primitive of the Northern camps, the Briarpatch had no electricity and the "inside walls of the cells were dabbed with cement and painted with muddy water which gave them a cave-like appearance." The POWs constantly battled poor sanitation and meager rations. Rats, mosquitoes, ants, and cockroaches infested the cells, and "a mosquito net was necessary for survival." In April 1966 the North Vietnamese constructed a bath area for prisoners, but the Briarpatch officials gave prisoners only "ten minutes to draw water from the well, wash clothes, [and] bathe." Although the North Vietnamese attempted to boil drinking water, it was often "murky, very greasy, and tasted of wood smoke." The POWs consumed a diet comprising rice, greasy pumpkin soup, and "occasionally a piece of hairy pork fat," as well as three cigarettes per day. The Briarpatch was one of the few Northern prisons where POWs suffered from malnutrition.[25]

The entire camp, including prison cells, consisted of nine brick huts. Despite the compact logistical nature of the camp, the North Vietnamese were committed to keeping prisoners isolated from one another. As a result, POW organization and communication were limited. Fortunately, the captives at the Briarpatch had received instructions on resistance strategies while at their earlier places of confinement. During indoctrination and interrogation sessions the North Vietnamese used various torture methods such as the ropes and punishment stools, as well as sleep, food, and water deprivation. In seeking biographical and military information, the North Vietnamese prepared a questionnaire of "approximately twenty pages in length." The captors placed propaganda materials in the cells, including the *Vietnam Courier*, an English-language communist news weekly. In April 1966 the North Vietnamese installed a public address system "powered by a gasoline generator" and broadcast indoctrination lessons about the four-thousand-year history of Vietnam and its struggle for independence.[26]

Security at the Briarpatch was extremely tight, and increasingly so after early August 1966. The camp was within two miles of a North Vietnamese military complex; the complex was a frequent bombing target of US planes. Concern over a possible camp bombing prompted the North Vietnamese to dig "a series of six-feet deep trenches" as a type of bomb shelter or foxhole, and they made special preparations so that they could evacuate the prisoners at a moment's notice. As a result, the POWs had their hands "loosely cuffed" behind their backs each day "from the end of the morning meal [at dawn] until the second meal [at dusk] was served." After three weeks the captors replaced the cuffs with "short ropes," and late in September 1966 the North Vietnamese allowed the ropes to "be worn on one arm like a bracelet," a practice that continued until the camp closed. The North Vietnamese also used these camp evacuation preparations as part of their torture rituals, forcing bound and blindfolded POWs to sit "for several days" in the damp, dirty, rodent-infested trenches before taking them to interrogation sessions. More than fifty Americans spent time at the Briarpatch. In early February 1967 the camp closed, presumably because of severe water shortages, and the POWs were sent to the Little Vegas complex at the Hilton or on to the Zoo.[27]

Opened in early summer 1967, the prison camp known as the Plantation served as a place of detention but also as a stage for propaganda. Situated just outside of Hanoi, the two-acre Plantation had been the domicile of the capital city's colonial mayor. Navy Lieutenant Commander John S. McCain, who spent two years at the facility, described its physical features in one of his memoirs, *Faith of My Fathers*. A large mansion, which the POWs called "the Big House," served as the place of "initial interrogation" and a receiving area for visiting delegations. The POWs were held in cells in warehouse-like structures that encircled the Big House. "The cells in the Plantation were large compared to those at other prisons," McCain recalled, "mine was approximately fifteen by fifteen feet. Each cell had a wooden board for a bed and a naked light bulb dangling on a cord in the center of the ceiling." The North Vietnamese kept the light on twenty-four hours a day as a form of harassment. McCain also recalled that "the building's tin roof . . . must have increased the summer heat by ten or more degrees," and the boarded windows stifled both ventilation and communication.[28]

The North Vietnamese designated the Plantation with the specific intent of producing and disseminating propaganda. In the summer of 1967 the North Vietnamese used an East German film company to produce *Pilots in Pajamas*. The documentary portrayed the prisoners living in clean rooms with ready access to showers, reading rooms, and an adequate diet. Staged scenes showed the POWs sweeping the grounds, exercising, and digging foxholes for protection during a potential air raid. A four-hour version of the film played "on East German television over four nights and later, in an abbreviated one-hour version, in the United States." Office of the Secretary of Defense Historians Stuart I. Rochester and Frederick Kiley called *Pilots in Pajamas* "one of the major propaganda coups of the war."[29] Additional propaganda successes occurred in 1968 and 1969 when the North Vietnamese released nine prisoners, in three separate incidents, as a show of goodwill.

The first took place on 16 February 1968 when three prisoners received a "red-carpet sendoff . . . in front of a pack of foreign newsmen, [Communist] party officials, and distinguished guests as a battery of cameras and taping devices recorded the proceedings." As part of their release, each prisoner expressed their thanks to their captors for the humane and lenient treatment and expressed remorse over the war. The prisoners were then placed in "the custody of peace activists Daniel Berrigan and Howard Zinn." The other two releases followed a similar format. These early releases violated policies set by the SROs, which stated that the order of release would be sick and injured first, then enlisted personnel, and the remaining officers by order of shoot-down. Only one POW, Navy apprentice seaman Douglas Hegdahl, had the permission of the seniors to accept early release. Hegdhal, who was captured when the concussion from the guns on the USS *Canberra* knocked him overboard during a night bombardment, possessed an incredible memory. He could "recite the Gettysburg Address forward and backward," and he was ordered home because he had memorized the names of his fellow prisoners and other valuable information.[30]

Excepting Hegdahl, the release of the other eight POWs caused a great deal of resentment, anger, and demoralization among the remaining prisoners. In his National War College thesis, published less than thirteen months after the release of all POWs from Hanoi, then Commander John S. McCain described the early releases as "evil." He maintained that the communists had been successful, in part, because they "used the promise or prospect of parole" to entice cooperation from POWs. The North Vietnamese also used paroles as a way to incite competition between POWs, who sought to gain special favors or early release. McCain defined special favors as anything—whether it was exercise activity, receipt of letters and packages, or even the opportunity to draw pictures—that was not available to all prisoners. As a hard-line resister, McCain worried about the "favorable publicity and propaganda value" that these actions afforded the North Vietnamese communists. He even chastised the US government for not publicly advocating the SROs' policy on early releases, calling the US peace negotiators' response to the propaganda releases "inexcusable."[31] By almost any standard the North Vietnamese succeeded quite well in exploiting the Plantation for propaganda purposes and delivered a sharp blow to the psyche of the American prisoners held at the camp.

Figure 8.4 POWs meeting with Canadian journalists. The communists tortured POWs into behaving well for visitors, who would then report that the prisoners were being cared for adequately. Visits to Hanoi by American anti-war activists, including Jane Fonda, Tom Hayden, and Daniel Berrigan, added to POW suffering.

US Air Force.

In July 1970 the North Vietnamese closed the Plantation and reassigned the prisoners to the Zoo, the Hilton complex, and other camps.

THE POWs AND THE HOME FRONT

In response to the prisoner of war issue in Vietnam, the administration of President Lyndon B. Johnson believed that the humane treatment and the eventual release of POWs would be more easily achieved by not condemning publicly the North Vietnamese government. Conflicted and uncertain over America's war aims and military strategy, Johnson struggled with the press, suffered some intense criticism, and never fully marshaled the country behind the war effort.

One consequence of his general failure with the media was that he never rallied public support for the POWs. The administration of President Richard M. Nixon abandoned Johnson's "quiet diplomacy" and initiated the "Go Public" campaign in the spring of 1969. The goals of the Go Public campaign were to obtain a complete list of POWs in captivity, the release of infirmed prisoners, third-party inspections of prison camps, and compliance with the Geneva Convention. The Nixon administration also encouraged individual citizens and private organizations to promote the objectives of the Go Public campaign.[32]

The largest of the family-led organizations was the National League of Families of American Prisoners and Missing in Southeast Asia (NLOF). The group, comprising primarily the wives of prisoners, formed in June 1969, incorporated in May 1970, and opened a national headquarters in Washington, DC, in June 1970. Local branches in military communities such as Norfolk and Virginia Beach on the east coast and San Diego on the west coast were vital components of the NLOF's work. The original leaders of the NLOF were Sybil Stockdale, first chair of the board of directors, and Iris R. Powers, first full-time national coordinator. Louise Mulligan and Jane Denton were very active members, as were Doris Day, Anne Purcell, Maureen Dunn, Phyllis Galanti, and Valerie Kushner. NLOF representatives met, or attempted to meet, with North Vietnamese representatives in Paris on several occasions. The Texas businessman and US Naval Academy graduate H. Ross Perot sponsored one of the largest NLOF visits, which took place in December 1969 when fifty-eight wives and ninety-four children boarded *The Spirit of Christmas*, bound for Paris. Only three wives were allowed to meet with the four-member North Vietnamese delegation; they produced no concessions. Members of the NLOF also testified before the US Congress on several occasions.[33]

In *Love and Duty*, Anne Purcell, wife of Colonel Benjamin H. Purcell, the highest-ranking Army officer held in captivity during the Vietnam War, describes the various activities organized through the NLOF in Columbus, Georgia. "Several times each month," Purcell explains, "we would set up tables at shopping centers, at Fort Benning, at fairs, and at conventions, from which we could distribute bumper stickers, buttons, and information leaflets." Bumper sticker messages included "POWs Never Have a Nice Day," "Don't Let Them Be Forgotten," and "Free POWs in Hanoi." They urged supporters to write letters and send petitions to North Vietnamese representatives demanding that prisoners be treated in accord with the Geneva Convention and that agreements be reached for the release of all prisoners.[34]

In May 1970, Voices in Vital America (VIVA) began developing one of the most enduring popular culture symbols of the entire war, the POW bracelet. Each bracelet contained the name, rank, and date of loss of a POW or MIA (person missing in action), and people wore them as an expression of concern and commitment, and vowing not to remove the bracelet until the POW was released or the MIA accounted for. Celebrities who publicly wore the bracelets included Billy Graham, Bill Cosby, Bob Hope, Cher and Sonny Bono, and Princess Grace of Monaco. At $2.50 for nickel-plated bracelets and $3.00 for copper bracelets, VIVA raised millions of dollars for the POW/MIA cause.[35]

THE FINAL YEARS

A confluence of events between September 1969 and November 1970 radically reshaped the captivity experience of both Northern and Southern prisoners. The first took place on September 3, 1969, the day Ho Chi Minh died. Prisoners recalled that their guards openly wept and the entire nation mourned the loss of their leader. For reasons not fully known, prisoner treatment improved dramatically following the death of Ho Chi Minh, and, most importantly, the systematic program of torture came to an end. To be sure, hard-line resisters, SROs, and new shoot-downs experienced some episodes of torture and severe abuse, but the propaganda-driven reign of terror came to an end. Also, on November 21, 1970, the US military launched Operation Ivory Coast, a daring but unsuccessful attempt to rescue POWs at the Son Tay Prison Camp. In the aftermath of the Son Tay Raid, North Vietnam enacted a prisoner consolidation program that moved POWs from two camps, Camp Faith and the Zoo, to a reconfigured Hanoi Hilton. With nearly 350 prisoners in a single camp, the Americans began referring to the prison as Camp Unity. The POWs now found themselves in much larger rooms, with as many as thirty to sixty roommates. The close quarters made sleeping arrangements difficult, and the toilet facilities produced some rather obnoxious odors. Still, the reuniting of old friends and the certainty of companionship more than made up for the inconveniences. To pass the time and to feed their minds after years of deprivation, the POWs devised a number of educational classes. Prisoners who possessed advanced college training or just personal expertise conducted classes in history, political science, foreign languages, business, and even music.

Coinciding with the changes in the North, American prisoners of war in the South embarked on a new era in their captivity experience. For most of the 1960s the number of prisoners captured in the South remained relatively small, averaging twenty-five per year from 1963 to 1967. Although nearly 100 Americans had been captured by the end of 1967, escape, release, and death had reduced their numbers to just twenty-five remaining in captivity.[36] As one Southern POW suggested, they had been "transformed [from] civilized human beings into primal animals struggling to cling to some fleeting sense of what it means to be alive, and why. . . . At best, it was a half-life."[37] The 1968 Tet Offensive added another seventy-five prisoners to the total number in the South. A piecemeal effort commenced, as early as late summer 1968, to transfer most of the Southern POWs to the North, to give Hanoi greater control over the prisoner of war issue. The process of forced marches took more than three years to complete. Some POWs went to Skid Row, five miles southwest of Hanoi; some went to Farnsworth, eighteen miles southwest of Hanoi; and another contingent moved to the Plantation. These camps were a radical departure from the jungle camps of the South.

A very candid discussion of these differences appears in Frank Anton's memoir *Why Didn't You Get Me Out?*. Warrant Officer Anton, an Army helicopter pilot, had been captured during the time of the Tet Offensive and had spent time with the "Kushner group." The Kushner group, named after senior officer Captain Floyd Kushner, an Army medical doctor, endured some of the most extreme hardships of any POW group during the entire war. Variously numbered at between ten and twenty, and the largest contingent of Southern POWs, the Kushner group suffered a death rate of nearly 50 percent. Anton acknowledged that the early Northern captives had undergone "dehumanizing confinement" and had been "tortured unmercifully." However, Anton contended that "such barbarity was not the norm by the time I had arrived in Hanoi in August 1971." For prisoners in both North and South, the final years of captivity were primarily years of waiting.[38]

On January 27, 1973, the Paris Peace Agreement outlined the conditions for the release of American POWs. In total, 591 POWs returned to the United States as part of Operation Homecoming. Beginning on February 12, 1973, 116 prisoners departed Hanoi for Clark Air Force Base in the Philippines, where they began the debriefing process and underwent medical examinations. From there the POWs returned to various military bases in the United States before making the final journey home. There would be three more releases that followed this pattern, the last on March 29, 1973.[39]

CONCLUSION

The American POW experience in Vietnam varied according to region of captivity and date of capture. Of the nearly 600 POWs released during Operation Homecoming, slightly more than 100 had spent time in the South, and yet their experiences have been neglected by most students of the Vietnam War. In terms of sheer survival, the POWs in South Vietnam confronted a mortality rate of 20 percent, as compared to 5 percent for those held in North Vietnam. The only successful escapes, approximately two dozen, occurred in the South.

Even the basic profile—rank and branch of service—of Southern and Northern prisoners differed. For the most part, POWs in the South were enlisted men and non-commissioned officers, with only a few commissioned officers, who served in the Army or Marines. In contrast, most of the POWs in the North consisted of commissioned officer aviators who served in the Air Force or Navy. Prior to September 1969, American POWs confronted a hellish existence, whether in the jungle pestilence of the South or the torture chambers of the North. During the latter years of captivity the work of the National League of Families and the Go Public Campaign helped define the American POWs as the gallant heroes of a tragic war. In many respects the American POW experience in Vietnam was not a singular narrative, but a mosaic of stories, as complex as the war itself.

DISCUSSION QUESTIONS

1. What were the defining characteristics of the Southern POW experience?
2. What were the defining characteristics of the Northern POW experience?

3. How did the North Vietnamese use the POWs for propaganda purposes?
4. How did the POW experience change from 1969 to 1970?
5. What is the legacy of American POWs of the Vietnam War?

SUGGESTED READING

Anton, Frank. *Why Didn't You Get Me Out? Betrayal in the Viet Cong Death Camps*. Arlington, Texas: Summit, 1997.
Doyle, Robert C. *Voices of Captivity: Interpreting the American POW Narrative*. Lawrence: University Press of Kansas, 1994.
Franklin, H. Bruce. *M.I.A. or Mythmaking in America: How and Why the Belief in Live POWs Has Possessed the Nation*. New Brunswick, NJ: Rutgers University Press, 1993.
Gargus, John. *The Son Tay Raid: American POWs in Vietnam Were Not Forgotten*. College Station: Texas A&M University Press, 2007.
Grant, Zalin. *Survivors: American POWs in Vietnam*. New York: W. W. Norton, 1975.
Hirsch, James S.. *Two Souls Indivisible: The Friendship That Saved Two POWs in Vietnam*. Boston: Houghton Mifflin, 2004.
Howes, Craig. *Voices of the Vietnam POWs: Witnesses to Their Fight*. New York: Oxford University Press, 1993.
Johnson, Sam, and Jan Winebrenner. *Captive Warriors: A Vietnam POW's Story*. College Station: Texas A&M University Press, 1992.
Norman, Geoffrey. *Bouncing Back: How a Heroic Band of POWs Survived Vietnam*. Boston: Houghton Mifflin, 1990.
Philpott, Tom. *Glory Denied: The Saga of Jim Thompson, America's Longest Held Prisoner of War*. New York: W. W. Norton, 2001.
Purcell, Ben, and Anne Purcell, *Love and Duty*. Clarksville, GA: The Patriotism Foundation, 2006.

NOTES

1. Stuart I. Rochester and Frederick Kiley, *Honor Bound: The History of American Prisoners of War in Southeast Asia, 1961–1973* (Washington, DC: Office of the Secretary of Defense, 1998), 60–1.
2. George E. Smith, *P.O.W.: Two Years with the Vietcong* (Berkeley, CA: Ramparts Press, 1971), 78; Donald L. Price, *The First Marine Captured in Vietnam: A Biography of Donald G. Cook* (Jefferson, NC: McFarland, 2007), 129–31.
3. James N. Rowe, *Five Years to Freedom* (Boston: Little, Brown, 1971), 99.
4. *American Prisoners of War in Southeast Asia, 1971*, Hearings before the House of Foreign Affairs Subcommittee on National Security Policy and Scientific Development, Ninety-second Congress, First Session, Part 2, 49–63, http://www.vietnam.ttu.edu/star/images/220/2201904005a.pdf.
5. Smith, *P.O.W.*, 121–32.
6. Rochester and Kiley, *Honor Bound*, 60, 81.
7. Ibid., 156.
8. Commander Cole Black interview, no. 560, Andersonville, GA, National Historic Site.

9. William J. Duiker, "Ho Chi Minh and the Strategy of People's War," in *The First Vietnam War: Colonial Conflict and Cold War Crisis*, ed. Mark Atwood Lawrence and Fredrik Logevall (Cambridge, MA: Harvard University Press, 2008), 173.
10. William S. Turley, "Civil–Military Relations in North Vietnam," *Asian Survey* 9 (December 1969): 890–1.
11. Carlyle Harris television interview transcript, pp. 8–9, McCain Library and Archives, University of Southern Mississippi, Hattiesburg, MS.
12. Ibid., 9–12.
13. Rochester and Kiley, *Honor Bound*, 135–40.
14. Stephen A. Rowan, *They Wouldn't Let Us Die: The Prisoners Tell Their Story* (Middle Village, NY: Jonathan David, 1973), 44–6.
15. Jeremiah Denton, *When Hell Was in Session* (1976; reprint, Mobile, AL: Traditional Press, 1982), 101–2.
16. Lori Lyn Bogle, *The Pentagon's Battle for the American Mind: The Early Cold War*, College Station: Texas A&M University Press, 2004), 119–24.
17. For a comprehensive look at the bounce back concept as it impacted Navy lieutenant commanders Al Stafford and Richard Stratton, see *Bouncing Back*. Their captivity narratives also overlap that of John McCain on several occasions. Geoffrey Norman, *Bouncing Back: How a Heroic Band of POWs Survived Vietnam* (Boston: Houghton Mifflin, 1990).
18. For a concise but informative review of the three policy stages and the interpretive dilemmas regarding the Code of Conduct, see Craig Howes, *Voices of Vietnam POWs: Witness to Their Fight* (New York: Oxford University Press, 1993), 20–32; Rochester and Kiley, *Honor Bound*, 298.
19. *The Prisoner of War Problem*, study prepared for Ninety-first Congress, Second Session, by the American Enterprise Institute, December 28, 1970, 15–17.
20. Ibid., 7–10. Quoted material is the actual language in the Geneva Convention, 7–10.
21. Ibid., 10–11, 18.
22. Ibid., 19–23.
23. An excellent account of the Hanoi March can be found in John G. Hubbell, *P.O.W.: A Definitive History of the American Prisoner of War Experience in Vietnam, 1964–1973* (New York: Reader's Digest Press, 1976), 183–99.
24. *Congressional Record*, Senate, July 15, 1966, 15853.
25. Armand J. Myers et al., *Vietnam POW Camp Histories and Studies* (Maxwell Air Force Base, Montgomery, AL: Air War College, 1974) vol. 1, 75–8, 87.
26. Ibid., 82–6.
27. Ibid., 78–9, 92–4.
28. John McCain, *Faith of My Fathers: A Family Memoir* (New York: Random House, 1999), 216–17.
29. Rochester and Kiley, *Honor Bound*, 345.
30. Ibid., 346–56, 366–7.
31. John McCain, "The Code of Conduct and the Vietnam Prisoner of War" (National War College thesis, Washington, DC, April 8, 1974), 216–17.
32. Vernon E. Davis, *The Long Road Home: U.S. Prisoner of War Policy in Southeast Asia* (Historical Office of the Secretary of Defense: Washington, DC, 2000), 532.
33. For Sybil Stockdale's experiences, see Jim Stockdale and Sybil Stockdale, *In Love and War: The Story of a Family's Ordeal and Sacrifice during the Vietnam Years* (1984; reprint, Annapolis, MD: Naval Institute Press, 1990), 295–325, 361–91.
34. Ben Purcell and Anne Purcell, *Love and Duty* (2002; revised addition, Clarksville, GA: The Patriotism Foundation, 2006), 118–20.
35. H. Bruce Franklin, *M.I.A. or Mythmaking in America: How and Why the Belief in Live POWs Has Possessed the Nation* (New Brunswick, NJ: Rutgers University Press, 1993), 54–7, 83.
36. Rochester and Kiley, *Honor Bound*, 446–7.
37. Frank Anton, *Why Didn't You Get Me Out? Betrayal in the Viet Cong Death Camps* (Arlington, TX: Summit, 1997), 42–3.
38. Ibid., 41.
39. Davis, *The Long Road Home*, 491–518.

TIMELINE EVENTS

1973 – Final US withdrawal from Vietnam

1975 – Fall of South Vietnam

1980 – Post-traumatic stress disorder formally recognized in the *Diagnostic and Statistical Manual of Mental Disorders,* volume III

1982 – Dedication of the Vietnam Veterans Memorial.

1990 – Publication of the National Vietnam Veterans Readjustment Study

August 1990 – February 1991 – Gulf War

March 2003 – Invasion of Iraq

Chapter 9

Post-traumatic stress disorder and healing from the war

Raymond M. Scurfield

CHAPTER SUMMARY

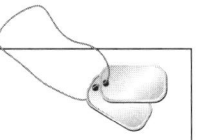

This chapter provides an overview of the impact of the Vietnam War on combatants, including post-traumatic stress disorder (PTSD), and central elements in postwar healing from being exposed to war trauma. It examines the incidence and prevalence of PTSD among Vietnam veterans, several profound myths about the impact of war and trauma—and the corresponding realities, and methods that combatants utilize to survive war trauma—and the impact of such survival modes after returning home. Also, there is a description of PTSD symptoms, warning signs and common triggers that can precipitate negative reactions. Finally, there is a discussion of the two unique characteristics of being in war that have a profound impact on postwar healing, and the essential elements involved in healing from war experiences—to include the vital role of the veterans' relationship with their country and major institutions.

I had the misfortune to have a mental breakdown three years ago and, as part of that healing process, discovered that my service and my cousin's services to the United States were full of soul-rendering terror.... There is nothing honorable in killing. Nothing is as horrible as the inner soul-rendering scream that comes with the first time. Then the numbness comes to silence it. Numbness is a narcotic to the soul. Numbness takes over your life and has a death grip on you until (or if) you finally reach a point of total security by being home among family and friends. There is nothing to glorify what we do in war.[1]

POST-TRAUMATIC STRESS DISORDER AND PHYSICALLY DISABLED VETERANS AND THEIR FAMILIES: THE LIVING CASUALTIES OF THE WAR

Why should we care about understanding what post-traumatic stress disorder (PTSD) is, and how it impacts on Vietnam and other war veterans? If for no other reason, consider that some 3.14 million veterans served in Vietnam or in the contiguous waters and air space from 1964 until 1975. And that some 1.7 million men and women have been deployed to Afghanistan and Iraq to date. These figures do not include the millions of families with whom so many veterans returned to live following deployment and who have themselves been impacted by what returning veterans have brought back home from the war.

In addition to the 58,209 who died from their Vietnam service, there are a number of additional casualties who survived but suffered physical wounds and injuries—some 153,303 Vietnam veterans who were wounded and over 80,000 who were severely physically disabled. And even these significant numbers pale in comparison to the over 829,000 Vietnam veterans suffering from full-blown or partial post-traumatic stress disorder, as estimated by the National Vietnam Veterans Readjustment Study (NVVRS).[2]

The NVVRS study was the first and is the only national epidemiologic psychiatric study ever conducted on an entire era of veterans. The NVVRS findings some fifteen years after the war officially ended in 1975 sent shock waves through the federal government and the American people:

- Almost 25 percent (15.2 percent male, 8.5 percent female) of theater veterans at the time of the study (1985–8) had full-blown post-traumatic stress disorder.
- An additional 18.9 percent (11.1 percent male, 7.8 percent female) of theater veterans were suffering some degree of PTSD symptoms or "partial PTSD" that did not meet the full diagnostic criteria for a PTSD psychiatric diagnosis.

The NVVRS also documented that there was a very strong "dose–response" relationship between amount of exposure to combat and the development of PTSD. In other words, the more a service member was exposed to combat stressors, the more likely he or she was to develop PTSD. This was an extremely important finding, in that many critics and disbelievers of the magnitude of PTSD among war veterans had continued to argue that it was not the war per se that "caused" PTSD but, instead, "pre-morbid" factors such as a troubled history before the war and/or purposeful or inaccurate exaggeration of PTSD symptoms. Unfortunately, there has been no subsequent national study capable of determining whether the number of Vietnam veterans with full-blown and partial PTSD has increased, stayed about the same, or decreased over the ensuing two decades since the NVVRS study data collection.[3]

Clearly, the extent and duration over time of PTSD symptoms among Vietnam veterans is a major health problem among a significant group within the US population. And currently, of course, the United States is engaged in Operation Iraqi Freedom (OIF) and Operation Enduring Freedom (OEF; in Afghanistan). These wars have resulted in enormous numbers of medical and psychiatric casualties, to include alarming suicide rates among veterans returned from deployment. For example, a military-conducted study found that clinicians identified 20.3 percent of active and 42.4 percent of reserve component soldiers three to six months after return from deployment as requiring mental health treatment.[4] And yet, in talking with various United States Department of Veterans' Affairs (VA) health-care providers at different VA facilities, it becomes clear that *the majority of veterans being treated at VA medical facilities nationwide continue to be Vietnam-era veterans*.

The above tells us at least four things: (1) that war-related PTSD is an extremely durable condition; (2) that it is *still* a major problem for untold numbers of Vietnam veterans; (3) that we can expect the numbers of OEF and OIF veterans who will require VA services only to grow over time; and (4) that OEF/OIF veterans might not be willing to utilize or be trusting of the VA this early following their war deployment.

We know that the third of these points is inevitable, because of one of the many lessons we should have learned from the Vietnam War: <u>The incidence of acute PTSD is always less than that of</u>

Figure 9.1 Raymond M. Scurfield working with Vietnamese civilians during his tour on one of the US Army's two psychiatric teams in Vietnam.

Courtesy of Raymond M. Scurfield.

longer-term PTSD.[5] Indeed, from my experiences as a social work officer on one of the Army's two psychiatric teams in Vietnam in 1968 with the 98th Medical Attachment, 8th Field Hospital, and from communications with many other military providers, I can say that it is extremely rare that any troops break down psychiatrically while in the midst of battle. While in a war zone, the vast majority of combatants have their innate survival modes kick in—survival modes that have served humanity since time immemorial to enable us to survive as a species ("fight or flight"). Along with our innate survival instinct and behaviors, military training, leadership, and organization buttress our drive to stay alive under the most extreme of conditions. It is only later, some time after the "emergency" of the trauma is past, that breakdowns typically occur—and "later" can be days, weeks, months, years, or even decades later. (For example, I have treated World War II veterans who came in for the first time in their late sixties seeking mental health treatment for their war-related PTSD.)

MYTHS AND REALITIES ABOUT THE IMPACT OF WAR

People believe a number of myths about war, its impact, and PTSD. I am going to address a number of these pervasive myths[6] and what the corresponding realities of such myths are. These are vital to address as part of the post-healing readjustment process.

> Simultaneously everyone leveled his weapon at him and fired. "Jesus Christ!" somebody gasped behind me as we watched his body reverse course back toward the trees; chunks of meat and bone flew through the air and stuck to the huge boulders. One of our rounds detonated a grenade the soldier carried, and his body smashed to the ground beneath a shower of blood.[7]

Myth: Heroes and "normal" or healthy persons don't continue to have problems after being exposed to war. If they do, that means that they already had problems and were "predisposed" to having such problems anyhow.

Reality: War is so catastrophic that it will evoke symptoms in almost everyone regardless of their background or pre-morbid factors. Indeed, it is abnormal *not* to have strong reactions to a trauma. As Viktor Frankl, concentration camp survivor and founder of logo-therapy stated:[8] *An abnormal reaction to an abnormal situation is normal behavior*. Indeed, trauma *always* has a significant impact on those who experience it, although they do not necessarily develop PTSD.

- As one Iraq war veteran stated: *My body's here, but my mind is there* [in Iraq].[9]
- As one Katrina survivor said: *I can't get what happened during Katrina out of my mind; I still remember vividly how terrifying it was.*[10]

Myth: Time heals all wounds.
Reality: Not necessarily. For example, long-term follow-up studies of World War II, Korean War, and Vietnam War veterans indicate that not only do psychiatric symptoms not necessarily disappear over time, but in a significant subgroup the symptoms have become worse, probably exacerbated by the aging process—that is, triggered by greater likelihood of exposure to deaths of significant others as they grow older, age-related losses of job or career, worsening health, and increased realization of their mortality.

Myth: Vietnam is the cause of *all* of the problems that I am having. Or: I'm behaving or feeling this way just because of Vietnam.
Reality: No one was a "blank tablet" before going to Vietnam; we were all persons with strengths and weaknesses, positives and negatives. You may be having problems now that existed before Vietnam, or that have become worse in the aftermath of Vietnam. If this is so, you must be truthful with yourself as to the cause(s) of your current problems, or you will put blame and responsibility where it does not belong, and you will not address what truly needs to be addressed.

Myth: I must have been bad or somehow deserved what happened to me.
Reality: Bad things can happen to good people and through no fault of their own. However, many survivors tend to blame someone for their trauma: themselves, others, institutions—or God.

Myth: I can never trust myself or anyone else again. I didn't respond during the war in a way that I feel good about, or my judgment was bad, and the environment was dangerous. So, I need to isolate myself and be constantly wary and careful of my surroundings.
Reality: Trust in yourself or trust in others is not an all-or-nothing proposition.

Myth: I must be crazy or weak to still keep remembering and still be bothered by what happened during the war (or homecoming or postwar in how I was treated as a Vietnam vet) after this many years have gone by.
Reality: War (and other) trauma is unforgettable (unless one has psychic amnesia). It is absolutely normal *not* to be able to totally eradicate the memories of war, and to be bothered to at least some degree by the trauma experienced during Vietnam—for months, years, or decades afterwards.

Myth: If I can just forget about the traumatic memories, I can move on with my life.
Reality: Since war (and other trauma) is unforgettable, if you are a survivor of the Vietnam War (or another trauma that happened a while ago), you have become an expert at detachment,

denial, minimization, or avoidance in an attempt to forget about the unforgettable traumatic experience.

Myth: Most war veterans who experienced significant trauma during the war or as part of readjusting postwar are highly motivated to eliminate or reduce PTSD-related symptoms such as isolation, numbing, and physical arousal or hyper-alertness to the environment.
Reality: A number of such PTSD symptoms also are survival modes that were learned during or following the war, and many veterans are very reluctant to give them up, or ambivalent about or not interested in giving them up[11] (to stay removed and apart from others, to not let themselves feel emotions once again, and to believe it is wise not to trust and wise to be wary of the environment, and so hyper-arousal is a necessary protection).

Myth: If I fully remember and re-experience aspects of my original (war-related) trauma (through talking about it, thinking about it, focusing on it), I will lose control and either become sucked back into the vortex of that memory and never be able to come back out again—or I will go crazy, or start crying and not be able to stop crying, or become so enraged that I will hurt someone or myself.
Reality: War veteran survivors do *not* go crazy from remembering and talking about their trauma. But they may go "crazy" trying so desperately to deny the undeniable: that the trauma happened, that it hurt then and it hurts now, that it has not gone away and that it needs to be dealt with.

SURVIVAL MODES IN THE WAR ZONE—AND WHAT IS BROUGHT HOME

Once the realities about war are understood and the myths countered, this leads to the question of *what is the nature of the problems* that so many deployed military personnel bring home after the war—where do these problems come from?

> And I froze, 'cos it was a boy, I would say between the ages of twelve and fourteen. When he turned at me and looked, all of a sudden he turned his whole body and pointed his automatic weapon at me, I just opened up, fired the whole twenty rounds right at the kid, and he just laid there. I dropped my weapon and cried.[12]

Just what do veterans do while deployed in a war zone to survive day after day after day?[13] It is my clinical experience that the vast majority of war-zone veterans become so conditioned to one or more survival modes that *they bring them home and into the family and community*. I have come to understand these several war-zone survival strategies from my tens of hundreds of clinical contacts with war veterans while in Vietnam, my remaining three years on active duty and my subsequent twenty-five-year mental health career with the US Department of Veterans' Affairs.

Fight or flight

You meet and engage the enemy, destroying or repelling them. Conversely, in the face of overwhelming odds you choose strategically to retreat to fight another day. Fight or flight: these are the two classic instinctual survival strategies that have been genetically imprinted in human beings over the millennia, instinctual responses that have ensured the survival of the human species from the days of the cave dwellers and up through modern times.

The potential downside to this survival strategy is that a number of vets, after they have left the war zone, or even while still there, have found themselves plagued by feelings of guilt, shame, grief, or unremitting rage over what they had to do to fight and/or flee in order to survive in the war zone. These feelings may be bothering the vet now, and/or may come back to haunt the vet months or years afterward.

Detachment, numbing, and denial

You learn how to protect yourself against the horrors of what you are witnessing and do so by convincing yourself that "it don't mean nothin'," no matter what happens. You learn to self-anesthetize, to *not* feel what otherwise would be overwhelming: anxiety, fear, shock, horror, depression, loss, grief.

In Vietnam, a prevalent mantra that helped many to survive was "F—— it, it don't mean nothin'." If you were walking and saw a dead Vietnamese civilian lying alongside the road, "F—— it, it don't mean nothin'." No matter if it were a child, woman, elderly person, "F—— it, it don't mean nothin'." As you repeated this to yourself day after day after day, you were able to detach yourself to some degree from having the kind of profound reactions that you might otherwise have had—and preserve your ability to concentrate on getting through yet another day.

And the potential downside was that you might get so proficient at detachment, denial, and emotional numbing that you take this with you out of the war zone and back to the civilian world. For example, a number of family members have described their veteran family member as not able to show, or perhaps even feel, normal emotions like everyone else and that they are emotionally inaccessible.

Tunnel vision

You learn how to maintain an intense, focused, full attention on completing the immediate task or objective in order to complete a particular task and to exclude whatever else is going on around you. A Vietnam vet nurse who was stationed at an evacuation hospital once told me:

> When a group of mass casualties would be flown in on the med evacs and would be laid down in a long row, or when they totally filled up the ward, I learned very quickly not to ever look around—not look to the right, nor to the left, or ahead or behind. No, if you did that it was too overwhelming. So, you just looked directly at the wounded vet lying there directly in front of you. And when you were done doing what you could do, you moved on to the one immediately next to you and gave him your full attention. But you never looked all around. It was just too much to take in.

Back in the civilian world, a vet might find that tunnel vision helps to get through tough times in civilian life. Conversely, tunnel vision may become so second nature that there it becomes very difficult, or indeed impossible, *ever* to turn it off. And this can be devastating to relationships or to the ability to enjoy life fully.

External discharging of emotions

Finding an outlet for the inevitable cumulative buildup of stress, frustration, grief, fear, and rage that are inevitable in a war zone is crucial to surviving. Typically, this is expressed through rage towards the enemy, which can be very functional, or it can fuel an internal anger and resolve to persevere.

> By the time I got out of Basic, I had so much rage built up in me that I wanted to go to Vietnam—so I could kill and prove to them that I was a man . . . what I hate the most is that I became abusive towards others just like I was abused.[14]

Conversely, there may be an absence of regular opportunities to discharge such pent-up emotions. This can be because you don't use a weapon as part of your normal duty (as a medic or corpsman, mess hall worker, etc.). And even for those whose primary role is to engage with the enemy, opportunity might not be there very often. This is especially likely in a war waged by guerrillas, insurgents, or terrorists. Thus, pent-up emotions can erupt strongly and unexpectedly, possibly to include emotions toward innocent or apparently innocent civilians, and even toward those on one's own side. This is because the pent-up emotions have to go somewhere. If they are not expressed outwardly, you may well redirect such feelings inwardly or suppress them, keep pushing them down.

And when you are back home, discharging your emotions can be helpful to release pent-up feelings. On the other hand, this can make it very difficult to share what is going on with you with your family members. You might keep it all bottled up within—and then you explode in anger, frustration, or grief. Or you may isolate yourself in an attempt to avoid possibly having your deep emotions and memories triggered or to prevent venting your emotions against others.

"Comparing" war traumas[15]

Some troops who are wounded, suffer losses, or have other traumatic experiences while deployed will "compare" (both while on deployment and afterwards) their trauma with what others have experienced.

One comparison is that you tell yourself that you "did not suffer nearly as much as many others." This can be used as a positive. For example, some wounded troops focus on how much more badly some others were injured (or were killed) or what others faced in combat; this can be used as motivation to help them to persevere and get through the tough times, and to count their blessings and see the glass as half full rather than half empty. Conversely, this can result in *denying*, or not admitting to yourself, how much you were impacted, and/or feeling that you "do not deserve" to have negative or troubling reactions over what has happened to you. Or such comparisons can lead to feeling guilty, ashamed, or very self-critical of your "weakness" in not being "strong" enough, in that you are having troubles even though you went through "so much less."

The opposite form of comparison is that you "suffered much more than many others." Focusing on how much worse off you are can lead to bitterness, blame, anger, depression, self-pity, or being very judgmental of others and having a distorted sense of entitlement because you went through so much more than they did.

The reality is that *any* comparisons are a no-win proposition; your traumatic experiences were your traumatic experiences, period. It was and is meaningful to you, and to compare your traumas to anyone else's trauma is not fair to anyone.

Belief in fate/randomness/a higher power

Many military personnel rely on their long-standing faith in a higher power or Supreme Being to sustain them through the horrors of war. Some find their faith and beliefs strengthened. Conversely, others find their beliefs severely challenged when they come face to face with the horrors and inhumanity and a Catch-22 conundrum: having to kill in order to save the lives of self and others.

> [While in Vietnam] I called out many times to God, and . . . He didn't answer. He left me alone . . . to do what I had to do. . . . How could He have deserted me like that—when I most needed Him?[16]

The first question that some troops often ask after something bad has happened in the war zone is "Why me, God?" Or "Why did this have to happen to ———, God?" Others will ask, "Why me, God?" but continue, "There is a God and I need to reconnect." Also, there is the issue of morality in a war zone, such as "Thou shalt not kill" (especially women and children) and

"What you do to the least of my brethren you do unto me." Chaplains are a source of great comfort and counsel to many troops; conversely, some combat vets may perceive a marked conflict, viewing chaplains as blessing their own side's troops to kill and emphasizing that "God is on our side"—but not on the enemy's.[17] And you may wonder how there can be a God or higher power who would allow people, and you, to do what is done to each other during war. You may carry such issues back home.

Figure 9.2 Raymond M. Scurfield (right) at the 98th Medical Attachment, 8th Field Hospital, during the Vietnam War.

Courtesy of Raymond M. Scurfield.

Dehumanizing the enemy

Training for war inculcates the new recruit in the classic detachment strategy: dehumanize the enemy. "They are not human beings like we are; they are horrible, evil, heartless, immoral." And racism and extreme ethnocentrism are key dehumanizing strategies in which there is a promotion of racial and ethnic negative stereotypical attitudes and language directed toward the enemy—Krauts, Japs, slant-eyes, gooks, towel-heads, A-rabs, Muslim radicals, hajis.

> "You just sort of try to block out the fact that they're human beings and see them as enemies," he said. You call them hajis, you know? You do all the things that make it easier to deal with killing them and mistreating them.[18]

One Iraq veteran described how what happened to Vietnam veterans parallels what is now happening with a number of Iraq veterans, beginning with the realization that the original mission or justification given for the war proved to be false.

> There was a progression of thought that happened among soldiers in Vietnam. It started with a mission [in Vietnam]: contain Communism. That mission fell apart, just like it fell apart now—there are no weapons of mass destruction. Then you are left with just a survival instinct. That, unfortunately, turned to racism. That's happening now, too. Guys are writing me saying, "I don't know why I'm here, but I hate the Iraqis."[19]

It is much easier to seek out an enemy whom you have dehumanized to kill rather than an enemy who is regarded as human, good, an honorable adversary, fighting for a just cause. And you can become cut-throat, cold, uncaring, and develop an intense hatred and loathing that stays with you for a very long time. For example, I have met a number of World War II veterans who still have a vitriolic hatred toward the Japanese or the Germans—any Japanese or Germans. And I continue to meet too many Vietnam veterans who still maintain a vitriolic hatred toward the Vietnamese, any Vietnamese—be they living in Vietnam or in the United States. And such profound hatred can inevitably poison and pollute attitudes toward those who are of differing races, creeds, religions, and ethnic heritages.

Social isolation and alienation

Isolating oneself from others, not letting anyone get close emotionally, is another common way to promote detachment. The remarkable bonding that occurs among brother and sister soldiers in a war zone is a two-edged sword. It helps you to survive the otherwise unsurvivable. On the other hand, when you lose a close comrade it can be devastating. And so at some point during deployment a number of soldiers decide not to let anyone get too close—because it hurts too much when they die or are maimed. And they carry this attitude home. And then back home some vets only want to be around other vets, because they find that they cannot feel very comfortable with almost anyone who isn't a vet—or even with anyone who did not fight in the same war as they did. Still other vets find themselves avoiding meaningful discussions or interactions with other veterans; it brings back too many disturbing memories and too much pain. As one Vietnam veteran shared with me:

> When I came home after the war, I felt that other vets were the only people I could relate to. But they were the last ones I wanted to be with.

Drinkin' and druggin'

Substance use and abuse are two common tactics by which fighting men and women achieve detachment and relief—and the military historically has made cheap or even free alcohol readily available. To compound this problem, there is an unmatched ingenuity and enterprise in the military for troops to somehow be able to procure or manufacture substances to get intoxicated from—even in the middle of nowhere. And so, many vets who may have entered the war zone with substance-use problems leave with a bigger problem. A number of vets who did not enter the war zone with substance-use problems can leave the war zone with them. And this can become or continue as a habit back home; or you revert back to such, especially when things get rough or you're feeling down. Finally, substance usage can at least help to temporarily drown out the unrelenting traumatic memories and associated emotions.

Risk-taking/thrill/sex addiction

Another survival strategy is to become immersed in and "addicted" physiologically, psychologically and behaviorally to the thrill, the risk, the danger, the adrenaline rush. And sex is *always* available in a war zone, always. Sex can be bought with local civilians; or the intensity and loneliness of life in the war zone will spark sexual encounters that are mutually sought—or forced. You can become an action junkie, which can be a powerful elixir to help you survive, or can lead to increasingly dangerous attitudes and behaviors. And needing this "rush" becomes extremely difficult simply to turn off when returning to civilian life.

However, some vets will be able to satisfy some or most of this high risk/adrenaline habit through successful postwar employment in high-risk, high-thrill occupations and jobs such as emergency medical, fire and rescue, law enforcement, offshore and oil pipelines, or contract positions in support of military operations. Conversely, others try to live life on the edge, on the wild side, engaging in extremes of food, drink, or high-speed or dangerous driving—whatever extremes are available. Or they stay immersed in danger, and in memories and feelings about the war—"being there while living here."

As an example of dangerous risk taking, an alarming number of recently returned Iraq Army and Marine veterans have been killed in single-occupant vehicle accidents.

> We absolutely have a problem. . . . The kids come back and they want to live life to its fullest, to its wildest. They get a little bit of time to let their hair down, and they let their hair all the way down and do everything to excess. They drink to excess. They eat to excess. They party to excess. And then, some drive. . . . They want something that goes fast and keeps that high up they had during the war . . . speed fills some indescribable urge for excitement that they've felt since returning from war . . . Going fast is like a drug—the newest crack out there.[20]

Bizarre or gallows humor

In the midst of horror and chaos, resorting to what otherwise would be seen as gross or inappropriate humor can be at least a partial antidote to the relentless horrors of war. Humor and irreverence can be very healthy and adaptive during challenging times. They help to stop you from crying, or becoming overwhelmed by what you're facing day after day after day. Instead, you can get a deep belly-laugh, a moment of absurdly hilarious respite, a closeness of comradeship with the only people who could possibly get it or tolerate such humor—your war buddies.

> Hey, John: we seem to have an extra leg among all these body parts from the last mass casualties we received. Since I can't figure out which body it belongs to, I'm going to give this here guy a third leg—that'll give the body handlers Stateside a little surprise when they open up the body bag.

It is a very relief-providing respite, but it does not erase the horrors, feelings, and indelible images from your mind or from your heart. And you can carry that bizarre humor back home with you in either a positive or a negative way. Positively, you may be able to have an irreverent attitude, an enjoyable or refreshingly unexpected or amusingly sarcastic or humorous attitude that might be a welcome respite, especially during tough times. Or you can become pejorative, cynical, nasty, insulting, critical, derogatory toward others in the face of mounting frustrations—and you couldn't care less. Or perhaps you fall somewhere in between (as I have been accused of at times).

X factors

Several factors distinctive to the Vietnam War are essential to bear in mind in trying to understand more fully the psychological impact of the Vietnam War on returning veterans.

Some of the most important distinctive elements are that Vietnam was (1) in substantial part a guerrilla war (hence it oftentimes was difficult or impossible to discern enemy from innocent civilian); (2) quite protracted (lasting over ten years); (3) up close and nasty (hence many veterans had first-hand exposure to the gruesomeness of death and maiming); (4) mostly a fixed one-year or thirteenth-month deployment for individual personnel (which had a very negative impact on unit cohesion, as various unit members would rotate in and out of combat singly and not as a unit); (5) extremely unpopular and denigrated by a substantial portion of Americans (resulting in too many returning Vietnam veterans being denigrated and demeaned, called "baby killers" and drug addicts, and causing many veterans to "go underground" about their status as a veteran); and (6) involving a high percentage of conscripts or draftees (many of whom were strongly against the Vietnam War or participating in any war, and hence were beset with anguished issues of morality for participating).

THE DIAGNOSIS OF PTSD: A BREAKTHROUGH IN UNDERSTANDING WAR TRAUMA

In 1980, for the first time there was a diagnostic category of mental disorder that could account for psychiatric symptoms that might occur short- or long-term following exposure to a trauma. This diagnosis, PTSD, appeared in the *Diagnostic and Statistical Manual of Mental Disorders*, volume III.[21] Finally, it was officially recognized that *anyone* could be impacted following exposure to a severe enough stressor—regardless of whether they had had prior mental health problems.

The *DSM–IV–TR* (2000)[22] recognizes two categories of stress disorder: acute stress disorder and post-traumatic stress disorder. Acute stress disorder describes reactions to extreme stressors from two days to four weeks following exposure, and PTSD describes reactions later than four weeks following exposure. The PTSD diagnostic criteria include the following:

- The person is exposed to a traumatic event in which both of the following are present:
  (a) The person has experienced, witnessed, or been confronted with an event/events that involve actual or threatened death or serious injury, or a threat to the physical integrity of oneself or others.

    My buddy, Johnny, was killed right in front of me—and *there was nothing I could do about it*. I can still see his body blowing apart—and my total helplessness to save him. This experience haunts me still.—Vietnam veteran

  (b) The person's response involved intense fear, helplessness, or horror. Note: in children, it may be expressed instead by disorganized or agitated behavior.

    Vietnam vet describing when he had been wounded in the battlefield: "It was terrible; right after I was hit, I was lying there, all exposed, couldn't move and no one could get to me. I was in such pain, and I was terrified I was going to bleed to death or be hit again."[23]

- The inclusionary symptoms are *persistent* and occur *sometime following* exposure to the trauma (note that *only* the re-experiencing of symptoms is unique to PTSD):
  (a) re-experiencing of the trauma in some way: intrusive recollections, thoughts, dreams, reactivity to external or internal cues that symbolize or resemble the event.

  One day I was out in the bush, killing gooks, seeing buddies get killed, covered in mud, trying to sleep at night with the threat of ambush by the VC and two days later I was trying to talk to my family at the dinner table. I couldn't tell them what I had been through. They couldn't have understood it.[24]

  (b) avoidance of stimuli associated with the trauma; numbing of general responsiveness, denial.

  I still never watch a war movie. It is too painful and brings back too many terrible memories.

  (c) increased arousal: hyper-vigilance, startle response, sleep disturbance, anger outbursts.[25]

  It is difficult for me to sleep in the same bed as my wife. I am always so "wired" that the slightest movements by her can result in my lashing out at her as an impulsive defensive response to "protect myself." So, it's better if we aren't in the same bedroom.

Just reading through the official list of PTSD symptoms might not suffice adequately to help a non-mental health professional fully understand what PTSD is all about. To that end, I have developed a more descriptive listing to help people understand when a veteran might be experiencing significant war-related issues.

> Our government sends us to war, our military uses us in war and our country forgets us after war.
>
> (Ray Scurfield, Vietnam veteran)[26]

There are a number of warning signs that strongly suggest that the imprint of war and the transition postwar is continuing to have a significant negative impact on troops returned from deployment. Such symptoms might be part of having PTSD, or might be present without the veteran having full-blown PTSD—and yet suffering at least in part because of war and/or postwar re-entry experiences. Rather than repeat the core symptoms of PTSD mentioned above, I will elaborate on important warning signs to be alert for:

- Perhaps most tellingly, there is the reaction from family and friends: "This is not at all the same person who went on deployment." Or: "The war changed him [or her]." The changes can be very troubling—or just changes. The reality is: the one thing you never believe is when a war veteran tells you that "the war had no impact" on him or her. Bull. *Everyone* who goes to war is impacted by war and comes back different—everyone. And, of course, such differences are not necessarily "disordered."

- The vet just cannot forget one or several very disturbing experiences and is very bothered by them.
- There is significant sleep disturbance—nightmares, trouble getting to or remaining asleep, waking up prematurely and not being able to go back to sleep.
- There is excessive boredom with normal living and/or excessive thrill-seeking to get kicks.
- The vet feels cut off and isolated, "distant" emotionally from almost everyone, different, having nothing in common with almost anyone, except possibly with some other vets, and perhaps feeling alienated.
- The vet feels that life is aimless or has little or no worthwhile meaning and perhaps yearns to be back in the war. As one Iraq vet said,

    I miss it. At least there was a purpose. I wish I was in Iraq because my buddies are there.[27]

- The vet may be very confused, pessimistic, angry, cynical about his (or her) fate in life, hopeless about his future and any possibility of changing what is in the future.

    I'm getting older now, but what I experienced in Vietnam becomes a kaleidoscope of events and the emotional impact it has on me continues. Today I feel lost, empty, detached, alone, and dead. I'm afraid to let go and feel. I'm afraid I might become lost and never return.—Vietnam veteran.

- Finally, there can be preoccupation with bitter or disappointed feelings and thoughts toward the government, society, and/or the military about broken promises— how they have been mistreated or ignored.[28] This can become a "me-against-the-world" mistrust of what's to come, an indistinct but entirely accurate perception that the United States has failed veterans of past wars. The war will stay with them, but after a point the Army won't.[29]

One Vietnam veteran in 1999 poignantly expressed his post-war angst:[30]

Even today, I feel like so much of me died in Vietnam, that at times I wished all of me had died over there. For those who came back, the price of living is never easy or cheap. Laughter and happiness is rare. The nightmares, the flashbacks, the pains, waking up soaked in sweat, hyper-alert, and sleeplessness . . . are the norm. The sounds and smells of combat, the smell of sweat and dust, of the damp earth and vegetation, of the hot sun and exhaustion, of ambushes and firefights to full-blown battles, and of blood and death, enter my daily life. The moans of the wounded, some cursing, others calling for their mother, someone screaming for the corpsman or moans of "Oh God, Oh God." Like so many other Vietnam vets, I feel so much rage in me that it exhausts me and isolation is my only sanctuary.[31]

ESSENTIAL ELEMENTS OF HEALING FROM WAR: IT TAKES A COUNTRY

There are many possible paths to healing from war and other traumas. Beware of false prophets who claim that their way, and only in its "pure" form, is *the* way. I do not accept that any one approach is the way to help veterans heal. Various approaches have their strengths, whether applied to World War II, Korean War, Vietnam War, Gulf War I, OEF/OIF, or any other veterans.

I have found that several elements are critical to forge a legitimate relationship with veterans and promote a healing path from the ravages of war. First, it is essential to earn the trust of someone who has been in effect violated by the environment—because war trauma is inflicted on the service member by someone outside of him- or herself. Too many veterans come to mistrust the motivations of others. *Why should a veteran trust you?* You must let the veteran see that you truly care and genuinely want to better understand his or her experiences and viewpoints, and that you are not sitting in judgment of his or her survival actions during deployment.

Figure 9.3 Raymond M. Scurfield (in hat) seated with Vietnam veterans Roy Ainsworth and Charles Brown (in camouflage shirt) during a trip back to Vietnam in 2000.

Courtesy of Raymond M. Scurfield.

Involving significant others (counselor, family members, close friend, spiritual or religious adviser) is crucial as part of the recovery process and to challenge the John Wayne/Lone Ranger mentality. Indeed, the impact of trauma inherently is a family problem: the family is inevitably and deeply impacted and hence *must* be part of the recovery process—at the appropriate time.

Furthermore, fellow and sister comrades-in-arms or battle buddies have a *very* special salient, clarifying, and supportive role in recovery. They each know what the other has been exposed to, and they know that other vets know. This helps with truth telling and with giving meaningful, realistic feedback to each other. Also, if the war veteran has any belief in God or a higher power, or in the interconnectedness of humanity, how his or her war experiences affect and are affected by such beliefs and attitudes must be addressed as part of the healing process. To come to terms with forgiveness of the perpetrator, such as the enemy, is nice to have as a goal if the veteran sees that as necessary. However, it is not necessarily essential; what is essential is *to be able to let go of hatred* toward the perpetrator and/or toward others being blamed by the veteran.

Finally, a vital element of postwar healing that typically is not addressed much or at all in traditional counseling approaches is to allow veterans to address their relationship with their communities, government, and society. This is essential, in that for many veterans this has become an altered relationship involving major trust issues, victim blaming, being forgotten—when perceiving or experiencing that the United States is violating that sacred covenant to honor its veterans' sacrifices and provide humane and timely war-related financial benefits, health services, and mental health services. The results can include despair, isolation, rage, and alienation that cascade in turbulent waves over the war-wounded and their families. As one mother of a severely wounded Iraq vet said, "When he was no longer of use to the military, they forgot about him."

In other words, for veterans their healing is intrinsically linked with their relationship with their country—because the country sanctioned them to go into harm's way, and to kill and be exposed to death and dying. And in too many instances the country then has reneged on commitments made to honor and support veterans after their return home. And unless this relationship is "made right," many veterans will not complete their postwar healing journeys.

This is why it takes a country to help service members, veterans, and their families to truly heal from war. In reality, historically a substantial segment of faculty and students at many universities and colleges typically have had quite negative attitudes toward military personnel and veterans, fostered by a prevailing climate that is anti-war if not anti-military. Hence, faculty and students have a particularly crucial role to play in helping to heal the wounds of war. This is because the worst thing that can happen to anyone who has gone into harm's way is to be the target of protests or denigration for having served his or her country. Rather, former combatants need to be understood concerning the terrible toll that war can exact, and to be reached out to, talked with, and shown that they are cared about—and appreciated. And speaking as a Vietnam veteran who also is a university professor, I can say that for this to come from students and academics is particularly meaningful.

DISCUSSION QUESTIONS

1. Identify and explain four common myths, and the corresponding realities, about the impact of war and other trauma.
2. What are four common "survival modes" that military personnel who are deployed utilize as a means of coping in the face of the horrors of war?
3. While each of these survival modes is functional to survival while deployed, they also have a potentially negative impact that is brought home following the veteran's return. What are these potentially negative impacts of the survival modes during war?
4. What are five of the warning signs or symptoms of PTSD?
5. What are three of the essential elements that it takes to heal from any war?

SUGGESTED READING

Figley, C., ed. *Stress Disorders among Vietnam Veterans*. New York: Brunner/Mazel, 1978.

Grossman, Dave. *On Killing*. Boston: Little, Brown, 1995.

Kulka, R. A., W. E. Schlenger, J. A. Fairbank, R. L. Hough, B. Kathleen Jordan, C. R. Marmar, and D. S. Weiss. *Trauma and the Vietnam War Generation: Report of Findings from the National Vietnam Veterans Readjustment Study*. New York: Brunner/Mazel, 1990.

Lanham, Stephanie Laite. *Veterans and Families' Guide to Recovering from PTSD*. Annandale, VA: Military Order of the Purple Heart Service Foundation, 2007.

Scurfield, R. M. *Healing Journeys: Study Abroad with Vietnam Veterans*. New York: Algora Publishing, 2006.

Scurfield, R. M. *Vietnam Trilogy: Veterans and Post-traumatic Stress, 1968, 1989 and 2000*. New York: Algora Publishing, 2004.

Scurfield, R. M. *War Trauma: From Vietnam to Iraq*. New York: Algora Publishing, 2006.

Sonnenberg, S., A. Blank, and J. Talbott, eds. *Stress and Recovery in Vietnam Veterans*. Washington, DC: American Psychiatry Press, 1985.

NOTES

1. J. P. McDonald, Letter to the Editor, *The SunHerald*, Biloxi, MS, November 12, 2004, D-2.
2. R. A. Kulka, W. E. Schlenger, J. A. Fairbank, R. L. Hough, B. Kathleen Jordan, C. R. Marmar, and D. S. Weiss, *Trauma and the Vietnam War Generation: Report of Findings from the National Vietnam Veterans Readjustment Study* (New York: Brunner/Mazel, 1990).
3. However, a more recent reanalysis of the NVVRS data not only confirmed the strength of the relationship between amount of exposure to combat and subsequent development of PTSD and other mental health problems, but found it to be even more significant; Bruce P. Dohrenwend, J. Blake Turner, Nicholas A. Turse,

Ben G. Adams, Karestan C. Koenen, and Randall Marshall, "The Psychological Risks of Vietnam for U.S. Veterans: A Revisit with New Data and Methods," *Science* 313 (5789) (2006): 979–82. A different major study upheld the consistency of what veterans report about their war experiences over a fourteen-year period; K. C. Koenen, S. D. Stelelman, B. P. Dohrenwend, J. F. Sommer Jr., and J. M. Stellman, "The Consistency of Combat Exposure Reporting and Course of PTSD in Vietnam Era Veterans," *Journal of Traumatic Stress* 20 (1) (2007): 3–13.

4. Charles S. Milliken, Jennifer L. Auchterlonie, and Charles W. Hoge, "Longitudinal Assessment of Mental Health Problems among Active and Reserve Component Soldiers Returning from the Iraq War," *JAMA* 298 (18) (2007): 2141–8.
5. Raymond M. Scurfield, *War Trauma: Lessons Unlearned from Vietnam to Iraq* (New York: Algora Publishing, 2006).
6. Because of space limitations I will provide very brief descriptions of most of the myths and realities; see Scurfield, *War Trauma*, for more detail.
7. Dave Grossman, *On Killing* (Boston: Little, Brown, 1995), 265–6.
8. V. Frankl, *Man's Search for Meaning* (Boston: Beacon, 1959).
9. This quotation is from an Iraq veteran who stated that he could not get past the memories of Iraq and that his experience there felt unresolved. Sarah Corbett, "The Permanent Scars of Iraq," *New York Times Magazine*, February 15, 2004, 34.
10. Raymond Scurfield, "Post Katrina Storm Disorder and Recovery in Mississippi More than Two Years Later," *Traumatology* 14 (2) (2008): 88–106.
11. See R. T. Murphy, R. P. Cameron, L. Sharp, G. Ramirez, C. Rosen, K. Dreschler, and D. F. Gusman, "Readiness to Change PTSD Symptoms and Related Behaviors among Veterans Participating in a Motivation Enhancement Group," *The Behavior Therapist* 27 (4) (2004): 33–6.
12. Grossman, *On Killing*, 88.
13. From two sources: Unpublished manuscript, 2007, by Raymond M. Scurfield and Kathy Platoni, "Warning Signs, Triggers, Survival Strategies and Coping from War"; and adapted and summarized from Scurfield, *War Trauma*.
14. Author's interview with Vietnam veteran, 1996.
15. This survival strategy is not included in my Vietnam Trilogy books, although I have described how "comparing" traumas with those suffered by others is one of the important myths that survivors must honestly face to avoid the issues described above.
16. Author's interview with Vietnam veteran, 1998.
17. Frank and realistic dialogue is absolutely necessary to address such real, not just imagined, conflicts in a war zone, and such dialogue may well have to go beyond private one-on-one conversations and occur in the very circle that is the sustaining lifeblood of military combatants—in the small-unit peer group. For a more detailed discussion of the conflicts between faith and behavior in a war zone, see Raymond Scurfield, *A Vietnam Trilogy* (New York: Algora, 2004); also see William Mahedy, *Out of the Night: The Spiritual Journey of Vietnam Vets* (New York: Ballantine, 1986).
18. Bob Herbert, "'Gooks' to 'Hajis,'" *New York Times*, May 21, 2004 (accessed online January 8, 2008).
19. Scurfield, *War Trauma*, 87.
20. From October 2003 to September 2004, when troops first returned in large numbers from Iraq, 132 soldiers died in vehicle accidents, a 28 percent jump from the previous twelve months. Two-thirds of them were veterans of Iraq or Afghanistan. And there was a 23 percent increase in deaths from vehicle accidents in the past seven months. Gregg Zoroya, "Survivors of War Take Fatal Risks on Roads," *USA Today*, May 2, 2005 (accessed online May 2, 2005).
21. American Psychiatric Association, *DSM-III-R, Diagnostic and Statistical Manual of Mental Disorders*, 3rd ed., rev. (*DSM-III-R*) (Washington, DC: American Psychiatric Press, 1987).
22. American Psychiatric Association, *DSM-IV-TR: Diagnostic and Statistical Manual of Manual Disorders*, 4th ed., text revision (*DSM-IV-TR*) (Washington, DC: American Psychiatric Association Press, 2000).
23. R. Scurfield and S. Tice, "Interventions with Medical and Psychiatric Evacuees and Their Families: From Vietnam through the Gulf War," *Military Medicine* 157 (2) (1992): 90.

24. Joel Brende and Erwin Parson, *Vietnam Veterans: The Road to Recovery* (New York: Plenum Press, 1985), 723.
25. *DSM-IV-TR*, 465–6, identifies distinctive symptom clusters for two populations: in children, and in such chronic interpersonal stressors as childhood sexual or physical abuse and domestic battering (this is in contrast to single-event or shorter-lasting trauma): impaired affect modulation; self-destructive and impulsive behavior; dissociation; somatic complaints; feelings of ineffectiveness, shame, despair, or hopelessness; feeling permanently damaged; hostility; impaired relationships; and change in personality characteristics. One can argue that *prolonged combat exposure* fits these criteria.
26. Scurfield, *War Trauma*.
27. Corbett, "The Permanent Scars of Iraq," 38.
28. For example, many veterans are very aware that, while the government boasts it has boosted for the Department of Veterans Affairs in 2004 by $1.9 billion, the government neglects to inform America's citizenry that because of an increasingly older veteran population with increased health-care needs, and more and more veterans being killed (thus increasing survivor benefit payments to widows/widowers and their children) and wounded in Iraq and even still in Afghanistan, the VA budget falls considerably short of the $3.1 billion increase the House Veterans Affairs Committee said in February 2004 was needed just to maintain the current level of services and benefits. It is this kind of doublespeak that generates more distrust and rage. Editorial, *SunHerald*, Biloxi, MS, December 6, 2004, B2.
29. Corbett, "The Permanent Scars of Iraq," 38.
30. Andrew Wiest, Leslie P. Root, and Raymond M. Scurfield, "Post-traumatic Stress Disorder: The Legacy of War," in *War in the Age of Technology*, ed. Geoffrey Jensen and Andrew Wiest (New York: New York University Press, 2001), 316–17. That this is not confined to Vietnam veterans is reflected in the recently published high numbers of suicides committed by OEF and OIF veterans, which now exceed any previous suicide numbers among military veterans since such statistics began in 1980.
31. Just some of the many books on Vietnam veterans: S. Sonnenberg, A. Blank, and J. Talbott, eds., *Stress and Recovery in Vietnam Veterans* (Washington, DC: American Psychiatry Press, 1985); T. Williams, ed., *Post-traumatic Stress Disorders of the Vietnam Veteran* (Cincinnati: Disabled American Veterans, 1980); C. Figley, ed., *Stress Disorders among Vietnam Veterans* (New York: Brunner/Mazel, 1978); R. J. Lifton, *The Broken Connection: On Death and the Continuity of Life* (New York: Simon & Schuster, 1979); W. Mahedy, *Out of the Night: The Spiritual Journey of Vietnam Vets* (New York: Ballantine Books, 1986); K. Walker, *A Piece of My Heart: The Stories of Twenty-six American Women Who Served in Vietnam* (New York: Ballantine Books, 1985); Wallace Terry: *Bloods: An Oral History of the Vietnam War by Black Veterans* (New York: Ballantine Books, 1984); J. P. Wilson, *Identity, Ideology and Crisis: The Vietnam Veteran in Transition. A Preliminary Report on the Forgotten Warrior Project* (Cincinnati: Disabled American Veterans, 1977); and A. Egendorf, C. Kadushin, R. Laufer, G. Rothbart, and L. Sloan, *Legacies of Vietnam: Comparative Adjustment of Veterans and Their Peers* (Washington, DC: Government Printing Office, 1981).

TIMELINE EVENTS

1968 – Norman Mailer's New Journalism account of the 1967 anti-war march on the Pentagon, *The Armies of the Night*, wins both the Pulitzer Prize and the National Book Award

1973 – Early combat memoir: Tim O'Brien's *If I Die in a Combat Zone, Box Me Up and Ship Me Home*

1973 – Early, important book on America's misapprehension of Vietnamese culture: Frances Fitzgerald, *Fire in the Lake: The Vietnamese and the Americans in Vietnam*. Awarded the Pulitzer Prize and the National Book Award.

1978 – Tim O'Brien's first Vietnam novel, *Going After Cacciato*, which wins the National Book Award.

1982 – First full-length critical studies of Vietnam war literature: Philip D. Beidler, *American Literature and the Experience of Vietnam*, and Jeffrey Walsh, *American War Literature 1914 to Vietnam*

1985 – First scholarly conference on Vietnam War literature: Asia Society conference entitled "The Vietnam Experience in American Literature"

1997 – First novel by a Vietnamese American: Lan Cao, *Monkey Bridge*

1997 – Philip Roth (arguably America's greatest living writer) tackles the anti-war movement in *American Pastoral*, which wins the 1998 Pulitzer Prize for Fiction

Chapter 10

The Vietnam War and literature

Maureen Ryan

CHAPTER SUMMARY

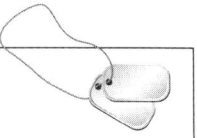

The large canon of creative literature—fiction, drama, and poetry—about the Vietnam War and its legacy in the United States is diverse in genre, authorship, and theme. Beginning with the first wave of published Vietnam literature in the mid- to late 1970s, through recent offerings such as Denis Johnson's 2008 National Book Award-winning novel *Tree of Smoke*, this vast assemblage of literary treatments of the war, its aftermath, and the home front testifies to the lingering influence of the Vietnam War on American society.

"ALL THE NAMES IN AMERICA": LITERATURE OF THE VIETNAM WAR

Barack Obama's 2008 election to the presidency of the United States has been lauded and analyzed as a transformative event for African Americans and racial relations in America. But there is a less acknowledged aspect of the Obama presidency that also marks a significant development in American politics and culture: Barack Obama is the first post-baby-boomer president.

In his stump speeches and his best-selling manifesto, *The Audacity of Hope*, Obama called for a political philosophy that—and a president who—transcends the divisive ideologies that have prevailed in American politics for the past half-century. Claiming that the real and important social advances of the 1960s were compromised by an attendant loss of a "quality of trust" in American democracy, the new president suggests that a renewed liberal agenda (and an Obama presidency) can surmount the "psychodrama of the Baby Boom generation" that has defiled

American politics and public life in recent years.[1] Barack Obama is the first—but only the first—American politician to repudiate as fractured and outmoded the social and political legacy of the baby boomers and the 1960s.

And yet the presidential campaign that yielded a president who rejects the polarized politics that prevailed in America in the years after (and because of) the controversial Vietnam War was itself largely defined by the after-effects of America's longest war, which continue to reverberate in American society. Obama's defeated opponent, Arizona senator John McCain, is widely honored as an American hero-patriot for his valorous survival of many years as a North Vietnamese prisoner of war. And in the campaign, McCain's Republican operatives attacked Obama for his alleged relationship with William Ayers, a former member of the late 1960s anti-war group the Weather Underground, whom Republican vice-presidential candidate Sarah Palin and others labeled a "domestic terrorist." In the thirty-five years since the end of the Vietnam War, social attitudes toward the war's combat veterans have gradually improved; public responses to the current wars in Iraq and Afghanistan demonstrate that if America learned anything from the debacle in Vietnam, it was to *not* blame the warriors. Yet the recent animus against Bill Ayers showed that contemporary attitudes toward the well-known veterans of the Vietnam anti-war movement are less forgiving. It also indicates that Obama's election, despite his hopes, will not automatically signal the demise of the legacy of the 1960s.

Another notable political marker of the Vietnam War and its era's relevance in contemporary American life is Louisiana voters' late-2008 election of Anh "Joseph" Cao, the first Vietnamese American to be elected to the House of Representatives. So Barack Obama, fulfilling the dreams of countless activists who created the early 1960s movement to obtain civil rights for historically disenfranchised African Americans, defeated Vietnam War hero John McCain and will work with a Congress that includes a man who fled his war-torn home at the age of seven for a new life in the country whose long sojourn in Vietnam has marked American life for now nearly half a century. Yes, the legacy of the Vietnam War is with us still.

It is hardly surprising that a war that lasted as long as the Vietnam War and that was so entangled with important concurrent events (the anti-war movement, the civil rights and women's movements, and more) has inspired countless assessments and artifacts. Widespread journalistic and television coverage of the war, beginning in the mid- to late 1960s and continuing through America's withdrawal from Vietnam in 1973 and the defeat of the South Vietnamese (the fall of Saigon) in 1975, swelled, beginning in the early 1980s, to an outpouring of history, journalism, movies, television series, music, comic books, video games, and other treatments of the war that shows no signs of stopping. Among the most numerous and powerful testaments to the war's lingering legacy are literary texts—novels, memoirs, drama, and poetry—that personally and powerfully recreate a variety of experiences of the war and its era.

In his introduction to *Coming to Terms*, a 1985 anthology of American plays about the Vietnam War, James Reston Jr. suggests that for memories and assessments of the Vietnam War, traditional historical method is inadequate. Facts and men in power are not at the core of this story, but rather the emotions of the generation that shouldered this ill-conceived enterprise. The Vietnam generation, reacting to the decisions from on high, changed American society forever, and so the heart of the matter is emotional and cultural.[2]

"The novels, the plays, the painting and sculpture, the poetry . . . are worth more than a mountain of books on the military campaigns or . . . the facts about the era," Reston continues. "With the Vietnam experience, the history is the subtext."[3] Or, as Ernest Hemingway, that great chronicler of earlier American wars, asserted, "all good books are alike in that they are truer than if they had really happened."

Reston's assertion, written as the Vietnam War became a lively, contested subject in the national conversation in the 1980s, was prescient, for indeed the creative literature inspired by the Vietnam War—much of it written by veterans of the war—is a large and multitudinous component of the cultural commentary about the war and its repercussions in American society. Acolytes of the modern women's movement that arose out of the Civil Rights and anti-war movements famously insisted that "the personal is political," a truism underscored by the literary artifacts of America's longest war, which—given its scope and the broad home-front war against the war—directly touched many Americans (and, of course, the too often overlooked Vietnamese) and yielded powerful personal testimonies that present the impact of the war—on the battlefield, on the home front, and in the war's aftermath.

LaSalle University's special collection of Imaginative Representations of the Vietnam War currently includes some 10,000 short stories, plays, film scripts, works of graphic art, paintings, videos, TV productions, and sound recordings, including 9,000 novels and books of poetry—which LaSalle calls "fictive writing." Colorado State University's Vietnam War Literature Collection is more narrowly defined, including "imaginative accounts" of only the Vietnam combat experience—and it too comprises over 4,000 texts. Because of the large (and growing) number of literary texts about the war, and because of their varying literary quality, the interested student may well need some guidance about where to begin.

THE TRADITIONAL COMBAT NOVEL

John Dos Passos' 1921 novel *Three Soldiers* and Norman Mailer's 1948 *The Naked and the Dead* are two of the iconic combat novels of the World Wars I and II respectively. Each, in a wartime collective version of the classic initiation or coming-of-age narrative, offers multiple, diverse protagonists and a panoramic, naturalistically detailed representation of the horrors and boredom of the combat experience. The canon of Vietnam War literature includes many ambitious novels which offer that war's variation on the collective fictional story of the so-called melting pot platoon. James Webb, Vietnam veteran and current US senator from Virginia, creates a solid example of the genre in *Fields of Fire* (1978). Webb's novel, which is avowedly autobiographical, strives for verisimilitude (with detailed descriptions, a map of the area in Vietnam in which the action occurs, a glossary of military terms in the back of the book) in the story of a Marine platoon's combat experiences in 1969. In three distinct sections the novel's third-person narrator offers the points of view of three main characters: Hodges, a noble young lieutenant from a Southern military family; Snake, a tough, lower-class character who finds purpose in the war; and Goodrich (Bush-named Senator), a peevish college boy who is ambivalent about the war.

Though perhaps not the most sophisticated Vietnam combat novel, *Fields of Fire* is a worthy representative of the form because it deftly incorporates so many of the common themes that recur in most narrative treatments of America's most controversial war. It privileges the enlisted man's—the grunt's—experience of and account of the war in its familiar acknowledgment that *you had to be there*. Bagger, a member of Hodges's platoon, describes his recent R&R:

Figure 10.1 *Combat scenes: ARVN–Helioborne: Heavily laden infantrymen of the 1st Battalion, 1st Regiment of ARVN First Division dash from a helicopter that lifted them to a recently "cleared" mountaintop landing zone overlooking Ba Long Valley in Quang Tri Province.*

Photograph VA002367, November 1969, Douglas Pike Photograph Collection, The Vietnam Archive, Texas Tech University.

THE VIETNAM WAR AND LITERATURE

"I hate this bullshit. But all the time I was [on leave], I kept thinking about the bush. Like I belong here, and all the other stuff is only important because I *earned* it here, because it's a part of being *here*. Like I been here all my life, and the people in the bush are real, are my people. Like nobody in the world except for us understands this, or gives one flying fuck about it."[4]

Though the imaginative literature from all wars has emphasized the special knowledge that combatants share, Webb reflects the widespread acceptance that the Vietnam War was unique, and that the extreme youth and almost universal working-class provenance of its combatants created a special claim on this war by its participants, who are, the title of Part 1 of *Fields of Fire* notes, "the best we have."

And if Snake and Hodges are men of honor in a morally ambiguous universe, their enemies are equally clear: craven military officers and pogues (rear-area clerks) who put the grunts in harm's way, often disastrously, in a mindless adherence to bureaucratic rules or a selfish quest for glory; the press ("goddamn leeches, sucking off other people's blood"); America's corrupt, inept, or cowardly South Vietnamese allies; and, most abhorrent (here as in most Vietnam combat novels), anti-war activists.[5] A Marine in *Fields of Fire* who survived his thirteen-month tour of duty and returned to "the World" re-enlists because of the indifferent or hostile reception he has met back home; and when, at the end of the novel, the unsympathetic Goodrich returns (wounded and the cause of Snake's death) to college, his clueless class-mates exploit his veteran status by enlisting him to speak at an anti-war rally. Goodrich, the callow college boy, is, as a result of the crucible of the Vietnam War, now a mature pragmatist. He calls for an end to the war, but the rest of his remarks to the naïve Harvard students are the novel's final words: "I DIDN'T SEE ANY OF YOU IN VIETNAM. I SAW . . . TRUCK DRIVERS AND COAL MINERS AND FARMERS. . . . WHAT DO YOU CARE IF IT ENDS? YOU WON'T GET HURT. . . . WHAT DO ANY OF YOU EVEN KNOW ABOUT IT."[6] *You had to be there.*

Many other ambitious conventional combat novels (most written by veterans of the war) recount these and other themes of the Vietnam combat experience (the complexity of race relations among the soldiers; the frustrations of conducting war in unfamiliar jungle conditions, against a tenacious enemy who looked all too much like America's Vietnamese allies, with technology and equipment often ill-suited for guerrilla warfare; the temptations toward and repercussions of extreme violence and atrocities; the close fraternal bonds and community created by men struggling to stay, and keep each other, alive). Other readable variations on the traditional combat story include:

Josiah Bunting, *The Lionheads* (1972)
William Pelfrey, *The Big V* (1972)
Larry Heinemann, *Close Quarters* (1977)
Winston Groom, *Better Times than These* (1978)

John Del Vecchio, *The 13th Valley* (1982)
David Halberstam, *One Very Hot Day* (1967)
Susan Fromberg Schaeffer, *Buffalo Afternoon* (1989)

EXPERIMENTAL FICTION

Historians and commentators have long accepted that the Vietnam War was unique in the annals of American warfare. It was a war without a front line, where progress was measured by often illusory body counts, and the only movement seemed to be endless, circuitous marches through the hot, unfamiliar bush; a war in which American soldiers were never certain which of the odd-looking natives around them were enemies, which friends; a war fought in the dark of night. It was a war about which Tim O'Brien writes, "the old rules are no longer binding, the old truths no longer true."[7] Much as Joseph Heller's satirical 1961 novel *Catch-22* captured the absurdities of World War II, much of the literature of the Vietnam War reflects authors' efforts to reflect the often surreal, absurdist characteristics of America's jungle war. *Going After Cacciato*, the 1978 novel by Tim O'Brien—the accomplished veteran-author whose many narratives on the war have most compellingly transformed various aspects of the Vietnam experience into enduring literature—presents the bizarre, fantastical journey of point-of-view character Paul Berlin as he and his squad follow a fellow soldier named Cacciato, who has fled the Vietnam War and is headed, on foot, for Paris.

Cacciato is a tour de force, a dazzling and imaginative fiction; O'Brien's 1990 collection *The Things They Carried* is a more readable and teachable book that similarly outlines its author's perceptions of the ambiguities of the Vietnam War. *The Things They Carried*, a unified collection of short stories and prose pieces, exemplifies the more compelling commonplaces about the war. In "The Ghost Soldiers," for instance, the first-person narrator (called Tim O'Brien) articulates the exclusivity and camaraderie of the combat experience and its ironic allure when he notes, on being moved out of harm's way after his second wound, that he

"missed the adventure, even the danger, of the real war in the boonies. It's a hard thing to explain to somebody who hasn't felt it, but the presence of death and danger has a way of bringing you fully awake . . . you pay attention to the world. . . . You become part of a tribe and you share the same blood."[8]

His chronicle in the title story of the grunts' equipment, weapons, personal items—the literal things they carry—approaches the realistic detail of more conventional narratives. Yet *The Things They Carried* is unconventional or experimental in form, in part because the collection of twenty interrelated but discrete narratives transcends its wartime subject matter (Alpha Company's experiences in and after the Vietnam War) to become a subtly sophisticated narrative about writing and storytelling.

Throughout the collection, whose varied assortment of short stories, essays, notes, and fragments underscores its emphasis on the technique of making narrative sense of an inherently senseless experience, O'Brien reiterates his central precept, that "story-truth is truer sometimes than happening-truth."[9] In O'Brien's fictional universe—in America's Vietnam—nothing is what it seems. The cowardly decision that the newly drafted, anti-war narrator makes at the end of "On the Rainy River" is to fight in Vietnam. The civilian who is seduced by the dark, dangerous allure of the jungle is a soldier's high school girlfriend smuggled into a remote encampment in "The Sweetheart of the Song Tra Bong." At the end of the story, which Rat Kiley insists is true, Mary Anne "had crossed to the other side. . . . She was wearing her culottes, her pink sweater, and a necklace of human tongues. . . . She was ready for the kill."[10] The narrator Tim O'Brien relates the story of "the man I killed" in the story of that name, but sixty pages later, in "Good Form," he discloses that he in fact did *not* kill the enemy soldier. Throughout *The Things They Carried*, O'Brien illustrates that the peculiar surrealism of the Vietnam War demands a new kind of narrative; in Vietnam, as in his fiction, "the only certainty is overwhelming ambiguity."[11]

Another readable example of experimental fiction about the Vietnam War is Stephen Wright's *Meditations in Green*.

THE HOME FRONT AND THE AFTERMATH

Despite—or perhaps because of—veteran-authors' insistence that only the combatants who directly engaged this singular, complex war can ever understand it, much of the imaginative writing about the Vietnam War is about American society during and after the United States' ill-advised adventure in Vietnam. It is, of course, the breadth and depth of writing about the war that does *not* directly engage the combat experience that testifies to the lingering influence of the Vietnam War in American culture for the past forty years.

The thematic post-combat reverberations are myriad and complex. Larry Brown's 1989 novel *Dirty Work* and Larry Heinemann's *Paco's Story* (1986) are spare, elegant novels about veterans enduring the trauma of persistent physical combat-inflicted wounds. The damage is psychological for the veteran-protagonists of Tim O'Brien's *In the Lake of the Woods* (1989) and Philip Caputo's *Indian Country* (1987). Beverly Gologorsky recounts the postwar lives of the wives of a group of variously damaged vets in the 1999 novel *The Things We Do to Make It Home*. And in one of the more accessible aftermath narratives, *In Country* (1985), Bobbie Ann Mason offers a female variation on the coming-of-age novel in the story of Sam(antha) Hughes, who in the summer after her high school graduation becomes preoccupied with her father, who died in Vietnam before she was born.

As she supplements her reading about the war with inquiries to her mother and her uncle Emmett and his vet pals about Vietnam and her young father, Sam is told repeatedly that her quest is ill-advised. "Women weren't over there . . . so they can't really understand," Emmett snarls in angry solidarity with a veteran-buddy whose wife has left him.[12] And Sam's remarried

Figure 10.2 "A female demonstrator offers a flower to military police..."

By S.Sgt. Albert R. Simpson, Arlington, Virginia, October 21, 1967 (ARC Identifier: 594360); Color Photographs of Signal Corps Activity, 1944–81; Records of the Office of the Chief Signal Officer; Record Group 111; National Archives.

mother has long ago forgotten about her long-dead husband and moved on with her life. Sam confronts Tom, a vet whose psychological combat wounds have left him sexually impotent; a vet who after twenty years still misses the war, "the intensity of it, what you went through together"; and an uncle whose breakdown late in the novel, when he confesses to Sam the combat trauma that has left him "damaged . . . like something in the center of my heart is gone and I can't get it back," an ineffable wound far more debilitating than the Agent Orange-induced acne that so worries his niece.[13]

As Sam negotiates the typical challenges for adolescent girls in her small Kentucky town in 1984—whether to marry her high school boyfriend or attend college; whether to stay with the brother-like uncle, Emmett, or leave town with her pregnant, unmarried friend—she discovers, through his Vietnam diary, her father's cavalier, thoughtless response to killing Vietnamese soldiers and recognizes that "she will never really know what happened to all these men in the war." But on a trip to the recently built Vietnam Veterans Memorial (a pilgrimage to which concludes many aftermath novels and movies), Sam—when she sees her own name on the Wall—realizes as well that it is "as though all the names in America have been used to decorate this wall."[14]

Like the many stories of the resonance of the war in American life now into the twenty-first century, *In Country* demonstrates Michael Herr's oft-quoted aphorism "Vietnam Vietnam Vietnam, we've all been there."[15]

THE VIETNAM MEMOIR

The veteran's persistent insistence that "you had to be there" in order to understand the war—the claim of exclusive ownership of the experience—intersects, throughout the literature of the war, with the common assertion that no one back home really wants to know about the horrors of war anyway. As the ghost narrator of Larry Heinemann's *Paco's Story* notes, "the people with the purse strings and apron strings gripped in their hot and soft little hands denounce war stories . . . as a geek-monster species of evil-ugly rumor."[16] The logical result of these truisms—the war belongs to its combatants; non-combatants can't understand it and don't want to—should be silence. And, indeed, many Vietnam texts echo Frederic Henry's famous declaration, in Hemingway's 1929 World War I novel *A Farewell to Arms*, that "I had seen nothing sacred, and the things that were glorious had no glory. . . . There were many words that you could not stand to hear."[17] But one of the ironies in this ironic war is that the insistence that *you* can't understand it, that the experience was unspeakably horrid, recurs in hundreds, *thousands* of personal testimonies that repeat and repeat the restrictive news. And, as the privileging of the combatant's voice suggests, many veterans of the war told their personal tale in memoirs. Early memoirs include Tim O'Brien's first book, *If I Die in a Combat Zone, Box Me Up and Ship Me Home* (1973) and Ron Kovics's *Born on the Fourth of July* (1976). Philip Caputo's *A Rumor of War* (1977) is representative of war-era combat memoirs.

Caputo's memoir of what he calls "the dominant event in the life of my generation" is his account of his year as a marine with the "first U.S. combat unit sent to Indochina."[18] Caputo served in 1965 and 1966 as a second lieutenant in charge of a rifle platoon and, later, as a casualty reporting officer; his story concludes with his return to Vietnam a decade later as a journalist and his account of the chaotic fall of Saigon in late April 1975, which ended the war for the Vietnamese. Caputo's narrative reiterates many of the standard assertions about all war—the boredom, the powerful camaraderie shared by fighting men, the "fact that it had been an experience as fascinating as it was repulsive, as exhilarating as it was sad, as tender as it was cruel." It insists as well on familiar truisms about the exceptionality of the crucible of Vietnam:

> We were fighting in the cruelest kind of conflict, a people's war. It was no orderly campaign, as in Europe, but a war for survival waged in a wilderness without rules or laws; a war in which each soldier fought for his own life and the lives of the men beside him, not caring who he killed . . . and feeling only contempt for those who sought to impose on his savage struggle the mincing distinctions of civilized warfare—that code of battlefield ethics that attempted to humanize an essentially inhuman war.[19]

In his anger at the cruelty of the conflagration, Caputo finds his most powerful theme. *A Rumor of War* conveys compellingly Caputo's gradual cynicism about America's presence in Vietnam. Though he enlisted in the Marines, and welcomed the opportunity to prove his manhood and encounter adventure, Caputo comes to question the morality of the "organized butchery" that is the war. Late in his rotation, with his C Company enduring high casualties and a low kill ratio, Caputo is complicit in his men's brutal retaliation against the resourceful enemy; the author both admits and explains his own and his comrades' actions when he reflects that "the war had awakened something evil in us, some dark, malicious power that allowed us to kill without feeling," but he decides that the murder is "a direct result of the war. The thing we had done was a result of what the war had done to us."[20]

Caputo's examination of the moral and psychological dimensions of combat is similar to Lynda Van Devanter's in the earliest and best-known personal account of the female experience of the Vietnam War. In *Home before Morning: The True Story of an Army Nurse in Vietnam*, her 1983 memoir, Van Devanter recounts the trajectory of her disaffection with the war. Inspired to enlist, like Caputo, by the "noble sentiments of John Fitzgerald Kennedy," the idealistic young nurse comes to question the corruption of the South Vietnamese government, the "inane regulations" of army life, the nightmare of the constant deaths of friends, patients, and Vietnamese civilians. "Maybe there were [Americans] who could spend 365 days in that crazy environment and never once ask why," Van Devanter asserts. "If there were, I never met them."[21]

Like many veteran-memoirists, Van Devanter devotes a substantial portion of her book to her difficult adjustment to life back in "the World" after her return from Vietnam. Having "lost an important part of" herself in Vietnam, Van Devanter learns that the "real war" begins *after* Vietnam.[22] Suffering from the lingering emotional numbness that allowed her to survive the operating-room horrors of Vietnam, exacerbated by her friends' and families' indifference to the reality of her war experience and a vituperative anti-war movement, on her return home Van Devanter endures the nightmares and flashbacks that are the characteristics of post-traumatic stress disorder (PTSD). As a woman, her difficult adjustment is a solitary experience: she is unwelcome at the local Vietnam Veterans Against the War chapter. Her nursing skills are undervalued in a stateside military hospital. Only after a troubled postwar decade does Van Devanter become involved with the new Vietnam Veterans of America organization, for which she established and administered the VVA Women's Project. *Home before Morning* ends in 1982, and for the next twenty years of her life (until her 2002 death, ostensibly from the effects of exposure to Agent Orange in Vietnam), Van Devanter devoted herself to healing and support for women veterans of the Vietnam War. Her memoir inspired subsequent similar accounts of women veterans, such as Keith Walker's oral history *A Piece of My Heart* (1995) and Winnie Smith's *American Daughter Gone to War* (1992).

THE NEW JOURNALISM

Much has been written about the role of the media in reporting on—and shaping public opinion about—the war in Vietnam and the home front protest movement that is the inextricable parallel to America's long imbroglio in Southeast Asia. *Reporting Vietnam*, a two-volume Library of America anthology dating from 1959, presents nearly 2,000 pages of journalism about the war, from straightforward news articles in publications such as *Time* and the *Wall Street Journal* to examples of the more personal journalism popularized in the era by Hunter S. Thompson and Tom Wolfe. Indeed, the reporting and commentary on the war were often influenced by the response of non-fiction writers to the social transformations of the 1960s with a new kind of writing that combined the conventions and techniques of fiction and journalism. In a changing world in which "everyday events continually blurred the comfortable distinctions between reality and unreality, between fantasy and fact," wrote scholar John Hollowell in 1977, fiction writers turned to "documentary forms" while journalists incorporated a more personal voice into their reporting.[23] Norman Mailer's 1968 account of the 1967 anti-war March on the Pentagon, *The Armies of the Night*—which Mailer subtitled *History as a Novel, the Novel as History*—is an exemplar of the new, hybrid genre called the New Journalism.

Many mainstream journalists (some of whom, like Ward Just, later also wrote fiction about the war) returned from their assignments in Vietnam to craft compelling non-fiction books based on their experiences covering the war. Ward Just's *To What End* (1968), Frances Fitzgerald's *Fire in the Lake: The Vietnamese and the Americans in Vietnam* (1972), and Gloria Emerson's *Winners and Losers* (1976) were important books by journalists who worked in Vietnam that helped Americans understand the issues and mistakes of the war.

The most lauded and most influential non-fiction book by an American journalist, however— a book that illustrates perfectly the new infusion of fictional techniques into a factual account of the war—is Michael Herr's 1977 *Dispatches*. *Dispatches* was perhaps the earliest narrative to suggest, in its fragmented, asymmetrical structure and prose style, that the ambiguous, absurdist undertaking in Vietnam could be captured only through a new kind of writing. As Herr asserts, "conventional journalism could no more reveal this war than conventional firepower could win it."[24] Thomas Myers maintains that "as a model of how the successful union of form and function may transmute private vision into public understanding, *Dispatches* remains the war's most distinctive and eloquent voice, its most abundant and demanding compensatory history."[25]

Herr's structure (six discrete sections) and prose style (described best by the title of one of those sections, "Illumination Rounds") only underscore his thematic preoccupation with the complexities and ambiguities of the American experience in Vietnam, which he evocatively captures through the image of the outdated, humidity-damaged map of ancient Vietnam that opens the book and the "one-pointed and resonant" *non*-war story that introduces his account of his time in-country: "Patrol went up the mountain. One man came back. He died before he could tell us what happened." This, writes Herr, was "as . . . resonant as any war story I ever heard, it took me a year to understand it."[26]

Herr includes reporting and commentary on the January 1968 Tet Offensive, the prolonged battle at Khe Sanh, the grunts' and military command's complicated relationship with the press (as well as an insider's introduction to some of the more colorful journalists who worked in-country). He tells the stories of ordinary enlisted men: Marines Mayhew and Day Tripper and their friend Orrin, whose wife's letter confesses her infidelity and who thereafter becomes "the crazy fucking grunt who was going to get through the war so he could go home and kill his old lady"; and the much-wounded Special Forces sergeant who is on his third tour of duty but refuses to go home to his wife and children because "as far as he was concerned, there was no place in the world as fine as Vietnam"; and the African American soldier who won't shoot his gun for fear that he might kill one of "'th' Brothers, you dig it?'"[27] What distinguishes *Dispatches* from other powerful reportage on the war, and has made it one of the iconic books on the subject, is Herr's transcendence of journalism into art. In *Dispatches*, Herr audaciously interweaves the terrors and beauty of combat, the dazzling technology of the US fighting force, and the untruths and unknowable elements of the undertaking, into a breathless, bold narrative that captures the "Inscrutable Immutable" and inimitable story of America's misadventure in Vietnam.

POETRY

Perhaps more than any of the genres represented in writing about the Vietnam War and the 1960s, poetry has featured a variety of voices and perspectives. From early in the war years, veterans' poetic responses to combat have been complemented by protest poetry, written by both men and women, and—discovered and translated in later years—the voices of the Vietnamese. In more recent years the popularity of the World Wide Web has allowed amateur poets to make their work accessible. As H. Bruce Franklin notes in *The Vietnam War in American Stories, Songs, and Poems*, "the Vietnam War has helped to erode the barriers between 'poetry' as literature of the elite and poetry as relished by the masses."[28]

The earliest Vietnam War poetry was by established poets who sought—in individual volumes and several early (now out-of-print) anthologies—to protest the war. Lawrence Ferlinghetti, Denise Levertov, and Robert Bly published early, important statements against the war. In "At a March against the Vietnam War" (from his 1968 National Book Award-winning book, *The Light around the Body*), Bly imagines a November 1965 anti-war march shadowed by "something moving in the dark somewhere / Just beyond / The edge of our eyes." It is a boat in the jungle, moving in "that darkness among pine boughs / That the Puritans brushed / As they went to kill turkeys." For Bly, the Vietnam War is only the most recent manifestation of the violence inherent in the American story.

Similarly, the best veterans' poetry about the combat experience evokes the terrors of war in precise, detailed, lyrical descriptions but transcends the immediate to offer powerful statements about the loss of personal and national innocence, and about guilt and responsibility. In 1972, D. C. Berry, in *Saigon Cemetery*, and Michael Casey, in *Obscenities*, published the first full-length books of poetry by Vietnam veterans. Berry's experimental, e. e. cummings-influenced form contrasts with Casey's colloquial, accessible style, but both capture the immediacy and authenticity of the combat experience.

Two Vietnam War poetry anthologies edited by W. D. Ehrhart Jr. (himself an accomplished poet and memoirist) brought Vietnam poetry to a larger audience. His 1976 collection *Demilitarized Zones*, co-edited with Jan Barry, and especially 1985's still-available *Carrying the Darkness*, included poetry by male and female veterans with a variety of non-veteran voices. *Carrying the Darkness*, reprinted in 1989, includes now-canonical Vietnam poems such as John Balaban's "After Our War," which wonders, "After the war . . . will the ancient tales tell us new truths? / Will the myriad world surrender new metaphor? / After our war, how will love speak?" Now-well-known poets such as Yusef Komunyakaa, Bruce Weigl, and Basil T. Paquet are also represented.

Lynda Van Devanter and Joan A. Furey's 1991 anthology of poetry by women who served in Vietnam, *Visions of War, Dreams of Peace*, and John Balaban's editions of Vietnamese folk poetry added relevant voices to the poetic conversation. Today, the most comprehensive collection of Vietnam War poetry available is Philip Mahony's *From Both Sides Now: The Poetry of the Vietnam War and Its Aftermath* (1998). Organized chronologically, Mahony's anthology includes 135 well-known and lesser-known veteran poets, as well as anti-war poetry and poetry by Vietnamese combatants, Vietnamese displaced by the war, and the second-generation Vietnamese Americans who grew up in the United States.

DRAMA

As with the early poetry about the war, the first dramatic works to take the war as their theme or context were polemical, often technically innovative protests against the war. Many early plays were street theater, staged by the madcap counterculture and, often, never published. Most drama broadly about the Vietnam War addresses the home front and the aftermath. Theater, notes David J. DeRose, is not a likely medium "for recreating the physical realities of a hostile jungle environment, the intensity of combat, and the suddenness of death. Thus, with notable exceptions, the theater has not proven to be a primary venue for the realistic representation of in-country experiences."²⁹ For instance, among early plays, Megan Terry's 1966 *Viet Rock* is an experimental anti-war rock musical with an ensemble cast; Barbara Garson's satiric *MacBird* (1967) is a counterculture parody of *Macbeth* with a Lyndon Johnson-like character as MacBird. Arthur Kopit's *Indians* (1969), like Robert Bly's poem "At a March against the Vietnam War," suggests that America's involvement in Vietnam echoes the country's brutal treatment of Native Americans.

Some of the best American plays about the war from the 1970s and early 1980s were collected in the 1985 anthology *Coming to Terms: American Plays and the Vietnam War* (now out of print). Most notably, the book includes David Rabe's 1976 play *Streamers*, an army barracks drama about a varied group of Vietnam-bound soldiers whose violent confrontations about race and homosexuality culminate in multiple deaths before they even get to Vietnam. "The melting pot, macho army, the repository of . . . a whole accumulated legacy of warrior myth, hemorrhages to death in a frenzy of internal combustion," notes scholar Philip Beidler of the play. Like *Streamers*, Rabe's 1971 play *The Basic Training of Pavlo Hummel* traps a diverse group of military men in the violence and insanity of the Vietnam War. The hapless draftee Pavlo Hummel dies in the opening scene, in a Saigon brothel; the play is his posthumous return to basic training, guided by a Virgilian black GI named Ardell; on his visit to his past life, Pavlo learns only, as Philip Beidler notes, that "as in his abortive American life, so in his quick, inglorious American death, he has truly experienced nothing."³⁰

The second of the three plays now commonly known as Rabe's Vietnam trilogy, *Sticks and Bones*, won the 1972 Tony Award for best play; in it Rabe brings the war home to a banal America that willfully refuses to confront the moral consequences of its fatal incursion into Vietnam. The blind combat veteran David returns to his family and home in a dark, satiric turn on the long-running 1950s and early 1960s television situation comedy *The Adventures of Ozzie and Harriet*, which has come to represent the perfect suburban American family and the romanticized, nostalgic ideal of a post–World War II, affluent, stable American society. David is dispatched to his childhood home by a military convoy that will deliver its cargo throughout the United States, where the casualties will be "layin' there all over the grass, their backs been broken, their brains jellied, their insides turned into garbage. No-legged boys and one-legged boys."³¹ Though David insists that something is wrong, that he does not know the family that welcomes him, his parents, Ozzie and Harriet, continue to insist that he is fine, that he is safely home, and, Harriet says, "we're all together, a family." As the chirping Harriet prepares food for her men, World War II vet Ozzie happily reminisces about the camaraderie of men at war, and teenaged brother Ricky snaps family photographs, David struggles with his guilt over Vietnamese fatalities and his abandonment of his Vietnamese lover Zung (who hovers in her *ao dai*). By the end of the play the hidden fissures in this ostensibly perfect family have erupted, Ozzie and Harriet revealing their repressed anger and disappointments, and David refusing to pretend that he is OK. Near the end of the play, David summons the death convoy and insists on inviting the corpses into the family home: "We'll stack them along the walls. . . . They will become the floor and they will become the walls, the chairs. We'll sit in them, sleep in them. We will call them 'home.'

... They will call it madness. We will call it seeing." The blind veteran has challenged the metaphorically blind family to see clearly; but the loving parents and brother calmly kill the "yellow" Zung, whom they despise, and direct David to slit his wrists. And the play ends. "I like David like this," Rick suggests. Harriet: "He's happier." Ozzie: "We're all happier."[32] As *New Yorker* theater critic John Lahr asserts, *Sticks and Bones* "marked better than any other play of its era the bitter spiritual divide between American generations."[33]

David Rabe is the most important dramatist to find art in the Vietnam experience. In the Afterword to the 1993 two-volume edition of *The Vietnam Plays*, Rabe recognizes, looking back twenty years, that the Vietnam War was a watershed event in the modern American psyche that unleashed the country's innate capability for evil. The nightmare of the war and the country's refusal to confront its culpability created a tipping point that, Rabe suggests, nudged America toward the mindless violence that characterizes contemporary American society; the war

> cut the last moral tether by which certain ideals and urges and forces were balanced, and with their release and commingling the serial killer was hatched, the plague of drug dealers and child molesters and wife beaters, the corruption in government and business, the army of teenagers bearing guns through high school halls.[34]

Situating in the Vietnam War the death of American innocence, Rabe, like the best writers on the war, in his theatrical alchemy, transforms the dross of America's shameful experience in Vietnam into the gold of literary art.

Less challenging, popular dramatic representations of the Vietnam War include Shirley Lauro's often-produced *A Piece of My Heart* (based on Keith Walker's collection of oral histories) and the musical *Miss Saigon*.

VOICES OF THE VIETNAMESE

Like Michael Herr's *Dispatches* and Tim O'Brien's fiction, Bao Ninh's *The Sorrow of War: A Novel of North Vietnam* foregrounds a fragmented literary technique that seems particularly appropriate for the chaos and ambiguity of the Vietnam War; it is, in fact, a book about the writing of a book. Combat veteran Bao Ninh's 1991 autobiographical, metafictional narrative is the story of Kien, a former soldier who is one of the few survivors of his North Vietnamese battalion. In 1975, after the war is over, Kien has returned to Vietnam's central highlands—where much of his fighting experience occurred a decade earlier—as part of the Missing in Action Remains-Gathering Team. He has not recovered from the trauma of combat, and he writes his manuscript to exorcise the demons of his ten long years of war. Kien's narrative—the novel *The Sorrow of War*—is "the ash from this exorcism of devils." For Kien, in fact, writing about the war is an irresistible compulsion; he "cannot stop writing war stories, stories of rifles firing, bombs dropping, enemies and comrades . . . [he] can't write about anything else."[35]

Figure 10.3 Viet Cong soldiers moving forward under covering fire from a heavy machine gun during the Vietnam War, ca. 1968.

Photo by Three Lions/Hulton Archive/Getty Images.

Kien remains obsessed with his wartime experiences because of their powerful and profound effect on his life; in his preoccupation, he is like many American veteran-narrators, though Kien was a combatant for the full ten years of his country's war against the Americans and the South Vietnamese. Through his protagonist, Bao Ninh evokes the brutal nightmares of dehumanizing combat for soldiers as well as the tragic lives of millions of Vietnamese civilians who were inevitably damaged by the protracted war. He recognizes that "war was a world with no home, no roof, no comforts. A miserable journey, of endless drifting. War was a world without real men, without real women, without feeling" and that "the cruelty and the destruction of war had warped his soul."[36]

Novels like Bao Ninh's and Duong Thu Huong's *Novel without a Name* offer the perspective of the North Vietnamese combatant. Despite the length of their combat experience and the deprivations of their combat conditions, Kien and Huong's Quan are not unlike American combat veteran protagonists in their disillusionment with war.

A more unusual variation on the Vietnamese experience of the war appears in literature by and about the 1.2 million persons of Vietnamese ancestry currently residing in the United States. The stories of the Vietnamese who fled their war-torn country to create new lives in the land of their vanquished invaders and their American-born or American-raised children who

Figure 10.4 *Arrival of South Vietnamese refugees, Eglin Air Force Base, Florida, May 1975.*

Photograph VA002580, May 1975, Bryan Grigsby Collection, The Vietnam Archive, Texas Tech University.

struggle to reconcile the sad legacy of their heritage with the allure of contemporary America are captured in Lan Cao's 1997 novel *Monkey Bridge*, lê thi diem thúy's *The Gangster We Are All Looking For* (2003), Dao Strom's *Grass Roof, Tin Roof* (2003), and American veteran Robert Olen Butler's Pulitzer Prize-winning story collection *A Good Scent from a Strange Mountain* (1992). These poignant stories of the real victims of the war challenge Americans' provincial perception of the war; demonstrating that the Vietnam War was, for the majority of those who engaged it directly, daily, often disastrously, an American war. It is the creative narratives of the Vietnamese displaced by America's sojourn in Vietnam— and their children—that disclose most evocatively the inclusive apprehension of the war that all of these literary texts offer.

SCHOLARSHIP AND FURTHER READING

The vast assemblage of literature about the Vietnam War, its aftermath, and its era has of course demanded—and yielded—substantial scholarly commentary. The important full-length critical cultural studies include Philip Beidler's *American Literature and the Experience of Vietnam* (1982) and *Re-writing America: Vietnam Authors in Their Generation* (1991), Thomas Myers's 1988 *Walking Point*, Jeffrey Walsh's *American War Literature 1914 to Vietnam* (1982), Susan Jeffords's *The Remasculinization of America: Gender and the Vietnam War* (1989), Philip Melling's *Vietnam in American Literature* (1990), Tobey C. Herzog's *Vietnam War Stories* (1992), Andrew Martin's *Receptions of War: Vietnam in American Culture* (1993), Donald Ringnalda's *Fighting and Writing the Vietnam War* (1994), Jim Neilson's *Warring Fictions: Cultural Politics and the Vietnam War Narrative* (1998), Katherine Kinney's *Friendly Fire: American Images of the Vietnam War* (2000), and Maureen Ryan's *The Other Side of Grief: The Home Front and the Aftermath in American Narratives of the Vietnam War* (2008). Journals such as *War, Literature and the Arts* (published at the United States Air Force Academy) regularly present new literary material and cutting-edge scholarship on the capacious canon of Vietnam War literature.

An interested reader approaching this material for the first time might begin with novelist Stewart O'Nan's affordable 1998 anthology *The Vietnam Reader: The Definitive Collection of Fiction and Nonfiction on the War*. Readers who wish to engage a more comprehensive literary treatment of the Vietnam War and the Vietnam era might look to oral histories (Christian G. Appy's 2004 *Patriots: The Vietnam War Remembered from All Sides* is an excellent starting point); to memoirs by Vietnam prisoners of war; to poetry, memoirs, and novels by and about anti-war activists; and to the many texts by women who waited at home for their husbands, brothers, and fathers to return from the war.

DISCUSSION QUESTIONS

1. While most of the combat fiction written by Vietnam War veterans insists that you can't understand the war unless you were there as a combatant, the broad variety of literature about the war suggests, like Michael Herr, that "we've all been there." How does reading the literature about the war comment upon—perhaps reconcile—this apparent contradiction?
2. Elsewhere in *Dispatches*, Michael Herr writes that "War Stories aren't really anything more than stories about people anyway." Discuss.
3. In his introduction to *Coming to Terms*, James Reston Jr. writes that for understanding the Vietnam War, "traditional historical method is inadequate. Facts and men in power are not at the core of this story, but rather the emotions of the generation that shouldered

this ill-conceived enterprise." How does the imaginative literature of the war affirm or deny this assertion?
4. Scholars and commentators have suggested that it is impossible—or inadvisable—to discuss the Vietnam War without considering the transformative American social movements of the Vietnam era: the peace movement that opposed the war; the Civil Rights movement that preceded it; the women's rights, gay rights, and environmental movements that coincided with it. What do you know about the domestic turmoil in the United States during the war years? Are the scholars correct?
5. Is there evidence in contemporary America that President Obama is correct when he suggests that the issues and conflicts of the 1960s are over (or should be)? Or will America's fascination with the Vietnam War and the Vietnam era die with the last of the baby boomers?

SUGGESTED READING

Beidler, Philip D. *American Literature and the Experience of Vietnam*. Athens, GA: University of Georgia Press, 1982.
Caputo, Philip. *A Rumor of War*. New York: Ballantine, 1977.
DeRose, David J. "Drama." In *Vietnam War Literature: An Annotated Bibliography of Imaginative Works about Americans Fighting in Vietnam*, edited by John Newman. Lanham, MD: Scarecrow Press, 1996.
Duong Thu Huong. *Novel without a Name*. New York: Wm. Morrow, 1995; 1991.
Ehrhart, W. D. Jr., ed. *Carrying the Darkness: The Poetry of the Vietnam War*. Lubbock: Texas Tech University Press, 1985; 1989.
Franklin, H. Bruce. *The Vietnam War in American Stories, Songs, and Poems*. New York: Bedford/St. Martin's, 1995.
Herr, Michael. *Dispatches*. 1977. New York: Vintage Books-Random House, 1991.
Hollowell, John. *Fact and Fiction: The New Journalism and the Nonfiction Novel*. Chapel Hill: University of North Carolina Press, 1977.
Lahr, John. "Land of Lost Souls: David Rabe's America." *New Yorker*, November 24, 2008, 114–20.
Lan Cao. *Monkey Bridge*. New York: Viking, 1997.
Mason, Bobbie Ann. *In Country*. New York: Harper & Row, 1985.
Myers, Thomas. *Walking Point: American Narratives of Vietnam*. New York: Oxford University Press, 1988.
Bao Ninh. *The Sorrow of War*. 1991, 1993. New York: Riverhead Books, 1996.
O'Brien, Tim. *The Things They Carried*. 1990. New York: Broadway Books, 1999.
Rabe, David. *The Vietnam Plays*. 2 vols. New York: Grove Press, 1993.
Reston, James Jr., ed. *Coming to Terms: American Plays and the Vietnam War*. New York: Theater Communications Group, 1985.
Van Devanter, Lynda, with Christopher Morgan. *Home before Morning*. 1983. New York: Warner Books, 1984.
Webb, James. *Fields of Fire*. 1978. New York: Bantam Books, 1979.

NOTES

1. Barack Obama, *The Audacity of Hope: Thoughts on Reclaiming the American Dream* (New York: Crown Publishers-Random House, 2007), 37.
2. James Reston Jr., *Coming to Terms: American Plays and the Vietnam War* (New York: Theater Communications Group, 1985), vii.
3. Ibid., ix.
4. James Webb, *Fields of Fire* (New York: Bantam Books, 1979), 265.
5. Ibid., 146.
6. Ibid., 451.
7. Tim O'Brien, "How to Tell a True War Story," in *The Things They Carried* (1990. New York: Broadway Books, 1999), 88.
8. O'Brien, *The Things They Carried*, 219–20.
9. Ibid., 203.
10. Ibid., 125.
11. Ibid., 88.
12. Bobbie Ann Mason, *In Country* (New York: Harper & Row, 1985), 107.
13. Ibid., 134, 25.
14. Ibid., 240, 245.
15. Michael Herr, *Dispatches* (1977. New York: Vintage Books–Random House, 1991), 260.
16. Larry Heinemann, *Paco's Story* (1986. New York: Penguin, 1987), 3.
17. Ernest Hemingway, *A Farewell to Arms* (New York: Charles Scribner's Sons, 1929, 1957), 184–5.
18. Philip Caputo, *A Rumor of War* (New York: Ballantine, 1977), xx, xiii.
19. Ibid., xvi, 217–18.
20. Ibid., 218, 309.
21. Lynda Van Devanter, *Home before Morning* (1983. New York: Warner Books, 1984), 209–10.
22. Ibid., 199, 4.
23. John Hollowell, *Fact and Fiction: The New Journalism and the Nonfiction Novel* (Chapel Hill: University of North Carolina Press, 1977), 5.
24. Michael Herr, *Dispatches*, 218.
25. Thomas Myers, *Walking Point: American Narratives of Vietnam* (New York: Oxford University Press, 1988), 169.
26. Herr, *Dispatches*, 6.
27. Ibid., 127, 172, 180.
28. H. Bruce Franklin, *The Vietnam War in American Stories, Songs, and Poems* (New York: Bedford/St. Martin's, 1995), 221.
29. David J. DeRose, "Drama." In *Vietnam War Literature: An Annotated Bibliography of Imaginative Works about Americans Fighting in Vietnam*, ed. John Newman (Lanham, MD: Scarecrow Press, 1996), 438.
30. Philip D. Beidler, *American Literature and the Experience of Vietnam* (Athens, GA: University of Georgia Press, 1982), 181, 115.
31. David Rabe, *Sticks and Bones*, in *The Vietnam Plays*, vol. 1 (New York: Grove Press, 1993), 104.
32. Ibid., 170, 175.
33. John Lahr, "Land of Lost Souls: David Rabe's America" (*New Yorker*, November 24, 2008), 117.
34. Rabe, *Sticks and Bones*, 194.
35. Bao Ninh, *The Sorrow of War* (1991, 1993. New York: Riverhead Books, 1996), 114, 56.
36. Ibid., 31, 30.

TIMELINE EVENTS

1968 – *The Green Berets*

1969 – *MASH*

1976 – *Taxi Driver*

1978 – *The Deer Hunter*

1979 – *Apocalypse Now*

1982 – *First Blood*

1986 – *Platoon*

1987 – *Full Metal Jacket*

1994 – *Forrest Gump*

2008 – *Stop-Loss*

Chapter 11

Vietnam and film

Thomas Doherty

> **CHAPTER SUMMARY**
>
> Many of us have images of the Vietnam War from the movies that we have watched. Few of us can forget Forrest Gump in Vietnam or John Wayne walking with a young orphan boy as the sun sets in the east instead of the west. What few people know is that one of the first films about America's involvement in Vietnam was based on a Graham Greene novel, *The Quiet American*. This was also the only movie actually filmed on location in Vietnam. This chapter makes sense of films about the conflict in Vietnam and puts them into perspective.
>
> For many of us, the film that we remember the most, perhaps because it was so controversial, was *The Green Berets*, which starred John Wayne, who vehemently believed, despite resistance, that the movie had to be made. Although reception of the film was not what Wayne wanted, or even anticipated, it forced filmmakers and viewers to take a new look at the war. Noting the two waves of Vietnam movies, the chapter analyzes films that were about the war without being explicitly about the war, those that were critical of the war, and others that attempted to persuade the viewer that Vietnam veterans were heroes. It argues that the films have come full circle and accomplished what *The Green Berets* did not—they have "turned Vietnam into a WWII movie."

Stardate: 4211.4. New frontier spokesman and Starship *Enterprise* captain James T. Kirk is—yet again—disobeying the Prime Directive, the anti-imperialist dictate that forbids meddling with new life and new civilizations. Being ready to bear any burden and pay any price in the defense of earth-style democracy, he has decided to boldly intervene in the domestic affairs of an alien people. The off-world in question is home to two primitive warring tribes, puppets for the rival superpowers who dominate the bipolar galaxy of the twenty-third century, the militaristic warrior race known as the Klingons and the liberal peace-mongers allied with the Federation. Learning that the Klingons have supplied gunpowder and flintlocks to their pre-industrial surrogates, Kirk resolves to do likewise and thereby "equalize both sides" of a civil war.

Dr. McCoy, Kirk's crusty medical officer, is characteristically apoplectic. "Jim, that means you're condemning this whole planet to a war that may never end!" he sputters. "It could go on for year after year, massacre after massacre!"

"Bones," replies the Captain patiently, prefacing apt history lesson, "do you remember the twentieth-century brush wars on the Asian continent? Two giant powers involved, much like ourselves? Neither side felt they could pull out?"

"Yes, I remember," spits back Bones. "It went on for bloody year after bloody year!"

Kirk counters the doctor's passionate intensity with a dose of hard-nosed *realpolitik*. "The only solution is what happened back then—balance of power," he insists, "the trickiest, most difficult, dirtiest game of all—but the only one that preserves both sides."

For twentieth-century viewers, the telecast date of *Star Trek*'s "A Private Little War"—Friday, February 2, 1968, at 8:30–9:30 p.m. EST—must have been more resonant than the star date entered in the captain's log. Three days earlier, the Viet Cong launched the Tet Offensive, the high-stakes semi-suicidal assault that turned allegedly pacified regions of South Vietnam into raging combat zones. Beamed by satellite from Japan, the first news images of the carnage and chaos in the cities of Hue and Saigon, thought to be citadels of American control, hit the nightly news shows of the three major networks just hours before the didactic episode of NBC's short-lived but eternally syndicated series. Looking back over the week, Jack Gould, television critic for the *New York Times*, marveled at the surreal warp speed of the transmissions from a world away, a materialization akin to the special effects wizardry of a science fiction film. "Television's extraordinary motion pictures of the assault on Saigon, hastened by the speed of their relay over the communication satellite connecting Japan and the United States, has made the Vietcong attacks a vivid reality in living rooms not only here but also around the world," he commented, before venturing a sage prediction: "Television's depiction of chaos may register more deeply in a viewer's mind than diplomatic or military contentions"—whether from Secretary of Defense Robert McNamara, Secretary of State Dean Rusk, or USS *Enterprise* captain James T. Kirk.[1]

Star Trek's allegorical ruminations on American involvement in Vietnam (the projection of a present-day crisis onto the final frontier of space was a favorite ploy of series *auteur* Gene Roddenberry) marked one of the rare intrusions of the Vietnam War into the flow of prime-time programming while the war was taking place. The living-room war entered the living room by appointment only. However much the images saturated the "consensual nightly séance" of the network news, incited angry point-counterpoints on Sunday morning talk shows, or filled the occasional hour-long news special, the Vietnam War, either as plotline or setting, was missing in action from the entertainment line-up. Literary critics would term the dead air around all things Vietnam a "structured absence": something that should be there but is not.

Just how structured the absence was can be seen, or not seen, in a popular situation comedy whose uniformed cast members would seem on sight to be a stark *memento mori* of the off-screen military ranks. Telecast on CBS from 1964 to 1970, dates that track precisely with the peak years of American involvement in Vietnam, *Gomer Pyle U.S.M.C.* was a goofball service comedy about a good-natured but low-IQ recruit tormenting his spit-and-polish drill sergeant. Week in, week out, zany antics ensued in barracks, on parade ground, and off post without a single mention of the tour of duty that real Marines were being shipped off to. The most noteworthy challenge to the prime-time blackout was *The Smothers Brothers Comedy Hour*, telecast on CBS from 1967 to 1969, a variety show embroiled in almost weekly controversies over an antiwar wisecrack or performance: Joan Baez dedicating "Green, Green Grass of Home" to her draft resister husband David Harris; banjo-playing George Segal and the brothers harmonizing on Phil Ochs's "Draft Dodger Rag"; or, most notoriously, folk singer Pete Seeger defiantly belting out "Waist Deep in the Big Muddy" on February 25, 1968, in the wake of Tet, after having had the song censored from the show the previous September. Otherwise, on television all was quiet on the Vietnam front.

The projection of the living-room war in the more expansive space of the motion picture theater was, if anything, even dimmer. To survey the box office hits and artistic gems Hollywood produced about the Vietnam War, *during* the Vietnam War, is to view a blank marquee. Civil rights, the sexual revolution, the generation gap, and the myriad countercultural revolutions that roiled America in the 1960s were all assimilated into big-budget Hollywood cinema, but the most violent, melodramatic, and spectacular story of the decade—a made-to-order scenario, ripped from the headlines, seemingly picture-perfect raw material—was denied a green light. During the height of the escalation and the grimmest toll of the dead, Hollywood in the 1960s was more timorous about Vietnam than Hollywood in the 1930s was about the Great Depression.

From the start (and even that was problematic: no obvious starting gun like December 7, 1941, or June 25, 1950, could kick off the first act) there was something motion picture-unfriendly about Vietnam. Vietnam was distant and Asian, like Korea, but muddier and murkier. Where Korea immediately spawned rousing combat films such as *The Steel Helmet* (1950) and *A Yank in Korea* (1951), live television dramas such as the *U.S. Steel Hour* and *Studio One*, and a continuous stream of postwar meditations that ultimately went over the top with *The Manchurian Candidate* (1962), Vietnam was forbidding territory—narratively difficult, ideologically touchy, and commercially dubious. Like no other American war since the dawn of cinema, it sent out radioactive waves.

The singular exception was John Wayne's *The Green Berets* (1968), a labor of love from Hollywood's most durable icon of broad-shouldered, tight-lipped masculinity. Universally reviled and ridiculed by critics and soldiers alike, the film remains fascinating as an attempt to graft the tropes of the World War II combat film onto the surface of Vietnam, a cinematic operation in which the host rejected the transplant.

Based on Robin Moore's popular book about the J.F.K.-endorsed US Special Forces unit and buoyed by the name recognition from S.Sgt. Barry Sadler's number one 1966 hit, *The Green*

Berets dutifully ticks off a checklist of required gear from the World War II combat film genres: the multiethnic combat squad of American types and ethnicities is present and accounted for, including character Aldo Ray (an icon of the genre in himself) as the gruff but lovable Sarge, and the venerable practice of indiscriminate Asian casting wherein Japanese and Chinese actors play the Vietnamese. Wayne fights the vicious Viet Cong and befriends a spunky war orphan, but his main mission is to turn a dovish newsman into a hawk. Clunky, didactic, palpably inaccurate in locale, lingo, and planetary orbit (in the final scene, Wayne and the orphan, in dappled silhouette, are looking into the sunset in the South China Sea—in the East on the wrong side of the ocean—when he drawls his curtain line, "You're what this war's about, kid." For all its retro-sensibility, however, the film is a reliable predictor of one future trend in the Vietnam combat film: the real enemy is not the Viet Cong or the North Vietnamese, but the fellow American.

Significantly, *The Green Berets* defied its generic progenitor in at least one bellwether way: though made with the cooperation of the Department of Defense and shot at Fort Benning, Georgia, the credit lines failed to gratefully acknowledge the generous cooperation of the US military. The seal of approval from the American military—long a mark of authenticity and patriotism—was already a token of compromise. Few of the artistically ambitious Vietnam films would seek the imprimatur.

Showcased at the Warner Theatre in Times Square, *The Green Berets* attracted huge crowds—and angry pickets. Protesters chanted slogans ("Green Berets—SS") and carried signs ("Green Berets—Saga of Fascist Terror") that give a fair inkling of the heated rhetoric of the era. Renate Adler, the newly installed film critic for the *New York Times*, penned a review of legendary vitriol. "A film so unspeakable, so stupid, so rotten and false in every detail, that it passes through being funny, through being camp, through everything and becomes an invitation to grieve," she frothed. "It is vile and insane."[2] Even the trade weekly *Variety* panned it as a "pro-Vietnam war meller, poorly written, acted, directed, edited," and predicted a "spotty b-o in exploitation payoff."[3]

Variety was wrong: the box office was not spotty but boffo. *The Green Berets* ranked among the top ten grossing films of 1968, buoyed by a solid silent majority of filmgoers for whom buying a ticket, perhaps, was like casting a vote against the kind of people who carried signs comparing the Green Berets to Nazis.[4]

The World War II combat film would always be the generic ghost haunting the Vietnam combat film, but, *The Green Berets* aside, it would be as a vision to be debunked and a specter to be exorcised. Few memoirs by Vietnam combat veterans fail to resurrect the mythos of the World War II combat film, often by specifically citing the film title and movie-house location, in order to ridicule the purblind ignorance of their juvenile selves and to foreshadow the horrific epiphany brought about by a baptism under real fire. The rules of engagement fought under the Production Code—the sanitized violence ("it's only a flesh wound"), the moral clarity, and the certainty of American victory—were not heeded in Vietnam. None of the "crap civilians have seen in Jack Webb's Hollywood movie *The D.I.* [1957] and in Mr. John Wayne's *The Sands of Iwo*

Figure 11.1 *Generic incompatibility: director-star John Wayne on the Hollywood set of* The Green Berets *(1968), his World War II-style combat film about Vietnam. Aldo Ray as the gruff but lovable Sarge stands on the right. (1968, Warner Bros.–Seven Arts.)*

Print from the collection of Thomas Doherty.

Jima [1949]," as Gustav Hasford acidly put it in his Vietnam war novel *The Short-Timers*, published in 1979, applied.[5] Writing from his wheelchair, Ron Kovic remembered a gullible boyhood spent bedazzled at matinees. "Every Saturday afternoon we'd all go down to the movies in the shopping center and watch gigantic prehistoric birds breathe fire, and war movies with John Wayne and Audie Murphy," he recalled, imagining himself in the starring role, charging up Mt. Surabachi or jumping atop a flaming tank.[6] Like Horace, Hollywood told the old lie that it was sweet and fitting to die for one's country. Like the poets and soldiers of the Great War, the Hollywood filmmakers who came to take on the Vietnam War were determined to expose old Hollywood's lies.

EXPOSING OLD HOLLYWOOD'S LIES

The work began early with generic dissections of two venerable military-minded Hollywood genres, the service comedy and the epic war film. *M*A*S*H* trashed the khaki-colored farces epitomized by *Buck Privates* (1941) and *No Time for Sergeants* (1958); *Patton* transformed the uplifting World War II spectacle into an unnerving psycho-biopic. The word "Vietnam" was not uttered on the dialogue track of either film, but by then it didn't need to be.

A shaggy-dog picaresque fueled by overlapping dialogue and ensemble improvisation, Robert Altman's *M*A*S*H* (1969) purported to chronicle the exploits of a mobile army surgical hospital within mortar range of the thirty-eighth parallel, but for all but the densest spectator it was a connect-the-dots allegory for that other Asian land war. Written by Ring Lardner Jr., a member of the lately untouchable Hollywood Ten, the film oozed irreverence—indeed, contempt—for all that was once held sacred: God, country, and the military. Also, and not least, Altman and Lardner hacked away at previous Hollywood war movies, funny or solemn. In its sign-off credit sequence the hectoring camp loudspeaker that has acted as Greek chorus and wiseass chatterbox offers a self-reflective summary of the action and attitude:

> Attention: tonight's movie has been *M*A*S*H*. Follow the zany antics of our combat surgeons as they cut and stitch their way along the front lines, operating as bombs and bullets burst around them, snatching laughs and love between amputations and penicillin.

For all its vanguard pose on the politics of war and cinema, *M*A*S*H* remained firmly entrenched in its time—1969, not 1952—in the realm of gender. The camp is more frat house than military post, a raucous boys' club where the guys bond over golf, football, and sex, and the girls are dubbed Hot Lips and Lieutenant Dish.

Twentieth Century Fox was "edgy" about the obvious association and insisted *M*A*S*H* be inoculated with a post-credit crawl firmly setting the action in Korea. No matter: everyone connected the dots. "I wanted people to mix it up," director Altman confirmed years later.[7] The film's distinctive advertising logo (a collage of the V-for-victory fingers of an upraised peace sign superimposed atop a pair of shapely female legs) served as a visual synecdoche for the anti-war slogan "Make love, not war." "For me, *M*A*S*H* contains as much depression as humor," mused film critic Gene Siskel. "I don't think I ever recovered after a soldier says about a Korean, 'he's a prisoner of war.' The reply is, 'So are you.'"[8]

Like *Bonnie and Clyde* (1967), *M*A*S*H* administered its generic shock treatment not just through irony and irreverence, but from its radical shifts in generic tone. The head-spinning switchover from zany comedy to surgical gore—actually, the suturing together of both elements in the same scene—was as transgressive as the anti-war ethos; it packed a wallop on spectators in 1969–70 hard to conjure up in retrospect. The operating room sequences were explicit, bloody, and gory—unprecedented not just for a war film, but for a comedic laugh riot. Rave critical notices and strong box office success (*M*A*S*H*—"as in smash") greeted the black comedy.

Sharing marquee space with *M*A*S*H* was *Patton* (1970), directed by Franklin J. Schaffner, based on the book by Patton biographer Ladislas Frigo and the memoir by General Omar Bradley, and written by Edmund H. North and Francis Ford Coppola. The filmmakers pulled off a remarkable sleight of hand, a World War II combat film that managed to straddle both ends of the generation gap and political divide. To the right, Patton was an American hero, military genius and anticommunist visionary. To the left, Patton was a loony warmonger and reckless glory hound as lethal to his troops as the enemy ("Our blood, his guts," cracks a GI, ducking artillery fire). "There is no conventional way of explaining a man like Patton," said producer Frank McCarthy, who had been struggling to make a film on Patton since 1951. "Had we attempted to take a stand one way or the other . . . we would have been unfair to the man and at the same time limited our audience to those pre-sold on either a liberal or conservative view."[9] Eschewing hagiography, McCarthy had to shoot without the cooperation of the US military, in Spain, where both the terrain and the World War II-period hardware (from both the United States and Germany) lent verisimilitude.

The direct address prologue tells the story: with a wall-sized American flag filling the entire screen, out strides Patton in full regalia (the outfit is more a costume than a regulation military uniform, especially the trademark pearl-handled pistols). "No one ever won a war by dying for his country," he growls. "He won it by making the *other* poor bastard die for his country." Head case or military genius? In an inspired narrative hook the screenwriters mull the question by having a Nazi intelligence officer create a psychological profile of Patton for his superiors. (His conclusion: Patton is "a magnificent anachronism, a romantic warrior lost in modern times.") For channeling the general, actor George C. Scott won, and famously refused, an Oscar. Of course, the most famous connection between *Patton* and Vietnam is extra-textual. In April 1970, prior to ordering the invasion of Cambodia, Richard Nixon screened *Patton* twice at the White House, by way of either diversion or inspiration. Liberal critics averred that the invasive militarism of Hollywood's megalomaniac inspired Washington's.[10]

Over the next several years, a period now lauded as Hollywood's Second Golden Age, a storied high renaissance when artistic ambition met box office validation, Vietnam was deep background to scenarios of explosive violence (*Straw Dogs*, 1971), dark conspiracy (*The Parallel View*, 1974; *Three Days of the Condor*, 1975), and criminal corporate greed (*Chinatown*, 1974; *The Godfather*, 1972), but it would be years before the background was foregrounded as a place on the map and an event from history.

The exceptions were mostly independent ventures out of the commercial Hollywood mainstream, mainly documentaries limited to small art houses and college film societies that catered to undergraduates already primed for anti-war agitprop. A pioneering example was Emile de Antonio's *In the Year of the Pig* (1968), in which the animal in the title did not refer to the cycles of the Chinese calendar. The only below-the-radar anti-war documentary that broke into popular consciousness was Peter Davis's *Hearts and Minds* (1974), perhaps the most technically accomplished of the anti-war archival documentaries of the era. The editing was blunt and heavy-handed, the message was telegraphed in bold letters: when General Westmoreland opines that life is less valued by the Oriental mind, the sequence jumps to a wailing, heartbroken Vietnamese mother; when the camera pulls back on a veteran, a fuller picture reveals that he is confined to a wheelchair; at home, American boys play football and pray; in Nam, they set hamlets ablaze and consort with hookers.

Like most documentaries in the American marketplace, *Hearts and Minds* was not widely distributed or seen, but it gained notoriety at the Academy Awards ceremony that year after nabbing the Oscar for Best Documentary. On April 8, 1975, as North Vietnamese troops advanced inexorably towards Saigon and America braced itself for an ignominious defeat, Hollywood's glittering soiree was interrupted by a surprise diplomatic overture. Accepting the Oscar on behalf of director Peter Davis and himself, producer Burt Schneider hailed the looming "liberation" of Vietnam and read a message of greetings to the American people from the Viet Cong ambassador to the Paris Peace Talks. After a hasty conference backstage, Howard Koch, producer of the Oscar telecast, authorized Frank Sinatra to read a statement (written by Bob Hope) disclaiming Schneider's initiative. Schneider was unrepentant. "It is indeed the liberation of Vietnam—as far as the Vietnamese people are concerned."[11]

CONFRONTING THE PAST IN FILM

Two historical events and one motion picture encouraged Hollywood to confront a political past long deemed box-office poison: the humiliating images of American retreat in Saigon, now Ho Chi Minh City, the resignation of Richard M. Nixon in the wake of the Watergate scandal, and the surprise commercial and critical success of *All the President's Men* (1976). As if closure was necessary before retrospection was permitted, the first wave of Vietnam combat films rolled in only after military defeat, political disillusionment, and the possibility of formal defeat.

"Four years after our troops left Vietnam, and almost 20 years after they went there, Hollywood appears at last ready to come to grips with the Vietnam war," the *New York Times* noticed in 1977. "At least six pictures are being prepared these days in which the war, or its victims and veterans, will be placed under the microscope of moviemakers." Soon to come into focus were an anti-war love story, *Coming Home* (1978); the gritty combat films *Go Tell the Spartans* (1978) and *The Boys of Company C* (1978); a scruffy crime film about running heroin from Vietnam in the bodies of dead GIs, *Who'll Stop the Rain?* (1978); and two certified cultural landmarks, *The Deer Hunter* (1978) and *Apocalypse Now* (1979).

Hal Ashby's *Coming Home* (1978) was a home-front melodrama that might have been titled "The Worst Years of Our Lives." The romantic leads were Jon Voight and Jane Fonda, two Hollywood stars extra-textually linked to the anti-war movement, with Bruce Dern, ever the psycho, as the gung-ho marine captain rattled by what was not then called post-traumatic stress disorder. Fonda plays a military wife who volunteers to work in a veterans' hospital during her husband's tour of duty. On her rounds, she meets and mates Voight, an embittered, wheelchair-bound veteran, now an anti-war warrior. The old masculinity—repressed, violent, and lousy in the sack—is easily outmatched by the new masculinity—sensitive, pacific, attentive to his partner's sexual needs. Even in a wheelchair, paralyzed, the anti-war Vietnam vet possesses the potency that has been sapped out of the pro-war Vietnam vet. The anti-war warrior gets the girl and the pro-war warrior walks to his death in the surf.

Wary of "the conflicting attitudes on the Vietnam debacle," *Variety*'s review of *Coming Home* gingerly broached the lingering audience resistance to dredging up a painful past. "Even though there are no battle scenes, the pic must overcome a psychic revulsion to reliving a major national embarrassment."[12] Mindful of the aversion, the advertising for the film avoided typesetting the word "Vietnam" and instead publicized a love story laced with big-star sexual chemistry and explicit coupling. Despite critical raves and major awards, *Coming Home* was only modestly successful.[13]

Coming home to America, the Vietnam veteran would ever be crippled in body or mind. In Martin Scorsese's *Taxi Driver* (1976), the most searing of the Return of the Repressed Vietnam Veteran films, the scarred body and warped mind of Travis Bickle embodied the Vietnam vet as ticking time bomb, let loose on the streets of America as avenging angel, popping pills, decked out in fatigues, sporting a Mohawk haircut. Painfully inarticulate in conversation, if not in his diary ("someday a real rain will come and wash all the scum off the street"), Travis cruises the mean streets of New York in his taxi on a personal search-and-destroy mission. Lock, load, and fire with no internal guidance system—a drug dealer or a political candidate, it's all the same to Travis.

Deranged, dangerous, and "disgruntled" (the incessant adjectival tag), the Vietnam veteran presented a clear and present danger to the domestic tranquility. In *Black Sunday* (1977) a disgruntled Vietnam vet plans to slaughter a stadium full of football fans during that most American of peacetime rituals, the Super Bowl. In *Twilight's Last Gleaming* (1977) a disgruntled general framed for manslaughter because of his opposition to the Vietnam War goes rogue and takes a nuclear missile silo hostage. And in *Rolling Thunder* (1977) a near-catatonic disgruntled former POW terminates the thugs who murdered his family (at least he has good reason). By the time of *Heroes* (1978), in which the Vietnam veterans were merely troubled and nutty, *Variety* was also disgruntled, lamenting, "It's also unfortunate that the few films dealing with the survivors of Vietnam depict the veterans as borderline psychotics."[14] Actually, the psychic portrait of Hollywood's veterans had long since gone over the borderline.

True to its frontier mythos, Michael Cimino's *The Deer Hunter* (1978) was the pathfinder, the first cinematic version of Vietnam to contribute a storehouse of images as vivid and visceral as the nightly news. Deep in the Pennsylvania coal-mining country, three blue-collar buddies are proud to go and do their patriotic chore. Steeped in the atmospherics of James Fenimore Cooper's primal westerns, these heroes (like Natty Bumppo) practice the ancient American arts of hunting and marksmanship, and (like Kit Carson) consider it a matter of honor to slay the deer with one shot. The "Indian country" of Vietnam is a natural projection, only now the trio are the prey, captured in tiger cages and bound like deer meat. Ultimately, one is crippled, one kills himself, and one returns to join the shattered community in a version of "America the Beautiful" that sounds less like a proud anthem than a funereal dirge.

The Deer Hunter bequeathed an indelible tableau and a surefire metaphor: a game of Russian roulette that the Viet Cong (VC) force their prisoners to play, a spectator sport that has eluded verification in the historical record. Here Cimino's depiction of the VC took on none of the romanticism then so fashionable on the American left—they are savages, screaming in an (to the Anglophone ear) atonal barking. Cimino delivers a master class in the art of audience manipulation and excruciating, Hitchcockian suspense, as the prisoners count down the chambers and squeeze the trigger. "Look, the film is not realistic—it's surrealistic," Cimino said at the time, when called on the fantasy. "If you attack the film on its facts, then you're fighting a phantom because literal accuracy was never intended."[15] As history, it was sheer fabrication; as metaphor, it was inspired: America in Vietnam, shooting its brains out.

Despite its three-hour-plus running time and meandering first act, *The Deer Hunter* proved that Vietnam was no longer box-office poison. Critical praise for the sprawling, ungainly epic was immediate; no one denied the faults, but its virtues as melodrama, action adventure, and bravura on-location filmmaking were undeniable. "Vietnam was no apocalypse," said Cimino, with an eye to the competition.

The competition was Francis Ford Coppola, the most commercially successful and critically esteemed *auteur* in Hollywood. Propelled by his twin blockbusters *The Godfather* (1972) and *The Godfather Part II* (1974), Coppola played maestro by declaring his intention to compose the definitive cinematic symphony about Vietnam. Not since *Gone with the Wind* (1939) had a motion picture endured a longer period of gestation or generated more anticipation. At first breathless, and later increasingly skeptical, press reports revealed that *Apocalypse Now* was to be a serpentine adaptation of Joseph Conrad's *Heart of Darkness*. "It's a descent into hell—the loss of all sense of civilization," screenwriter John Milius told *Variety* in 1975. "It's just an evil dark screenplay."[16] The statement would apply not only to the screenplay but also to production.

Unveiled to a ravenous international press at the 1979 Cannes Film Festival and released in the United States on August 14, 1979, *Apocalypse Now* pulsated with jungle rhythms scored to a kaleidoscopic swirl of painterly tapestries: the jungle treeline exploding in slow motion as napalm fireballs erupt in time to "The End" by the Doors; surfer dude grunts waterskiing on the Mekong River to the boom-box beat of "Satisfaction" by the Rolling Stones; and (in what is certainly the most oft-quoted line in all of Vietnam cinema) the sensuous admission by the crazy war-lover Colonel Kilgore, whose surname and sensibility would have made him welcome around the war-room table in *Dr. Strangelove*: "I love the smell of napalm in the morning."

Coppola intuited that the woozy jump-cut disorientations peculiar to the Vietnam War demanded a surrealistic approach. In the blink of an eye, combat horror ricocheted into the comforts of home and zinged back again. Motoring upriver, deep into Indian country, hell or heaven may await on the next shore landing. In a phantasmagorical USO sequence, *Playboy* bunnies, helicoptered into the jungle by none other than rock impresario Bill Graham, beckon like sirens and whip a mob of howling, horny GIs into testosterone frenzy.

The most sustained metaphor wrapped around *Apocalypse Now* was an unintended bit of extra-textual irony: the Hollywood location shoot as the perfect allegory for the American quagmire. "The most important thing I wanted to do in the making of *Apocalypse Now* was to create a film experience that would give its audience a sense of horror, the madness, the sensuousness, and the moral dilemma in the Vietnam war," Coppola declared in the credits booklet to the 70mm version of the conspicuously creditless film.[17] For an *auteur* stuck in the big muddy with cost overruns, typhoons, and a corrupt dictatorship in the Philippines, he backed into a double meaning. Later the topic of a documentary film and book, Coppola's incursion into the Philippines jungle became a kind of location-shoot version of the American war in Vietnam: overlong, messy, well intentioned, and wastefully extravagant. (At least no one died.)

Despite Coppola's location shoot from hell, the Philippines became the preferred stand-in for Vietnam. Though not quite a topographic body double for the real terrain, the country was a source of cheap Asian labor, plentiful period-appropriate American military hardware, and a dictatorial regime under Ferdinand Marcus more cooperative than Ho Chi Minh's successors in Hanoi. Michael Cimino preferred Thailand, "which is more like Vietnam than the Philippines where Francis shot *Apocalypse Now*," he sniffed.

MAKING THE VIETNAM HERO

After so excessive an expenditure of cash and cultural cache, *Apocalypse Now* seemed to suck all the available oxygen out of the Vietnam genre—as if creative energies and production financing alike were all tapped out. After a long hiatus a new foreign policy crisis (the Iran hostage crisis) and a new Vietnam-friendly president would redirect the trajectory and reshape the thematics of the Vietnam combat film. "Ours was a noble cause," affirmed President Reagan, without apology, in defense of American involvement in Vietnam. The second great wave of Vietnam films in a sense revised the revisions of the first wave. It would be heralded by a Vietnam vet hero who was as psychically damaged as Travis Bickle but whose aggressions were channeled into more commercially advantageous directions.

Based on a hard-boiled novel by David Morrell, *First Blood* (1982) introduced a battered Vietnam veteran named John Rambo who took to the woods of the Pacific Northwest and, VC-like, cut a swathe through a hapless American police force. Rambo's army of one would re-enlist for service in Vietnam in 1985, Afghanistan in 1988, and eventually Burma in 2008.

In *Rambo: First Blood Part II* (1985), Hollywood delivered what the US military could not: a breathtakingly efficient extraction of American hostages, here in the skeletal figures of American POWs in tiger cages, still confined in Vietnam by Russian communists. The deep background here and in a whole cycle of action-adventure films was not only Vietnam but the humiliation of the Iran hostage crisis of 1979–81, and the video images of the tangled wreckage of American helicopters in the aftermath of a failed rescue mission. *Missing in Action* (1984), *Let's Get Harry* (1986), technically set in the jungle of Colombia, and *Bat 21* (1988) all rectified on film the failures in the news.

Sent on a mission to prove conclusively that no American POWs still languish in Vietnam, Rambo discovers the opposite, an inconvenient political fact that sniveling American bureaucrats seek to conceal. When Rambo escapes with a POW, his rescue helicopter lifts off without him, a callous act of betrayal and desertion that leaves him howling in rage, not at the VC, the North Vietnamese Army (NVA), or the USSR, but at the United States (or its government; not the concept or country). All muscle and monosyllable (he was not only a grunt; he grunted), Rambo is captured and strapped to the wire frame of a bedpost for electrical torture, the lacerated and bloody body of the vet as Christ figure, suffering for America's sins. "I'm coming to get *you*," he rasps at his real enemy, the civilian bureaucrat backstabber. The nation had indeed left something

Figure 11.2 Retrieving what was left behind: Rambo (Sylvester Stallone) rescues American POWs still languishing in Vietnam in Rambo: First Blood Part II *(1985, Tristar Pictures.)*

Print from the collection of Thomas Doherty.

behind in Vietnam. On the strength of his cartoonish exploits, Rambo soon replaced John Wayne as the epithet of choice for the guts-and-glory macho posturing of the Hollywood war movie.

In 1986–7 a second wave of Vietnam combat films rode in on a culture-wide tide of renewed respect for the US military. Hollywood had already picked up on the trend in a very un-*M*A*S*H*-like cycle of service comedies such as *Private Benjamin* (1980) and *Stripes* (1981), in which a pampered princess and shiftless boomers are whipped into shape by the discipline of army boot camp, and in military-friendly melodrama-cum-action adventure such as *An Officer and a Gentleman* (1982), a by-the-numbers update on *The D.I.* injected with cross-gender romantic appeal, and *Top Gun* (1986), in which navy jet pilots feel the need for speed and homoerotic volleyball games. By then, with the draft over for more than a generation, the military was a mysterious and exotic realm for many young moviegoers.

The cinematic and cultural landmark was *Platoon* (1986), directed and written by Oliver Stone, whose high-profile off-camera persona as a Vietnam veteran lent the film not just its aura of verisimilitude (the action is laden with the kind of inside-dopester details that only a participant-observer would know) but its moral authority. Stone knew, as Walt Whitman knew, that "the real war will never get in the books," still less be projected on a motion picture screen, but he could say, also like Whitman, and almost alone in a Hollywood where the workforce graduated from film school, not basic training, "I was the man, I suffered, I was there" (although the aggrandizing celebration of the director's military background in the advertising campaign—that he was the only man in Hollywood with a Purple Heart and an Oscar—forgot a World War II generation that included Lee Marvin). By contrast, Michael Cimino had been an army medic Stateside, and Coppola's military experience, as *Patton* producer Frank McCarthy joked, "was limited to two weeks as a flourish with a New York military academy band."

Not that Stone was content to rest on his service record—or let his actors be prima donnas. Stone's ethos of verisimilitude required his performers to endure a kind of faux boot camp. "We're going into a heavy duty training program at the end of the month," Stone declared prior to shooting. "All the actors are going to become a rifle platoon." Knowing that overt Vietnam message mongering was the commercial kiss of death, Stone promised "no political messages" in *Platoon*; "just the truth as I saw it." But of course political and historical motivations informed every frame. *Platoon* will "educate the younger generation to what a war is really like as opposed to Rambo theatrics."[18] *Platoon* was billed as the anti-*Rambo*.

Setting a pattern for the second wave, *Platoon* is not about the Vietnam war in any didactic way; the hawk–dove divide had long since congealed into a consensus that saw Vietnam as a tragic misadventure whose real victim was the American soldier. (The Vietnamese are almost always extras, stick figures in an American playground.) A sentimental paean to a band of brothers, the film wallows in the hyper-masculinity of an in-country world of men without women. Stone's Manichean vision is incarnated by two dueling non-coms of light and darkness, angel and demon, the warrior who perpetrates war crimes and the warrior who stops them. At the end of the film, in the voice-over narration of the soldier who has withstood his crucible of war and aligned himself with the forces of light, Stone's grunt-surrogate reflects, "I felt like the

Figure 11.3 *Once an insult, now an honorific: Charlie Sheen and Keith David as grunts in Oliver Stone's* Platoon *(1986, Hemdale Film Corporation/Orion Pictures.)*

Print from the collection of Thomas Doherty.

child born of those two fathers," neatly eliminating the female even from reproduction. Stone's womb is the platoon.

The subject of endless exegesis and magazine covers, the winner of the Best Picture and Best Direction Oscars, *Platoon* broke the "philosophical logjam" that blocked the production of Vietnam films in Hollywood. The pipeline would flow smoothly for Vietnam-set combat films, juvenile action adventure, and melodramas, an atmosphere so favorable it also spurred the theatrical re-releases of *Apocalypse Now* and *Go Tell the Spartans*.

The most widely heralded was Stanley Kubrick's *Full Metal Jacket* (1987), a cold-as-ice duplex based on Gustav Hasford's scabrous *The Short-Timers* and written by Hasford and journalist Michael Herr, author of *Dispatches*, a New Journalistic account of his time in Vietnam that is a masterpiece of the form. Having taken on the futility of World War I in *Paths of Glory* (1957) and the insanity of the Cold War in *Dr. Strangelove or: How I Learned to Stop Worrying and Love the Bomb* (1964), Kubrick—inevitably?—turned his talents to the other great absurd war. (Significantly, Kubrick never tackled World War II, a site whose moral clarity may not have been suited to his coldly ironic gaze.)[19]

Shot in England at Bassingbourn Barracks in Cambridgeshire and Beckton Gasworks factory in east London (stand-ins, respectively, for the US Marine training ground at Parris Island and the bombed-up city of Hue), *Full Metal Jacket* eschews the verisimilitude its generic kindred craves: the set design and exterior locations are palpably studio-bound and backlot, but the psychic, not combat, landscape is what Kubrick seeks to map. The film is chopped into two distinct parts: first, a grueling training session in Marine boot camp; and second, a run through the jungle in Vietnam as the Tet Offensive explodes (the transition is cued by the bass line to Nancy Sinatra's "These Boots Are Made for Walking," and a tracking shot following not the footwear of the grunts but the high heels of a Vietnamese hooker whose broken-English come-hither ("Me so horny—me love you long time") became a pop culture mantra sampled for a rap song by 2 Live Crew). Both environments, boot camp and the boonies, form one continuous line of male-on-male violence and the denigration and elimination of the feminine life principle. "How do you kill women and children?" a marine, more curious than appalled, asks a helicopter gunner. "Simple," he chortles above the roar of the engines, "you just don't lead 'em so much!"

As the enforcement agent for same-sex marine asceticism, Lee Ermey, a real-life former marine drill sergeant, delivers the most charismatic incarnation of a larger than life military tyrant since George C. Scott played *Patton*. His fluency with the obscene poetry of military

Figure 11.4 Vietnam vernacular: Marine drill Sergeant Hartman (Lee Ermey) expresses his displeasure about jelly doughnuts to Private Pyle (Vincent D'Onofrio) in Stanley Kubrick's Full Metal Jacket (1987, Warner Bros. Pictures.)

Print from the collection of Thomas Doherty.

245

vernacular—a non-stop patter of racist, sexual, scatological, misogynist, homophobic, and homoerotic wordplay—is positively Shakespearean ("What's your major malfunction, numb-nuts?" being one of his more printable interrogations). The nicknames he bestows upon the recruits are meant to dehumanize, not endear: Joker, Snowball, Cowboy, and—inevitably—Private Pyle, the doughnut-eating powder-puff and designated sacrificial lamb that will turn the pack of raw puppies into wolves, who lives "in a world of shit" and who will crack and explode prematurely.

Released in the wake of the twin powerhouses *Platoon* and *Full Metal Jacket*, John Irvin's *Hamburger Hill* (1987) was overshadowed in what was already becoming a glutted market. Chronicling the May 1969 assault by the 101st Airborne on a hill of dubious military value in the A Shau Valley, the operative theme is waste. In a war that was about hearts and minds, not conquering territory, the taking of a hill, any hill, is a Sisyphean exercise in futility. Not for nothing does the scenic backdrop of burnt-out trees, charcoaled terrain, and mud-caked troops invoke the no man's land moonscapes of World War I: despite the high-tech aerial support, this is a meat grinder of trench warfare, the men mere cannon fodder. When a trio of survivors gains the summit, the bleak pointlessness of the achievement could not be more different than the triumphal flag rising atop the summit of Mount Surabachi in *The Sands of Iwo Jima* or, for that matter, the solemn tone of its obvious cinematic echo, *Pork Chop Hill* (1957), a Korean War combat film of similar theme. The waste, the futility, and meaninglessness are underscored in a line of dialogue repeated like an incantation to ward off total psychic meltdown when a brother in arms falls, a mantra that applies to the war but not the man: "It don't mean a thing."

Shot in the Philippines and made with the cooperation of the Department of Defense, *Hamburger Hill* is an early example of the *mea culpa* compulsion in Vietnam cinema, a kind of cinematic penance for the excesses of the antiwar movement in the 1960s, a cadre known to celebrate the Heroic People's Liberation Army of Vietnam and demonize the American combat soldier as a wanton baby killer. "War at its worst . . . fought by young men at their best," intoned the voice-over in the film's trailer. When a grunt gets a "Dear John" letter, his girlfriend not only kisses him off but calls him immoral. When a sergeant remembers a trip back home, he confronts hippie girls ready to toss bags of excrement at him. Not exempted from reproach are the media. Staggering down Hamburger Hill, bloodied and bedraggled after a day at the slaughterhouse, the exhausted veterans are approached by a crisp and clean newsman with a microphone and dumb questions. "Fucking vulture," seethes one grunt. "You haven't *earned* the right to be here," says another. Lurking in the background is Hollywood's own role: of Burt Schneider cozying up to the North Vietnamese during his acceptance speech for the Oscar for *Hearts and Minds*, of Travis Bickle and his ilk, of Jane Fonda smiling and applauding by North Vietnamese anti-aircraft guns.

By the late 1980s, in film and—finally—television, Vietnam had become fit for filming and fictionalizing. As a historical event repackaged by Hollywood narrative, the war would always carry a special weight and anxiety-ridden significance, but it was approaching something like normalization and familiarity. Francis Ford Coppola's elegiac *Gardens of Stone* (1987), a sensitive depiction of the duties of the honor guard at Arlington National Ceremony, was infused with an air of reverence and solemnity light years away from the rock-and-rolling chaos of *Apocalypse Now*; *Good Morning, Vietnam* (1987) was basically a star vehicle for motor-mouth comedian Robin Williams; combat veteran Peter Duncan's *84 Charlie Mopic* (1989) filtered the war from the point of view of a combat cameraman; and Brian de Palma's *Casualties of War* (1989) might best be described as a deranged Vietnam vet film set in Vietnam.

For a time, television, the true arena of normalized relations between the media and Vietnam, sustained two network shows about Vietnam: *Tour of Duty* (CBS, 1987–90), about the grunts, and *China Beach* (ABC, 1988–91), about the nurses. A Vietnam background had also become acceptable, in some ways necessary, for a TV action hero. Telecast on CBS from 1980 to 1988, *Magnum P.I.* celebrated a rakish private investigator who was a veteran of naval intelligence in Vietnam, a man who oozed congeniality and psychic stability and who maintained a bond with his equally capable crew of war buddies—the kind of postwar bond that was common in 1940s cinema. Though the great wellspring of traumatic stress and residual shame, the Vietnam War was also the only credible back story for a mature action hero to have acquired skill in weaponry and certification of his courage on the field of battle. Periodically tormented by flashbacks and night terrors, he was, by and large, a functioning human being whose Vietnam experience informed his police work and dexterity under fire.

Under a self-congratulatory headline ("Hollywood Alters American Attitudes toward Vietnam"), the *Hollywood Reporter* commented on the sudden zeitgeist shift in the company town. "Just a few years ago, presenting a Vietnam manuscript to a studio exec was a sure way to be shown the door," it gushed. "Today however Vietnam tales proliferate in motion pictures and television." And then a bow to itself: "Although it has taken America more than a decade to come to grips with the Vietnam experience, it is Hollywood that has led the way to a new public acceptance of the men who lived through it."[20] Of course, Hollywood's less than flattering portraits of "the men who lived through it" was a part of motion picture history edited from the official version.

By then, under the cumulative influence of the first and second waves, the conventions of the Vietnam combat film had hardened into cement. Among the requisite ingredients:

- **The classic rock soundtrack**. Whether on the soundtrack to pump up a florid montage or wafting through camp from transistor radios, a Top Forty playlist of 1960s-era rock and roll is the essential musical accompaniment for the Vietnam War. Where the unit cohesion of the World War II combat film was expressed in the GI appreciation of the Big Band swing of Glenn Miller or the harmonies of the Andrews Sisters, the dissonance of Vietnam found sonic reflection in the dark, Dionysian rock songs of Jimi Hendrix ("Purple Haze," "All Along the Watchtower," "Hey Joe"), the Rolling Stones ("Satisfaction," "Gimme Shelter," "Paint It Black"), and the Doors ("Light My Fire," "The End"). The swamp-rock thump of Credence Clearwater Revival is in heavy rotation as play-by-pay commentary on in-country firefights or home-front backfire: "Bad Moon Rising," "Run through the Jungle," and

"Who'll Stop the Rain?" (cribbed as the title for the 1979 film). A playlist of about twenty songs comprises a sort of greatest hits for the Vietnam jukebox. More sentimental moments tend to favor the smooth, silky soul of Motown, perhaps best captured in the interracial kinship of the grunts in *Platoon*, who drove, stoned, to Smokey Robinson's "Tears of a Clown." Sometimes the music may lead to disharmony: the soul music favored by the black troops as opposed to the country songs preferred by southern whites, an aesthetic-cum-racial division. In *Hamburger Hill* the trio of black troops sardonically croons a twangy country-and-western parody, mocking the lyrical obsession with cars, prison, and adultery. In the Vietnam context, lyrics written to be played on AM radios stateside suddenly send out new layers of meaning. In *Hamburger Hill*, "We Gotta Get Outa This Place," by Eric Burdon and the Animals, blares as the 101st Airborne are helicoptered into the A Shau Valley, the lines suddenly ominous: "you'll be dead before your time is due."

- **Vietnam vernacular**. A blunt contrast to the choirboy lingo spoken by military men under the language policing of the Production Code Administration, the dialogue track of the Vietnam combat film is peppered with the rich, irreverent, and vulgar vernacular of the grunts (itself an in-country coinage: World War II troops were GIs). Often the acronyms (FNG, fucking new guy; REMF, rear-echelon motherfucker), broken English, battered Vietnamese, and combinations thereof (did e mos, the all-purpose modifier "beaucoup," number one, mama-san, deep kimchi), and sundry period- and place-specific slang ("the World," "the land of the Big PX," "Indian country") is snarled and spat out quickly, without translation or subtitles. If the home-front auditor cannot follow, too bad. The ironic use of the official language of the military bureaucracy is also deployed for local color and effect, no phrase more ominously than the euphemism for killing: "to terminate with extreme prejudice." Along with the ubiquitous "Charlie," a litany of racial slurs for the enemy ("Luke the Gook," "zipperheads") can be heard, not always disrespectfully. In *Hamburger Hill* a wily non-com cautions against the racist diminution that can breed a lethal overconfidence. "You will call him Nathaniel Victor or *Mister* Nathaniel Victor," he informs his troops, speaking of the North Vietnamese regulars.

- **Visceral violence**. In tandem with the end of Production Code censorship in 1968, advances in makeup artistry and special effects technology facilitated a gruesomely realistic depiction of the impact of modern weaponry on the human body. In the Vietnam combat film, limbs fly, blood spurts, and guts spill out with anatomical correctness. During the opening seconds of *Hamburger Hill* the blasted body of a mortally wounded soldier falls into frame from above and lies supine in the foreground, his stomach burst open and intestines hanging out, as if to rub the spectator's face in the consequences of molten shrapnel: *this* is a "flesh wound," this is not your father's war film. Unlike the gleeful "gross-out" response encouraged by the contemporaneous teenager slasher flicks, the medicinal verisimilitude is meant to appall, not delight. In *Platoon*, when a soldier blasts the brains out of a Vietnamese villager, he responds as if he is watching a horror film, not committing a war crime: "Holy shit! Did you see that head come apart, man?"

- **Film- and video-framed Vietnam**. Vietnam was framed by two screens, the television box and big-screen cinema, the war news in the living room and the glorious spectacles at the local Bijou. Both the small and the big screen lied, says the Vietnam combat film, insisting that this Hollywood version of combat unspooling now before you is real. The television version of Vietnam the home front saw on the networks news is false, mediated, censored. In *Apocalypse Now*, Francis Ford Coppola himself plays an intrusive news cameraman hectoring the troops with inane questions, and in *Full Metal Jacket* Stanley Kubrick's camera plays the television news camera in a self-reflexive Steadicam shot, hand-held and jerky to imitate combat photography. Being the Americans, the soldiers play to the camera, joking about John Wayne, "Vietnam: The Movie," and "the gooks" playing the Indians. Just as the Great War doughboys filtered their war through the romantic poetry of Kipling and Tennyson, the media-saturated grunts of Vietnam see war through the lens of the movies and TV. Almost always the misunderstanding is fatal, as when the fresh-faced would-be hero in *Go Tell the Spartans* learns too late that the enemy fires live ammunition. Hence too the line first quoted in Michael Herr's *Dispatches*: "I hate this movie."
- **Frag-able leadership**. In films about World War II, such as *Command Decision* (1948) and *Twelve O'Clock High* (1949), leaders who sent their men to certain death grieved and paid a terrible psychic cost, sometimes breaking down under the pressure. In Vietnam films, the men making the command decisions are incompetents at best, more often sadists and sociopaths, heartlessly wasting their own troops as expendable casualties of war, mere numbers in a body-count competition. The civilian leadership is even worse, killing friend and enemy alike from a safe distance.
- **Sonic booms**. Pioneered by Walter Murch for *Apocalypse Now*, the art of sound design is a trademark orchestral maneuver of the Vietnam combat film. Multi-track and, later, digital sound recording render the layered sonic wraparound distinct to Vietnam. No sound was more spookily evocative on the soundtrack than the whoop-whoop-whoop of the rotor blades of the Huey helicopter mixed with the precision of a backbeat—hovering, approaching from afar, ascending back into the sky and trailing off into the distance. The aerial screech of birds of prey swooping in for the kill, conducting most famously in *Apocalypse Now* when a flock of helicopters soars in for the kill to the strains of Wagner's "Ride of the Valkyries." The concussion-inducing boom of artillery shells, the zing and whistle of rocket-propelled grenades, the racket of automatic weapons fire—all are mixed LOUD and un-cued so the spectator-auditor will experience some of the deafening shock and awe of being bushwhacked by an ear-splitting explosion. Again, *Apocalypse Now* provides the sheet music. The most stunning sonic effect (especially in digital re-releases, where it emanates from a remote speaker on the theater wall) is the sudden natural roar of a tiger in the jungle—a strange primal fear amid all the noisy man-made terror. Finally, after the orchestration of the metallic cacophony of war, the Vietnam combat film makes wise use of another terrifying combat sound to men on patrol—silence.

- **Fratricide**. Not to be confused with fragging, the harshest death blow delivered in the Vietnam combat film was aimed at a comrade in arms. Where the World War II combat unit took a motley crew of American types and bound them together to fight the enemy, the Vietnam unit was ripped apart by suicide and fratricide: in *Apocalypse Now*, Captain Willard kills Colonel Kurtz; in *The Deer Hunter* the solders put guns to their heads and pull the trigger; in *Full Metal Jacket*, Private Pyle shoots his drill sergeant and himself; in *Platoon* the good soldier kills the bad sergeant; and in *Hamburger Hill*, friendly fire cuts down the soldiers of the 101st airborne more efficiently than the North Vietnamese Army. "We did not fight the enemy," reflects the narrator of *Platoon* in voice-over. "We fought ourselves." More than a narrative device, the impulse borders on repetition compulsion. In the Vietnam combat film the enemy is us. The VC and the NVA are secondary targets.

Like the tropes of the World War II combat films, the once-fresh conventions of the Vietnam War could easily calcify into cliché. They could also be transfused into kindred genres in accord with the promiscuous cross-breeding of film forms so characteristic of post-classical Hollywood cinema. Intriguingly, the science fiction film seemed most congenial to transplanting the tropes and topography of Vietnam into futuristic firefights, high-tech grunts, and strange creatures in the bush. James Cameron's *Aliens* (1986) is a virtual extraterrestrial projection of the Vietnam combat film. Recruited to terminate (with extreme prejudice) the acid-blooded creatures infesting a deserted off-world colony, an airborne assault team is helicoptered onto a purple-hued industrial city. The platoon comprises African Americans, Latinos, and working-class whites who communicate in Vietnam vernacular ("stay frosty," "lock and load", "rock 'n' roll!") while an incompetent officer and callous bureaucrat monitor their battles from the safety of video screens well out of artillery range. "He's just a grunt," blurts out the smarmy company man, before spotting the object of his condescension. "No offense," he adds. "None taken," the grunt hisses back, the insult now a badge of honor. Likewise, in *Predator* (1987), when an alien warrior picks off a squad of Green Beret-like commandos, he resembles nothing so much as a Viet Cong insurgent, cloaked in invisibility, master of his jungle environment.

Of course, any period piece that harkens back to the 1960s cannot avoid the longest-running and most momentous historical event of the era. *Forrest Gump* (1994), Hollywood's most elaborate and self-conscious act of excavation in the 1960s, followed an idiot savant who meanders his way through the pageant of baby boom-centric American history—from Elvis, to JFK, to Vietnam. The film's extended Vietnam sequence valorizes a genuinely heroic warrior, albeit one too dense to experience the pangs of post-traumatic stress disorder. Back home the protesters are self-righteous pigs, the man in uniform a noble knight.

CONCLUSION

In the years since the second major wave of Vietnam war films broke, in the late 1980s, no comparable cyclical crest has fueled the Hollywood production line. For America, successor wars—the 1991 war in Iraq, the post-9/11 wars on terror, and the wars in Afghanistan and Iraq—have competed with and in many ways supplemented Vietnam as a site of combat action and polemical rumination. In Hollywood and Washington alike, however, the two most instructive back stories to America at war—the moral clarity of World War II, with its lesson that aggression undeterred is aggression encouraged, and the moral ambiguity of Vietnam, with its lesson that an unwarranted intervention is a lethal quagmire—dominate the tonalities of cinema and politics when confronting subsequent American wars. Sometimes, like generals, Hollywood filmmakers can seem to be fighting the last war. In *The Valley of Elah* (2007) and *Stop-Loss* (2008), the ethos of the first wave of Vietnam films has been grafted whole onto the Iraq War, with the Deranged Vietnam vet morphing seamlessly into the Deranged Iraq War vet and the American military a force for sinister conspiracy.

Yet eventually, against all odds, the two wars and two film genres converged, united at last by the healing power of Hollywood cinema. Based on the memoir by Lieutenant General Harold G. Moore, Randall Wallace's *We Were Soldiers* (2002) pays reverent homage to the first Army regiment to engage battle-hardened veterans of the North Vietnamese Army in the Central Highlands of Vietnam, a three-day bloodbath commencing on November 14, 1965. Starring Mel Gibson as the heroic Colonel Moore, the stern but loving leader of a band of equally courageous brothers, *We Were Soldiers* did what *The Green Berets* could not: turn Vietnam into a World War II movie. "Mel Gibson has the closest thing to a John Wayne part that anyone's played since the Duke himself rode into the sunset," commented Todd McCarthy in *Variety*, not entirely disapprovingly.[21] The lack of ideological conflict, the presumption of American nobility, and the certainty that the filmmakers have come to salute, not slander—Vietnam might as well be World War II. With the end of the twentieth century and the beginning of a War on Terror even more confounding and open-ended, Vietnam finally joined with the other wars in American history as a place, event, and mythology fit for the frames of Hollywood cinema.

DISCUSSION QUESTIONS

1. This chapter discusses a series of movies that were not set in Vietnam, but were really about the war in Vietnam. Why were filmmakers hesitant to make films that were explicitly about Vietnam? Include a discussion of one of the films in your answer.

2. What constituted the first wave of Vietnam films? What were their characteristics? Which film best fits this chapter's classification of "first wave" Vietnam movies? Explain which film you have chosen and why.
3. In 1968 John Wayne produced and starred in *The Green Berets*. Although it was panned by the critics, the movie was a box-office success. Why was there a paradox about *The Green Berets*? Be sure to explain the paradox as well as the possible reasons for it.
4. What constituted the second wave of Vietnam films? What were their characteristics? In what ways were these films different from, or similar to, those in the first wave? Which film best fits this chapter's classification of "second wave" Vietnam movies? Why?
5. What were the requisite ingredients, according to this chapter, in a Vietnam film? Explain each, and discuss whether or not you agree that each is critical to a Vietnam film.

SUGGESTED READING

Devine, Jeremy M. *Vietnam at 24 Frames a Second: A Critical and Thematic Analysis of over 400 Films about the Vietnam War*. Austin: University of Texas Press, 1999.
Dittmar, Linda, and Gene Michaud. *From Hanoi to Hollywood: The Vietnam War in American Film*. New Brunswick, NJ: Rutgers University Press, 1991.
Doherty, Thomas. *Cold War, Cool Medium: Television, McCarthyism, and American Culture*. New York: Columbia University Press, 2005.
Doherty, Thomas. *Projections of War*. New York: Columbia University Press, 1993.
Feeney, Mark. *Nixon at the Movies: A Book about Belief*. Chicago: University of Chicago Press, 2004.

NOTES

1. Jack Gould, "TV: Vietnam War Turned Into Nightly Experience," *New York Times*, February 5, 1968: 71.
2. "Picket, 'Green Berets' on B'Way; Anti-Vietnam Angles; Biz Big; Reneta Adler, 'Cleo'-Like Slam," *Variety*, June 26, 1968: 5; 16.
3. Arthur D. Murphy (Murf), "The Green Berets," *Variety*, June 18, 1968: 6.
4. "Big Rental Films of 1968," *Variety*, January 8, 1969: 15.
5. Gustav Hasford, *The Short-Timers* (New York: Bantam Books, 1979), 7.
6. Ron Kovic, *Born on the Fourth of July* (New York: Simon & Schuster, 1976), 54.
7. Robert Altman, DVD commentary track, *M*A*S*H* (Twentieth Century Fox Home Entertainment, 2004).
8. Gene Siskel, "The Movies: *M*A*S*H*," *Chicago Tribune*, March 30, 1970: A11. Vincent Canby dissented somewhat from the chorus by calling MASH, at heart, "an ultra-sophisticated, high ranking *Buck Privates*—Abbott and Costello for the Pepsi Generation." Vincent Canby, "Blood, Blasphemy, and Laughs," *New York Times*, February 1, 1970: D1, D20.
9. Addison Verrill, "Left, Right Hail War Pic," *Variety*, February 11, 1968: 3.

10. Mark Feeney, *Nixon at the Movies: A Book about Belief* (Chicago: University of Chicago Press, 2004), 67–72. Feeney argues that "liberal critics [who] said Nixon fastened on *Patton* as a way to stiffen his resolve to invade Cambodia" are guilty of an "interpretation as unnuanced as Scott's performance."
11. Will Tusher, "Oscars Aftermath Torn by Viet Nam Passions," *Hollywood Reporter*, April 10, 1975: 1, 3.
12. Arthur D. Murphy (Murf), "Coming Home," *Variety*, February 15, 1978.
13. "Big Rental Films of 1978," *Variety*, January 3, 1979: 17.
14. "Heroes," *Variety*, November 2, 1977: 17.
15. Leticia Kent, "Ready for Vietnam? A Talk with Michael Cimino," *New York Times*, December 10, 1978: D15.
16. Dale Pollack, "An Archival Detailing of UA's 'Apocalypse Now' since 1967 Start," *Variety*, May 23, 1979: 5, 46.
17. Dale Pollock, "Reaction to Edited 'Apocalypse'; Coppola Improves His Odds," *Variety*, April 15, 1979: 30, 46.
18. Louis Chunovic, "Stone Working on 'Platoon' Film," *Hollywood Reporter*, February 20, 1986: 3, 24.
19. Film critic James Naremore opines, "Kubrick's vision of military indoctrination and combat is distinctly unsentimental and unmelodramatic, especially compared with the patriotic distortions of *The Deer Hunter*, the operatic pretensions of *Apocalypse Now* and the emotion manipulations of *Platoon*." James Naremore, *On Kubrick* (London: British Film Institute, 2007), 222.
20. Jeffrey Jolson-Colburn, "Hollywood Alters American Attitudes toward Vietnam," *Hollywood Reporter*, August 13, 1987: 14.
21. Todd McCarthy, "We Were Soldiers," *Variety*, February 22, 2002.

TIMELINE EVENTS

1963 – Bob Dylan releases "Masters of War"

1965 – Phi Ochs releases "I Ain't Marching Anymore"

March 1965 – First US combat forces arrive in Vietnam

July 1965 – Bob Dylan first performs live with electric guitars at the Newport Folk Festival

1966 – Sergeant Barry Sadler releases "Ballad of the Green Berets"

1967 – The Beatles release *Sgt. Pepper's Lonely Hearts Club Band*

1968 – Tet Offensive

1969 – Woodstock Music and Art Fair

1970 – The Temptations release "Ball of Confusion"

1973 – The last US troops leave Vietnam

Chapter 12

The soundtrack of Vietnam

Kim Herzinger

CHAPTER SUMMARY

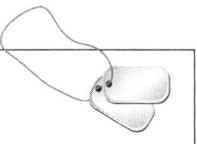

Rock and roll, in all of its various forms from alternative to pop, has long been a cultural barometer in the United States, especially as regards the concerns of teens of all races and regions. Rock was particularly well suited to express the complex ideas and emotions of the Vietnam era. Especially early in the war, rock and roll captured the generational feeling that a new time in the world's history had dawned in which anything was possible. As the war went on, though, the mood of both the nation and its music began to change. Especially in the period after the Tet Offensive of 1968, rock and roll became more reflective of a country that was alienated from and confused by its distant war.

We might begin with what seems a simple truth: it has become almost impossible to remember, or even imagine, the Vietnam War era without the accompanying background of rock music. Filmmakers have long since discovered this, and the sound tracks of their films about the war or about American life during the war years are infused with the memory-evoking sound of rock. And, too, almost no one who has written about American social and cultural experience during the Vietnam era has failed to recognize the degree to which that period was dominated by political, social, and cultural confrontations with established authority, and few have written about those confrontations without attempting to take into account the significance of rock music. My job here will be to attempt to trace some of the reasons why rock music achieved this extraordinary cultural resonance, why it came to be such a fitting expression of the Vietnam era's sensibility, and to suggest some of the ways that rock expressed that sensibility.

Rock music in its various forms (and that includes soul, "alternative," hip-hop, most contemporary pop, etc.) has been with us for over five decades now, and has established itself almost without question as the central musical expression of our time. Rock has become the musical expression around which we organize our most interesting thoughts about ourselves. There are no other serious contenders, actually: "art" composers from Berg and Boulez to Reich, Riley, and Varese have not been able to sell the culture on Schoenberg's new scale, on the glories of cacophony, on electronic music generally, on serial music, on minimalist music, or anything else much. In fact, it could be said that it has been rock music that has come the closest to making the central features of much modern "art" music—cacophony, electronics, repetition with nuance—acceptable, maybe even recognizable, forms of musical expression in the culture as a whole. Jazz remains a significant form, of course, but no one would claim for it the cultural vitality that rock has; folk music blew away in the first high winds of the 1960s and is now mainly embedded in the jangling, acoustic earnestness of certain alternative rock bands and alt-folk performers. To music hall music, a fond goodbye; to the soft pop of Tin Pan Alley, farewell; show music? Get serious; New Age music? Your twenty minutes of airtime was quite enough, thank you.

Rock is a music of instincts, something we all have, rather than of training, something we don't. Rock and roll, especially early rock and roll, is and wants to be amateurish; it's homemade, out-in-the-yard-and-in-the-garage music. This is not the music of ordinary working people as played by highly polished musicians; these are the ordinary people themselves. As one rock and roller has said, rock is "just an attitude. You don't have to play the greatest guitar." Indeed, part of the charm of early rock and roll is that we all thought we could do it, and we all did do it: in the shower, at the hop, in front of the mirror. Indeed, the rough amateurishness of rock music is one of its essential elements, and one of the most important things about it. Its amateurishness declares rock's insistent democratic non-elitism, the cultural equivalent of participatory democracy, and an alternative to traditional cultural authority. Rock's resistance to established authority confirms that it was at its origins, and remains still, one the most compelling modes of expression ever devised for the disenfranchised, the unfranchised, and the marginalized.

Until the early 1950s the thoughts, feelings, and concerns of young teens of all races and regions—but especially urban blacks, small-town country whites, unvoguish high school kids, and other particularly marginalized subgroups—were simply unavailable in savory form to the dominant culture as a whole. Blacks had "race music"; whites had Tin Pan Alley, show tunes, and country music; teens had a commercial music made for adults but just dorky enough to include them. But this changed with the emergence of rock and roll. Rock gave them a voice, a means by which the marginal could make their case, nationwide, as an expression of revolt, aimed at subverting established ideological codes and stereotypes. All of a sudden, there they were, speaking up and, for the first time, being heard: poor white kids from Memphis and Liverpool; poor black kids from Macon; white teen hicks from Lubbock; working-class kids from Minneapolis, Seattle, and Boston; street kids from the Bronx and East LA; Rude Boys from

Figure 12.1 *Jimi Hendrix performing live at the Royal Albert Hall, London, February 24, 1969.*
Photo by David Redfern/Redferns.

Kingston; women, especially young women, from everywhere. There they were—the angry, dazed and confused, suicidal, strung-out, broke; there they were—feeling sexy, feeling lusty, feeling puppy-love, feeling mistreated, unjustly treated, untreated. Rock was, and remains, their music, their say in the culture.

Even now, when rock is dominated by white, middle-class performers from some art school somewhere, the music still remembers its emotional and experiential base. When it wanders too far from that base, some form of "correction" follows: the mid-1960s return to blues, R&B, and early rock and roll foundations; 1970s punk; 1980s "alternative" and hip-hop; grunge and riot grrrls records in the 1990s; the White Stripes and the Strokes in the early 2000s. Rock is always a backbencher, it is always oppositional—sometimes against itself; and if it does embrace some notion of community, as it did in the 1960s, it always embraces a community that is in opposition to the perceived system of power. As Pete Townshend of the Who said, "I think you should keep on playing rock for as long as you have an axe to grind, and if you haven't got an axe to grind, you should go into cabaret." *Pace* Elvis.

EVERYTHING WAS POSSIBLE

Of all the products of popular culture, it is rock music that has its finger most firmly on the pulse of what Americans are feeling at any particular moment. The reasons for this are many, but two are particularly obvious. The first is that rock music has, historically, always been a transient musical form that interested itself in the transient obsessions of the culture. The second is that because it takes such a comparatively short time from the moment of the studio performance to the moment that a record is released, rock tends to reflect social obsessions much more immediately than other cultural products—television programs, movies, clothes, etc.—all of which take much longer to produce and distribute. Consequently, when a new or different set of concerns, or a new and different mood (no matter how transient it will eventually prove to be), takes hold in American life, one can hardly do otherwise than to look to rock music as a reflection of those new concerns and new mood.

Rock, then, was particularly well suited to suggest and express the complex of ideas and emotions which monopolized the sensibility of the Vietnam era—dominated as it was by political, social, and cultural confrontations with authority, and by the emergence of a counterculture that celebrated its outsider status, its marginality. During the Vietnam era, rock was what generational solidarity sounded like. Its sound pitched a statement of difference between the "baby boom" generation and the generations of Americans that preceded it— between those generations that were managing the war and the one that was fighting it, or desperately hoping *not* to fight it. This was a generation particularly given to confrontation, one that felt marginalized by traditional authority and chafed by traditional cultural habits and attitudes. For that generation, rock was right, and—given its own history—inevitably right. Rock became the sound track for the generation that grew up during the Vietnam era, a brilliantly effective reflection of the shifting, volatile moods of the period, and—in time— powerful and expressive enough to function as a catalyst for those moods. The music had found its perfect audience, and the audience had found its perfect music.

One of the dominant "moods" that rock music both fueled and was fueled by was the visionary—the widely shared feeling among many at home, if not necessarily by soldiers in Vietnam, that *everything was possible*, that people were living in a moment of universal liberation, a time of unbinding energies. Rock music in the 1960s was without question a powerful cultural manifestation of that shared feeling. Nothing else came as close to expressing and conveying the sense of liberating energies as rock did. The music was, of course, much less adept at locating and promoting a political focus for those energies, which would have required a grounding in real-world politics, something very few rock musicians would claim, or *should* claim, to have. Instead, rock's arguments were emotional, and only occasionally practical, ethical, or theological.

It is impossible to say with certainty how much public reaction to the Vietnam War alone—as opposed to the civil rights movement, drugs, the mushrooming youth market, and other phenomena of the 1960s—specifically had to do with this emerging sense of new possibilities. But there is little question that the youth culture's general disengagement from traditional lines of authority created a desire to break boundaries and test new possibilities, or at least that it enhanced the idea that the old possibilities were in fact limitations, and that America, as a culture, should hardly be satisfied with such limitations.

Many of the most telling rock songs of the era consistently reminded listeners that they should not be satisfied with things as they are, and that a new and more exhilarating world was within the grasp of those who kept their eyes on what might be possible. In their own rather different ways, songs such as "Something's in the Air" (Thunderclap Newman, 1969), "People Just Got to Be Free" (the Rascals, 1968), "Time (Has Come Today)" (the Chambers Brothers, 1968), "White Rabbit" (Jefferson Airplane, 1967), "Purple Haze" (Jimi Hendrix, 1967), "War" (Edwin Starr, 1969), "Love the One You're With" (Stephen Stills, 1970), "Imagine" (John Lennon, 1971), and, most importantly, the Beatles' *Sgt. Pepper's Lonely Hearts Club Band* (1967) all stand as rock testaments to the notion that new possibilities were simply out there waiting to be fulfilled, that the assumptions and restrictions of the old world were exhausted, and that complacency or acceptance of the old was tantamount to a kind of death. The music would "love to turn us on" to this generational truth.

Sgt. Pepper, by far the most significant rock document of the period and one of its most significant cultural documents of any kind, introduced an extraordinary new *sound* in rock music. It was a sound sufficiently sophisticated and culturally conscious to propose to the 1960s generation a sense of importance (confirmed by the likes of Leonard Bernstein, Glenn Gould, and other musical elders); it was still *their* music, yes, but it was music that meant serious business, music that was clearly not made merely to be consumed and then forgotten. *Sgt. Pepper* was *aware* of itself as being something important, but quite intentionally undercut any sense of the *self-importance* (the Beatles introduce themselves, music hall-style, as "guaranteed to raise a smile" and hope the audience will simply "sit back and let the evening go") that would soon come to dominate rock for the remainder of the 1960s until the middle of the 1970s (Zagar and Evans' excruciating "In the Year 2525"; almost anything by the Doors; all of prog-rock).

Sgt. Pepper declared that the old ways of making that music were simply no longer sufficient because the old ways of going about the business of living were no longer sufficient, either. By "picturing" ourselves in new ways ("Lucy in the Sky with Diamonds"), by leaving home to find "something inside that was always denied" ("She's Leaving Home"), by discovering the love "that could save the world" ("Within You Without You"), by refusing to accept aging complacently

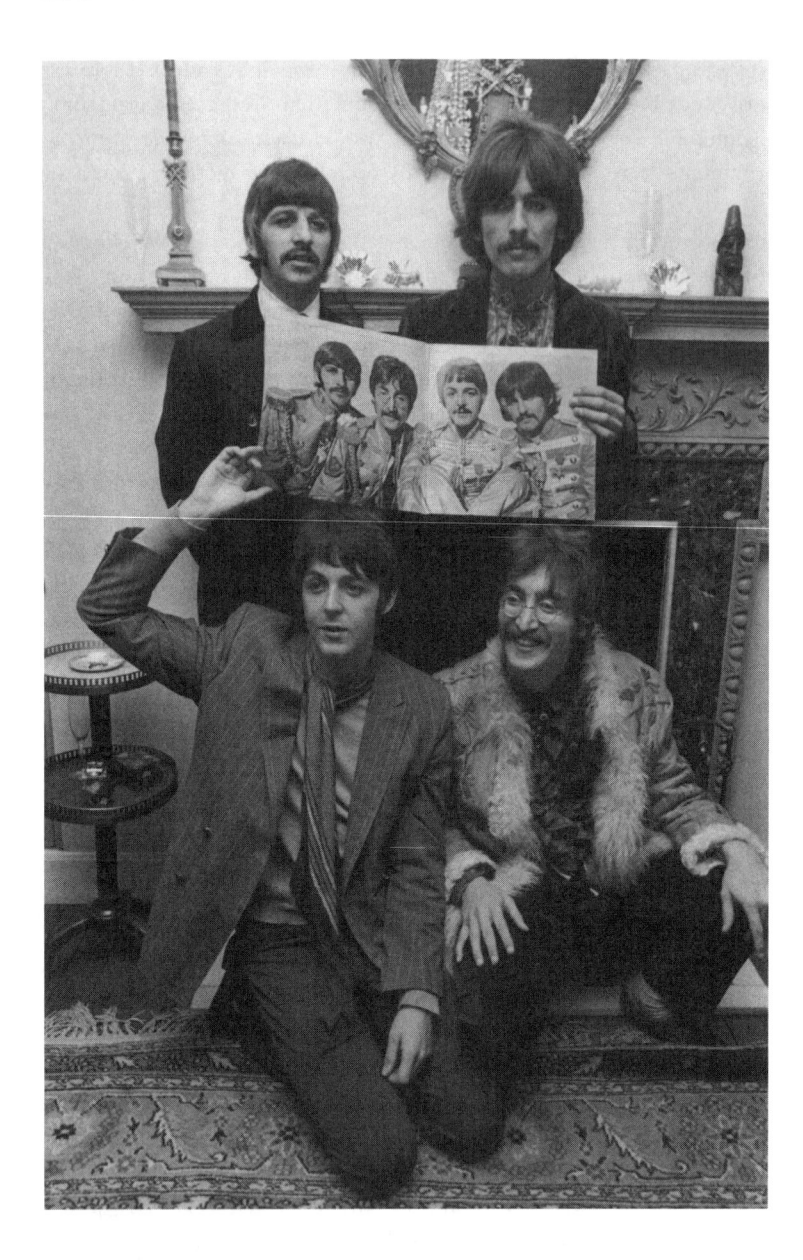

Figure 12.2
British pop group the Beatles (clockwise from top left: Ringo Starr (b. 1940), George Harrison (1943–2001), John Lennon (1940–80) and Paul McCartney (b. 1942)) pose with the cover of their new album, Sgt. Pepper's Lonely Hearts Club Band, at manager Brian Epstein's west London home, May 22, 1967.

Photo by John Downing/ Daily Express/ Hulton Archive/ Getty Images.

("When I'm Sixty-Four"), and with a little help from our friends, *Sgt. Pepper* insistently proposes that "it's getting better all the time"—or could, at least, be getting better.

Sgt. Pepper suggests that "a splendid time is guaranteed for all" ("Being for the Benefit of Mr. Kite") if only we would "fix the holes" and disallow the "people standing there who disagree and never win" ("Fixing a Hole") and those who "hide themselves behind a wall of illusion"

("Within You Without You") from retaining control. These are the people, the album suggests, for whom "nothing had changed it's still the same" and have "nothing to say but it's O.K." ("Good Morning, Good Morning"). In "A Day in the Life," the Beatles sing of a "lucky man who made the grade," but who "didn't notice that the lights had changed." For him, and for others who hadn't noticed—the Kinks' "Well-Respected Man," Dylan's "Mr. Jones"—the inevitable consequence was a kind of senseless self-destruction. The Beatles' "lucky man" blows "his mind out in a car."

Sgt. Pepper's Lonely Hearts Club Band explicitly references war only once, and it is not even the Vietnam War. In "A Day in the Life," the speaker sees a film in which the English army has "just won the war," but the crowd of people turns away. The speaker has to look, however, "having read the book."

Why does the crowd "turn away"? Boredom? Disgust? And who are they? The young? The experienced? The speaker doesn't say, but the implications are clear enough. *That* book has been written, *that* film has been seen—and all too often. The lights have indeed changed, and it is time to be "turned on" to other possibilities. The old, familiar habits—war among them—are no longer viable. As "Getting Better" has it, if we can "finally hear" the "word," if we can reject the "teachers" who were "holding me down, turning me round, filling me up with [their] rules," we can change everything—"Man I was mean but I'm changing my scene and I'm doing the best that I can."

Was *Sgt. Pepper* an "anti-war" album? Not explicitly, no. But there is little doubt that in 1967 practically everyone *understood it to be just that*. *Sgt. Pepper* stood in opposition to those versions of authority that run lives and wars, and it, like almost every significant rock song of the late 1960s and early 1970s, is an anti-war song, whether directly "about" the war or not.

ROCK AND VIETNAM

Much of the rock music of the 1960s proposes itself as visionary, and the visionary is almost always opposed to what it sees as the mean and ancient machinery of war and war-making. But rock music also found itself willing and able to take up Vietnam as a specific case. So what did the music have to say, explicitly, about the Vietnam War? And how did rock say it? That, of course, very much depends on what music we're talking about, and when it was produced.

Simply put, and not surprisingly, the attitude of rock music changed with the attitude of the American public—from lack of interest at the war's beginnings, to apprehension and queasiness by 1967, to disgust, anger, and protest from 1968 until 1972, then back to lack of interest until the war's official end. Rock did not lead, as some (mainly conservative) social commentators would have it; rock followed the pulse of the people. But the pulse of the people it followed, of course, was the pulse of the young and the disenfranchised, and—as the only cultural product on a national scale that was insistently, even inherently, oppositional—it often seemed to be leading because it was so visible and invasive.

Samuel Hynes has told us that the Vietnam War "was a rock-and-roll war."[1] This is not simply because of the sheer *physicality* of rock music, its high-adrenalin high rev that was the closest musical equivalent of running through a jungle with guns on automatic fire. He is also talking about how the soldier in the field was buoyed up by an army that "zealously . . . nurtured the back-home needs of the troops."[2] Hynes claims:

> It was as though the generals had persuaded themselves that the American spirit and loyalty of troops in the field could be sustained forever, regardless of how the war went, if only they had enough American products to consume. Those consumer goods litter the memoirs [of American soldiers] like empty beer cans along an American highway, and help to give them their characteristic dissonant note of the totally familiar in the totally strange.[3]

Rock music was one of America's most important and energizing products.

Nevertheless, perhaps the most beloved songs among the troops in Vietnam were those that reminded them of the totally familiar, or those that dramatically expressed the soldier's desire to get out of the situation he found himself in. Soldiers in Vietnam certainly embraced rock songs that seemed to speak of the world they found themselves living in—"Run through the Jungle" by Creedence Clearwater Revival, "Paint It Black" by the Rolling Stones, and so on—but it appears that the music that most endeared itself to the troops was that which reminded them of what they had left behind, or which expressed their desire to get back to what they had left behind. It has often been remarked that the Animals' "We Gotta Get Out of This Place," which has nothing specifically to do with Vietnam, was a primary example of the kind of thing the soldier responded to. The soldier was responding, of course, to a sentiment which he felt very strongly, and the song—first produced in 1965—had a long life in Vietnam. Indeed, "going home" songs like "Leaving on a Jet Plane" and "Homeward Bound," as well as songs that provided idealized images of America ("The Dock of the Bay," "Galveston," "A Rainy Night in Georgia," for example) were particularly popular among the troops.

It might be reasonable to suppose that such songs would have solidified the soldier's notion of exactly what he was fighting for, as Georgian pastoral poetry about the English countryside is said to have done for some British Tommies during World War I, but an examination of statements by soldiers in the field would seem to suggest that it had the opposite effect, reminding them instead of what they were missing, and of the excruciating difference between their situation and that of the place and people from which those songs emanated.

It is not surprising that the more insistent anti-war songs in rock's arsenal were not necessarily the most popular among the in-country troops. Such songs were certainly present, however, and not only provided the war with its own distinctive music but also "offered the men who were there a rhetoric and a set of attitudes—brash, anti-establishment, often explicitly anti-war."[4] Although some attempts were made to control what the troops heard (a central feature of the movie *Good Morning, Vietnam*), it could never be done successfully. Short-timers were already aware of the anti-war songs, and there were too many tape recorders, stereos, and radio broadcasts—many from pirate radio stations set up by the soldiers themselves—available to make suppression a viable possibility. So part of what the soldiers inevitably heard was the brash, anti-establishment, and anti-war mood of life back in the States, at least life as it was being lived and felt by the same generation as that of those who were doing the fighting.

ROCK AFTER TET

A crucial moment for rock, as it was for the war as a whole, was the Tet Offensive of 1968. Before Tet, rock music may have shown concerned opposition to what was happening in Vietnam, but it did not yet show the degree of anger, frustration, drooping cultural morale, confusion, and general disgust with the entire Vietnam escapade that began to be felt in 1968. For those opposed to the war, Tet confirmed their worst suspicions; for those yet undecided, the consequences of the Tet Offensive exposed the likelihood that American political and military policy in Vietnam might well be wrongheaded and fruitless. Such a realization was necessarily a devastating political blow to those who were administering (and, often, to those who were fighting) the war, and had dire consequences not only for those who were in Vietnam but also for those who were observing it and judging it back home in the States. Like almost nothing else, Tet affected American perceptions of the war effort and caused, for many in and out of the armed forces, serious distrust, a decline in morale, increased frustration and anger, and genuine opposition. The rock music of mid-1968 to 1972 reflects those changes in perceptions: during and after Tet, the music, like the culture, becomes angrier, more disjointed, more insistently oppositional, and far more pointedly political than it had been before it.

This is not to say that there were not anti-war protest songs written and produced before 1968. There were, of course, many. The most famous, perhaps, are Bob Dylan's "Masters of War" (1963), Phil Ochs's "I Ain't Marching Anymore" (1965), Arlo Guthrie's "Alice's Restaurant" (1967), and Country Joe and the Fish's "I-Feel-Like-I'm-Fixin'-to-Die Rag" (1967). Of these, only "Fixin'-to-Die," which was never a "hit," expresses the anger and bitterness that would mark the songs of the post-Tet years. But unlike the major anti-war and protest songs of 1968–72, it delivered its bitterness with irony. Still, there is enough in "Fixin'-to-Die" of what later became the sound of rock protest that it became perhaps the best-known protest song of the era—the first, really, to become a rallying cry for Vietnam War dissidents, and effectively the first to argue that complacency about the war was tantamount to agreeing to "be the first ones on your block / to have your boy brought home in a box."

Dylan's and Ochs's songs are generic anti-military/industrial complex folk songs that owe more to the long-standing Cold War folk-protest tradition than to the Vietnam conflict, and Arlo Guthrie's famous narrative song is more about tolerance for difference than it is about resistance to the draft. In any case, Guthrie could, in 1967, afford a kind of gentle humor that became increasingly tough to come by after mid-1968.

In fact, the only pre-Tet rock song that sounds the anger and accusation of the post-Tet period is one that very few people at the time ever heard: "Kill for Peace" by the Fugs, a Greenwich Village group including Beat poet and lyricist Ed Sanders, whose chant "Kill, kill, kill for peace" fairly accurately predicts the peculiar ironies that so many Americans would feel later, especially after the My Lai incident, and the now-notorious formulation that so undercut the United States' pacification program—the notion that US troops might have to destroy a village in order to save it. But even here, The Fugs' song is as much about American Cold War postures, and reactions to the threat of nuclear war, as it is, specifically, about Vietnam.

And, too, before 1968 it was possible for performers such as Sergeant Barry Sadler, Dave Dudley, the Spokesmen, Pat Boone, and even Senator Everett Dirksen to release songs that harkened back to the patriotic tunes of World War II. Boone's "Wish You Were Here, Buddy" (1966) is a particularly egregious example of this, a song that takes up the usual "just-doing-my-duty-and-don't-you-wish-you-could-pitch-in-as-well" sentiments widely used as recruiting tools during previous wars. The song's title alone would be an impossible sentiment to offer after 1968, when no one—not even Pat Boone—would wish for his stateside buddies that they ought to be with him in Vietnam.

Sergeant Barry Sadler's "The Green Berets" (1966) is perhaps the most famous pro-military song of the era. It reached number 1 on the pop charts in mid-January 1966 and stayed there for five full weeks, and remained somewhere on the charts for eleven weeks. This is quite a feat for any pop tune, let alone one produced during the heyday of the Beatles, Stones, and Supremes. The song declares the kind of bracing patriotism that makes itself officially welcome during any war. In it the Green Berets are brave, heroic, and capable of extreme sacrifice; they are "America's best," and their legacy—should a Green Beret die on his mission—will be passed on to their sons. The "sound" of the song, not surprisingly, is firm, unperplexed, convinced, and its rhythm is that of a slightly dirge-like march, established by military drum rolls. Those who liked it—and there were many—found it the perfect expression of military purpose and patriotism; those who didn't found it stiff, blind, and an embarrassing tribute to what they found most worrisome and objectionable in the official military and government attitude toward the war and the qualities of character necessary to carry it on.

Before 1968 it could be argued that rock music was engaged in a democratic wartime debate about Vietnam. But after Tet the debate was over, at least as far as rock was concerned. After 1968, songs like "The Green Berets" and "Wish You Were Here, Buddy" were almost never played on American pop radio, and the songs that might be considered "pro-war" were country songs by country singers (such as Merle Haggard's "Okie from Muskogee"), which in fact were not so much pro-war as they were songs that declared themselves in opposition to anti-war public sentiment in general and anti-war protesters specifically, especially since anti-war protesters were associated with, and sometimes felt to be indistinguishable from, counter-cultural icons such as hippies.

SONGS OF CONFUSION AND RAGE

The rock songs that did dominate the airwaves after Tet no longer seemed to have time for ironies ("Fixin'-to-Die") or gentle humor ("Alice's Restaurant"), or even generalized pacifist sentiments like "I Ain't Marchin' Anymore" or "Masters of War." What they did have time for were various other kinds of anti-war responses, mainly of three different but related types: (1) expressions of confusion, perplexity, and instability; (2) expressions of a doomed sense of political, cultural, or moral sickness, combined with a sense of demoralized helplessness about the ongoing war; and (3) expressions of direct anger and accusation, aimed at a spectrum of targets—the military, the draft, public complacency, the perceived intolerance and inflexibility of those who supported the war, or the very idea of war itself. A few examples of these three different kinds of "anti-war" songs should suffice.

The songs of confusion, perplexity, and instability are perhaps the most interesting. They are most interesting, in part, because they reflect not only a complex of ideas and emotions about the war, but also the stress caused by changes associated with the transformation of American culture itself, brought on by the civil rights movement, lifestyle changes, gender dislocation, and the emergence of a very powerful and visible anti-authoritarian counter-culture. It does not seem in any way a stretch to argue that the *sound* of groups such as Jefferson Airplane, the Doors, Love, Cream, the Jimi Hendrix Experience, Captain Beefheart and His Magic Band, and the Mothers of Invention, to name a few, was as suggestively anti-war as any anti-war lyrics they might have written—and they did of course write some. But it was the *sound* of these bands—heard in everything from the psychedelic distortions coming out of the West Coast to the edgy, slightly crazy ravings of many bands across the country and in Britain—that had by 1968 become the sound of cultural transformation and the center-lessness of a youth culture that found itself unable to accept the traditional directions mapped out for it by those in charge of the country. Hendrix's "Star-Spangled Banner" is a particularly suggestive case in point. Better than almost any other example from the era, its gnarled, bent, grotesquely distorted sound conveys the gnarled, bent, and distorted feelings so many had about the times they were living in and the loaded meanings that America's national anthem had come to represent. That it *is* the national anthem, and not just any tune, makes it a primary example of one kind of anti-war sentiment, of course, but its sound is what makes it distinctive, and what makes it a primary example of the culture's state of mind at the time.

Some songs, of course, were much more explicit about cultural confusion and instability. "Ball of Confusion" (1970) is a Motown gripe-fest that attempts to express such notions with both lyrics and rhythm. The pulse of the song is hurried, as if the Temptations barely have time to catch their breath with things moving at such a frenetic pace. The lyrics, "Segregation, determination/Demonstration, integration/Aggravation, humiliation, etc.," are jammed up against each other so as to suggest the hurried rush of sometimes colliding concerns and feelings that made up the emotional map of American life in those years. The upbeat doom-saying of

"Bad Moon Rising" is perhaps the best-known example of a rock song that expresses the public feeling of disillusion and helplessness during and after 1968—despite John Fogerty's disclaimer that it wasn't really a political song at all. In a very different way, Marvin Gayes' "What's Going On" expresses those same feelings of disillusion and helplessness, combined with yearning for relief.

Jamaican Jimmy Cliff's lesser-known (at least at the time) "Vietnam" is also useful as an example of this, if only because it suggests the way in which disillusionment about the war was beginning to stretch far beyond American boundaries. In it, the speaker talks to a Mrs. Brown, who—like so many from the Caribbean—had left Jamaica with her family to seek opportunity in the United States. But the war catches up with her, just as it had caught up with everyone. She has just received a telegram telling her of her son's death. "Don't be alarmed," the telegram says, "but Mistress Brown, your son is dead." The inevitable coldness of such a message is, of course, apparent, but it is exacerbated by its asking her to do the impossible: not to be alarmed by the most alarming thing a mother can hear. All Cliff has to add is "and it came from Vietnam," and then repeat the word "Vietnam" over and over, as if to begin to count the number of similar messages received by mothers everywhere. So much for Mrs. Brown's dreams for her son, so much for her aspirations. The war had put an end to those.

"Fortunate Son" (1969) by Creedence Clearwater Revival is perhaps the most successful and, arguably, best known of the angry anti-war songs of the era. John Fogerty wrote it the day he got his release papers from the US Army Reserves. His anger, it appears, was in having been one of the unfortunate sons who had been directed to fight in the war, hoodwinked by false inducements of glory and by the recognition that privileged young men managed to elude it while young urban blacks and poor white Southerners seemed to shoulder far more of the war's burden than a general "draft" should have made possible. "Some folks are . . . made to wave the flag." All right. But when the country calls them to serve, "Ooh, they'll point the cannon at you." Fogerty's lyrics argue his disconnection from a country that bestows special privileges on those who are "born [with a] silver spoon in hand." Fogerty is furious about the unjustness of the draft, and he sings his complaint furiously.

The general suspicion after Tet that the United States was not giving peace a chance, but instead undercutting the chances for peace by committing to a policy of escalation, stands behind "Give Peace a Chance," the John Lennon–Yoko Ono mantra which even now raises conservative hackles. Recorded in Room 1742 of Hotel La Reine Elizabeth in Montreal, Lennon uses a technique similar to that of "Ball of Confusion," spewing buzzwords and nonsense words: "Revolution, evolution, masturbation/flagellation, regulation, integration/meditations, United Nations" and then punctuating it with, "All we are saying is give peace a chance," as if—amidst the confusing babble of the time—this is all that really needs to be said.

THE SOUNDTRACK OF VIETNAM

Figure 12.3 Creedence Clearwater Revival, ca. 1970.
Photo by Michael Ochs Archives/Getty Images.

CONCLUSION

"Give Peace a Chance" was, of course, not all that needed to be said about the Vietnam War, and songs like "Bring the Boys Home" (Freda Payne, 1971), "Draft Morning" (the Byrds, 1968), "Draft Resister" (Steppenwolf, 1970), "Military Madness" (Graham Nash, 1971), "Peace Train" (Cat Stevens, 1971), "America" (Simon and Garfunkel, 1968), "War" (Edwin Starr, 1969), "2 + 2 = ?" (Bob Seger, 1968), "War Pigs" (Black Sabbath, 1970), and even "Street Fighting Man" (Rolling Stones, 1968) all stand as testaments to just how much more was said, and to the various ways rock found to say it. What is most remarkable, however, is the degree to which songs as different in their attitude and attack as "Fortunate Son," "A Day in the Life," and "A Rainy Night in Georgia" all seem, then and now, to be permeated with implications having to do with the war. If one gave voice to the anger and frustration of the period, the others gave voice to attitudes equally present and pervasive: disillusion on the one hand, and on the other an idyllic version of America that seemed to be teetering on the edge of collapse. The power of rock music was that it was capable of speaking across an entire spectrum of attitudes and positions, and to articulate them so memorably and expressively that—as subsequent films about the war confirm—it has become practically impossible to remember, or even imagine, the Vietnam War without its rock soundtrack.

Vietnam was a "rock-and-roll war," as Samuel Hynes has said, both for the soldiers on the ground and for American culture as a whole. It was so, in great measure, because the history and ideology of rock—its brash anti-authoritarianism, its history of giving voice to the marginalized and disenfranchised, its instantaneous cultural pulse taking—was a perfect match for the complex of attitudes, ideas, and emotions that the war in Vietnam inevitably evoked. Some years ago I would certainly have claimed, in fact did claim, that because the Vietnam War so deeply scarred the American psyche, because all subsequent conflicts would likely rouse the ghastly specter of that war, and because of rock's established oppositional—and sometimes visionary—nature, it would seem likely that all war-making in the foreseeable future would somehow have to deal with rock's sonic commentary. This appears not to be the case: the war in Iraq, for instance, has perhaps found its most heady anti-war expressions from two venerable rock refugees from the Vietnam era: Mick Jagger and Neil Young. Rock is here to stay and so, it seems, is war. But the generational solidarity and the impulse to kick down the jams of institutional authority are certainly of a quite different nature, a quieter, less oppositional nature, than the impulses that animated the 1960s. Rock seems barely to have cracked the silence.

It feels a bit like something lost, somehow, as if rock had lost its nerve. Perhaps, though, it must wait for the next transformational moment, when the entire culture—or a significant part of it—involves itself in confronting the major moral, political, and institutional embroilments that bedevil it. This remains to be seen, of course, and when and if it is seen, it will very probably also be heard.

DISCUSSION QUESTIONS

1. Why is rock and roll arguably the central mode of musical expression of our time?
2. In what ways was *Sgt. Pepper's Lonely Hearts Club Band* an important cultural document of the 1960s?
3. Discuss the "visionary" qualities of rock and roll in the period before 1968.
4. In what ways can the music of the Vietnam era before 1968 be described as a "democratic wartime debate"?
5. In what ways did rock and roll change after the Tet Offensive?

SUGGESTED READING

Friedlander, Paul. *Rock and Roll: A Social History*. Boulder, CO: Westview Press, 1996).
Gillett, Charlie. *The Sound of the City: The Rise of Rock and Roll*. New York: Pantheon, 1984.
Hynes, Samuel. *The Soldier's Tale: Bearing Witness to Modern War*. New York: Penguin, 1997.
Lipsitz, George. "Who'll Stop the Rain? Youth Culture, Rock 'n' Roll, and Social Crises." In *The Sixties: From Memory to History*, edited by David Farber. Chapel Hill: University of North Carolina Press, 1994.
The Rolling Stone Illustrated History of Rock and Roll. New York: Random House, 1992.
Werner, Craig. *A Change Is Gonna Come: Music, Race and the Soul of America*. Ann Arbor: University of Michigan Press, 2006).

NOTES

1. Samuel Hynes, *The Soldier's Tale: Bearing Witness to Modern War* (New York: Penguin, 1997), 185.
2. Ibid., 184.
3. Ibid., 185.
4. Ibid.

TIMELINE EVENTS

January 27, 1973 – Paris Peace Accords signed

July 1, 1973 – Beginning of the All-Volunteer Army

April 30, 1975 – Saigon falls

June 1973 – General William DePuy assumes command of Training and Doctrine Command

July 1976 – FM 100-5, *Operations*, is published

July 1977 – General Donn Starry assumes command of Training and Doctrine Command

August 1982 – New FM 100-5, *Operations*, is published, promulgating AirLand Battle

April 24, 1980 – Iranian hostage rescue mission fails

October 1980 – US Army National Training Center opens

October 1983 – Invasion of Grenada

October 1986 – Goldwater–Nichols Department of Defense Reorganization Act is signed into law

October 1989 – Berlin Wall comes down

December 1989 – Operation Just Cause

August 2, 1990 – Saddam Hussein's forces invade Kuwait

January 17, 1991 – Operation Desert Storm begins

March 20, 2003 – US and Coalition forces invade Iraq

December 2006 – FM 3-24, *Counterinsurgency*, published

Note: The views expressed in this chapter are those of the author and do not reflect the official policy or position of any department or agency of the US government.

Chapter 13

The legacy of the Vietnam War for the US Army

James H. Willbanks

CHAPTER SUMMARY

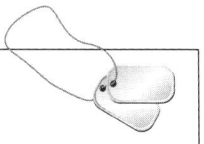

The US Army was nearly destroyed as an effective fighting force by the Vietnam War. It would take nearly two decades for the Army to reform itself into the force that performed so magnificently in the hundred-hour First Gulf War. This reformation included changes in doctrine, organization, recruitment, and technology. The Army was transformed into a modern force trained and equipped to prevail on the conventional battlefield. However, this transformation had some unintended effects as well, which caused difficulties for the Army when it was confronted with different kinds of conflict in Iraq and Afghanistan.

In 1991 the US Army performed magnificently in the first Gulf War, routing the forces of Saddam Hussein in a war that lasted only one hundred hours. That Army—technologically sophisticated, highly trained, and confident—bore little resemblance to the Army that left the Republic of Vietnam so ignominiously in 1973. However, in a very real sense the Army of 1991, arguably one of the finest forces that the United States had ever put in the field at the beginning of an international conflict, was shaped by the legacy of the Vietnam War, and in turn today's Army continues to be shaped by the Army's response to that war. The US military in general and the US Army in particular were severely damaged by the war in Southeast Asia; while much of the discussion that follows is applicable in varying degrees to the other services, this chapter will focus on the impact of the Vietnam War on the Army.

The US Army came unraveled in Vietnam. Although the Army entered the war as a trained and disciplined force, it emerged from the conflict deeply scarred by the Vietnam experience, and it took over twenty years to overcome the corrosive effects of the war. The road from the ruin of the Vietnam War resulted in a change in military culture that led directly to the force that performed so magnificently in 1991. However, the legacy of the Vietnam War had some unintended effects as well, and some of those continue to have an impact on the Army today.

The decline of the US Army in Vietnam can be traced to President Richard Nixon's decision in 1969 to "Vietnamize" the war and begin withdrawing American ground combat units. The Army had already begun to show the signs of the stress caused by the demands of the war, but the long and bloody withdrawal that ensued from Nixon's announcement to transfer the responsibility for the war to the South Vietnamese undercut morale. As more and more US forces departed South Vietnam, but the fighting continued, the troops who remained began to ask themselves whether it was worth it to risk dying in a war from which the United States was withdrawing. This situation only exacerbated the downward trend in motivation of the force, which was already suffering the effects of high casualties and personnel turbulence caused by the policy of twelve-month individual tours. Additionally, as a draftee army, the Army experienced the same drug abuse and racial unrest as the rest of American society during this period. As historian Shelby L. Stanton put it, "America's military sword—which had been thrust so quickly into Southeast Asia—became dulled and eroded."[1]

Flaws in the Army's institutional culture hastened the service's decline. A 1970 Army War College professionalism study noted that careerist "ticket-punching," micromanagement by senior officers, over-reliance on statistical indicators like the body count, and the promotion of marginally qualified career personnel contributed greatly to the deterioration of the Army as a fighting force. These flaws significantly impeded the service's ability to deal with the terrific challenges that it faced in the war, particularly as it began to disengage itself from the fighting.

The result of the confluence of these factors was an Army beset by problems that threatened to destroy it. The latter years of the Vietnam War saw an almost total breakdown in discipline and order in the Army. "Fragging" was soldier slang for the murder or attempted murder, usually by the use of fragmentation grenades, of strict, aggressive, or merely unpopular officers and non-commissioned officers (NCOs). Between 1969 and 1971, Army investigators recorded eight hundred instances of attacks involving hand grenades in which forty-five officers and NCOs were killed.[2] There were also numerous reported cases where bounties ranging from $50 to $1,000 were placed on the heads of leaders by disgruntled soldiers. In 1969 the GI underground newspaper in Vietnam, *G.I. Says*, publicly offered a $10,000 bounty on the battalion commander who ordered the attack on Hamburger Hill in May of that year.[3]

"Combat refusal," an Army euphemism for disobedience of orders to fight, began to occur in 1969. The 1st Cavalry Division admitted to some thirty-five individual cases of refusal in 1970 alone, and in one case in mid-1969 an entire company of the 196th Light Infantry Brigade publicly sat down on the battlefield and refused to go on patrol.[4] In another demonstration of the growing indiscipline that afflicted the Army as more and more US troops were withdrawn, there were increasing occurrences of "search and evade" whereby units in the field tacitly avoided combat by not aggressively seeking out the enemy to do battle.

As for drugs and race, the Army suffered greatly on both fronts. Racial strife had a serious impact on morale and combat readiness. The Army, particularly in Europe, was rife with racial conflict. In 1971, major US Army installations at Augsburg, Krailsheim, and Hohenfels saw serious violent confrontations between black and white soldiers.[5] A number of commanders attempted to initiate race relations programs to address the situation, but service-wide problems in this area continued to have a negative impact on the Army and its readiness.

The situation with regard to illicit drug use was no better. A 1971 congressional investigating committee reported that the Army had 17,742 drug investigations the previous year. At Fort Bragg, North Carolina, the Army's third largest post at the time, a 1971 survey revealed that 4 percent of the 36,000 soldiers stationed there were on hard drugs, ranging from heroin to LSD.[6]

The problems were not just with the Army in Vietnam; they affected the Army wherever it was stationed. The Seventh Army in Europe, theoretically the Army's highest-priority unit since it was nose to nose with the Soviet Army, was in a debilitated state because of the replacement system in Vietnam, which had used other commands as replacement pools. This resulted in extreme personnel turbulence in Europe and drastic shortages of officers and non-commissioned officers (NCOs) in the Seventh Army as both officers and men were drawn from there to fill the needs of the Army on the ground in Vietnam. Additionally, the US Army in Europe experienced the same morale and discipline problems that plagued the Army in Vietnam, including racial strife and drug abuse. Forty percent of the Army in Europe confessed to drug use, with a significant number admitting to being hooked on heroin. Drug abuse also manifested itself in increased crime, AWOL (absence without leave), and desertion, further degrading unit readiness.

By 1972 the Army was demoralized and in desperate trouble; only four of its thirteen active divisions were rated as ready for combat. The Army's worldwide combat effectiveness had deteriorated to a drastically low level because of the demands of the war in Vietnam. The signing of the Paris Peace Accords in January 1973 and the subsequent withdrawal of the last remaining US troops from Vietnam the following March did not put an end to the deterioration of the Army. The process had gone too far for too long.

It is difficult to dispute the words of historian Roger Spiller, who observed that "the United States Army was an institutional wreck by 1973."[7] The wreckage that Spiller describes was a direct legacy of the Army's experience in Vietnam. The Army came out of that experience as a demoralized, disoriented, undermanned, and ineffective force that was unable to carry out its assigned mission: the defense of the nation. Given that situation, many officers and NCOs decided to leave the service, but those who stayed resolved to do whatever was necessary to turn things around. It would prove a daunting task that would take nearly two decades. As Shelby Stanton observed, "When the war was over, the United States military had to build a new volunteer army from the smallest shreds of its tattered remains."[8]

History is replete with examples that demonstrate that disaster is a much more effective catalyst for reform in organizations like the Army that are, by their very nature, conservative and resistant to change. However, the US Army's experience in the Vietnam War provided a catalyst that would lead to major reforms which would, over the next twenty years, transform this demoralized force from the ashes of that experience into an army that was better prepared for war than any American Army in history. In a sense, this transformation was also a legacy of the Vietnam War.

The initial attempts at reform began at the top. General Creighton Abrams, a protégé of General George S. Patton and commander of US forces in Vietnam from 1968 to 1972, became Army chief of staff in 1972. He was determined to get the Army on the road to recovery following the trauma of Vietnam. However, it was not just the senior officers who were involved in beginning the long process of internal reform. The malaise that affected the Army in the latter years of the Vietnam War and immediately after US withdrawal from Southeast Asia caused a re-examination of the military's culture and values among mid-level and junior officers. As we have seen, the problems that beset the Army were so severe that it would take a number of years to overcome them. These problems—doctrine, manning, organization, training, and matériel—were all intertwined and interdependent; they could not be attacked sequentially but had to be attacked simultaneously, a demanding task.

The most immediate problem to be dealt with in the aftermath of the war was the transition to an all-volunteer force. However, this proved very difficult. As Major Paul Herbert observed, "Racial tensions and drug abuse among soldiers compounded the sense of defeat that, however gilded, attended the withdrawal from Southeast Asia."[9] More often than not, the blame for the American defeat in Vietnam and subsequent disillusionment with war and all military institutions among many Americans fell on the Army. How far the Army had fallen was clearly revealed in a 1973 Harris Poll in which the American public ranked the military only at about the level of sanitation workers in relative order of respect.[10] This would have an impact on the Army as it tried to recruit the best young people to man the all-volunteer Army.

In the wake of Vietnam and suffering from such a poor public image, the US Army could not entice the best young Americans to join up and thus was forced to accept lower-quality recruits. The end result was that nearly one of every two enlisted volunteers in the mid- and late 1970s was either a high school dropout or scored in the lowest acceptable mental category. Nor could the Army retain the soldiers that it already had; by 1974, it was 20,000 soldiers below authorized levels and missed its annual re-enlistment objective by 11 percent.

The low quality of volunteers contributed to the continuing problems in discipline and training, created morale problems among NCOs and junior officers, and limited the number of soldiers suitable for use in building the NCO corps. Thus, the Army had to deal with a twofold personnel problem: first, it had to rid itself of the ill-disciplined and untrainable; and second, at the same time it had to recruit better soldiers, all during a period of fiscal constraint that would not improve until the 1980s.

While trying to find a way to man the all-volunteer force, the senior Army leadership also had to wrench the Army out of the malaise caused by the Vietnam experience. The 1973 Arab-Israeli War provided a stimulus for the Army to review its way of fighting. The war began on Yom Kippur Day, October 6, 1973, when the armies of Egypt and Syria attacked Israel. The

Arab forces that had been wiped out in six days by Israel in 1967 were, in 1973, much better equipped, better trained, and better led. The Egyptian Second and Third Armies launched a surprise attack across the Suez Canal, penetrated the Bar Lev Line, and drove deep into the Sinai in an operation that stunned the Israelis. At the same time, five Syrian divisions stormed the Golan Heights, resulting in an intense tank-on-tank battle. In the end the outnumbered Israelis prevailed, but it had been a near thing. The Syrians and Egyptians, equipped with modern Soviet tanks and other weapons, had fought much better than they had in 1967. The war lasted only eighteen days before diplomacy brought it to an end, but it was characterized by bitter fighting in which both sides lost vast amounts of weapons and equipment. Although the war was short, it demonstrated a new and more lethal kind of warfare that resulted when forces that were armed with modern weapons systems collided on the battlefield.

The Arab–Israeli War helped the Army leadership, which, with the Vietnam War over, wanted to renew its focus on what was considered the main threat: the Soviet forces' overwhelming numerical superiority in Europe. While the United States had been tied up in Vietnam, the Soviets had used the decade to modernize their tanks and missiles, to improve their doctrine, and to beef up their manpower in Europe. American intelligence agencies in the early 1970s noted an increase of five Soviet armored divisions in Europe, a restationing of Soviet Army divisions further to the west, and a major improvement in equipment, with T-62 and T-72 tanks replacing older models, and corresponding modernization of other classes of weapons systems. The result was that the US Army, coming out of its devastating experience in Southeast Asia, found itself confronted on the plains of Europe by forces of the Soviet Union and its Warsaw Pact allies that were both numerically and qualitatively superior.

To the senior Army leadership, wanting to refocus the Army from Southeast Asia and facing a troubling imbalance of forces in Europe, the Arab–Israeli War provided two valuable lessons. First, the new high-tech battlefield was extremely lethal; the new destructiveness of tank guns and anti-tank and air defense missiles had resulted in heavy losses on both sides; in one month of fighting, the Israeli, Syrian, and Egyptian armies lost more tanks and artillery than existed in the entire US Army, Europe. Second, the outnumbered Israelis had prevailed against their larger enemies, proving that an outnumbered force could win. This implied that the outnumbered US forces and their allies in Europe, like the Israelis, could fight and win against superior numbers, but only if they changed their concept of warfare to take into account the new lethality on the battlefield. Therefore, the Yom Kippur War provided an impetus to turn away from the lessons of counterinsurgency and jungle warfare to reorient the Army toward its more traditional mission of defending Western Europe against the Soviet Army and its Warsaw Pact allies. The Army clearly aimed to look ahead to winning the next war instead of trying to figure out how it could have fought the last war better.[11]

Not many Americans outside the Army will recognize his name, but General William E. DePuy played a seminal role in the revitalization of the Army after Vietnam. DePuy, an energetic and forceful leader who had commanded troops in World War II and Vietnam, assumed command of the newly formed Training and Doctrine Command (TRADOC) in June 1973. This was a key post, since TRADOC had been established to coordinate the Army's doctrine development and training programs. As commander of this new organization, DePuy would be in a unique position to oversee the reform of the Army. The Arab–Israeli War further convinced him that there was a need to "reorient and restructure the whole body of Army doctrine from top to bottom."[12] DePuy then set about leading the Army in a process designed totally to rethink the way it trained its forces and fought its wars.

To DePuy, the 1973 Arab–Israeli War was a compelling argument in support of sweeping modernization and reform in the Army; it provided the Army with "a measure for its professional focus, gave guidance for its development in weaponry and tactics, and helped concentrate it on the nature of the threat in Europe."[13] Moreover, according to historian Roger Spiller, the Arab–Israeli War "supplied the American Army with a new professional reference point, uncontaminated by association with Vietnam."[14]

Using the war in the Middle East as a model, DePuy hoped to "optimize the fighting capabilities of limited numbers by training each soldier to fight to his full capacity and to create a superior war-fighting method through progressive doctrinal reform."[15] Under DePuy's leadership, TRADOC developed a new doctrine embodied in Field Manual (FM) 100-5, *Operations*, published in 1976. Traditionally, the Army's operations manual defines how the

Figure 13.1 General William DePuy, chief architect of the new American military doctrine of "Active Defense."

Army would train, fight, and equip the force. DePuy's new manual was focused almost exclusively on the challenges of confronting the Soviet Army in Western Europe. It was designed to change the thinking of the Army and take "the Army out of the rice paddies of Vietnam and place it on the Western European battlefield against the Warsaw Pact."[16] DePuy would use doctrine to provide an operational concept of how to wage war that would permeate the Army and lend coherence to all the myriad activities required to restructure it and enable it to recover fully from the war in Vietnam.

This new doctrine came to be known as "active defense" and it was designed to prepare the Army to "fight outnumbered and win the first battle of the next war." It was focused on armored warfare, Soviet weapons systems, emerging Western technology, and US numerical inferiority on the NATO battlefield in Europe. Emphasizing the indirect approach and the suppression of enemy forces with indirect fire, the new doctrine was based on economy of force and the need to strike at penetrating enemy forces with surprise and with carefully husbanded combat power at the critical place and time. The manual emphasized "battle calculus" and focused on "servicing" targets. It acknowledged the armored battle as the heart of warfare, with the tank as the single most important weapon in the Army's arsenal. Success, however, hinged on a deft manipulation of all the arms, including infantry, engineers, artillery, and air power, to give free rein to the tank maneuver forces.

Published in a camouflage-patterned cover and illustrated with colored charts, the new manual was meant to be "a break with the past—especially the Vietnam War—and to prepare the Army doctrinally to win the next war, not its last."[17] DePuy hoped to use the new manual to present an overarching concept of warfare that would rationalize everything the Army did, from training recruits to designing tanks.[18] It was designed to be the capstone of a family of Army manuals that would completely replace the doctrine current at the end of the Vietnam War.

The new manual quickly became one of the most controversial field manuals ever published by the US Army.[19] It was widely criticized because it was focused too narrowly on combat in Europe. Moreover, it appeared too preoccupied with weapons effects and emphasized defensive operations while virtually ignoring the psychological and human dimensions of warfare. Between 1976 and 1981 the criticisms against the manual grew, but in the end the publication of the 1976 manual proved to be a very important event in the long road to reforming the Army after Vietnam. The controversial manual caused a dialogue on doctrine to occur within the Army that brought about a fundamental change in the way that the Army viewed itself.[20] The manual would be revised and "active defense" would ultimately be abandoned, but DePuy and his manual caused a renaissance in doctrinal thought that would eventually result in rediscovery of the operational art within the Army and the creation of an entirely new doctrine that would ultimately prove so successful in the First Gulf War.

With his emphasis on conventional doctrine, DePuy and the others involved in remaking the Army after Vietnam gave the Army "a mighty shove that . . . rolled it out of its preoccupation with the Vietnam War and on the road to the twenty-first century."[21] However, in the process, the Vietnam conflict became a "non-subject."[22] The Vietnam War came to be seen as an aberration, and consequently there was no detailed study of lessons learned. More importantly, counterinsurgency rapidly disappeared from the curricula in Army schools.[23] Effectively, the Army turned away from the distasteful experience in Vietnam, setting aside counterinsurgency doctrine in favor of conventional operations. This would have an unintended effect that will be addressed later in this chapter.

The doctrinal dialogue that flowed from the publication of the 1976 version of FM 100-5 played a critical role in the evolution of the Army after Vietnam, but these doctrinal reforms would not mean much if the Army could not attract and retain the soldiers it needed to field a quality force. The Army continued to suffer from funding constraints into the late 1970s; low soldier pay and drastic cuts in the Army budget for training and maintenance had a serious impact on the Army's readiness. By 1979, six of ten Stateside Army divisions were rated "not combat ready."

The all-volunteer force was in trouble. The Army recruited so many poor-quality soldiers during the late 1970s that it dismissed 40 percent for indiscipline or unsuitability before they had completed their first enlistments. Only 50 percent of those recruited in 1980 had high school diplomas. At the same time, statistics for drug addiction, unauthorized absences, and crimes, while still below the immediate post-Vietnam War figures, were alarmingly high.[24]

Army Chief of Staff Edward C. Meyer shocked President Jimmy Carter and many of his own peers by publicly declaring in 1980 that America had a "hollow Army" that was incapable of carrying out its assigned missions. The failure of the hostage rescue mission in the Iranian desert later that year demonstrated the impact of the maladies that affected the US armed forces, and marked one of the lowest points in American military performance since the end of the Vietnam War.

The failure of the hostage mission caused a furor that led to a defense buildup that began under Carter and increased in velocity under Ronald Reagan, and would help revive American military forces. Congress took several measures to increase the quality of the all-volunteer force. Legislation was passed that increased soldiers' salaries by 25 percent between 1981 and 1982. Congress also reinstated the GI Bill and initiated the Army College Fund. Armed with the increase in pay and the new programs, the Army launched a new recruiting campaign designed to increase the quality of new recruits. Under the leadership of General Maxwell Thurman, commander of the US Army Recruiting Command, the "Be All You Can Be" campaign contributed greatly to presenting the Army as a "caring, challenging high-tech outfit."[25]

The increase in recruit quality was not immediate, but it began steadily to climb. By 1991 more than 98 percent of Army enlistees were high school graduates, with more than 75 percent scoring in the upper mental categories on the Army entrance examinations. As quality increased, traditional indicators of indiscipline dropped; desertions and unauthorized absences dropped by 80 percent and courts-martial by 64 percent; drug positives dropped to less than 1 percent by 1989.[26]

While the Army focused on the emerging doctrinal debate and the Recruiting Command focused on attracting more qualified soldiers, the Army was still beset by austere budgets, and there was little funding for equipment modernization. This was a critical situation because the Army had lost a generation's worth of technical modernization while in Vietnam. With the war in Southeast Asia over, and having identified the conventional combined-arms battlefield in Europe as the focus, the Army had to modernize its equipment. There was an urgency to this effort because, as already stated, in Europe the US Army would have to fight an enemy that would almost certainly be numerically superior. To address this problem the Army turned to technologically superior hardware. However, the austere defense budgets in the years following Vietnam mitigated against developing all the weapons systems that the Army thought it needed to defeat the Soviets in Europe. Given the funding constraints that precluded the development of the wide range of systems needed fully to modernize the force, the Army decided to focus on a few key weapons systems that were essential to prevailing on the NATO (North Atlantic Treaty Organization) battlefield of Europe. Accordingly, the Army identified five weapons systems that were "must have." These five programs included a new main battle tank, an infantry fighting vehicle, a new attack helicopter, a new utility helicopter, and a new air defense missile. In a very real sense, emerging doctrine helped to justify the expense of the new weapons systems without which that doctrine would not work. The Army packaged these five programs as an interdependent group, and it sacrificed other programs to protect them from budget fluctuations that could impede their development. This strategy helped protect the "Big Five" from budget cuts, but the normal development process, some technical problems, and limited budgets meant that the weapons would not be fielded until the 1980s. Nevertheless, when the Army went to war in 1991, it would do so with M1 Abrams tanks, M2 Bradley fighting vehicles, Black Hawk and Apache helicopters, and the Patriot air defense missile, all state of the art.

Meanwhile, the doctrinal debate continued. General DePuy at TRADOC, using the 1976 version of FM 100-5 as the basis, instituted new training programs focused on performance training in the field. He caused to be written a number of "how to" manuals derived from FM 100-5 as the capstone document that set out the tasks, conditions, and standards to focus individual and unit training. These manuals provided the guidelines for a completely new approach to performance-oriented training. In doing so, according to Richard Lock-Pullan, they established the instructional nature of DePuy's training reforms and were "a crucial feature of the self-regeneration by the Army."[27]

An extension of this effort to codify individual and unit training was the Army Training and Evaluation Plan (ARTEP), which was introduced in 1975 to provide a vehicle for training readiness. It was focused on evaluating the level of training in field situations to assess the actions and behaviors addressed in the "how to" manuals. Although this was a leap forward in assessing training, the ARTEP still did not provide a realistic yardstick for predicting how units would perform in actual combat. The ARTEP was scripted and could not adequately replicate combat conditions. Something else would be needed to increase realism in training, but the solution was still a few years off.

Figure 13.2 US Marines from Alpha Company, 1st Tank Battalion, provide security in an M1A1 Abrams tank, one of the weapons systems critical to the restructuring of the US military after Vietnam, while Marines from Regimental Combat Team 2 search for weapons caches along a section of the west bank of the Euphrates River, March 9, 2007, north of Hit, Iraq.

US Marine Corps photo by Cpl. Shane S. Keller.

In 1977, General Donn Starry took over from DePuy at TRADOC. Starry, one of the original proponents of "active defense" and the 1976 version of FM 100-5, presided over the continuing dialogue about that manual and the operational concepts on which it was built. In June 1979, Starry, directed by General Meyer, Army Chief of Staff, instigated a re-examination of Army doctrine in response to the continuing criticisms of the 1976 version of the operations manual. Over the next two years, Starry presided over a process that resulted in the development of a new operational concept that, unlike "active defense," was offensive-oriented and focused on the need for "deep battle" on the "extended battlefield." This meant the attrition of the second and third echelons of an attacking Soviet force; since the Army did not have the weapons to reach out to the necessary range to do this, Starry enlisted the aid of the Air Force and drew it into the dialogue. The development of the new doctrine became a cooperative effort. The new concept was subjected to outside analysts and criticism from politicians, military analysts, and traditionalists within the US military. Additionally, the Army submitted the concept to its NATO counterparts for their input. The result of this effort was AirLand Battle, published as

FM 100-5, *Operations*, in August 1982. This manual moved away from the force ratios and "battle calculus" of the 1976 version of the manual to focus on the human element of combat and the operational level of war that tied the outcome of tactical battles to the achievement of a defined strategic end state. AirLand Battle was based on four tenets: initiative, depth, agility, and synchronization. Rather than mathematical formulas determining the outcome of battles, the victor would be the one who seized the initiative, was agile and adaptive in the face of changing situations, and could synchronize all the weapons and resources at his disposal. Thus, leadership was listed as an element of combat power equal to firepower and maneuver; the manual went on to underscore the validity of training and motivation. AirLand Battle would provide the Army's fighting doctrine that would dictate how the US Army would go to war when called upon to do so against the forces of Saddam Hussein in 1991. This new doctrine, besides defining how the Army would go to war, also provided a strategy for training, organization, and procurement.

With the development of the new doctrine, there was an intensified need for more realistic training. Historical studies revealed that units suffered very high casualties in their first exposure to actual combat. What was needed was a demanding and realistic force-on-force training assessment to supplant the old one-sided ARTEP approach. Using the Navy's Top Gun program

Figure 13.3 General Donn Starry, chief architect of the US doctrine of AirLand Battle.

as a model, the National Training Center (NTC) was created at Fort Irwin, California. The NTC provided an opportunity in which combat units could be pitted against each other in the vast maneuver area of the California desert in relatively free-play, force-on-force engagements. Using electronic data collection methods, winners and losers in each engagement could be determined and the engagements could be replayed in critical after-action reviews. This environment provided the training units with iterative opportunities to see how they operated in simulated, but relatively realistic, combat engagements against a living, thinking opposing force.

This approach worked so well that two other combat training centers were established, at Fort Polk, Louisiana, and Vilseck, Germany. In order to exercise senior officers, the Battle Command Training Program was established at Fort Leavenworth, Kansas, where division and corps staffs were subjected to command-post exercises to improve their combat planning and execution skills.

With the renaissance in Army training came a concurrent improvement in the Army education system. By the summer of 1990 the Training and Doctrine Command had created a coherent series of schools that trained officers at each turning point in their careers. New lieutenants began with an Officer Basic Course that introduced them to the duties of their branch of service and, after service as senior lieutenants and junior captains, returned for an Officer Advanced Course designed to prepare them to serve as company, battery, and troop commanders. The Combined Arms Staff Service School (CAS3) was a new school established to enhance the staff officer skills of senior captains. The premier officer school remained the Command and General Staff Officer Course, where junior majors went before service as executive officers and operations officers of battalions and brigades. This course focused on the concepts and language of AirLand Battle doctrine.

As part of the Army renaissance and a re-emphasis on officer education, senior Army leadership established the Advanced Military Studies Program (AMSP) at Fort Leavenworth in 1983 as a follow-on year at Command and General Staff College for selected students. The purpose of this program was to provide an advanced military education at the operational level and then to infuse a common body of thought—a common cultural bias—throughout the Army by means of its graduates.[28]

At the top of the Army officer education system was the Army War College, attended by lieutenant colonels with successful battalion command behind them. With the new emphasis on officer education, the career officer was expected to spend roughly one year in every four in some sort of school, either as a student or as a teacher.

The Vietnam War had devastated the NCO corps; back-to-back combat tours and high casualties nearly ruined it. The senior Army leadership realized that part of the process of rebuilding the Army needed to be a complete revitalization of the NCO education system. Consequently, by 1990 the non-commissioned officer education system paralleled the structure of officer schools, resulting in a comprehensive new program that included four successive levels of training and education. The first step in this program was the primary leadership development course, where young specialists and sergeants received instruction on how to be effective sergeants. The basic non-commissioned officer course trained sergeants to serve as staff sergeants in their branch of service. This was followed by an advanced NCO course, where the curriculum prepared them to serve as platoon sergeants. At the apex of the structure stood the US Army Sergeants Major Academy at Fort Bliss, Texas, where a twenty-two-week course qualified senior sergeants for the top non-commissioned officer jobs in the Army. This comprehensive program resulted in a transformation of the NCO corps that was marked by a high level of professionalism and vastly improved job performance and leadership ability.

By the early 1980s the doctrinal, recruiting, training, and education reforms had begun to achieve a level of traction. The first test of the improved Army came with the 1983 invasion of Grenada. When Grenadian prime minister Maurice Bishop was overthrown and killed in an internal power struggle, President Ronald Reagan ordered an invasion by 10,000 US troops to evacuate American citizens from the island. While the Reagan administration and the military declared the mission a "success," after-action analysis identified that there were a number of problems during the operations, most of which had to do with the application of joint doctrine and the ability of the Army, Navy, Marines, and Air Force to work together efficiently and effectively.

The Goldwater–Nichols Bill, signed in 1986, was designed to alleviate many of the problems that were revealed in the Iranian hostage rescue and the invasion of Grenada. It reworked the entire command structure of the US military and made other sweeping changes aimed at improving communications and coordination between the different branches of the US armed forces. Meanwhile, the Army had begun to reap the benefits of the many reforms that had been instituted in the post-Vietnam years. This was aptly demonstrated in 1989 during Operation Just Cause, in which the US Army, supported by the other services, took down the regime of Manuel Noriega. The near-simultaneous achievement of twenty-seven different objectives clearly demonstrated the capabilities of the revitalized Army.

By 1990 the US military, including the Army, seemed to have turned the corner in distancing itself from the ravages of the Vietnam War. For the Army, the years since the departure of US forces from Vietnam had witnessed some desperate times marked by austere budgets and other difficulties, but still the Army had been able to reform itself in all the critical areas: doctrine, training, manpower, and technology.

The result of that reformation would be tested on August 2, 1990, when the forces of Iraqi strongman Saddam Hussein invaded Kuwait. After Hussein refused an ultimatum from the United Nations, the US-led coalition began preparations to liberate Kuwait. The defensive phase, Operation Desert Shield, began on August 7, 1990, when US troops deployed to Saudi Arabia to prevent Iraqi forces from attacking the Saudi oilfields. After several months of United Nations resolutions, Saddam Hussein was given a deadline of January 15, 1991, to withdraw his troops from Kuwait. A day after the deadline passed with no response from Iraq, US and Coalition forces launched a massive air campaign which began the general offensive that would become known as Operation Desert Storm. After more than a month of intense bombing, the Coalition ground forces launched a lightning-like strike, which included a masterful giant left hook against the Iraqi rear. Saddam's forces were decisively defeated. One hundred hours after the ground war began, President George H. W. Bush ordered a cease-fire and on April 16 he declared that Kuwait had been liberated. The US Army, which had come out of Vietnam in such a debilitated state, by all accounts had performed magnificently.

President Bush proclaimed, "By God, we've kicked the Vietnam syndrome once and for all!"[29] Barry McCaffrey, an Army general who had commanded the 24th Infantry Division during Desert Storm, testifying before the Senate Armed Services Committee shortly after the war, upon being asked how the war was won in just one hundred hours, replied, "This war didn't take 100 hours to win, it took 15 years."[30] This was true. The US Army had been seared by the Vietnam experience; as historian Roger Spiller described the situation, "The shadow of the Vietnam dragon was long, and it was very dark."[31] In a very real sense that dark shadow ultimately served as a catalyst for a total transformation of the Army.

Figure 13.4 *An Army AH-64 Apache helicopter, one of the chief weapons systems of the AirLand battle that made possible the coalition victory in Operation Desert Storm, provides air support for US Army soldiers from the Alpha Battery, 3rd Battalion, 320th Field Artillery Regiment, and Iraqi army soldiers from the 1st Battalion, 1st Brigade, 4th Division, during a raid in Remagen, Iraq, on Feb. 24, 2006.*

Department of Defense photo by Petty Officer 3rd Class Shawn Hussong, US Navy. (Released.)

A generation of Army officers, who as young soldiers watched the Army fracture itself in Southeast Asia and then devoted their lives to the task of reforging the institution, led the Army to victory in the Iraqi desert. According to Robert Scales, "the Army that met Saddam Hussein was fundamentally different from the Army that emerged from the jungles of Vietnam twenty years before."[32]

The victory against Iraq was stunning, but the legacy of Vietnam also had several second- and third-order effects. Coming out of Vietnam, the Army had focused on preparing itself almost exclusively for the mission that seemed to provide both the greatest and the most traditional challenge: large-scale, theater warfare. It had done a masterful job in preparing for that challenge, as evidenced by the victory over Saddam Hussein's forces. However, in doing so it had consciously decided never to get involved in a conflict like the Vietnam War. The Army departed from Vietnam determined never again to be drawn into such a war, which was laden with acute civil–military tension over its conduct. The Army had been almost destroyed by the war in Vietnam, and to many who would ascend to Army leadership in the 1980s and 1990s the war there had been lost because of political interference and unrealistic restrictions on the military's conduct of the war. Army General Colin Powell, chairman of the Joint Chiefs of Staff during Operation Desert Storm, wrote in his autobiography, "Many of my generation . . . seasoned in [Vietnam], vowed that when our turn came to call the shots, we would not quietly acquiesce in halfhearted warfare for half-baked reasons that the American people could not understand or support."[33] This thought was codified in the Weinberger–Powell Doctrine, which some have argued was an attempt by the military to pick where, when, and how it would fight—essentially guaranteeing "no more Vietnams."

The seeds of this outlook took root in the years immediately after the departure from Vietnam when the Army consciously put the war behind itself, choosing to focus on conventional warfare and to avoid at all costs any type of conflict that even remotely resembled the Vietnam War. This tendency was reinforced by the 1973 Arab–Israeli War, which dominated Army thinking and seemed to be a model for the type of warfare that the Army would face. Andrew Krepinevich said that the 1973 Arab–Israeli War was a "godsend" for the Army, which then dismissed counterinsurgency as a "fad" and turned back to preparing for conventional conflict.[34] Consequently, counterinsurgency files were purged from Army schools. The result was an army that was organized, trained, and equipped to fight almost solely conventional operations. In the 1980s there was a small resurgence of interest in counterinsurgency, but the El Salvador model prevailed, in which the mission was handled with minimal US military involvement other than by a small handful of Special Forces soldiers. In the 1990s there was a dialogue in the Army about what was variously called low-intensity conflict or military operations other than war, but the focus of Army doctrine and training remained on conventional conflict.

The reaction to the Vietnam experience and the resultant focus on conventional conflict produced an Army that performed magnificently in Operation Desert Storm. However, it also produced a force with attitudes, doctrine, and force structure focused on large-scale conventional operations. It did not produce a force compatible with counterinsurgency, peacekeeping, or stability operations. The loss in Vietnam forced the US Army to redefine its way of war, and led to a reliance on technology and a repudiation of the lessons of Vietnam. As General Wesley Clark observed in 1997, the US Army "junked the doctrine of counter-insurgency warfare."[35] This situation resulted in a force that was supremely organized, trained, and equipped to conduct conventional warfare, but arguably a force unprepared to face situations in Iraq and Afghanistan strikingly similar in some ways to the conflict in Vietnam. Therefore, when faced with conflicts that did not fit the type of war for which the Army had both prepared and preferred to fight, the Army had to go back and relearn many of the lessons of Vietnam.

The Vietnam War had left a significant legacy for the US Army. The conflict cast a long shadow in the twenty years after the fall of Saigon and served as a catalyst for a renaissance in the Army, but it also had second- and third-order effects on the Army that continue to have a significant impact on the US Army today.

DISCUSSION QUESTIONS

1. What problems did the US Army face in the aftermath of the Vietnam War?
2. What impact did the 1973 Arab–Israeli War have on the US Army?
3. What were the major factors that contributed to the ability of the US Army to rebuild itself in the aftermath of the Vietnam War?
4. What role did General William DePuy have in the reformation of the US Army in the aftermath of the Vietnam War?
5. What were some of the unintended effects of the US Army reformation movement after the Vietnam War?

SUGGESTED READING

Cincinnatus. *Self-Destruction: The Disintegration and Decay of the United States Army during the Vietnam Era.* New York: Norton, 1980.

Crane, Conrad C. *Avoiding Vietnam: the U.S. Army's Response to Defeat in Southeast Asia.* Carlisle Barracks, PA: Strategic Studies Institute, US Army War College, 2002.

Dunnigan, James F. and Raymond M. Macedonia. *Getting It Right: American Military Reforms after Vietnam to the Persian Gulf and Beyond.* New York: W. Morrow, 1993.

Griffith, Robert K. Jr. *The U.S. Army's Transition to the All-Volunteer Force, 1968–1974.* Washington, DC: Center of Military History, 1997.

Herbert, Paul H. (Major). *Deciding What Has to Be Done: General William E. DePuy and the 1976 Edition of FM 100-5, Operations*. Fort Leavenworth, KS: Combat Studies Institute, US Army Command and General Staff College, 1988.

Kitfield, J. *Prodigal Soldiers: How the Generation of Officers Born of Vietnam Revolutionized the American Style of War*. New York: Simon & Schuster, 1995.

Lock-Pullan, Richard. *U.S. Army Innovation and American Strategic Culture after Vietnam*. London: Routledge, 2006.

Powell, Colin. *My American Journey*. New York: Random House, 1995.

Scales, Robert H. *Certain Victory: United States Army in the Gulf War*. Washington, DC: Office of the Chief of Staff, US Army, 1993.

Stanton, Shelby L. *The Rise and Fall of an American Army: U.S. Ground Forces in Vietnam, 1965–1973*. Novato, CA: Presidio Press, 1985.

NOTES

1. Shelby L. Stanton, *The Rise and Fall of an American Army* (Novato, CA: Presidio, 1985), 365.
2. Robert H. Scales Jr., *Certain Victory: United States Army in the Gulf War* (Washington, DC: Office of the Chief of Staff, US Army), 5.
3. Col. Robert D. Heinl Jr., "The Collapse of the Armed Forces," *Armed Forces Journal* 108 (19) (June 7, 1971): 31.
4. Ibid.
5. Ibid., 34.
6. Ibid., 35.
7. Roger J. Spiller, "In the Shadow of the Dragon: Doctrine and the US Army after Vietnam," *RUSI Journal* 142 (6) (1997): 42.
8. Stanton, *Rise and Fall*, 368.
9. Major Paul H. Herbert, *Deciding What Has to Be Done: General William E. DePuy and the 1976 Edition of FM 100-5, Operations* (Fort Leavenworth, KS: Combat Studies Institute, US Army Command and General Staff College, 1988), 5.
10. Scales, *Certain Victory*, 7.
11. Richard Lock-Pullan, "'An Inward Looking Time': The United States Army, 1973–1976," *Journal of Military History* 67 (2) (April 2003): 488; Donn A. Starry, "A Tactical Evaluation—FM 100-5," *Military Review* 58 (8) (1978): 2–11.
12. John L. Romjue, *From Active Defense to AirLand Battle: The Development of Army Doctrine 1973–1982* (Fort Monroe, VA: Historical Office, United States Army Training and Doctrine Command, June 1984), 83.
13. Lock-Pullan, "'An Inward Looking Time,'" 500.
14. Spiller, "In the Shadow of the Dragon," 46.
15. Scales, *Certain Victory*, 10.
16. Quoted in Lock-Pullan, "'An Inward Looking Time,'" 488.
17. Herbert, *Deciding What Has to Be Done*, 7.
18. Ibid., 1.
19. Maj. Robert A. Doughty, *The Evolution of U.S. Army Tactical Doctrine, 1946–76* (Fort Leavenworth, KS: Combat Studies Institute, US Army Command and General Staff College, 1979), 43.
20. Scales, *Certain Victory*, 14.
21. Herbert, *Deciding What Has to Be Done*, 1.
22. W. Scott Thompson and Donaldson D. Frizzell, eds., *The Lessons of Vietnam* (New York: Crane, Russack, 1977), v.

23. Andrew J. Birtle, *U.S. Army Counterinsurgency and Contingency Operations Doctrine 1942–1976* (Washington, DC: Center of Military History, United States Army, 2006), 480–1.
24. Scales, *Certain Victory*, 16.
25. Ibid., p. 17.
26. Ibid.
27. Lock-Pullan, "'An Inward Looking Time,'" 511.
28. Scales, *Certain Victory*, 28.
29. Quoted in Ann McDaniel and Evan Thomas, "The Rewards of Leadership," *Newsweek*, March 11, 1991, 30.
30. Scales, *Certain Victory*, 35.
31. Spiller, "Shadow of the Dragon," 43–4.
32. Scales, *Certain Victory*, 36.
33. Colin L. Powell with Joseph Persico, *My American Journey* (New York: Random House, 1995), 149.
34. Andrew F. Krepinevich Jr., *The Army and Vietnam* (Baltimore, MD: Johns Hopkins University Press, 1986), 272.
35. Wesley Clark, "The Next War," *Washington Post*, September 16, 2007.

TIMELINE EVENTS

June 1973 – Nixon ends the draft

December 1979 – Iranian Revolution

August 1990 – February 1991 – First Gulf War

December 1992 – May 1993 – Operation Restore Hope in Somalia

September 11, 2001 – Attacks on the World Trade Center and the Pentagon

January 2002 – George W. Bush's "axis of evil" speech

March 2003 – Invasion of Iraq

November 2006 – Resignation of Secretary of Defense Donald Rumsfeld

December 2006 – Iraq Study Group releases its report

January 2007 – General David Petraeus takes command in Iraq

Chapter 14

Iraq as "the good war" as opposed to Vietnam, the bad war

Lloyd Gardner

CHAPTER SUMMARY

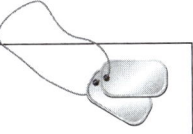

The present wars in Iraq and Afghanistan are being fought in the historical shadows of World War II and Vietnam. In an attempt to eschew the complicated legacy of the Cold War, President George W. Bush attempted to cast the Iraq War in light of the "good war" of World War II. However, as the conflict in Iraq stalled, Bush and his advisers were left to deal with a war that had come to resemble Vietnam. Complicating matters further, American policymakers and the military are conducting the war in Iraq even as the complicated legacies of Vietnam, ranging from the end of the draft to debates over the role of the military in counterinsurgency, have come to a head.

PROLOGUE: SEIZE THE MOMENT

According to the master chronicler of the Iraq War, Bob Woodward, George W. Bush keeps a diary. On the night of September 11, 2001, he wrote, "The Pearl Harbor of the 21st Century took place today. We think it's Osama Bin Laden." Then he added a curious comment: "We think there are other targets in the United States, but I have urged the country to go back to normal." He hoped, nevertheless, that now there would be an opportunity "for us to rally the world against terrorism."[1] But even more than that objective, Bush hoped that he could use the new situation to reorient the American self-image along the patriotic lines of World War II—or the "Greatest Generation," as chronicled in recent popular books about that era. That self-image sustained Americans during most of the Cold War years, had been one of the nation's most valuable assets in rallying the "free world" to oppose the menace of "international communism," but then lost much of its power in the Vietnam years. His father, George H. W. Bush, had famously declared that the nation had "kicked" the Vietnam syndrome, a supposed collection of guilt feelings and inhibitions, with the victory over Saddam Hussein in the Gulf War, as CNN's path-breaking war reporting from inside Baghdad showed the "rockets' red glare, bursting in air" over Iraq's capital city.

But it really wasn't so. The Vietnam syndrome appeared to haunt the Clinton years with the infamous "Black Hawk Down" fiasco in Somalia and the debate over American policy in the Kosovo wars, where Washington seemed unwilling to put "boots on the ground" out of fear at becoming embroiled in another "quagmire." However that may be—and historians will continue to argue the question—it did not take long for Bush to recognize that 9/11 presented an immediate opportunity to correct what his administration believed had been serious blunders after the Gulf War, when Saddam Hussein was left in Baghdad in the vain expectation that he would meet his ultimate fate without further American actions, and be overthrown by internal forces. Certainly Bush II felt it had been a blunder that helped to end his father's political career. From the first days of his administration he had targeted Iraq. More than that, however, Bush and his advisers all realized that the World War II analogy could serve as a break point with the increasingly ambiguous post-Cold War difficulty policymakers faced in defining the nation's role and opportunities as the only superpower. Underneath all this sense that Vietnam could finally and truly be kicked into the ash can of history, however, there was, ironically, a simultaneous debate going on in the military over why American strategy had failed in Vietnam—with one side arguing that it was because it was too much beholden to World War II concepts!

PERFECTING THE ANALOGY

In the first moments after the 9/11 attack, Bush had focused on Osama bin Laden and the opportunity to rally world opinion against terrorism, but, he confessed to Woodward later, he had not really had terrorism high on his agenda since taking office nine months earlier. Despite explicit warnings about the danger of an attack from intelligence experts, he had focused on his desire for a huge tax cut. "I didn't feel that sense of urgency. My blood was not nearly as boiling."[2]

The original World War II analogy reached its fullest oratorical expression in Bush's January 2002 State of the Union message. In that speech he described the "axis of evil" that confronted the United States. The regimes in Iran, Iraq, and North Korea, he said,

> and their terrorist allies, constitute an axis of evil, arming to threaten the peace of the world. By seeking weapons of mass destruction, these regimes pose a grave and growing danger. They could provide these arms to terrorists, giving them the means to match their hatred. They could attack our allies or attempt to blackmail the United States. In any of these cases, the price of indifference would be catastrophic.

IRAQ AS "THE GOOD WAR"

Figure 14.1 President George W. Bush speaks to an audience in the Pentagon auditorium on March 19, 2008. Bush addressed members of the armed forces, Department of Defense employees and Department of State employees about the progress made in Iraq and the Global War on Terror. Bush approved the Iraq War and tried to connect the coming conflict more with World War II in his "axis of evil" speech.

Department of Defense photo by R. D. Ward. (Released.)

The speech accomplished several things. First, it focused on states—Iraq, Iran, and North Korea—rather than individuals such as Osama bin Laden as sponsors of terrorism. Second, it removed from the front pages the embarrassing fact that Bin Laden had not been tracked down. Third, it began a serious campaign to make it seem as if the real culprit for 9/11 was Saddam Hussein rather than Bin Laden's suicidal fanatics. And finally, it conjured up enemy states in a way that recalled the opposing sides in the "good war" fought by the "Greatest Generation." Little wonder Bush speechwriters vied for the credit of having authored the phrase "axis of evil."

Perhaps most important of all, however, it made it seem that the war on terror could not be confused with anything like Vietnam—even, as we will see, while there was a growing feeling among younger (and some not so young) army officers that it resembled (and should resemble!) not only Vietnam but also the American effort in the Philippines and Central America, and that of the French in Algeria. Ironically, the importance of placing the Iraq War solidly within the narrative of the "good war" only grew more intense as it became clear that evidence of Saddam Hussein's responsibility for 9/11 did not exist. In the recent past, books such as Tom Brokaw's *Greatest Generation* (1998) extolled the feats of ordinary citizens called upon by the nation in time of world crisis, reaching a very large audience obviously perplexed about the state of the world, and American stakes in the multiple conflicts going on simultaneously in different parts of the globe, topped by the new terrorist menace that had overtaken assumptions about victory in the Cold War and an end to ideological conflicts. Similarly, the celebratory writings of Stephen Ambrose filled entire pages of online booksellers such as Amazon or Barnes & Noble, with titles that almost rivaled pulp fiction in their recording of heroic deeds of derring-do and simple narratives of good and evil.

It was not surprising, therefore, that television networks turned to Ambrose for special comments on President Bush's first speech to Congress after 9/11. In a raspy voice well suited to the occasion, the popular historian assured the national audience that Bush spoke with the steely determination and convictions of his World War II heroes. Almost immediately, nevertheless, there was a surprise development that did not easily fit the model without some hauling and tugging. Although it is already largely forgotten, the anthrax scare that emerged in the weeks after 9/11 was in many ways a more alarming follow-up to the attacks on the World Trade Center because of the simplicity of delivering the deadly toxin, and the implications of an "enemy within," yet directed—as Bush said in the "axis of evil" speech—by some foreign nation (aka Iraq). The idea of an enemy burrowing within had been a staple of mobilization techniques in the Cold War but did also recall the "fifth column" sensations of World War II, and films like *The House on 92nd Street*, which featured the FBI as the nation's first line of defense at home. Bush declaimed against the "feel-good" culture of recent years in that speech, and called upon all American citizens to dedicate 4,000 hours of their lives for public service to nation and community. Yet he also asked Americans to return to shops and malls to carry on economic life as before, and there was no hint here that the $30 million per day he said was being spent on the war on terror should come from taxes—even after the massive cuts already enacted:

> It costs a lot to fight this war. We have spent more than a billion dollars a month—over $30 million a day—and we must be prepared for future operations. Afghanistan proved that expensive precision weapons defeat the enemy and spare innocent lives, and we need more of them. We need to replace aging aircraft and make our military more agile to put our troops anywhere in the world quickly and safely.

Actually, Afghanistan had demonstrated that it took old-fashioned foot-slogging to root out Taliban forces, but who was really watching? The hi-tech military cost more, but it was what best accorded with American military doctrine under Secretary of Defense Donald Rumsfeld. It almost seemed as if, by some magical formula, military spending could be declared exempt from budgetary accounting, and that only "welfare state" spending produced deficits. As the "axis of evil" speech, so chock full of contradictory appeals demonstrated, the World War II narrative was also a bit tricky because it involved invoking the name of Franklin D. Roosevelt, anathema to conservatives for supposedly having betrayed Eastern Europe into Moscow's hands and surrendered China to the communists. That position had long dominated Republican critiques of American foreign policy, but in recent years there had arisen something of a counterargument that Democrats Dean Acheson and Harry Truman had, in fact, not been such bad fellows after all, and had pulled America out of the mess FDR left behind.

But there was also the other side of the World War II analogy that recalled FDR's New Deal, which the post-Eisenhower, post-Nixon Republican Party was determined to wash out of American politics. Even though the New Deal scarcely touched great wealth, and it was only with World War II that personal tax rates approached anything that could be called confiscatory, it was the ethos of the New Deal as much as anything that still infuriated conservatives far too young to remember or have lived in Roosevelt's day. Nevertheless, as matters unfolded when the war deepened into a protracted struggle that recalled the more recent history in Vietnam, the second President Bush frequently found himself calling up Roosevelt's role in saving capitalism in the American fight against fascism at the end of the Depression Decade in order to sustain support for his war in Iraq.

The authors of that now famous or infamous, depending upon your point of view, manifesto of the Project for a New American Century had indeed written that it would take a shock of the order of Pearl Harbor to make such an ideological mobilization possible. New American Century founders had worried ever since the end of the Cold War that America's world position was rapidly eroding, and that there must begin at once a process of rearmament. "Further, the process of transformation, even if it brings revolutionary change, is likely to be a long one, absent some catastrophic and catalyzing event—like a new Pearl Harbor."[3]

THE DOING AND UNDOING

The 9/11 attack offered the administration an opportunity to invoke the World War II analogy and to make it seem that this war would be as liberating as the crusade in Europe (and Asia), with local inhabitants welcoming GI Joes who showered chocolates and nylons on the people on the path to democracy. One problem was, there were no GIs in the wars in Iraq and Afghanistan—and therein was a clue to the undoing of the analogy. It was not that the American media failed to do their part, as was the charge during the Vietnam War. The *New York Times*, always obliging to the central premises of the nation's foreign policy, however much it might quibble about the details of tactics, constantly referred to GIs in Iraq and Afghanistan. A simple look at the *Times* index online reveals more than 300 references to GIs in the war zone—continuing today into the Obama administration. So, it is a non-partisan issue. Yet it is also a somewhat odd reference, of course, because while GIs were the backbone of the World War II army, the last time they fought was in Vietnam. Anti-war feelings engendered in part (a large part) by the draft finally persuaded Richard Nixon to end conscription in 1973. He may have calmed down anti-war fervor with that step, but it did not make much difference to the embarrassing way the war ended, with helicopters lifting off Vietnamese "loyalists" from atop the American embassy two years later.

Not only the administration but also those who had sons and daughters in Iraq were loath, however, to surrender the World War II narrative as casualty lists lengthened. Creating a link with the "good war" helped with a newly restive public disturbed by the reality of a war in which improvised explosive devices (IEDs) replaced the traps set by an enemy seemingly as elusive as the one American soldiers had faced in Vietnam, a war where once again America's technological advantages fell short both strategically and tactically. The press, almost in absent-minded fashion, continued to talk about the battles "GIs" fought in Iraq, though there had never been any draftees sent to the war. When I asked one of my classes what "GI," meant, I got a puzzled response, with one student venturing a guess, "Government Issue"? It was as good an answer as one was likely to get—from those who were as far removed emotionally as well as practically from the war.

Professor Andrew Bacevich, taking a different perspective on the alienation between the nation's leadership and the country, has recently called the post-Vietnam era the "Great Divorce," denoting the separation between the ideas of citizenship and obligation to perform military service:

> Contributing to the country's defense now became not a civic duty but a matter of individual choice. That choice carried no political or moral connotations. The Great Divorce gave birth to a new professional military with an ethos that emphasized the differences between soldiers and civilians.[4]

Still, it was necessary to mobilize the nation ideologically to achieve the "Great Expectations" —as Bacevich describes American foreign policy under George W. Bush—engendered by the war. It is always necessary, as Vietnam had demonstrated, to keep elevating the stakes the longer a war goes on, so as to make it more and more difficult to settle for anything less than some imagined victory. It was thus impossible to let go of the World War II analogy.

As Bacevich noted, a "standing army" had been anathema to the writers of the Constitution, as it suited kings and empires, not a republic. But in the post-Cold War era, empire was no longer a dirty word, and a standing army (after the Vietnam debacle) was the only way to sustain it and maintain the more than 700 overseas bases it required. Facing a shortfall in recruiting for the reserve—a large component of the Iraq force—the Pentagon upped bonuses across the board. While the wall between citizenship and military duty has grown higher, in other ways traditional boundaries have broken down. The prolonged Iraq War has revealed just how profound the changes have been. The regular Army, now on a volunteer basis, has scrambled to fill recruiting quotas by paying large bonuses and providing a fast track to citizenship for immigrants, among other methods of recruitment. But it was not enough, as, despite increasing age limits, accepting high-school dropouts, lowering passable grades on standard tests, and increasing immigrant access to citizenship, the Army still saw some goals go unmet.

The absence of a nationwide protest movement of the order of what happened during Vietnam is powerful evidence that, unlike World War II reality, America's soldiers will now come not from a cross-section of the populace but largely from the disenfranchised, while most citizens remain disengaged. In this way, it is hoped, draft-age protests will never become an issue in political calculations. The regular Army has become a safety valve for a variety of recruits, nevertheless, not only from poverty-blighted areas, but also, especially, from far-flung areas. Army recruiters turned to US territories in the Pacific, stretching from Pago Pago in American Samoa to Yap in Micronesia, 4,000 miles to the west, and found a small bonanza. Army salaries have no difficulty competing with the average income in such places.

> "You can't beat recruiting here in the Marianas, in Micronesia," said First Sgt. Olympio Magofna, who grew up on Saipan and oversees Pacific recruiting for the Army from his base in Guam. "In the States, they are really hurting," he said. "But over here, I can afford [to] go play golf every other day."[5]

The overall numbers from such areas are small, and little more than a finger in the dike. Meanwhile, by the end of 2006 the Army also faced serious shortfalls in funding, resulting in equipment shortages that caused serious morale problems in Iraq. "It's kind of like the old rancher saying, 'I'm going to size the herd to the amount of hay that I have,'" said the Army's top budget official. "[He] can't size the herd to the size of the amount of hay that he has because he's got to maintain the herd to meet the current operating environment."[6]

Army Chief of Staff General Peter Schoomaker took the dramatic step of withholding a required budget plan for 2008 after protesting to Secretary of Defense Rumsfeld that the service could not maintain its current level of activity in Iraq and its other commitments without billions in additional funding. All the services had relied on supplemental appropriations to cover war costs, but perpetual uncertainties over such funding which was not part of the budget cycle hit the Army the hardest, as the service most heavily involved in Iraq.

TOUGHING IT OUT

When Vice President Cheney was told in early 2008 that 65 percent of the public now opposed the administration's war, his only comment was: "So?" The comment came in response to ABC News interviewer Martha Raddatz's question while the vice president was on tour in the Middle East, a quest, it was said, to persuade Saudi Arabia to lower oil prices. "You don't care what the American people think?' Raddatz asked the vice president. "You can't be blown off course by polls," said Cheney. "This president is very courageous and determined to go the course. There has been a huge fundamental change and transformation for the better. That's a huge accomplishment."[7]

The analogy now reached up and grabbed the administration by the nape of the neck in his next answer, as it became clear that you couldn't on the one hand talk about vital national interests at stake and at the same instant rule out any of the sacrifices made by the "Greatest Generation." Instead of separating the Iraq War from Vietnam, it was becoming embedded in the same contradictory morass. How could the nation have been involved to a greater degree? Raddatz asked. "I suppose you could have created a sense of sacrifice if you'd gone back to the draft, but that would have, in my opinion, done serious damage to the state of our military." What went unsaid here was that it, a draft, would have also stirred yet more agitation along the lines that Iraq was indeed another Vietnam, the war that finally ended the draft. No one, Cheney now claimed, could have predicted "what course it's going to follow." At the outset of the war, he had used the World War II metaphor of the liberation of France to describe what was about to happen. "My belief," he told Tim Russert, "is we will, in fact, be greeted as liberators." It would be a short war. But in 2008 in the ABC interview, he had another view: "You do it as long as you have to until you get it right. You don't quit because it gets hard." Asked finally about soldiers in Iraq who agreed with Democratic candidates on withdrawing from Iraq, Cheney said, "They're a broad cross section of America. I think they've overwhelmingly supported the mission. Every single one of them is a volunteer."

Republican Senator Chuck Hagel, a war critic, was outraged by Cheney's words, which, he thought, revealed a new kind of "credibility gap," another Vietnam reference. "Here's a guy who got five deferments during the Vietnam War, [who] said publicly that [military service] didn't work into his plans." It was not fitting now for him to say, therefore, as Cheney did in this interview, that the president bore a greater burden than the 4,000 men and women killed in Iraq.[8]

The Iraq War was directed at the top by two men who had not served in Vietnam, something that had to be overcome in selling the war once the Mission Accomplished banners got taken down as presidential backdrops at photo ops. It was a real question about which of the two was the more powerful, but it was a tricky business to play the volunteer card. There were (are) also real questions about whether a new draft would encourage adventurism in foreign policy, or, in the light of Vietnam, inhibit the president from going abroad in search of monsters to destroy, as John Quincy Adams once cautioned, but Cheney had no doubt that the draft would ill serve his career-long mission to make sure the imperial presidency had been restored to its full grandeur BV (Before Vietnam).

There were other armies in Iraq, however, besides American volunteers, who fared considerably better than the ordinary soldiers. Counting both security guards and private contractors, this force grew from 10,000 in December 2003 to over 100,000 by 2007. "The private sector is so firmly embedded in combat, occupation and peacekeeping duties that the phenomenon may have reached the point of no return: the U.S. military would struggle to wage war without it."[9] Eager mercenaries, who could earn thousands of dollars a month, were recruited from many countries, especially in Eastern Europe and Latin America. Blackwater, the security guard company protecting diplomats when they risked going outside the secure Green Zone, found Chile a particularly good recruiting ground for commandos who had received their military training in the days of the dictator Augusto Pinochet. El Salvador, to take another example, had sent three hundred regular soldiers to stand in the ranks of the "Coalition of the Willing," but twice that number to private companies doing everything from KP duty to guarding oil installations and senior personnel. They came from faraway Fiji, the Philippines and India. By March 2005 their numbers had doubled to 20,000—more than twice the British contingent.[10]

Ann Garrels, a reporter in Iraq for National Public Radio, discussed the contrasting lifestyles in these private armies, and the differences between them and regular forces, from the interior of the Green Zone, the four-square-mile redoubt in the center of Baghdad that houses the Iraqi government and the American and British embassies, as well as thousands of employees dedicated to building the new Iraq. After securing the seven different security badges one must obtain to travel around through the various offices, the post exchange, and the McDonald's restaurant, Garrels was taken to the Bunker Bar, where the ceiling is covered with parachutes, and the walls hung with automatic weapons. The manager or owner told her that army grunts are not allowed in the bar, which was filled with security men hired by the contractors. These men, the owner went on, have a once-in-a-lifetime (maybe) opportunity to earn a lot of money, $15,000–$20,000 a month. They come from the United States, from Sri Lanka, from Fiji—from all over the world. Garrels noted that they all looked like "Yul Brynner on steroids." Indeed, she went on, steroids seem to be the drug of choice in Iraq.[11]

Quite aside from the Yul Brynner types who serve as models for the computer games that rule the lives of teenage Americans (of all ages), the Iraq War has seen the "war service" industry expand and become a permanent fixture in the larger Pentagon "order of battle." The outsourcing of supplies and support to huge mega-companies like Halliburton and Kellogg, Brown and Root has created a host of new problems for the military, as well as serious legal and constitutional questions about how it is possible to hold to account contractors who fail to perform in combat zones out of an unwillingness to take risks. The contractors—whose numbers could not even be counted accurately because of the absence of real government oversight—were estimated in 2007 to number in the range of 130,000–160,000.

Outsourcing previously traditional tasks carried out by the military was supposed to be a less expensive way of paying for the American version of an empire. But there were all sorts of indications that this was not so, including, increasingly, the cost of paying bonuses for patriotic "volunteers." There even arose questions that led back, in a different way, to the World War II analogy. Here is Cheney proclaiming a sacred bond between the people and the president as the 2006 Congressional elections neared, suggesting that the Democrats would thwart that sacred compact embodying the general will if they took control. "Unfortunately, at this stage, I think there's some jeopardy, depending on how the election comes out, as to whether or not we'll be able to continue those policies," he told the Fox News Channel. After the election, again on Fox News, the questioner was Chris Wallace when Cheney resurrected the Arc of Crisis image first popularized by National Security Adviser Zbigniew Brzezinski in the Carter administration. "Iraq is just part of the larger war—it is, in fact, a global war that stretches from Pakistan all the way around to North Africa." For the United States to succeed in that global struggle, the Iraq War had to be brought to a successful conclusion:

> People have got to have confidence in the United States, that they can count on us. If the United States doesn't have the stomach to finish the job in Iraq, we put at risk what we've done in all of those other locations out there."[12]

DEBATING THE EMPIRE

Before 9/11 it was suggested by some that two foreign policy themes appeared to clash in the Bush administration: the "realist" tradition championed by Secretary of State Colin Powell and National Security Adviser Condoleezza Rice, and what has been called by Andrew Bacevich a "Great Expectations" faction, championed by Vice President Dick Cheney and Secretary of Defense Donald Rumsfeld.[13] There are several things to say about this formulation. First, the supposed clash was probably exaggerated, as Rice, especially, had no difficulty crossing over to the Cheney–Rumsfeld side, though she preferred to see it as neoliberal or muscular Wilsonianism. Second, it is often seen as leading to the triumph of second-level officials called neoconservatives; but there is little evidence that Cheney needed anyone to talk him into pushing for a war on Iraq or that Rumsfeld's ideas about a streamlined military to ensure maximum coercive force could be applied anywhere in timely fashion required tutoring from a Princeton professor of Middle Eastern studies. Like the administration they succeeded, only more so, the Bush-*ists* were all nineteenth-century "liberals" dedicated to preserving access to world markets and controlling supplies of the major fuel of late capitalism: oil.

IRAQ AS "THE GOOD WAR"

Figure 14.2 Army Spc. Anthony Dowden of the 3rd Infantry Division presents a plaque made from a piece of armor that saved him from a sniper's bullet to Donald H. Rumsfeld (Secretary of Defense under George W. Bush, and chief proponent of the transformation to a smaller, more technological US military) in Baghdad, Iraq, on April 12, 2005

Department of Defense photo by Tech. Sgt. Cherie A. Thurlby, US Air Force. (Released.)

Cheney in private life after the first Bush administration had long sought a way to get out of the bind created by the 1979 Iranian Revolution. After Vietnam, President Richard Nixon, in one of many vows of never again, declared that he would rely on regional stabilizers. That was a role assigned to the shah of Iran. Jimmy Carter doubled down the bet on the shah, referring to him only months before the revolution as a rock of stability. The shah's fall was a tumultuous event that threatened to leave America with no secure landing zone in the oil-producing regions. Cheney had even suggested at one point that sanctions on Iran were self-defeating. After 9/11, however, removing Saddam Hussein was seen as a better option—and by far the easier task. Here was another reason for not thinking about the lessons of Vietnam and counter-insurgency warfare: all eyes were on the desert kingdoms, where, it was thought, it would be difficult for the enemy to hide from hi-tech warfare. Almost obligingly, furthermore, Saddam Hussein had a Sovietized army opposite American forces, not a bunch of bicycle riders threading along jungle paths.

Don Rumsfeld tried to see far into the future of warfare as well as the current obstacle to a New American Century. The important thing for him was to depersonalize the war on terror, and get away from a fixation on Osama bin Laden. Hence, he wanted to increase the list of terror-sponsors by adding Syria and Cuba—and maybe some others later. It was from this perspective that younger military theorists, including John Nagl and Australian David Kilcullen, insisted instead on the distinctions between a war on terror and counterinsurgency (COIN). Rumsfeld's ideas of terrain were entirely different than this rising COIN contingent. The secretary of defense even liked to muse about how the world looked from an observation point far away in outer space. He kept a satellite picture of the two Koreas at night under a clear plastic cover on his desk, he told reporters. The South was a blaze of lights, while in the North only Pyongyang, the capital, showed up as a pinpoint against the vast darkness. The photo intrigued him as demonstrating the differences, economically and politically, between the light and dark places around the world, a world of absolutes. Another time he remarked, "Anyone looking down from Mars sees that the countries that are providing the greatest opportunity for people are the freer countries." The West had to confront the challenge of those in the dark places who "hate freedom." "It isn't just the United States, it's a way of life."[14]

It would be hard to improve on Rumsfeld's updating of the nineteenth-century rationale for the civilizing mission of Western efforts in what was now called the post-colonial world—a vision he *did* share, however, with COIN advocates. The rationale also had to work in harmony with a third important theme that 9/11 helped to reconcile. It might be called the Ayn Rand/*Atlas Shrugged* theme of extreme individualism championed by such conservatives as Grover Norquist, whose credentials dated to Ronald Reagan and whose most famous saying was "I don't want to abolish government. I simply want to reduce it to the size where I can drag it into the bathroom and drown it in the bathtub." Norquist has said, however, that he was a foreign policy conservative first, before he developed his views fully on domestic policy, an indication of neoconservative ability to justify the sacrificing of civil liberties, and separating out fears of Big Brother government from a general dislike of anything that could be called, to use the Reaganites' phrase, the "nanny state." The usefulness of the World War II analogy, then, depended upon whether it was possible to mobilize public opinion for a war without sacrificing tax cuts, or imposing rationing.[15]

DESPERATE FOR A SUCCESS: GETTING VIETNAM RIGHT THIS TIME

Success in Iraq had always depended on the conflict there being a short war, because the threat of backlash, economically and politically, was always a danger to the Bush political alliance. The administration's assurances that the Iraq War would require no World War II sacrifices such as gas rationing, but only infringe a bit on civil liberties, became untenable with the reality of a prolonged struggle that lasted longer than World War II. In Iraq, "Mission Accomplished" gave way to "Stay the Course." On October 6, 2005, Bush used another World War II-laden analogy, the supposedly ever-present threat of lapsing into "isolationism," as earlier Republicans—now, of course, repudiated by the party—had done. If the terrorists achieved their goals, he said, they could use their enhanced economic, military, and political power "to advance their stated agenda: to develop weapons of mass destruction, to destroy Israel, to intimidate Europe, to assault the American people, and to blackmail our government into isolation." His writers came up with a new term not quite so felicitous as "axis of evil," "Islamofascism," to identify the enemy, with its presumed goal of succeeding where Hitler failed by establishing a thousand-year caliphate centered in the Middle East.

Still, with no end in sight, Iraq had opened a credibility gap between the administration and the public unlike anything that happened since Vietnam. The central beauty of the Pearl Harbor analogy was that it promised a "war of liberation," a perfect opportunity to leapfrog the ambiguous "containment" wars: Korea, which had left a dictatorship in control of half the country, and Vietnam, which had scarred the national psyche as no other conflict in the nation's history since the Civil War. The very term "containment" suggested to conservatives an almost un-American tolerance of an enemy, and a willingness to put limits on the technology-blessed American dream. They truly believed that Ronald Reagan had defeated the Soviet Union in the Cold War by calling the Soviet Union an "evil empire" and challenging it to a Star Wars race. Defeat in Vietnam had been a failure of will, nothing else. On the other side, COIN devotees argued that it had been much more complicated than that, but defeat there had been avoidable if policies they advocated for the future had been implemented back at the beginning.

By late 2006 all the assumptions the Bush administration had attempted to sell to the nation about Iraq as the anti-Vietnam War had collapsed in a heap of used slogans littering Pennsylvania Avenue between Capitol Hill and the White House. Once the voice of Mission Accomplished and Stuff Happens, Don Rumsfeld went the way of Robert McNamara, out one of the side entrances of the Pentagon. Ultimately, then, TV commentator Wallace had challenged Cheney, the United States would do whatever it took to win. "I believe we will." "By choosing the policy you have," Wallace said about plans for the "surge," and rejecting the Iraq Study Group's proposals, "haven't you, Mr. Vice President, ignored the express will of the American people in the November election?"

CHENEY: Well, Chris, this president, and I don't think any president worth his salt, can't afford to make decisions of this magnitude according to the polls. The polls change day by day. . . .

WALLACE: Well, this was an election, sir.

CHENEY: Polls change day by day, week by week. I think the vast majority of Americans want the right outcome in Iraq. The challenge for us is to be able to provide that. But you cannot simply stick your finger up in the wind and say, "Gee, public opinion's against; we'd better quit."

On the sixtieth Anniversary of VJ Day, August 30, 2005, President Bush invoked F.D.R. in yet another, more somber, twist on the Pearl Harbor–World War II analogy. This time it was the president who was faced with opponents who believed democracy's day was over.

Figure 14.3 American troops during the Iraq War, a conflict that, to many in the American public, brought back uncomfortable reminders of Vietnam.

Department of Defense photo by Sgt. Curtis G. Hargrave, US Army. (Released.)

Franklin Roosevelt refused to accept that democracy was finished. His optimism reflected his belief that the enemy's will to power could not withstand our will to live in freedom. He told the American people that our liberty depended on the success of liberty in other lands. And he called on Americans to defend liberty, and millions answered the call. Within four years, we would fight and win a world war on two fronts.

Placing Cheney's comments beside those of President Bush appears to raise ultimate questions about the defense of liberty and which front is now the most dangerous for the future prospects of American democracy. What the Iraq War has accomplished, more than anything else, is the transformation of the American military and its role in policy decisions. One is hard pressed to find Roosevelt defending democracy by repeatedly declaring that he would wait upon the approval of a general or admiral before making a key decision. Lyndon Johnson ran the Vietnam War in its expansionist stages from the White House Tuesday Luncheons with a few top advisers; but when it came time for him to make a crucial decision about a full bombing halt in the summer of 1968, he began the practice of assuring the public that he would listen to the recommendations of his generals before acting. In other words, he hid behind the generals. In doing so, moreover, he did more to limit presidential control of the military than anything Congress did to tie the executive's hands, albeit from a different perspective than is usually presented by his critics.

However that may be, when Iraq came to the Tet moment, something very different happened. And it is time now to talk about what that was—and was not. The Democratic victory in the 2006 Congressional elections left President Bush without the automatic stamp of approval he had enjoyed going back to 9/11, although his predicament would have been the same even without that victory. In the event, he bowed to outside pressures by appointing a bipartisan study committee that he never really intended to listen to except as a last resort. The Iraq Study Group (ISG), as it was called, originated with an idea put forward by the United States Institute of Peace, and was chaired by James Baker and Lee Hamilton. The ISG assembled a team of experts and issued its final report on December 6, 2006, in the midst of rumors that it would recommend troop withdrawals—which it did, along with recommendations for bringing nations Bush had shunned, Syria and Iran, into discussions over Iraq's future. Baker averred that he had no "magic bullet" to offer for Iraq, and instead, said the British newspaper the *Guardian*, stressed that the bottom line was "there are no good options left in Iraq, just bad options and worse ones."[16]

The report stirred a hornet's nest, with the president's neoconservative supporters probably the most outraged. Baker was accused of all sorts of less than patriotic motives, including the accusation that he was really an agent for Saudi Arabia—though how this fitted exactly into the presumed scheme of things was hard to say. The Baker–Hamilton report did reprise another Vietnam memory that stung the administration, saying that Baghdad had misled the White House about the levels of violence in Iraq, in much the same way as Saigon had supposedly underreported the numbers of enemy combatants in that war. The day after the report's release, Bush held a press conference with the British prime minister, Tony Blair, the purpose of which was to reassert the core loyalties of the president's "Coalition of the Willing," and to put down rumors of a Blair defection. He dismissed the 160-page ISG report with classic faint praise. "It is certainly an important part of our deliberations," he said. But the real message was, "We will stand together and defeat the extremists and radicals and help a young democracy prevail in the Middle East." Blair looked on with something approaching an expression of puzzled sympathy on his face, and his aides were at pains to point out that he was in Washington to discuss the importance of seeking a new, post-Kyoto agreement on climate change with the leading contenders of both parties for the White House in 2008![17]

It went largely unnoticed that the ISG report was issued on December 6, 2006, one day before the sixty-fifth anniversary of Pearl Harbor, and that Bush's press conference was on the day itself. His defiant reaffirmation of his determination to stay the course—unlike LBJ and Vietnam—could not conceal, even from himself, that he desperately needed a new strategy. Actually, the report did contain a recommendation (as a possibility) of a temporary increase in American forces to quell the immediate violence in Baghdad and pave the way for an orderly exit, somewhat similar to French efforts to mount a stand in 1954 at Dien Bien Phu preliminary to negotiations. Serious proposals for a change in strategy were, in fact, being presented to the president by a variety of other sources, both from the military and elsewhere. Linda Robinson's book *Tell Me How This Ends* offers a good summary of what happened and how General David Petraeus emerged as the man selected to lead the "surge" that is now credited with turning the Iraq situation around from near-certain defeat to one where, at least, a more honorable exit path has opened, and perhaps more.[18]

Robinson stresses that the outcome in Vietnam was always on the minds of policymakers:

> Americans wanted out [of Iraq], but they had not yet come to grips with what it would mean for America to lose its first war since Vietnam. . . . Americans might react to losing a war with a retreat from global leadership and efforts to solve the many problems besetting the world. And, on balance, losers of wars could expect to experience diminished influence.[19]

One could almost hear Robert McNamara here vintage 1965, proclaiming that L.B.J.'s hopes for alleviating poverty and demonstrating the efficacy of modernization for the world would go smash with a loss in Vietnam, or, after he became disillusioned, Walt Rostow, who served as one of Lyndon Johnson's chief security advisers, in 1967 (and evermore) arguing that Vietnam was the end point for violent communist-style revolutions unless America faltered out of fear of the birth pains of a new world. Condoleezza Rice had said the same thing about the Middle East, of course, repeating Rostow's mantra. So, it was still Iraq as the anything but Vietnam War.[20]

THE PETRAEUS TEAM

Petraeus's chief advisers, however, took the threat of another Vietnam defeat as a launching platform for implementing changes according to COIN theories of defeating insurrections. The story is a complicated one, and can be told here only in the briefest form. But the most stunning conclusion proponents of these theories reached was that the United States had it right (or nearly so) in Vietnam to begin with, but then went astray with L.B.J.'s massive troop buildup to fight a conventional war. And then, after defeat became all but certain, it switched back to a "could-have-won" strategy, had it been implemented sooner. "Should have won" Vietnam post-mortems fall into several categories, of course, beginning with those who argue that Westmoreland's "request" for more troops to follow up after turning back the enemy during the Tet Offensive was the best strategy for victory. That view is associated often with Niall Ferguson's challenging book *Colossus: The Price of America's Empire*, in which he argues that at one point, "Westmoreland was inflicting heavy losses on the enemy as the Tet offensive floundered." The villain in this reading was new secretary of defense Clark Clifford, who persuaded LBJ not to send more troops and counseled the president to initiate another partial bombing halt.[21]

Variations on this theme all stressed a crucial failure of will, whether they posited the need for a different strategy than the Westmoreland search-and-destroy, or went along with the

Ferguson critique. As the years went by, however, a group of young officers with advanced degrees in political science and history, and academic advisers, coalesced around the task of writing a new "counterinsurgency field manual," with the product of their labors attracting so much attention that it was soon published by the University of Chicago Press.[22] General Petraeus and his coauthor General James Amos noted in their foreword that what linked American campaigns in the Philippines, Vietnam, and Iraq and Afghanistan was that these were all wars "amongst the people," and as such shared certain "common characteristics of insurgencies." Nagl's foreword argued in very harsh terms that the sort of war Colonel Harry Summers averred in his famous book *On Strategy: A Critical Analysis of the Vietnam War* (1995) could have won in Vietnam could be summarized as "a strategy of annihilation—destroying a village in order to save it." It demanded, therefore, said Nagl, that Americans "abandon their core values."[23]

As Nagl freely admitted, the proposed new COIN "doctrine," which stressed the need to work "amongst the people," produced not only adherents in large numbers, but powerful enemies inside as well as outside the military establishment. One could almost call the resulting

Figure 14.4 Commander of US Central Command Gen. David H. Petraeus, in charge of the "surge" in the Iraq War and proponent of counterinsurgency techniques, talks with members of Combined Joint Task Force 101 at Combat Outpost Marghah, Afghanistan, on November 6, 2008.

Department of Defense photo by Staff Sgt. Bradley A. Lail, US Air Force. (Released.)

furor the "Army Wars." That subject and debate are for another time and place. Suffice it here to say that the COIN advocates honor the memory of Colonel T. E. Lawrence as a symbol of the proper way to mobilize the people to rally to one side in a worthy struggle, setting aside, of course, that "Lawrence of Arabia" was fighting with insurgents in World War I, not against them, in the Arabs' struggle to end the Ottoman Empire's grip on their lands. The other "hero" to COIN enthusiasts was a French colonel, David Galula, who wrote about the post-World War II campaign in Algeria, where, it is argued, even in a losing battle the metropolitan power did better than in Vietnam.[24]

John Nagl's foreword to Galula's short book stressed that the author's place in the canon of irregular warfare was assured by his lucid explanation of how counterinsurgency forces could protect the populace and thereby gain information "on the identity and location of insurgents, and thereby defeat the insurgency."[25] Here was the key to understanding the defeat in Vietnam, and the threat of defeat in Iraq. Nagl argued in his own book, *Learning to Eat Soup with a Knife*, which compared British success in Malaya with the Vietnam debacle, that Kennedy had made a good start in Vietnam with the Green Berets and his emphasis on that kind of multi-tasking soldier and approach to the problem—but it was all thrown overboard by the Pentagon's decision to fight the war "their way," which Lyndon Johnson then pursued along an undeviating path into the quagmire, a misuse of firepower to rival Pickett's charge at Gettysburg.[26]

Nagl was one of Petraeus's chief advisers in Iraq as the "surge" got under way with the buildup of troops to a number of about 40,000 in Baghdad and environs. The reduction in violence there and elsewhere in the country made Petraeus an almost overnight hero, if not quite on the scale of a MacArthur or Eisenhower. The political success of the surge remains a matter for the future—at least in Iraq—but in US military thinking its advocates have the upper hand. One commentator writes:

> Counterinsurgency is known as a thinking man's war, and it has attracted some of the country's best and brightest. In many ways, the doctrine comes across as refreshingly law-abiding, a product of the post-Abu Ghraib era. . . . Counterinsurgency is big on hearts and minds. In the wake of the Iraq War, no wonder it has been embraced.[27]

Another Petraeus adviser, Australian army officer David Kilcullen, made it plain that the principal reason for embracing the doctrine was that it worked. He said in a Washington panel discussion that there was "B.C.—before COIN and "A.D.—after Dave (as in Petraeus).[28]

So, while the argument over whether the surge had brought about a safe exit from Iraq, by whatever combination of military means and purchasing peace with dollars to float the Sunni Awakening and other temporary expedients, COIN advocates have made the Vietnam War come out right in their alternative history, so that the next big thing, Afghanistan, can be envisioned with a newfound sense of purpose and confidence. It was a matter of finding the right doctrine all along. Nagl bridles at the word "colonialism" to describe the new formula for success. "It is such a bad word," he says. But America has an important role to play in the world. "Madeline

Albright got in a lot of trouble for the phrase 'The United States is the indispensable nation.' But to a large extent that's true."[29]

Nagl is an admirer of Graham Greene, whose classic novel *The Quiet American* portrays a Cold War "liberal" who believes in the democratic "Third Way" between colonialism and communism, and attempts to shape the first Vietnamese war with the French to make it come out that way, and ends by destroying innocent lives. The novel demonstrates, he argues, that with the best of intentions it was possible to screw up in Vietnam. "There are obviously parallels with our actions both in Iraq and Afghanistan." How he reconciles these matters—his admiration for Greene's jaded view of the American "Third Way," his feeling that the novel shows parallels with American actions in Iraq and Afghanistan, and the notion that COIN promotes a different end by using similar methods to Greene's Alden Pyle's work "amongst the people"—needs further examination not possible here.

Viewed from this distance, COIN's origins in J.F.K.'s Green Berets suggests that hopes for success are now being pinned on a military doctrine employed by the British in Malaya and the French in Algeria. There are many questions posed by the parallels that Nagl cites, most of them, indeed, unexamined so far. Petraeus and Nagl both advocate a large army for Afghanistan, for example, and neither really offers any explanation of how such a poor country will be able to pay for such a force, or how the army will solve economic problems at the root of the country's misery. But if we leave those questions for another time, the way the war is being fought in Afghanistan and its borderlands with Pakistan suggests an unwelcome comparison with Vietnam—if one that appears necessary to the Obama administration and the Pentagon to attack Al Qaeda strongholds. The use of drone aircraft to deliver bombs on selected targets has become nearly as ritualized as the "Rolling Thunder" campaign in Vietnam; and even though it is characterized as a selective use of force to take out "the bad guys," the numbers of "others" killed continues to rise. It would appear that COIN has its limits, big areas, in fact, where hi-tech warfare will continue to be the norm. Saying anything about the confusion and turmoil of Pakistani politics is a risky business, though the drone strikes certainly do not win hearts and minds in that country. "Predator strikes are not a strategy—not even part of a strategy," wrote a former Pakistani ambassador to the United States, General Jehangir Karamat, in a front-page article of the newspaper *The Nation*. "They are tactical actions to ratchet up body counts."[30]

As George W. Bush found out, "Shock and Awe" changed the strategy of graduated escalation in Vietnam but did not make Iraq a continuation of the "good war." A real change might start with simple things that seem small, like putting an end to calling American soldiers "GIs," which could begin to clarify what these "small wars" of peacetime are really about.

DISCUSSION QUESTIONS

1. Discuss the World War II analogy as it pertains to the Iraq War.
2. Discuss the "Vietnam syndrome" as it relates to the Iraq War.
3. How has allowing the draft to lapse affected the US military?
4. What are the roles and implications of private military forces in the Iraq War?
5. Discuss the role of COIN in the wars in Iraq and Afghanistan.

SUGGESTED READING

Bacevich, Andrew. *The Limits of Power: The End of American Exceptionalism*. New York: Metropolitan, 2009.
Ferguson, Niall. *Colossus: The Price of America's Empire*. New York: Penguin, 2004.
Gardner, Lloyd. *The Long Road to Baghdad: A History of U.S. Foreign Policy from the 1970s to the Present*. New York: New Press, 2008.
Gardner, Lloyd. *Three Kings: The Rise of an American Empire in the Middle East*. New York: New Press, 2009.
Robinson, Linda. *Tell Me How This Ends: General David Petraeus and the Search for a Way out of Iraq*. New York: Public Affairs Press, 2008.
Woodward, Bob. *Plan of Attack*. New York: Simon & Schuster, 2004.

NOTES

1. Dan Balz and Bob Woodward, "America's Chaotic Road to War: Bush's Global Strategy Began to Take Shape in First Frantic Hours after Attack," *Washington Post*, January 27, 2002. Interestingly, when he wrote his book *Plan of Attack* (New York: Simon & Schuster, 2004), describing the path to the invasion of Iraq, Woodward did not juxtapose the comment about Osama bin Laden or Bush's hope to rally the world next to the Pearl Harbor reference (p. 24.) By that time the idea that the "coalition of the willing," as administration figures called it, would wage the war had overtaken the idea that America's objective was limited to catching Osama bin Laden, or that the world could be rallied for a war against Iraq.
2. Woodward, *Plan of Attack*, 24.
3. Project for the New American Century (PNAC), *Rebuilding America's Defenses: Strategy, Forces and Resources for a New Century* (Washington, DC: PNAC), 51.
4. Andrew J. Bacevich, "The Great Divide: The Crisis of U.S. Military Policy," *Short Take*, March 28, 2008.
5. James Brooke, "On Farthest U.S. Shores, Iraq Is a Way to a Dream," *New York Times*, July 31, 2005.
6. Peter Spiegel, "Army Warns Rumsfeld It's Billions Short," *Los Angeles Times*, September 25, 2006.
7. Nitya Venkataraman and Jonann Brady, "Exclusive: Cheney Cites 'Major Success' in Iraq, Says U.S. Has Hit 'Rough Patch,'" *ABC News*, March 19, 2008.
8. "All Indicators Pointing Down," *The Progress Report*, March 28, 2008.
9. Ian Traynor, "The Privatisation of War," *Guardian*, December 10, 2003.
10. Jonathan Franklin, "US Hires Mercenaries for Iraq Role," *The Age.com*, March 6, 2004; Danna Harman, "Firms Tap Latin Americans for Iraq," *Christian Science Monitor*, March 3, 2005.

11. Ann Garrels Reporting from Baghdad, *All Things Considered*, October 3, 2005.
12. "Transcript: Vice President Cheney on 'Fox News Sunday,'" January 14, 2007
13. The difficulty one has in labeling these themes suggests the continuing fluidity of the post-Cold War era, and the frequently changing patterns of adherents and alliances. Years ago, historian Frederick Merck attempted a synthesis. A student of Frederick Jackson Turner, Merck suggested that the links between Wilsonian thought and the supposedly more nationalistic ideas of other expansionists were scarcely different in practice. *Manifest Destiny and Mission in American History* (New York: Random House, 1963). Given George Bush's strong religious beliefs, a recent exegesis on the Merck thesis is worth noting: "With their missionary work the Puritans entered foreign policy and introduced what today is called *nationalist globalism*, meaning the active participation of the USA in the world and the attitude that it is the duty of Americans to save the world with their pureness and religious conviction. In other words, they wanted to force their exceptionalism on others. The American way of globalizing the world thus meant to make everybody do what Americans did, think the way they thought, govern the way they govern." Lisbeth Aalberg, "'A Beacon to the World': Religion and Exceptionalism in American Foreign Policy," *The Americanist* (September–October 2004).
14. Lloyd C. Gardner, "Mr. Rumsfeld's War," in *Iraq and the Lessons of Vietnam: Or, How Not to Learn from History*, ed. Lloyd C. Gardner and Marilyn B. Young (New York: The New Press, 2007), 182–3.
15. Wikipedia, en.wikipedia.org/wiki/Grover_Norquist. At one point he was registered with the Department of Justice as an official agent of the right-wing Angolan government of Jonas Savimbi. Norquist is the author of a recent book, noted in this entry: Grover Norquist's book *Leave Us Alone: Getting the Government's Hands Off Our Money, Our Guns, Our Lives* was published on March 11, 2008 by HarperCollins. Karl Rove said about Grover's new book, "Grover Norquist is provocative, intellectually fearless, and always worth paying attention to. His new book is Grover at his best, which is very, very good. Read this important volume and you'll understand why Norquist plays such a key role in American politics." Dick Morris also said, "The old dichotomies of left vs. right or liberal vs. conservative have increasingly little relevance for the politics of America. But Norquist's formulation, the leave-us-aloners vs. the takers, is vital, relevant, and incisive. Viewed through this prism, politics makes sense." Historian William Appleman Williams once said the era of American *laissez-faire* in the nineteenth century should better be understood as *laissez-nous-faire,* to better explain that *laissez-faire* did not mean a weak central government, but rather one that carried out a strong foreign policy and protected the interests of the ruling elites. *The Contours of American History* (W. W. Norton, 1989). Norquist's career, and book title, suggest the continuing relevance of Williams's correction.
16. Julian Borger, "Baker's Panel Has 'no magic bullet' to End the Agony," *Guardian,* November 14, 2006.
17. Mark Tran, "Bush: Victory Still Important in Iraq," *Guardian*, December 7, 2006.
18. Linda Robinson, *Tell Me How This Ends: General David Petraeus and the Search for a Way out of Iraq* (New York: Public Affairs Press, 2008). The tentativeness of Robinson's title is worth noting.
19. Ibid., 44–5.
20. Lloyd Gardner, "Obama Says He's a Realist in the Mold of George H. W. Bush. What Does That Really Mean?" *History News Network,* December 1, 2008.
21. Niall Ferguson, *Colossus: The Price of America's Empire* (New York: Penguin, 2004), 100.
22. *The U.S. Army—Marine Corps Counterinsurgency Field Manual*, foreword by General David H. Petraeus and Lt. Gen. James F. Amos, and foreword to the University of Chicago Press edition by Lt. Col. John A. Nagl (Chicago: University of Chicago Press, 2007).
23. Ibid., xlv, xxxvii.
24. David Galula, *Counterinsurgency Warfare: Theory and Practice*, foreword by John A. Nagl (Westport, CT: Praeger, 2006).
25. Ibid., vii.
26. John Nagl, *Learning to Eat Soup with a Knife: Counterinsurgency Lessons from Malaya and Vietnam* (Chicago: University of Chicago Press, 2002), 124–8.
27. Tara McKelvey, "The Cult of Counterinsurgency," *The American Prospect*, November 20, 2008.
28. Ibid.
29. Ibid.
30. Jane Perlez, "Time Is Short as U.S. Presses a Reluctant Pakistan," *New York Times,* April 6, 2009.

Contributors

Curtis Austin is an Associate Professor of History and Director of the Center for Black Studies at the University of Southern Mississippi. Dr. Austin is an acknowledged leader in the study of the Civil Rights Movement and is author of *Up Against the Wall: Violence in the Making and Unmaking of the Black Panther Party* (University of Arkansas Press, 2006).

Mary Kathryn Barbier is an Associate Professor of History at Mississippi State University. Dr. Barbier has published widely in the field of military history, including *D-Day Deception: Operation Fortitude and the Normandy Invasion* (Greenwood, 2007), and regularly teaches a course on Vietnam War history into which she integrates the history of memory.

Thomas Doherty is a Professor of Film Studies at Brandeis University and has published widely on film and American culture, including *Cold War, Cool Medium: Television, McCarthyism and American Culture* (Columbia University Press, 2003) and *Hollywood's Censor: Joseph I. Breen and the Production Code Administration* (Columbia University Press, 2007).

Lloyd Gardner is a Charles and Mary Beard Professor of History at Rutgers University. He is the author of several books on the Vietnam War, including *Approaching Vietnam: From World War II through Dienbienphu, 1941–1954* (Norton, 1988), *Pay Any Price: Lyndon Johnson and the Wars for Vietnam* (Ivan R. Dee, 1995), *Iraq and the Lessons of Vietnam* (co-edited with Marilyn B. Young, New Press, 2007), and *The Road to Baghdad: A History of U.S. Foreign Policy from the 1970s to the Present* (New Press, 2008).

Kim Herzinger is retired from his former position as a Professor in the English Department at the University of Southern Mississippi. Dr. Herzinger is an expert on the music of the 1960s, a critic and fiction writer, and winner of a Pushcart Prize. His publications include *The Teachings of Don B.: Satires, Parodies, Fables, Illustrated Stories, and Plays of Donald Barthelme* (Counterpoint, 2008).

CONTRIBUTORS

Martin Loicano recently served as an Assistant Professor of History at the University of Southern Mississippi. His PhD dissertation, "Negotiating Strategy: Republic of Vietnam and United States Military Relations, 1968–1973," is currently under revision.

Matthew Masur is an Assistant Professor of History at Saint Anselm College. He is presently revising his book manuscript, "Hearts and Minds: Cultural Nation Building in South Vietnam, 1954–1963", and has published "Falling Dominoes: The United States, Vietnam, and the War in Iraq" in David Ryan and John Dumbrell, eds., *Vietnam in Iraq: Lessons, Legacies, and Ghosts* (Routledge, 2006).

Glenn Robins is an Associate Professor of History at Georgia Southwestern State University. Dr. Robins is author of *The Bishop of the Old South: The Ministry and Civil War Legacy of Leonidas Polk* (Mercer, 2006) and an article entitled "Race, Repatriation, and Galvanized Rebels: Union POWs and the Exchange Question in the Deep South Prison Camps of the South." He is in the final stages of editing the Civil War prisoner of war diary of Sergeant Lyle Adair, 111th U.S. Colored Infantry, and has begun researching the tentatively titled *The Longest Rescue: Bill Robinson, An American Prisoner of War in Vietnam*.

Maureen Ryan is a Professor in the English Department at the University of Southern Mississippi, where she specializes in twentieth-century literature. Dr. Ryan has written articles on American women writers and Vietnam, and is author of *The Other Side of Grief: The Home Front and the Aftermath in American Narratives of the Vietnam War* (University of Massachusetts Press, 2008).

Amy Scott is an Assistant Professor of History at Bradley University. Her publications include "Cities and Suburbs," in David Farber and Beth Bailey, eds., *The Columbia Guide to America in the 1960s* (Columbia University Press, 2001), and she has co-edited (with Kathy Brosnan) *City Dreams, City Scenes: Utopian Visions, Urban Design, and City Life in the Twentieth-Century American West* (University of New Mexico Press, forthcoming).

Raymond M. Scurfield is a Professor of Social Work at the University of Southern Mississippi who served as a social work officer of an army psychiatric team in Vietnam. After the war he worked for twenty-five years for the Department of Veterans Affairs and directed the PTSD mental health programs in Los Angeles. He has published widely on PTSD, including the award winning *A Vietnam Trilogy: Veterans and Post Traumatic Stress* (Algora, 2004) and *War Trauma: Lessons Unlearned from Vietnam to Iraq* (Algora, 2006).

Heather Stur is an Assistant Professor of History at the University of Southern Mississippi. Her PhD dissertation, "Dragon Ladies, Gentle Warriors and Girls Next Door: Gender and Ideas that Shaped the Vietnam War," is forthcoming from Cambridge University Press. Her articles include "Perfume and Lipstick in the Boones: Red Cross SRAO and Vietnam," *The Sixties: A Journal of History, Politics, and Culture* (December, 2008).

CONTRIBUTORS

Andrew Wiest is Professor of History and Co-director of the Center for the Study of War and Society at the University of Southern Mississippi. Dr. Wiest has published widely in the field of military history, including *Rolling Thunder in a Gentle Land: The Vietnam War Revisited* (Osprey, 2006) and *Vietnam's Forgotten Army: Heroism and Betrayal in the ARVN* (New York University Press, 2008).

James H. Willbanks is a Vietnam veteran. Professor Willbanks serves as Director of the Department of Military History at the US Command and General Staff College and has written widely on the military history of the Vietnam War. His books include *Abandoning Vietnam: How America Left and South Vietnam Lost Its War* (University Press of Kansas, 2004) and *The Battle of An Loc* (Indiana University Press, 2005).

Index

Abrams, General Creighton 54, 70, 74n, 106, 108, 274, 279
Adams, Sergeant 1st Class Betty L. 78
Afro-American Liberation Army (AALA) 111
Allen, Elizabeth 86–7
Alvarez, Everett 164–5
American Friends of Vietnam 44
American Friends Service Committee 130, 134
An Quang 27
  Buddhists 27
  Party 27
Anderson, David 37
Ang, Claudine 20, 31n
Anti-war Movement 2, 5–6, 8, 10–11, 121–40, 156–8, 161, 208, 210, 218, 239
Ap Bac, Battle of 34, 47
Apocalypse Now 2, 230, 238, 240–1, 244, 247, 249–50, 253n
Arab–Israeli War of 1973 274–6, 285–6
Ayers, William 210
  Weather Underground 163n, 210

Bacevich, Andrew 296–7, 300, 310, 310n
Ball, George 39
Bao Dai 14, 26, 34, 41

Bao Ninh 223–4, 227, 228n
  The Sorrow of War: A Novel of North Vietnam 223–4, 227, 228n
Beatles 1, 146, 254, 259–61, 264
  Sgt. Pepper's Lonely Hearts Club Band 254, 259–61, 268
Beidler, Philip D. 208, 222, 226–7, 228n
  American Literature and the Experience of Vietnam 208, 226–7, 228n
Beijing 38
Bennett, Captain 95
Bennet, Fred 111
Bennett, Thomas 156
Berrigan, Daniel 124–5, 179–80
Berrigan, Philip 124
Bin Laden, Osama 291–2, 294, 302, 310n
Black, Lieutenant Commander Cole 169–70, 184n
Black Liberation Army (BLA) – see also Afro-American Liberation Army 111–12
Black Nationalist Photograph Album (BNPA) 110
Black Panther Party (BPP) 11, 100, 101–17, 118n, 119n
  Black liberation 101, 104, 106, 109, 111
  Black Panther Party for Self-Defense 104
  Executive Mandate Number One 104–5

INDEX

Free Breakfast for Children Program 110
National Committee to Combat Fascism (NCCF) 100, 113–16
Ten Point Program: What We Want, What We Believe 103
The Black Panther 106, 118n
Bowles, Chester 38
Bradley, Mark 36, 42–5, 52n, 53n
   Imagining Vietnam and America 36, 42–5, 52n, 53n
Brennan, Charles 110
Briarpatch 165, 176–8
Buddhists 27, 38, 47, 124, 129, 133
Bundy, McGeorge 40, 123
Bunker, Ellsworth 128
Bush, President George H. W. 284, 292
Bush, President George W. 12, 159, 290–6, 300–5, 309, 310n, 311n

Camacho, Isaac 164, 167
Cambodia 4, 23, 54, 65, 109, 142, 151, 237
Caputo, Philip 215, 217–18, 227, 228n
   A Rumor of War 217–18, 227, 228n
   Indian Country 215
Carmichael, Stokely 100, 125
Carter, Alprentice "Bunchy" 110
Carter, James 16, 31n
   Inventing Vietnam 16, 31n
Carter, President Jimmy 76, 96, 142, 160, 278, 300–1
Carter, Susie 94–5
Cheney, Vice-President Dick 159, 298–301, 303–4, 311n
Cherry, Fred 164
China 4, 14, 17–24, 29–30, 31n, 42–3, 56, 109, 150, 173, 234, 238, 295
   Chinese People's Liberation Army (PLA) 18
Churchill, Ward 110, 118n
Civil Rights Movement 1–2, 101, 118n, 125, 158–9, 227, 259, 265
Clark, Major Charlotte 92, 98n, 99n

Cleaver, Eldridge 100, 105–6, 108–10, 112, 118n, 119n
   Soul on Ice 100, 105
Clergy and Laity Concerned About Vietnam (CALCAV) 125
Clifton, Major General Chester 45
Cold War 3, 10, 15–16, 20–1, 25, 30, 40–5, 56, 80–1, 83–4, 96, 121–3, 127–8, 132, 137–8, 139n, 173, 244, 263–4, 291–2, 294–5, 297, 303, 309, 311n
Collins, J. Lawton 44
Coming Home 238–9, 253n
Commission on the Education of Women (CEW) 83
Communist Party of Vietnam 16
Conscientious Objectors (CO) 10, 128, 142, 143–63
Coppola, Francis Ford 237, 240–1, 243, 246, 249, 253n
Counterinsurgency (COIN) 5, 13, 48, 58, 73n, 270, 275, 278, 285–6, 288n, 291, 301–2, 307–8, 311n
Creedence Clearwater Revival 262, 266–7
   "Fortunate Son" 266–7
Cronkite, Walter 62

Da Nang 4, 41, 69, 76–7, 102, 165
Daly, James A. 158, 163n
Dang Ngoai 21
Dang Trong or Cochinchina 21–3, 25–6, 30, 31n, 32n
Dao Duy Tu 23
Davis, Peter, 120, 238
   Hearts and Minds 120, 238, 246
Dear America: Letters Home from Vietnam 6
Demilitarized Zone (DMZ) 4, 16, 70, 221
Democratic Republic of Vietnam (DRV) – see North Vietnam
Denton, Jeremiah 164, 171–3, 185n
Department of Defense (DOD) 111, 173, 234, 246, 293
   Code of Conduct 171, 173–5, 185n

DePuy, General William 270, 275–80, 286, 287n
Dien Bien Phu 2, 4, 34, 102, 167–8, 305
Diggs, Frank 111, 118n
Doering, Major Anna Marie 77–8
Dong Hoi 21–3
Dos Passos, John 211
   Three Soldiers 211
Doss, Desmond 156
Douglas, Emory 113, 118n, 119n
Duong Thu Huong 224, 227
   Novel without a Name 224, 227
Duiker, William 37, 52, 170, 185n
Dulles, John Foster 39, 44, 46
Dylan, Bob 254, 261, 263
   "Masters of War" 254, 263, 265

Edwards, George 108
Eisenhower, President Dwight D. 3, 37, 39, 42, 44, 128, 173, 295, 308

Fai-Fo or Hoi An 22
Fall, Bernard B. 2
Federal Bureau of Investigation (FBI) 110–12, 118n, 131, 294
   Domestic Intelligence Division 110
First Blood 230, 241–2
First Republic of Vietnam 25
Fitzgerald, Frances 208, 219
   Fire in the Lake: The Vietnamese and the Americans in Vietnam 208, 219
Fonda, Jane 120, 135–8, 140n, 180, 239, 246
Forbes, Air Force Captain Juanita 87
Ford, President Gerald R. 6
Forrest Gump 2, 55, 230–1, 250
Forte, Reginald 104
Forte, Sherman 104
France 2–3, 14, 15, 18, 24–7, 30, 34, 36–8, 40–4, 48, 56–7, 60, 102, 167–8, 294, 298, 305, 308–9
"Free Speech" Movement 142, 146
Fryett, George 164, 166

Full Metal Jacket 230, 244–6, 249–50

Galbraith, John Kenneth 38
Geneva Accords of 1954 57, 167
Geneva Convention 34, 175, 181, 185
GI Bill 80, 109, 278
Ginsberg, Alan 125
Goldwater-Nichols Bill 283
Gorman, Colonel Emily 78, 97n
Graham, Billy 45, 181
Great Britain 38, 41, 43, 265
Greene, Graham 2, 231, 309
   The Quiet American (novel) 2, 231, 309
Greene, Stephen 113
Greene, General Wallace 45

Halberstam, David 2, 27, 47, 50, 52n, 214
Hamburger Hill 246, 248, 250
Hanoi 4, 6, 13n, 15–16, 18, 20–1, 26–30, 31n, 38, 40, 43, 57, 71, 108, 120, 124, 127, 131–2, 135–6, 169–70, 175–83, 241
Hanoi Committee for the Investigation of War Crimes 132
Hanoi Hilton 165, 170, 182
Hanoi March 164, 176, 177, 185n
Hanoi Radio 176
Harriman, Averill 38
Harris, Captain Carlyle "Smitty" 170, 185n
Harris, David 124, 233
Harrison, Colonel Benjamin 67, 73n
Hayden, Tom 135–7, 140n, 180
Heinze, Major Shirley 89, 98n
Herr, Michael 217, 219–20, 223, 226–7, 228n, 244, 249
   Dispatches 219–20, 223, 226–7, 228n, 244, 249
Herring, George C. 2, 13, 17–18, 20, 31n
High Potential Equal Opportunity Program (HIPOT) 109–10

INDEX

Ho Chi Minh 3, 9, 15–16, 18, 27, 34, 43, 46, 50, 52, 57, 133, 164, 167, 170, 175–6, 182, 185n, 241
   August Revolution 15, 18
Hoffman, Abbie 125
Hoisington, Colonel Elizabeth 88–92, 97, 98n, 99n
Holmes, Harold 113, 116
Howard, Elbert 104, 108, 118n
Hubik, Major Delores 96, 99n
Hudson, Victor 113
Hue 4, 17, 22–3, 32n, 62–5, 69–70, 73n, 102, 232, 245
Hue-Tam Ho Tai 43
Huggins, John 109
Hutton, Bobby 104

Indochina 2, 20, 27, 31n, 34, 38, 40–3, 90, 122, 129, 217
   First Indochina War 18, 34
   Indochina Peace Campaign (IPC) 120, 135
   Second Indochina War 16–18, 21, 37, 170
International Committee of the Red Cross (ICRC) 175
International Voluntary Service (IVS) 128–129, 139n
Introduction to the Enemy 120
Iran 241–2, 270, 278, 283, 290, 292, 294, 301, 305
Iraq 2, 8, 12, 37, 51, 72, 96, 163n, 186, 188, 190, 197, 199, 202, 204, 206n, 207n, 210, 251, 268, 270–1, 280, 283–6, 290–310, 310n, 311n
   First Gulf War 12, 271, 277, 290
   Hussein, Saddam 270, 271, 281, 283–5, 292, 294, 301
   Iraq War 12, 51, 96, 163n, 190, 206n, 251, 291–310
Iraq Study Group (ISG) 290, 303, 305

Jackson, George 111
Jackson, Staff Sergeant Rose 94
Jackson State University 120

Jaco, Major Tom 67, 73n
Jacobs, Seth 36, 44–6, 50, 52n, 53n
   America's Miracle Man in Vietnam 36, 44–5, 52n, 53n
Jebb, Lieutenant Colonel Margaret 95–6, 98n, 99n
Johnson, General Harold 45
Johnson, President Lyndon B. 13, 34, 36–40, 42, 45, 50, 52, 56–7, 60, 62, 72, 73n, 122–3, 125, 129, 131, 139n, 180–1, 222, 304, 306, 308
Johnson, Captain Marjorie 92
Jolly, Thomas 107
Jurgevich, Nancy 86, 96

Kahin, George 37
Karnow, Stanley 13, 17, 52n, 65
Kennedy, President John F. 36, 38, 40, 42, 48–9, 52n, 83, 122, 218, 308
Kennedy, Robert F. 142, 176
Kent State University 65, 120, 142, 151
Key Black Extremist (KBE) 110–11
Khe Sanh 67, 220
Kilcullen, David 302, 308
Kim Il Sung 109
King, Martin Luther, Jr. 100, 125–7, 139n, 140n, 142, 157–8
Kontum 69–70
Krepinevich, Andrew 5, 72, 73n, 285, 288n
Kuhl, Major Ruth G. 92
Kushner, Captain Floyd 181–3
   Kushner group 181–3
Kussman, Lynn 92–4

Lader, Lawrence 103–4, 118n
   Power on the Left 103–4, 118n
Lan Cao 208, 225, 227
   Monkey Bridge 208, 225, 227
Landeen, Dr. Robert 108
Lansdale, Edward 44
Laos 4, 23, 65, 67–70, 109
   Invasion of – see also Operation Lam Son 719

INDEX

Lawrence, Mark 36, 40–2, 52n, 53n, 185n
    Assuming the Burden 36, 40, 52n, 53n
Le Loi 18
LeMay, General Curtis 45
Li Tana 20, 30, 31n, 32n
Liberal Internationalists 10, 121
    Federation of Atomic Scientists 121
    United World Federalists 121
    World Citizen Movement 121
Lockhart, Lieutenant Hayden 165
Logevall, Fredrik 36–42, 48, 50–1, 52n, 53n, 185n
    Choosing War 36–42, 51, 52n, 53n
Long Binh 76, 80, 86–7, 89–90, 92–6, 99n
Luce, Don 128–9
    Indochina Mobile Education Project 129

Mahony, Philip 221
    From Both Sides Now: The Poetry of the Vietnam War and its Aftermath 221
Mailer, Norman 208, 211, 219
    The Armies of the Night 208, 219
    The Naked and the Dead 211
Malcolm X 100, 103, 107, 118n
Mansfield, Mike 46
Marshall, Roger 130
Martinez, Elizabeth "Bettita" 127–8
    El Grito del Norte 127–8
MASH 230, 237, 252n
Mason, Bobbie Ann 215–17, 227, 228n
    In Country 215–17, 227, 228n
May, Ernest 43
McCain, Lieutenant Commander John S. 164, 178–9, 185n, 210
    Faith of My Fathers 178, 185n
McClenahan, Linda 84, 86, 96, 98n
McCreary, Thomas 107–8, 118n
McEldowney, Carol 131–3, 138, 139n, 140n
McDonald, Admiral David 45
McNamara, Robert 13, 39, 45, 49, 52, 72, 73n, 123, 232, 303, 306

Mekong Delta 102
Mekong River 4, 122, 240
Miller, David 124
Miller, Edward 20, 26–7, 31n, 33n, 52
Missing in Action (MIA) 148, 181, 223, 232, 242
Moseby, Priscilla 92–3
Moss, George Donelson 17, 20, 31n
Moyar, Mark 5, 13, 17, 20, 31n, 36, 46–51, 52, 52n, 53n, 72
    Phoenix and the Birds of Prey: Counterinsurgency and Counterterrorism in Vietnam 5, 13
    Triumph Forsaken 17, 20, 31n, 36, 46–51, 52, 52n, 53n, 72
Mulford Act 104–5
Murphy, Audie 2, 235
Murphy, Captain Joanne 89–92, 98n, 99n
My Lai 102, 120, 264

Nagl, John 73n, 302, 307–9, 311n
Napier, Samuel 111
National League of Families of American Prisoners and Missing in Southeast Asia (NLOF) 164, 181, 183
    Powers, Iris R. 181
    Purcell, Anne 181, 184, 185n
    Stockdale, Sybil 181, 185n
National Manpower Council (NMC) 83
    Womanpower 83
National Mobilization Committee to End War in Vietnam ("Mobe") 120
National Vietnam Veterans Readjustment Study (NVVRS) 186, 188, 205, 205n
New Left 122–3, 129, 131–2
New Orleans 107, 113–17, 118n, 119n
    Desire Project 113–14, 119n
    New Orleans Police Department (NOPD) 114–15
Newton, Huey 100, 103–4, 108, 112, 117, 118n

INDEX

Ngo Dinh Diem 3, 9, 14, 26–7, 30, 34, 36, 38–9, 44–48, 50–1, 52n, 54, 57–60, 167
  Religious intolerance 47
  1963 coup against 34, 47–8, 50, 54
Ngo Dinh Nhu 38
Ngo Quang Truong, Lieutenant General 59, 64, 73n
Ngo Quyen 18
Nguyen Duy Hinh, Major General 24, 26, 32n
Nguyen Hoang 14, 21, 32n
Nguyen Kao Ky 60
Nguyen Van Thieu 14, 27–9, 60, 67, 134
Nixon, President Richard M. 8, 51, 54, 65–6, 69, 71, 76, 95, 134, 142, 145, 151, 181, 237–28, 252, 253n, 272, 290, 295–6, 301
  Policy of Vietnamization 54, 66, 69, 71–2, 95, 142, 145, 162n
Nolan, Keith 63, 73n
  Battle for Hue 63, 73n
North Atlantic Treaty Organization (NATO) 277, 279–80
North Korea 109, 150, 173, 292, 294
North Vietnam 6, 10, 16–18, 21, 25, 27, 38, 48, 54–65, 67, 69, 71–2, 108, 130–6, 143, 145, 151, 156, 158, 164–6, 169–72, 175–84, 185n, 210, 223–4, 234, 238, 242, 246, 248, 250–1
  Easter Offensive 54, 69–71, 73n
  Hanoi 4, 6, 13n, 15–21, 26–30, 31n, 38, 40, 43, 57, 71, 108, 120, 124, 127, 131–2, 135–6, 138, 139n, 140n, 164–5, 169–70, 172, 175–83, 185n, 241, 252
  National Liberation Front (NLF) 34, 38, 47–50, 108, 130, 132
  North Vietnam Peace Committee 130–1
  People's Army of Vietnam (PAVN) 13, 18, 30
  Provisional Revolutionary Government of South Vietnam – see Viet Cong
  Tet Offensive 54, 61–6, 72, 73n, 87, 89, 91–2, 94, 142, 145, 151, 182, 220, 232–3, 245, 254–5, 263–5, 268, 305–6
  Viet Cong (VC) 56, 60–6, 108–9, 116, 134, 145, 158, 164–7, 169, 184, 185n, 201, 224, 232, 234, 238, 240–2, 250
  Viet Minh 25–6, 36, 40–2, 58
  Vietnamese National Army (VNA) 57–8

O'Brien, Tim 208, 214–15, 217, 223, 227, 228n
  If I Die in a Combat Zone, Box Me Up and Ship Me Home 208, 217
  In the Lake of the Woods 215
  Going After Cacciato 208, 214–15
  The Things They Carried 214–15, 227, 228n
O'Daniel, Lieutenant General John W. 46, 57
Obama, Barak 209–10, 227, 228n, 296, 309, 311n
Ochs, Phi 233, 254, 263–4
  "Draft Dodger Rag" 233
  "I Ain't Marching Anymore" 254, 263
Offut, Karen 86, 96
Olson, Major Gloria 89, 98n

Paris Peace Accords (Agreement) 183, 270, 273
Peace Activists 121–4, 128, 132–4, 139n, 179
  Liberal internationalists – see above
  Radical pacifists – see below
Peace Corps 128
Pelley, Patricia 20, 31, 31n
Pentagon Papers 120, 137
Pepper, Claude 108
Perry, Merton 27
Petraeus, General David H. 290, 306–10, 311n
Phan Chu Trinh 43
Phillips, Rufus 3–5, 9, 13
  Office of Rural Affairs 3
Plantation 164–5, 178–80, 182
Platoon 230, 243–4, 246, 248, 250, 253n

Pleiku 87
Post-Traumatic Stress Disorder (PTSD) 6–8, 10, 186, 187–207, 218, 226, 239, 250
Potter, Paul 123, 139n
Powell, Colin 285, 287, 288n, 300
Pratt, Elmer "Geronimo" (Ji Jaga) 107, 109–13, 117, 118n, 119n
Presley, Elvis 1, 250, 258
Prisoners of War (POWs) 10, 124, 132, 158, 164–185, 226, 239, 242

Quang Tri City 70

Rabe, David 222–3, 227, 228n
  Streamers 222
  The Basic Training of Pavlo Hummel 222
  Sticks and Bones 222
Radical Pacifists 10, 121–122
  Committee for Nonviolent Action 122
  Committee for a Sane Nuclear Policy (SANE) 122
  Merton, Thomas 122–4, 127
  Radical Quakers 122, 134
  Women Strike for Peace (WSP) 122, 130–1
Rahim, Malik 107, 114–15, 118n, 119n
Rawls, Dwight 106
Ready, Captain Peggy E. 84
Reagan, President Ronald 241, 278, 283, 302–3
Red River Delta 15
Reed, Officer Raymond 114
Republic of Vietnam (RVN) – see South Vietnam
Reston, James, Jr. 210–11, 226, 227, 228n
  Coming to Terms 210–11, 226–7, 228n
Rodgers, Marie 87
Rolling Stones 146, 240, 247, 262, 268
Rossi, Lieutenant Colonel Lorraine 89–90, 98n
Roosevelt, President Franklin D. 41, 295, 304
Roth, Marilyn 86, 88, 96

Roth, Philip 208
  American Pastoral 208
Rowe, James "Nick" 164, 166, 184n
Rumsfeld, Secretary of Defense Donald 290, 295, 297, 300–3, 310n, 311n
Rusk, Dean 39, 123, 232

Sadler, Staff Sergeant Barry 233–4, 254, 264
  "Ballad of the Green Berets" 233–4, 254, 264
Saigon 4, 14, 17, 19, 21, 24–5, 27, 29–30, 32n, 37, 47, 54, 57, 60, 62–3, 71, 76–8, 84, 86, 90–2, 95, 129, 137, 140n, 166, 210, 217, 221–3, 232, 238, 270, 286, 305
Seale, Bobby 103–5, 108, 118n
Seeger, Daniel Andrew 144, 151
  United States v. Seeger 142, 144
Selective Service Act 124, 152, 156
Selective Service System (SSS) 124, 143–5, 148, 151–2, 156, 162n, 163n
  "Manpower Channeling" 124
Selective Training and Service Act (STSA) 151–2
Sexual Revolution 2, 233
Sheehan, Neil 2, 27, 47, 50
Shuman, Lieutenant Commander Robert 165
Sirgo, Deputy Superintendent Louis J. 113–15
Sloane, John 104
Smith, George 166–8, 184n
  P.O.W.: Two Years with the Vietcong 167
Somalia 290, 292
Son Tay Raid 164, 182, 184
  Camp Faith 182
  the Zoo 176, 178, 180, 182
South Vietnam 3, 5, 9–10, 14–18, 20–30, 31n, 32n, 34–9, 46–50, 55–73, 73n, 76–7, 84, 88, 97n, 108, 128–30, 133–5, 145, 158, 162n, 165, 172, 183, 186, 210, 213, 218, 224–5, 232, 272
  Army of the Republic of Vietnam (ARVN) 3, 5, 8–9, 13, 54, 57–73, 77–78, 212

INDEX

Buddhist crisis 38, 47
Hamburger Hill 65, 102, 246, 272
Saigon 4, 14, 17, 19, 21, 24–5, 27, 29–30, 95
Special Weapons and Tactics (SWAT) 102
Spiller, Roger 273, 276, 284, 287n, 288n
Starry, General Donn 270, 280–1, 287n
Steinglass, Matt 8, 13n
Sternberg, Brigadier General Ben 78, 97n
Stickney, David and Mary 130
Stop-Loss 230, 251
Students for a Democratic Society (SDS) 123, 131, 135
Student Non-violent Coordinating Committee (SNCC) 125
Summers, Colonel Harry G., Jr. 5–6, 13, 13n, 37, 71–2, 74n, 307
  On Strategy: A Critical Analysis of the Vietnam War 5–6, 13, 13n, 307

Taxi Driver 230, 239
Tan Son Nhut Air Base 80, 84, 90, 95
Taylor, Keith 17, 20–1, 31n, 32n
Taylor, General Maxwell 49, 60
Taylor, Ollie 111
Taylor, Philip 20–1, 24, 31n, 32n
Temptations 254, 265
  "Ball of Confusion" 254, 265–6
Tet Offensive 54, 61–6, 72, 73n, 87, 89, 92, 94, 142, 145, 151, 182, 220, 232–3, 245, 254–5, 263–6, 268, 305–6
The Deer Hunter 230, 238–40, 250, 253n
The Green Berets 11, 230–1, 233–5, 251, 252, 252n
The Resistance 124
  Harris, David 124, 233
  Heller, Lennie 124
The Sixties 1, 3, 5, 9, 11, 20, 28, 31n, 37, 42, 48, 51, 81, 84, 87, 96, 98n, 122, 124–5, 138, 139n, 144–6, 149, 151, 157–9, 182, 190, 209–10, 219–20, 222, 227, 233, 246–7, 250, 256–9, 261, 268–9

The Quiet American (movie) 2
"The Wall" see Vietnam Veterans Memorial
Thich Nhat Hanh 124, 127
Thich Tri Quang 47
Theriot, Captain Olivia 87
Thurman, General Maxwell 278
Tonkin, Gulf of 4
  Incident 34, 165
  Resolution 142–3, 151
Torres, Francisco 101–2, 118n
Tran Cam Huong, Major 78, 99n
Tran Dinh Tho 26, 32n
Tran Hung Dao 18–19
Tran Van Don, General 58, 72, 73n
Tran Van Huong 29–30
Trautman, Captain Konrad 171–2
Thieu Au 18
Trinh 21–3
Trung Sisters 18
Truman, President Harry S. 3, 37, 40–2, 76, 80, 295
  Truman Doctrine 41
Tu, Colonel 6
Tucker, Spencer 17

United Kingdom – see Great Britain
United States 1–13, 15, 18, 20, 26, 30, 31n, 34–45, 48, 50–1, 55–6, 58, 60–3, 66–72, 73n, 79–87, 96, 101–12, 122, 125, 129–34, 142–5, 148–56, 159–61, 162n, 163n, 167–9, 174, 179, 183, 187–9, 197, 202–4, 209, 215, 221–4, 227, 232, 237, 240–2, 255, 264–6, 271–5, 291–2, 299–306, 309
  Advanced Military Studies Program (AMSP) 282
  All-Volunteer Army 270, 274
  Army Training and Evaluation Plan (ARTEP) 279–81
  Battle Command Training Program 282
  Combined Arms Staff Service School (CAS3) 282

INDEX

Department of Veterans Affairs (VA) 6, 189, 192, 207n
Field Manual (FM) 100–5, *Operations* 276
Home front 3, 5–6, 11, 55, 62, 66, 80, 102, 106, 180–1, 209, 211, 215–17, 219, 221, 226, 239, 247–9
Military Assistance and Advisory Group (MAAG) 54, 57–60, 78
Military Assistance Command, Vietnam (MACV) 54, 60, 77, 84, 152, 166
National Training Center (NTC) 270, 282
Operation Desert Storm 270, 283–6
Operation Enduring Freedom (OEF) 189, 203, 207n
Operation Homecoming 164, 183
Operation Iraqi Freedom (OIF) 189, 203, 207n
Operation Just Cause 270, 283
Operation Restore Hope 290
Pierce Arrow 165, 169
Rolling Thunder 38, 165, 169, 239, 309
Training and Doctrine Command (TRADOC) 270, 275–6, 279–80, 282
United States Army Vietnam (USARV) 76, 86
United States Army 12, 73n, 76–9, 86, 95, 158, 168, 189, 266, 270–87, 287n
  "Combat Refusal" 272
  Drugs 259, 273
  Fragging 108, 118n, 250, 272
  Noncommissioned officers (NCOs) 108, 272–4
  Racial Strife 273
Universal Military Training and Service Act (UMTSA) 144

Valdez, Luis 127–8, 133–4, 139n, 140n
Van Devanter, Lynda 218–19, 221, 227, 228n
  Home before Morning: The Story of an Army Nurse in Vietnam 218–19, 227, 228n
  Visions of War, Dreams of Peace with Joan A. Furey 221

Vance, Cyrus 45
Vann, John Paul 47
Veterans and Volunteers for Freedom 134
  Brown, Robert K. 134–5, 140n
Veterans and Volunteers for Vietnam – renamed Veterans and Volunteers for Freedom
"Vietnam syndrome" 8, 12, 284, 292, 310
Vietnam Veterans 6–8, 10–11, 96, 102, 109, 113–16, 120, 138, 187–9, 197, 200, 202, 203, 205, 205n, 206n, 207n, 218–21, 231, 239
Vietnam Veterans Against the War (VVAW) 120, 138, 218
Vietnam Veterans Memorial 6–7, 55, 186, 217
Vietnamese Communist Party 26
Vo Van Sen 20
Voices in Vital America (VIVA) 181
Volunteers in Service to America (VISTA) 102

Wall, Jim Vander 110, 118n
Walsh, Jeffrey 208, 226
  American War Literature 1914 to Vietnam 208, 226
War Powers Act 120
Watts Riots 100, 109
Wayne, John 84, 204, 231, 233–5, 243, 249, 251, 252
Webb, James 211–13, 227, 228n
  Fields of Fire 211–13, 227, 228n
Weller, Dot 130
Welsh, Elliott Ashton, II 145, 151, 162n, 163n
  Welsh v. United States 142, 144–5, 152, 156, 162n, 163n
  Welsh-CO 156–7
Westmoreland, General William 54, 56, 60–2, 84, 238, 306–7
Wheeler, General Earle 45
Wiest, Andrew 8–9, 13, 72, 207n
Wilkes, Major Kathleen I. 78

INDEX

Williams, Lieutenant General Samuel 57–9
Women – South Vietnam
  Vietnam Women's Training Center 86
  Women's Armed Forces Corps (WAFC) 76–9, 84, 86, 95, 97n, 98n, 99n
Women – United States 76–99
  Army Nurse Corps 80, 87, 98n
  Uniforms 89–91
  Women Accepted for Voluntary Emergency Service (WAVES) 84
  Women's Armed Services Integration Act 76, 80
  Women's Army Auxiliary Corps (WAAC) 76–7, 80, 83, 98n
  Women's Army Corps (WAC) 9, 76–99
  Women in the Air Force (WAF) 84
Woodstock 1, 254
World Council of Churches 128–9

Xuan Loc, Battle of 54

Yang Baoyun 20, 31n, 32n
Yom Kippur War 275

eBooks – at www.eBookstore.tandf.co.uk

A library at your fingertips!

eBooks are electronic versions of printed books. You can store them on your PC/laptop or browse them online.

They have advantages for anyone needing rapid access to a wide variety of published, copyright information.

eBooks can help your research by enabling you to bookmark chapters, annotate text and use instant searches to find specific words or phrases. Several eBook files would fit on even a small laptop or PDA.

NEW: Save money by eSubscribing: cheap, online access to any eBook for as long as you need it.

Annual subscription packages

We now offer special low-cost bulk subscriptions to packages of eBooks in certain subject areas. These are available to libraries or to individuals.

For more information please contact webmaster.ebooks@tandf.co.uk

We're continually developing the eBook concept, so keep up to date by visiting the website.

www.eBookstore.tandf.co.uk